ENGLISH LOCAL GOVERN ... AND BEATRICE POTTER WEBB

Publisher's Note

The book descriptions we ask booksellers to display prominently warn that this is an historic book with numerous typos, missing text or index and is not illustrated.

We scanned this book using character recognition software that includes an automated spell check. Our software is 99 percent accurate if the book is in good condition. However, we do understand that even less than one percent can be a very annoying number of typos! And sometimes all or part of a page is missing from our copy of a book. Or the paper may be so discolored from age that you can no longer read the type. Please accept our sincere apologies.

After we re-typeset and design a book, the page numbers change so the old index and table of contents no longer work. Therefore, we usually remove them.

Our books sell so few copies that you would have to pay hundreds of dollars to cover the cost of proof reading and fixing the typos, missing text and index. Therefore, whenever possible, we let our customers download a free copy of the original typo-free scanned book. Simply enter the barcode number from the back cover of the paperback in the Free Book form at www.general-books.net. You may also qualify for a free trial membership in our book club to download up to four books for free. Simply enter the barcode number from the back cover onto the membership form on the same page. The book club entitles you to select from more than a million books at no additional charge. Simply enter the title or subject onto the search form to find the books.

If you have any questions, could you please be so kind as to consult our Frequently Asked Questions page at www.general-books.net/faqs.cfm? You are also welcome to contact us there.

General Books LLC™, Memphis, USA, 2012. ISBN: 9781458826886.

CHAPTER I THE KING'S HIGHWAY BEFORE THE SIXTEENTH CENTUEY

We propose, in this book, to tell the story of the King's Highway in England and Wales: not, indeed, the romance and picturesque incidents of travel on the road, but the more prosaic tale of the maintenance and management of the thoroughfares which make travel possible. And in this history, even more than in others, it is out of prolonged darkness that we emerge into light. We have to pass rapidly over the first thirteen or fourteen hundred years of historical knowledge about England, during which, of the actual methods and detailed facts as to the management and maintenance of the roads, there is next to nothing known. Of the fifteenth, sixteenth, and seventeenth centuries we can form some imperfect vision; whilst from the beginning of the eighteenth the records are abundant. To those who wonder what there can be of interest or instruction in so prosaic and mechanical a subject as road maintenance, we venture to suggest that they should give it a trial. In the evolution of road administration in England, we shall see exemplified, with many an instructive parallel, the whole story of English Local Government, from the Court Leet to the County Council. And in the dramatic eighteenth century struggle between the new users of the roads and those who were liable for their maintenance— between the rival assumptions that the traffic must be suited to theroads and that the roads must be suited to the traffic— we have a curiously exact precedent for the constant argument that went on yesterday about the bicycle and the automobile, and that is going on to-day between the Road Authority and the Motor Omnibuses.

Our forefathers had a short and ready method of local selfgovernment, in our volume on *The Manor and the Borough* we have described, in connection with the Court Leet, the characteristic mediaeval assumption of local administration, that the common services needed for social life were to be performed, not by any specialised organs of the community, but by being shared among all the citizens, serving compulsorily without pay. It was taken for granted that these services—allotted as they were among persons and classes according to their assumedly permanent status in the community—would themselves remain, year in and year out, unchanged in kind and quantity. This assumption it was that gave significance to the whole conception of nuisances, active and passive. If no man committed any new annoyance, or refrained from fulfilling any old obligation, it was assumed that all would be well. In no department of local government was this mediaeval assumption so persistent as in the Maintenance of Roads, and in no other service was its result so obviously disastrous Not until well into the nineteenth century was the old order wholly superseded by the modern device of a specialised organ of administration, alimented by compulsory taxation, and having, as its express object, the satisfying of the increasing needs of a progressive society. Between these two assumptions, and the characteristic ideals of road administration to which they gave birth, there waged, during the whole of the eighteenth century, and indeed from the Restoration to the Reformed Parliament, one prolonged struggle. What maintained this conflict between the old principles and the new was the fact that these rival conceptions of public administration corresponded, in the main, with the interests and needs of antagonistic sections of the community—on the one hand the inhabitants of the rural parishes, but little concerned with any means of locomotion on wheels, and on the other, the new users of the roads, the citizens of the rapidly growing ports and industrial centres, and all whose business or pleasure compelled them to travel up and down England and Wales. It is this conflict between rival principles and conflicting interests that lends some philosophic interest to the story of the King's Highway.

But before we can reach the point in our narrative at which this conflict between rival policies becomes, as we may almost say, dramatic in its intensity, we must run rapidly over those preceding centuries into which we have made no special research. And we may as well begin at the beginning. The earliest highways in England of which there is any sign are the ancient trackways— sometimes first marked out by passing animals— which were used by the British inhabitants. These ancient lines of traffic, we are told, "were probably irregular and winding, unmetalled and frequently worn below the level of the surrounding country.... They ran from the higher country to points where the rivers were fordable.... With some notable exceptions they were not durable roads but tracks from the high ground, where the Britons largely resided, to the shipping ports." So persistent and unyielding is popular usage, and so little thought has there ever been of changing the course of a public thoroughfare, that we may well imagine these ancient hollow-ways and ridgeways, from Cornwall to Northumberland, to survive, if not even in some lines of Roman road, at any rate in many a sunken lane or moorland track, in many a field path or right of way. Here and there, as in the rude stone trackways across a Devonshire moor, a Wiltshire down or a Yorkshire wold; or as in the remarkable stone bridges on Dartmoor or Exmoor, or as in the remnants of the foundations of the wooden pile causeway across Lambeth Marsh, we may believe that we see actual structure of pre-Roman age. But of the management and maintenance of these prehistoric highways nothing is known.

We are on firmer ground during the Roman occupation of Britain, when the four great roads, together with others of lesser note, were constructed across the island, of a straightness that was magnificent, if not altogether economical. Of these great through roads, and of some of the others, we can to-day trace the exact course, and they still form, here and there, the basis of existing thoroughfares. We need not repeat the well-known descriptions of the structural features of these Roman roads, nor yet indulge in speculations as to their place in the great system of communications which extended to the very limits of the Empire. Scholars have paid more attention to the geography and to the mechanics of these roads than to the social organisation involved in their maintenance. What particular form of "social tissue " was developed in Britain for these great works; how far the direction was centralised in Rome; what labour force was employed and how it was organised and subsisted; and how exactly the cost was borne, does not seem, so far as the present writers are aware, to have been made out. We must remember that the object of these great works was military rather than commercial; that they were probably constructed by the legions themselves; and that they may well have been in the same manner kept in repair. Moreover, though wheeled vehicles were used by the Romans (as, indeed, they had been by the Britons), the main use of these roads was to enable the legions to march quickly from place to place; and to make it possible to supply them easily by packhorses. Although a few officers or dignitaries might travel in chariots, and even messengers and light articles be thus carried, we imagine that the Roman roads were used, in fact, almost entirely by pedestrians and horses—a fact which in itself explains and justifies their being made to take always the most direct line, irrespective of hills and valleys. How systematically they were connected by other, less permanent, routes with other places, we know not, although various subsidiary lines of communication have been traced. But we may infer that the construction of new through routes across Britain led to the opening of many new tracks, of one sort or another, connecting the great thoroughfares with the various villages in the neighbourhood of which they passed. Of the actual organisation of the service of road maintenance in Britain under the Romans, or of the working of the administration in practice, there is, so far as we are aware, nothing known.

We have, perforce, to pass equally rapidly over the next six or seven centuries. We may assume that neither the ancient trackways nor the Roman roads fell, with the departure of the legions, quite out of use. We know that the great Roman thoroughfares across the country soon received from the English those names of Watling Street, the Icknield Way, Ermin Street, and the Fossway— not to mention the names of such lesser roads as the Saltway and Akeman Street—by which they are still known; whilst the innumerable Stratfords and Strattons and "Streets" that persist in local place nomenclature teftvis/the same tale of continued use of the Roman foundation We .? know, too, that the English kings always insisted on the mainten-. ance, by the inhabitants of each locality, of the roads and bridges of that locality uiery largely because, without the keeping up of thoroughfares,Vit would have been difficult either to have moved armies or to have exercised any central authority. The maintenance of the existing roads and bridgeB was, indeed, one of the three fundamental obligations—the *trinoda necessitas*— of the holder of land. But, here again, less attention seems to have been paid to social organisation than to some other matters. The present writers, at any rate, find themselves unable to piece together any authenticated description of how the roads of England were actually managed arid maintained prior to the twelfth or thirteenth century. ,/

So far as we are aware, indeed, anything like exact knowledge of road administration in England begins with the manorial records, and is largely derived from the lawyers' subsequent interpretation of manorial obligations. We have described in our volume on *The Manor and the Borough* how, as we understand it, the Manor was organised. The maintenance of the King's Highway was certainly one of the duties which the law imposed upon the Manor. We gather that the Lord of the Manor threw this duty upon the whole body of tenants of the Manor, their several obligations being in some way adjusted and enforced by the Court Leet.

We must not, however, think of the Manor constructing a road, either as practised by the Romans or as understood in our own day. We shall, in fact, fail to understand the position, or the conflicts which subsequently arose, unless we dismiss from our thoughts anything like the modern conception of a road. To the citizen of to-day,the " King's Highway" appears as an endless strip of land, with definite boundaries, permanently and exclusively appropriated to the purpose of passage, with a surface specially prepared for its peculiar function. To the citizen of the twelfth, the fifteenth, or even the eighteenth century, the King's Highway was a more abstract conception. It was not a strip of land, or any corporeal thing, but a legal and customary right—as tneTawyera said, "a perpetual *right oj passage* in the sovereign, for himself and his subjects, over another's land." In one of our oldest law-books it is definitely laid down that " the King has nothing but the passage for himself and his people." What existed, in fact, was not a road, but what we might almost term an easement—a right of way, enjoyed by the public at large from village to village, along a certain customary couise, which, if much frequented, became a beaten trac£ But the judges held that it was " the good passage" that constituted the highway, and not only "the beaten track," so that if the beaten track became (as it invariably did in wet weather) " foundrous" the King's subjects might diverge from it, in their right of passage, even to the extent of "going upon the corn." Of this liberty, it is clear, the riders and pedestrians of the time made full use. The great majority even of the main English highways were, like those of Australia, America, and India of the present day, not bounded by fences. But even fences were not respected. As late as 1610 we read, in the very first book about roads that is extant, of "great hurt and spoil of fences and grounds, with riding and going over the corn and such like, by shifting and seeking the bestway diversely." And we must add to this understanding ofhe customary highways (as they existed in the twelfth, and even in the fifteenth century), that they were used almost exclusively for foot traffic of man or beast. For this purpose the immemorial track from village tp-village across the waste sufficed in its primitive conditionand if, in the months of summer dryness, the rude sledges or carts carrying home the crops could find a reasonably firm passage, it was all that was desired. That the ways, in winter, must be impassable for wheel traffic was habitually taken for granted. This primitive conception of locomotive needs lasted, in remote corners of England, right down to the end of the eighteenth century. In Cumberland, we are told, " in the spring of the year the Surveyor used to call on the people to go with him *to open the tracks* over the common, from which the old tumble-wheel carts of the country had been excluded during the winter; for, in 1792, the principal part of the corn was conveyed to market on the backs of horses!"

Thus, the idea of road maintenance in the Middle Ages, and indeed, down to much later times, did not include anything in the nature of the construction of a special road surface. The very word "road," which some derive from the Anglo-Saxon "ridan," to ride, as being something that is ridden on, may really have some connection with the verb "to rid," meaning to free or clear, as being something that has been cleared from obstruction. The ideal of road maintenance which the oldfashioned Englishman set before himself was, in fact, no more than "removing every kind of impediment that incommodes or molests the traveller, such as want of proper drains, overhanging trees and hedges, timber-logs, etc."; in short, to quote an eighteenth century reformer, everything "that prevents the roads from growing better of themselves." VThe first statute to deal with roads, the Statute of Winchester in 1285, extends this same conception of clearing a passage to a further point, and reminds us of the existence of other kinds of obstruction, *J* by ordering "that highways leading from one market town ' to another shall be enlarged where as bushes, woods, or dykes be, so that there be neither dyke nor bush whereby a man may lurk to do hurt within two hundred feet of the one side and two hundred feet of the other side of the way." It was this limited idea of keeping open the free passage for the King and his subjects, that the Common Law sought to realise byholding someone responsible for the maintenance of evry public highway. In exceptional cases this might be a burden incidental to the tenure of particular lands, or even, by mere prescription, a special charge upon a particular corporate body./But unless some such special obligation could be proved, the duty of maintaining all the public highways within each Manor was cast, without remuneration or reward, upon the inhabitants of that Manor/ Exactly on which inhabitants the duty fell, in what manner it was performed, and how far the Court Leet or other tribunal enforced it on defaulters, remains, prior to the Act of 1555 which we shall presently describe, provokingly obscure. It would, however, be a mistake to assume, merely because we do not know exactly how the roads were managed and maintained, that this service was not performed; or to infer, because we know the roads to have been horribly bad in the eighteenth century, that they were equally bad in the fifteenth. We have reason to believe that there was, in the fourteenth and fifteenth centuries, a considerable amount of travelling. The more important landowners usually held separate estates in different parts of England, so that there was a perpetual coming and going between them. The practice of appeals to Rome involved an astonishing amount of journeying of ecclesiastics and legal agents of one kind and another. The common people—much like the Hindoos and the Japanese of to-day—

seem always to have been on the road, on pilgrimages, or seeking employment, or visiting the towns. The innumerable local markets, and still more, the periodical great fairs, must have required huge concourses of travellers from longer or shorter distances. We get, in fact, from *Piers Plowman* and Chaucer, from the municipal and manorial records, and from the pictures of the period, a vision of a really enormous amount of " wayfaring life," which seems to indicate the existence all over the kingdom of quite passable bridleways. Of wheel traffic, indeed, there was comparatively little, and that of the most primitive kind. Every one travelled on foot or on horseback, and nearly all goods were carried on the backs of animals. Heavy materials were taken by water, going by small boats far up the most insignificant streams. But some heavy carriage by road there must have been. The agricultural tenants of the Manor had their own rude carte, drawn by the stout horses used for ploughing. The "common carrier" existed in the fourteenth century, much as he does in i the country today; and Thorold Rogers has shown that hired 'waggon traction for grain was, in the fourteenth century, charged for at the rate of about one penny, and that for heavy wares. at about twopence per ton per mile, or a sum not far removed from the day's wages of a common labourer.

When exactly the decline of the roads set in does not seem clear. What is probable is that many causes co-operated in producing neglect. We notice, to begin with, an actual falling off in the use of the roads. Though, of course, no statistics exist, there seems reason to believe that between 1350 and 1550 the amount of travelling greatly diminished. Thus, we see the fairs declining in importance, and even the local markets to some extent superseded by new methods of trade and the growth of town populations. Landed estates, we are told, became consolidated in the extensive redistributions of property that accompanied the dynastic wars of the fifteenth century, the "Great Pillage " of the monasteries, and the agricultural revolution that was simultaneously going on. This consolidation of estates must have involved less going to and fro of an influential class. The very agricultural revolution itself, with its substitution of pasture for arable cultivation, meant that less of the produce of the farm needed to be carted, and that an everincreasing proportion walked away on its own feet, actually preferring the " soft going " which the carriers thought a bad road. With the break with Rome there stopped all the business of appeals to the Pope, which had, in the preceding centuries, led to a perpetual riding to and fro. At the same time, the pilgrimages came to an end, and even the local shrines ceased to be visited. High and low, the characteristic wayfaring life of the Middle Ages gradually passed away. _ Moreover, as the roads became less used, so the resources applicable to their maintenance dwindled. Much had been done for the roads in the previous centuries by pious founders on the one hand, and by the various religious orders on the other, especially in their capacity as owners of a large proportion of the land of the kingdom. The progressive impoverishment of the religious orders in the fifteenth century seems to have checked expenditure on road maintenance, and the confiscation of the monastic property by Henry the Eighth practically brought it to an end. The new proprietors of the monastic estates habitually ignored the merely customary obligations which the monasteries had discharged; and it seems that road maintenance was no exception. But the manorial organisation was itself in decay, and, especially in those parts of England in which parishes were being enclosed, the performance of manorial duties must have become increasingly difficult to enforce. "The roads suffered," says Dr. Cunningham, "because the institutions which had been accustomed to do repairs lost their resources, and no one else had sufficient public spirit to take up the matter in earnest." With the progress of the sixteenth century the neglected condition of the highways gradually becomes a subject of public concern. In the first half of the sixteenth century we come across half a dozen statutes dealing with road improvement in particular localities. At last, in 1555, we see provided by statute a new organisation for road administration for the whole kingdom, for the first time an organisation specially for this service. It is with this organisation that our Story of the King's Highway really begins.

APPENDIX TO CHAPTER I

Noras And References

Page 1. We have made no special research into the history of roads prior to the sixteenth century; and we can only refer the student to such works as *English Wayfaring Life in the Middle Ages,* by J. J. Jusserand (English translation by Lucy Toulmin Smith, 4th edition, 1892); *History of Agriculture and Prices in England,* by J. E. Thorold Rogers, 1866-1902, especially voL i. chap. viii. "Journeys and Markets," chap, xxvii. "On the Cost of Carriage," and voL ii. pp. 664, 693, 712; *The Growth of English Industry and Commerce during the Early and Middle Ages,* by Dr. W. Cunningham, 5th edition, 1910, especially voL i. pp. 79, 104, 280, 450, etc.; *England in the Fifteenth Century,* by W. Denton, 1888, p. 173, etc.; and *Social England in the Fifteenth Century,* by Annie Abram, 1909.

Page 2. "The phrase... 'the King's Highway' has passed into common use as a kind of ornament of speech, without any clear sense of its historical meaning" *(The History of English Law,* by Sir F. Pollock and P. W. Maitland, 1895, vol. i. p. 22). The phrase is intimately connected with "the King's Peace." "They come from the time when the King's protection was not universal but particular, when the King's Peace was not for all men or all places, and the King's Highway was in a special manner protected by it" *(ibid.).* The extension of the King's Peace to all travellers on the four great through roads seems to date from the eighth or ninth century. These were the "Quatuor Chimini" of the Norman laws (see *Origins of English History,* by C. I. Elton, 2nd edition, 1890, p. 325, and the authorities there cited). Its extension to all highways may date only from the end of the eleventh century (see *Oxford Lectures,* by Sir F. Pollock, 1890).

Page 2. See *The Manor and the Borough,* by S. and B. Webb, 1908.

Page 3. The quotation as to the British roads is from *Our Roman Highways,* by U. A. Forbes and A. C. Burmester, 1904, p. 34. For all that is known or conjectured about these pre-Roman routes and structures, see various articles in *Archceologia* (notably by Dr. Phene and Dr. Alfred Tylor in voL xlviii., 1885); in *Journal of the Royal Archaeological Society* for June 1877 (by Dr. Phene); *The Ancient History of North and South Wiltshire,* by Sir Richard Colt Hoare, 1812-19; *The Celt, the Roman and the Saxon,* by Thomas Wright, 4th edition 1885, pp. 221-6; *The Old Road* i-Y from Winchester to Canterbury, by Hilaire Belloc, 1910; *Ancient Dorset,* by Charles Warne, 1872, pp. 29, 130; *History of Somerset,* by William Phelps, 1836-9, voL i. p. 84; *History of Berkshire,* by Colonel Cooper King, 1887, p. 19; *Victoria History of Devonshire,* vol. i., 1906 (article by R. Burnard, pp. 371-2).

Dr. Alfred Tylor gives reasons *(Archceologia,* vol. xlviii., 1885) for thinking that the Britons had at least some roads passable for war-chariots, and many others passable for packhorees laden with tin. The ancient stone trackways and bridges on Dartmoor are described in the *Perambulation of the Ancient and Royal Forest of Dartmoor,* by Samuel Rowe, 1848; *An Exploration of Dartmoor,* by J. L. W. Page, 1889; or *A Book of Dartmoor,* by S. Baring-Gould, 1900; see *Lives of the Engineers,* by Samuel Smiles, 1862, p. 157. / Page 3. For the road system of the Roman Empire, see Mommsen's *History of Rome* (translation by W. P. Dickson, 1886), book viii. oh. v. For the Roman roads of Britain, see *Histoire des Grands Chemins de* f *Empire Remain,* by Nicholas Bergier, 1622, 1628, 1694 and 1728;
Britannia Romana, by J. Horsley, 1732, p. 391; *Observations upon certain* (r *Roman Roads and Towns in the South of Britain,* by Vigilo H. L. Long,
1836; Cresy's *Encyclopedia of Civil Engineering,* 1847; "The Four Roman Ways," by Dr. Guest, in *Archaeological Journal,* vol. xiv. p. 99,
included in his *Origines Celticce; The Roman Roads in Britain, with the / Ancient and Modem Names attached to each Station on or near the route,*
by A. H., 1852; *Roman Britain,* by H. W. Scarth, 1883, p. 121; *The Celt, the Roman and the Saxon,* by Thomas Wright, 4th edition, 1885, pp. 222-3, 524; "The Roman Roads of Britain," by W. B. Paley, in *Nineteenth Century,* November 1898; *Roman Roads in Britain,* by T. Codrington,
1903; *Our Roman Highways,* by U. A. Forbes and A. C. Burmester, 1904;
and Haverfield's *The Romanization of Roman Britain,* 1912.
Page 5. It should be noted that there might also be exemption
ratione tenures, of a particular person or township or parish, from the obligation to repair some road or bridge.

Page 5. As regards early history, see *The Growth of English Industry and Commerce, during the Early and Middle Ages,* by Dr. W. Cunningham (5th edition, 1910), voL L

Page 5. The quotations are from *The Law of Highways,* by R. H. Spearman, 1881, p. 1; and Rolle's *Abridgement,* under title "Chimin," p. 292.

Thus " the right of the public in a highway is an easement of passage only—a right of passing and repassing. In the language of pleading, a party can only justify passing along, not being in, a highway" *(Pratt and S Mackenzie's Law of Highways,* by William W. Mackenzie, 16th edition, 1911, p. 2). Hence it has been expressly held that there is no right to use a highway for racing, or for a public meeting *(ibid.);* nor may a man stand still on the road to shoot pheasants flying over it (R. v. Pratt, 1855, 4 £. and B. 860). He may not even walk up and down so as maliciously to interfere with others' rights (Harrison v. Duke of Rutland, 1893, 1 Q.B. 142),—see *The Common Law of England,* by Blake Odgers, 1911, voL L / pp. 7-10. It is only inferentially that it has quile recently been suggested that a passenger along a highway may lawfully stop to rest on it for a short time, or to take a sketch (per A. L. Smith, L.J. in Hickman *v.* Matsey, 1900, 1 Q.B. 756). Any other use of a highway is a trespass.

But in legal definitions, as in common parlance, the term highway is now used to denote the land as well as the easement. "The term highway in its widest sense comprises *all portions of land* over which every subject of the Crown may lawfully pass " *(Pratt and Mackenzie's Law of Highways,* by W. W. Mackenzie, 16th edition, 1911, p. 1).

Page 6. The quotation as to the right to diverge from the beaten track, even to the extent of "going over the corn," is to be found in *A Treatise of the Pleas of the Crown,* by W. Hawkins, edited by T. Leach, 1795, vol. i. p. 153. / See *A Profitable Work to this Whole Kingdom concerning the Mending of* IS *yall the Highways,* by Thomas Proctor, 1610. Modern lawyers have more respect for fences, and fences have become more common. But it is definitely held that " the right of passage or way *(prima facie* and unless

«r-f:*r* » - » .

there be evidence to the contrary) extends to the whole space between the fences; and the public are entitled to the use of the entire of it as the highway" (per Martin, B. and approved per Cur, R. *v.* United Kingdom Telegraph Co. 31 L. J. MC. 166).
This is important in connection with the frequent attempts of adjoining landowners to appropriate and enclose the grass margins, sometimes called "pads," on each side of the metalled roadway.

Page 6. For the Cumberland roads of 1792, 6ee a speech by W. Blamire in the *Cumberland Pacquet* for 2nd February 1830.

Page 6. These etymologies of the word "road" are given in Skeat's Etymological Dictionary. But the Oxford English Dictionary suggests a connection with the Dutch or Low German " reeden," to fit out. The word " road " (at first spelt " rode "), in its modern sense, does not appear to be older than Shakespeare.

Page 7. The "eighteenth century reformer" is W. M. Godschall; see his *General Plan of Parochial Police,* 1787, p. 60.

Page 7. For the Statute of Winchester (13 Edward I. stat. II. cap. 5), see *Constitutional History of England,* by Dr. W. Stubbs; *The Growth of English Industry and Commerce during the Early and Middle Ages,* by Dr. W. Cunningham, 5th edition, 1910, vol. i. p. 280.

Page 7. As to the amount of travelling prior to the sixteenth century, see *English Wayfaring Life in the Middle Ages,* by J. J. Jusserand (translated by Lucy Toulmin Smith), 4th edition, 1892; *History of Agriculture and Prices in England,* by J. E. Thorold Rogers, 1866, vol. i. pp. 133, 144.

Page 8. As to cost of carriage, and the common carrier, see chap, xxvii. (" On the Cost of Carriage ") of vol. i. of *History of Agriculture and Prices in Englat«d,* 1866, by J. E. Thorold Rogers. Professor Nicholson summarizes the evidence as under: "In the first period (1260-1400) the cost of carrying grain by cart with two horses and a man was about a penny a ton per mile.... The same rate seems to have prevailed up to 1542, when the general rise in prices began.... Heavy goods, *e.g.* tiles and lead, cost something under twopence per mile, while wine varies from twopence to fourpence.... From 1583 to 1613 the cost of carriage of a ton of firewood was about 5Jd. per mile; and during the next thirty years 8d., and by the end of the century a shilling per ton per mile is a common rate" *(Principles of Political Economy,* by J. Shield Nicholson, 1901, vol. iii. pp. 91-2). Comparing these prices with the contemporary wages of labour, we get, approximately, the result that from 1260 right down to 1800 the price for carrying a ton of goods for a mile did not depart far from one day's wages of a farm labourer, though the price in money went up twelvefold. We may put against this approximately constant rate of one day's labour per ton mile a recent American statement of the cost of haulage on roads at the opening of the twentieth century. This is given as from 15 to 25 cents per ton per mile on earth tracks, and from 8 to 15 cents per ton per mile on the best roads *S/(A Treatise on Roads and Pavements,* by Ira Osborn Baker, 1903, p. 7). Taking it for comparison at 20 cents, or tenpence, being equal to about one-fifth of a day's wages of a common labourer, we may reckon that the cost of waggon haulage on earth roads in the United States is five times as r great in money, but (what is more important) is only one-fifth, measured in human labour, of what it used to be in the England of 1300-1800.

Page 8. For the decline of travelling, and the decay of road maintenance, see *The Growth of English Industry and Commerce during the Early and Middle Ages,* by Dr. W. Cunningham, 5th edition, 1910, voL i. pp. 450-1; *History oj Agriculture and Prices in England,* by J. E. Thorold Rogers, 1866, voL i. pp. 134-144, 650-666; voL ii. p. 693.

With regard to the diminution in the use of highways for carriage on the decay of arable farming, it is interesting to see that, as late as 1794 it was noticed that, in a pasture-farming district, the farmers cared little for roads. "The small quantity of corn the farmer has to draw to market renders the state of the roads of less consequence to the natives—a bullock, a sheep, or a horse will travel where it would be difficult for a cart or a waggon " *(General View of the Agriculture of Derby,* by Thomas Brown, 1794).

Page 9. It may here be noted that the wayside chapel, common enough on roads abroad, seems to have been rare in England (apart from chapels on bridges). One such wayside chapel existed on the great Bath road, near the entrance to the town of Newbury. It was pulled down by the Municipal Corporation in 1791 *(History of... Newbury,* by Walter Money, 1887, p. 364).

Page 9. In 1523 an Act (14 and 15 Henry VIII. c. 6), which authorised the owner of the Manor of Hempstead in Kent to enclose an old road and make a new one, also provided "in consideration that many other common ways in the said County of Kent be so steep and noyons by wearing, and course of water, and other occasions, that people cannot have their carriages or passages by horses upon or by the same, but to their great pains, peril, and jeopardy," that any other landowners might lay out new roads, by consent of two Justices and a Jury of twelve men. Eleven years later (by 26 Henry VIII. c. 7, 1534) the same power was given for the County of Sussex. Between 1532 and 1540 three successive statutes provided for the paving of various great highways leading out of London, which were "very noyous and foul, and in many places... very jeopardous" to passengers, "as well on horseback as on foot, in winter and in summer, by night and by day" (24 Henry VIII. c. 11; 25 Henry VIII. c. 8; 32 Henry VIII. c. 17). There were half a dozen Road Acts in Queen Mary's reign and nineteen in that of Queen Elizabeth *(Knight's Pictorial History of England,* by G. L. Craik and C. Macfarlane, vol. ii. book vi. chap. iv. pp. 781-2 of 1855 edition—practically the only history that deigns to mention the subject of roads in the sixteenth century).

We may note, in particular, the temporary Acts of 18 Elizabeth and 35 Elizabeth, re-enacted permanently under Charles I., requiring all occupiers of land within five miles of Oxford, either to perform their Statute Labour and Team Duty on the roads, or else to pay a tax to the Vice-Chancellor of the University and the Mayor of the City, which became popularly known as "the Mileway Tax." The Privy Council, under Charles I., had the roads measured, and posts put up at the fifth mile (see *Three Oxfordshire Parishes,* by Mrs. Stapleton, 1893, pp. 282-3; and in the Bodleian Library, 8ymonds MSS. p. 348, and Gough MSS. No. 138).

CHAPTER II ROAD LEGISLATION UNDER THE TUDORS AND THE STUARTS

The famous statute of the Parliament of 1555, known as 2 and 3 Philip and Mary, c. 8, formed for nearly three hundred years the basis of the new organisation of road maintenance. With agriculture in revolution, and the Manorial Courts in decay, Parliament apparently set itself to construct, not so much new law as new social machinery for the administration, all over England and

Wales, of what was deemed an entirely local service. The ancient common law obligation, descended from the *trinoda necessitas,* was, for the first time, definitely allocated among the several parties, and the procedure to be followed was peremptorily laid down. We need not stay to particularise all the minor changes made by successive amending Acts. What we shall attempt to describe is the new legal framework which, between 1555 and 1698, Parliament provided for the administraTion of the King's Highway.''

Under these Acts, together with the Common Law, which they only slightly modified, the obligation to provide for the maintenance of all existing public highways rested on the Parish as a whole and on every inhabitant thereof; on the newly created Surveyor of Highways appointed for the Parish; on the Justices of the Peace within the Division in which the Parish was situated; and, as regards certain minor services, on the owners of the lands adjacent to the highway. All these persons could be independently informed against or presented before a judicial tribunal, and if they had failed to fulfil their legal obligations, could be separately fined for their respective defaults. But upon the Parish as a whole, and upon all the inhabitants thereof, was cast a pre-eminent obligation. Unless it could be definitely proved that some particular person was legally liable to maintain a particular bit of road, it was the Parish which had to do it. Moreover, even if each and every inhabitant had severally performed his own statutory duty, if the highway was, in the opinion of the Court, still insufficiently repaired, the Parish might be fined over and over again until the road was made good. This general and continuous collective liability was, however, merely an uncomfortable background to the onerous personal duty imposed upon each inhabitant.

The first duty cast on the Parish was to provide, from among its own inhabitants, one or more persons to serve gratuitously as Surveyors of Highways for the ensuing year. But except for the individual who found himself thrust into an unpaid and onerous office, this was the easiest part of the task. All the manual labour, tools, and horses and carts needed for repairing the roads, had to be furnished gratuitously by the parishioners themselves. "Every person, for every plough-land in tillage or pasture " that he occupied in the Parish—defined subsequently as a holding of £50 annual value—and " also every person keeping a draught (of horses) or plough in the Parish," had to provide and send " one wain or cart furnished after the custom of the country, with oxen, horses, or other cattle, and all other necessaries meet to carry things convenient for that purpose, and also two able men with the same." Finally, "every other householder, cottager, and labourer, able to labour, and being no hired servant by the year," was either to go himself to work or to send "one sufficient labourer in his stead." All these teams and labourers had annually to appear on the roads on the date and at the hour fixed by the Surveyor, there to work under his direction for eight hours on four, and afterwards on six, consecutive days.

Upon the Surveyor of Highways more onerous duties were imposed. From the day on which the Parish Constable brought him the warrant showing that he had been nominated by his fellow-parishioners and appointed by the Justices at their special "Highways Sessions," he found himself entangled in multifarious and perplexing obligations. First, he had to take over from his predecessor any balance of " highway money," and to learn, as best he could, the manner in which *tb.%.* highway accounts were made up, and how he would have to enter the complicated series of fines, compositions, and commutations in order to satisfy at the end of his year of office the audit of the magistrates and their clerk. What may be called the police duties of his office were numerous and troublesome. Three times during the year, at least, he had to "view all the-roads, highways, watercourses, bridges, and pavements within his precinct, and make presentment upon oath in what condition he finds the same to the next Justice." He had to see to it that the owners of the lands adjacent to the highways cleared these ways of " any timber, stone, hay, stubble," etc. that had been placed on them; cleansed and scoured the "ditches, gutters, and drains adjoining "; laid "sufficient trunks, tunnels or bridges" where any cartways entered the highway from their fields: cut down, grubbed, and"carried away" any trees,bushes, or shrubs standing or growing in the highway; and kept "their hedges cut and pared right up from the roots, and not spreading into or hanging over any part of the highway," in order that, from one end of the parish to the other, there might be "a clear passage for travellers and carriages," and that the sun may shine into the ways "to dry the same," and enable them, as the phrase ran, "to grow better of themselves." And, as if this was not enough, he was at all times to keep a look-out for and waylay waggons, wains, carts, and carriages, that were drawn by more than the statutory number of oxen or horses, or had these arranged in any but the statutory way. The very next Sunday after he had discovered any "defaults or annoyances" in breach of the above regulations, he was expressly required to stand up in the parish church, " immediately after sermon ended," and proclaim the offenders, giving notice that, if not amended within thirty days, he would himself put the matter right and charge the expenses to the defaulters. Possibly, after some weeks of this unpopular activity, he might find some relaxation in his journey to attend the special Highway Sessions at the neighbouring town, to listen to a solemn "charge" from the assembled Justices as to his duties, to make his presentments, and to answer the magistrates' questions upon them; or in his occasional jaunt to the Quarter Sessions at the county town, to do his best to defeat an indictment of the parish for neglecting its roads, or, from the end of the seventeenth century, to extract from the Justices the order to levy the sixpenny rate, by which alone he could hope to recover the outlay to which he had been driven. But any little interest or excitement he might get from these contacts with the greater world would be more than balanced by the invidious relations into which he necessarily came with all his fellow-parishioners. It was the Surveyor who had to fix the six days on which the whole parish had to turn out and work on the roads; it was for him to order the unwilling teams and carts to drag the stones, gravel, or quarry rubbish to the places where he judged them to be required; it was for him to see that the labourers were all at work, and to direct their labours with whatever knowledge of road-making he might possess. Finally, it was on him that fell the disagreeable duty of reporting all defaulters to the nearest Justice of the Peace, in order that they might be fined; and of collecting, from poor cottagers and niggardly farmers, whatever cash payments might be due from them. If, dismayed by the prospect of so much work without pay, he refused to accept office, he might promptly find himself mulcted in a penalty of five pounds. Moreover, for any neglect of his duty, he was liable to be summarily fined forty shillings for each default.

Compared with such onerous duties, the obligations cast upon the Justices of the Peace with regard to highway administration were indefinite, slight, and easily evaded. After the collapse of the centralised adniinistration of James the First and Charles the First, the Justices were, as we have pointed out in our volume on *The Parish and the County,* left in practice free to perform as they chose, or altogether to ignore, their statutory duties. It is true that the Act of 1691 talked of a penalty of £5 being incurred by the Justices of each Division if they did not, once in every four months, hold a Special Highway Sessions; but no one ever heard of the penalty being enforced. It was at one of these sessions that the assembled Justices had to audit the accounts of the outgoing Surveyors, and after considering the lists of qualified persons presented by the officers of the several parishes in the Division, to appoint, for each of them, " out of the said lists, according to their discretion, and the largeness of the parish... one, two or more as they shall think fit and approve of to be... Surveyors of the Highways. " And every Justice, either by himself or in Petty, Special, or Quarter Sessions, had to perform, when appealed to, a number of semi-judicial functions relating to the parish highways, such as hearing pleas of excuse for non-fulfilment of the Statute Labour, issuing warrants for levying the penalties and forfeitures imposed by the Act, and, as we shall presently see, occasionally sanctioning rates on the inhabitants of particular parishes to cover extraordinary expenses. Beyond these obligations, the action of the Justices, though it might, if they chose, become of great importance, was entirely optional. Any one Justice might " on his own proper knowledge" make "presentment to Quarter Sessions of any highway not well and sufficiently repaired," and any such presentment was " of the same force, strength, and effect in the law" as if it had been made by the Grand Jury. But the locally resident Justices could themselves practically take over the highway administration. Without in any way absolving the parish from its legal liability, or relieving the Surveyor of his personal responsibility, the Justices could, if they saw fit, convert him practically into a mere agent. They could order him to repair one bit of road before another, they could command him to put up guide-posts or direction stones at the cross-ways; in Quarter Sessions assembled they could decide whether the compulsory service should be made to suffice, or whether a sixpenny rate should be levied in addition; they could direct exactly how the Surveyor should expend any moneys thus placed at his disposal; and finally, they could direct any highway to be widened and the necessary land to be compulsorily taken for the purpose, at the expense of the extra rate.

From the foregoing summary of the law, the student will have noted that the statutory enactments from 1555 to 1697 differed from the Common Law by their inclusion, in a tentative and somewhat cryptic form, of two typical powers of modern local government—the power to enlarge an ancient customary service at the public cost, and the complementary power of raising a revenue by compulsory taxation.

The note of enlargement of the ancient customary service is given in the titles and preambles of nearly all the statutes after the Restoration, even when their clauses amount to little more than a specific enactment of the Common Law. The highways are to be " enlarged," "better amended," and repaired so as to promote trade, in a way for which, admittedly, "the ordinary course appointed by the laws and statutes of this realm is not sufficient." It is enforced in the Act of 1691 by the emphatic direction that " the Surveyors shall make every cartway leading to any market town eight foot wide at least, and as near as may be even and level," and that "no horse causey shall be less in breadth than three foot "—a sort of "National Minimum" of road administration to which every parish might be forced to attain, if the Justices chose to do their duty, or if any one would undertake the cost and trouble of an indictment. Moreover, the Justices in Quarter Sessions were expressly empowered to go beyond this Minimum, and " to enlarge and widen any highways" by the compulsory purchase of the necessary land, so long as they did not exceed an extension of eight yards in breadth, and not " pull down any house " or " take away the ground of any garden, orchard, court, or yard."

The transition from a service to be wholly rendered in kind to a mixed system of Statute Labour and money payments, and from this to a compulsory Highway Rate, is full of interest and instruction. From time immemorial amercements or fines had been imposed by the Manorial Courts on persons committing active or passive nuisances in connection with the highways or otherwise, but it was not until the Act of 1555 that these fines were definitely assigned to the parish officers " to be bestowed on the highways." When "the Statute for Mending of Highways" was made permanent in 1563, and the four days' Statute Labour were enlarged to six days, the Surveyors of Highways were expressly required "within one month next after default made contrary to the Statute of 2 & 3 Philip and Mary, or this Act, to present such default to the next Justice of the Peace under pain to forfeit forty shillings, and such Justice shall certify the same presentment at the next General Sessions, upon pain to forfeit £5, and the Justices of the Peace shall have authority to enquire of any such default or offence at their Quarter Sessions, and to assess such fines for the same as they or any two of them, whereof one to be of the Quorum, shall think meet." Presently the fine took the form of a fixed payment in default of service; settled by the Act of 1670, at Is. 6d. for the day's labour of one man, 3s. for a man and horse, and 10s. for a cart with two men.

The momentous and decisive step of instituting a compulsory tax for road maintenance was taken by the Government of the Commonwealth. To the historian the period between 1649 and 1660 has usually seemed one of constitutional experiments and religious controversies. The student who will examine the records of the Commonwealth from the standpoint of economic and social development will find in these troublous years the beginnings of many of the institutions of our own time. Among these is the Highway Bate. It is plain that the resources at the disposal of the Surveyors of Highways, whether in the way of Statute Labour or in that of commutations and fines, were inadequate for any advance in the standard of road maintenance. The incidence of the burden was felt to be unfair. The success of the Rebellion had, perhaps, thrown into confusion the old system of parish government. We find complaints that parishes have neglected to appoint any Surveyors of Highways. In many places, we are told, the Surveyors were quite unable to enforce the Statute Duty from the farmers, "who beat them if they approached their houses" with obnoxious demands, so that parishes "could not repair the roads." We find, in fact, in 1649 and 1650 respectively, two Derbyshire parishes begging the Justices in Quarter Sessions, apparently with success, to order an equal assessment on all the inhabitants, in order to repay the Surveyor of Taxes for his outlay. In the first case the "Supervisor of the Highways" for Newbold and Dunston asks that, as "but few of the inhabitants have helped or paid towards the mending of the said highways, and many do refuse both to help with their draughts or to give money," that" draughts might be hired according to law and custom," and as he is already five pounds out of pocket, an order may be granted "that an assessment may be made through the whole township of Newbold and Dunston." In the other case, the inhabitants of Calowe themselves petition " that all the occupiers " of lands within the said hamlet may be equally assessed for " repair" of the highways. We are aware of no statutory authority under which Quarter Sessions could at that date lawfully impose these compulsory rates. But such authority was not long delayed. In 1654 the Commonwealth Parliament enacted "An Ordinance for Better Amending and Keeping in Repair the Common Highwaies within this Nation," which had been drawn up, so it is alleged, by Baron Thorpe (1595-1665), one of the ablest of the Commonwealth lawyers, who was at once member for Beverley in the Parliament of 1654-55, and also one of the Exchequer Judges. This provided, not only for ensuring that Surveyors of Highways should be appointed in every parish, but also for a meeting of parishioners to make a rate not exceeding a shilling in the pound for "making and repairing and cleansing roads and pavements" in corporate towns and rural parishes alike. If the parishioners failed to make the necessary rate, the Surveyors of Highways might make it themselves and get it confirmed by the nearest Justice of the Peace. With the funds so provided, labourers and teams were to be hired, and the making, repairing, and cleansing of the roads and pavements was to be systematically undertaken. Nuisances were to be abated and encroachments removed; and special assessments were to be levied on the owners of adjoining lands from which nuisances arose. Finally, if any parish found its rate of a shilling in the pound inadequate to the proper fulfilment of its duties, the Justices in Quarter Sessions were expressly empowered to levy, on the adjoining parishes, a special rate in aid.

To what extent and in how many parishes this trenchant and far-reaching Ordinance was actually put in force we have no information. Subsequent critics of road administration looked back regretfully to what was done "during the times of the Usurpation," when " they in some places taxed the parishes by a pound rate for repairing the highways. Particularly it was done in Herefordshire about Leominster, where the tax was no less than sixpence a pound. This way did not last long, but it did so effectually do the business and it wrought such a reformation that the like was never seen before or since."

With the Restoration, all the legislation of the Commonwealth became invalid; and we see, in one department of social life after another, the Parliaments of the whole of the ensuing generation picking up and hesitatingly reenacting imperfect scraps of the bolder Cromwellian legislation. Thus, in the matter of road maintenance, we have, first, a temporary statute of 1662, entitled "An Act for enlarging and repairing the highways," by which every Surveyor was directed, " together with two or three substantial householders... to lay one or more assessment or assessments upon every inhabitant rated to the poor. .. for the repairing, amending, and enlarging the said public and common highways," such assessment or rate not to exceed " sixpence in the pound in any one year," and to be allowed and signed by a Justice of the Peace. This Highway Rate was to be levied in all parishes, unless it was proved to the satisfaction of Quarter Sessions, or of two Justices, that it was not required; but only for a term of three years, after which, it seems to have been assumed, the ordinary Statute Labour would suffice. The Act itself was also limited to the continuance of the existing Parliament. We have discovered only one parish in which any rate was made under this temporary legislation, which remained, we suspect, a dead letter. In 1670 Parliament once more tried to get a rate levied for mending the roads, this time placing the duty directly upon Quarter Sessions, but again limiting the dreaded power of rating to a period of three years. During this period, if the Justices in Quarter Sessions were satisfied that the highways in any parish could and would not be sufficiently amended otherwise, they were to order a rate to be levied on all the parishioners, not exceeding sixpence in the pound on lands, or sixpence on every £20 worth of personal estate in any one year, and to have the money expended on the roads under the Justices' own direction. To what degree of efficiency the Justices were stimulated by this Act we cannot say. That some action was taken we may infer from the entries in the MS. Churchwardens' accounts of the Parish of St. Mary's, Reading, which show that "a tax of twenty weeks" (by which we understand the customary weekly levy) was granted for " The Surveyors of the Highways" on 22nd May 1670, and again on 24th April 1671; whilst others of "ten weeks" were granted on 15th September 1671, and 31st March 1673.

It is, however, clear that these temporary laws failed to effect their object; and, to use the words of a contemporary writer, in the opening years of William and Mary, "the drowsy heads of the slumbering statutes made for the repairing and amendment of highways " had once more to be " roused up " by a new Act, that of 1691, in which, for the third time, Parliament tried to set going a Highway Rate. In some parishes there was a lack of suitable road material, and the Surveyor was therefore authorised, if he could procure proper material in no other way, to purchase what was necessary. To reimburse himself for this outlay, he was authorised to call upon the Justices in Special Sessions to make a rate on the Parish for that purpose. At the same time Parliament re-enacted, this time in permanent form, the provision of the temporary Act of 1670, empowering the Justices in Quarter Sessions, if they were satisfied that the roads within any parish could not be otherwise sufficiently repaired, to levy a rate up to sixpence in the pound on all the parishioners, to be expended as Quarter Sessions might direct. Beyond these two rates for maintenance, the Justice in Quarter Sessions could, under an Act of 1697, " order an assessment to be made upon all the inhabitants, owners or occupiers of lands, houses, tenements or hereditaments," in order to put in force the power of taking land to widen a highway.

Still the law remained ineffective, and very few parishes had a Highway Rate. There was discovered, however, an indirect method of getting a compulsory levy on all the occupiers of land in the parish, which the Justices in Quarter Sessions derived from the Common Law, and of which, as we shall presently describe, constant use was made. The parish, as we have mentioned, was at all times liable to be presented or indicted for neglect to keep in sufficient repair any part of the highway within its limits. If found guilty, the parish was fined in an amount left entirely to the discretion of the Court. Originally such a fine might be levied on any inhabitant of the parish, and it went through the Sheriff's annual accounts into the Royal Exchequer. Presently it was provided in 1691, that the person so mulcted on behalf of the parish might get himself reimbursed by a rate levied on all the inhabitants, and paid to the Surveyors to be applied to the repair of the highways. Here we discover, in the union of the penal jurisdiction of Quarter Sessions or the Assizes, with the administrative jurisdiction of the Special Highway Sessions, a power of levying a rate of unlimited amount. Combined with the power of any one Justice to "present" a road on his own view and knowledge, and with that of the Clerk of the Peace to prosecute any indictment, this ancient procedure might be used to raise, throughout each county, the standard of road maintenance up to any point that Quarter Sessions chose to regard as sufficient. Thus, by the beginning of the eighteenth century, at any rate, the parish, and its amateur and compulsorily serving Surveyors of Highways, were provided with ample legal authority for raising the funds required for efficient road maintenance. Nevertheless, so great was the reluctance to levy a rate, and so wedded were the parishioners to the system of a common sharing of the labour to be performed, that this so-called "Statute Labour" continued, for more than another century, to be the main resource of parochial road administration.

APPENDIX TO CHAPTER II

Notes And References

Page 14. We know of no study of the highway legislation of the sixteenth and seventeenth centuries, for which the sources are the Statutes themselves, to which reference is made below, together with the scanty glimpses afforded by Parish and Quarter Sessions records and the rare contemporary pamphlets hereafter mentioned.

Page 14. The "Statute of Philip and Mary" (2 & 3 Philip and Mary, c. 8), passed as a temporary Act, in 1555, was permanently re-enacted in 1563 (5 Elizabeth, c. 13); and was not repealed until the codifying Act of 1766 (7 George III. c. 42, sec. 57), which re-enacted its provisions, whilst the General Highways Act of 1835 carried on those relating to the Surveyor of Highways to the close of the nineteenth century.

We are not acquainted with any account of the origin or authorship of these statutes, or of the circumstances of their enactment. In particular, it is not at all clear how exactly the ancient Common Law obligation of the Manor was transferred to the Parish.

Page 14. The statutes summarised and quoted from in this chapter are the following:— 2 & 3 Philip and Mary, c. 8 (1555).
5 Elizabeth, c. 13 (1563).
18 Elizabeth, c. 10 (1576).
14 Charles II. c. 6 (1662).
22 Charles II. c. 12(1670).
3 & 4 William and Mary, c. 12 (1691).
7 & 8 William and Mary, c. 29 (1695).
8 & 9 William III. c. 16 (1697).
These statutes, in so far as they were not

temporary, were all repealed (and, in effect, re-enacted) by the codifying Act of 1766 (7 George III. c. 42).

Page 19. For the social position under the Commonwealth, see *The Interregnum,* by F. C. Inderwick, 1891, p. 175, from which the quotation on this page is taken. The Bedfordshire and Yorkshire Quarter Sessions records contain many complaints as to the non-appointment of surveyors *(Growth of English Industry and Commerce in Modern Times,* by Dr. W. Cunningham, 1903, voL i. p. 535).

Page 20. See *Three Centuries of Derbyshire Annals,* by J. C. Cox, 1890, vol. ii. p. 227.

Page 20. The Ordinances of the Commonwealth (which deserve more attention than they have received from the student of economic and social history) may now be consulted in the admirable *Ada and Ordinances of the Interregnum, 1642-1660,* by C. H. Firth and R. S. Bait, 1911,3 vols.; which at last makes obsolete the *Collection of Acts and Ordinances,* by Henry Scobell, 1658. The valuable collection of "Thomason Tracts" in the British Museum contains separately published copies of the main highway law, entitled *An Ordinance for Better Amending and Keeping in Repair the Common Highwaies within this Nation* (31st March 1654), and of two unimportant amending laws, *An Ordinance touching Surveyors of the Highwaies* (12th April 1654), and *An Ordinance of Explaining of a former Ordinance* entitled an *Ordinance for Better Amending and Keeping in Repair the Common Highwaies within this Nation* (16th May 1654). This legislation is alluded to in *The Interregnum* by F. C. Inderwick, 1891, p. 107; and in *The History of Local Rates in England,* by Edwin Caiman, 2nd edition, 1912, pp. 87, 119, 120.

Bylaws in pursuance of these ordinances, relating to the use of iron tyres, haokney coaches, the wandering of pigs, paving and sweeping by householders, etc., were made by various London parishes and allowed by the Justices *(e.g.* in St. Giles in the Fields, and in Shoreditch; see *Middlesex County Records,* by J. C. Jeaffreson, vol. iii. p. 226).

The Commonwealth Parliament did not rest satisfied with this legislation. It is interesting to learn that among the measures under discussion in 1657, when Cromwell peremptorily dismissed the Parliament, was " A Bill for Repairing of the Highways and Improving the Public Roads." Cromwell had actually appointed, by patent, an officer styled " SurveyorGeneral of the Highways," with authority throughout the whole kingdom. The bill would have given him large funds, and, it was declared by its opponents, emoluments equal to £10,000 a year *(Diary of Thomas Burton,* by J. T. Rutt, 1828, vol. i. pp. 294, 345, vol. ii. p. 464).

Page 21. The quotation is from *Proposal for Maintaining and Repairing the Highways,* by E. Littleton, 1692, a rare pamphlet in the British Museum. The same author tells us of a case in which a County Rate was levied for the highways, for which we know of no legal authority. He adduces "what hath lately been done in Kent, upon Canterbury road, which they have made very substantially good where it was extremely bad before, by a small tax of about a halfpenny in the pound laid upon the County."

Page 22. The quotation is from *A Guide to Surveyors of the Highways,* by G. Meriton, 1694.

Page 22. Parishes did not need statutory authority to purchase road material (see *The Parish and the County,* by S. and B. Webb, 1907). In the MS. Churchwardens' accounts of St. Mary's, Reading, we find the Vestry on 12th April 1680 ordering money to be spent in buying " stones for the highways out of Oxfordshire." What the statute of 1691 gave was power to the Surveyor of the Highways himself to purchase, without the authority of the Vestry.

Page 22. How little was effected by the Act of 1691 at the outset may be inferred from the fact that a well-known manual for magistrates, published two years afterwards, ignores it altogether. In *The Justice of Peace, his Calling and Qualification,* by Edmund Bohun (1693), we read: "There have been two or three temporary Acts made since His Majesty's Restoration to enable the Surveyors to repair the ways by a Rate or Land Tax, but they are all expired. Now if this course were settled for ever for the carriages, and only the cottagers tied to do so many days work, all the other Acts of Parliament might be spared." He also notes the ambiguity of the Statute of Philip and Mary as to " plough tilth "; "nobody knows what it is." A " plough tilth" or " plough till" of land, or a " ploughland," we learn from the Oxford Dictionary, was used in Fabyan's *Chronicle,* vii-ccxxii (1516) as being equivalent to " a knight's fee," and as being 160 acres. But it is clear that varying interpretations were put upon the term; and the Act 7 & 8 William HI. c. 29 (1697) defined it as a holding worth £50 a year.

The earliest Highway Rate after the Restoration—the only one that we have found under the 1662 Act—was apparently at Spittal and Tweedmouth in Northumberland in 1663; where we read of "the assessment that was gathered for repairing the highways " (MS. Records of the " Court of View of Frankpledge with Court Baron "; see *The Manor and the Borough,* by S. and B. Webb, 1907, vol. i. p. 95).

CHAPTER III PAROCHIAL ROAD ADMINISTRATION

It was, as we have seen in the preceding chapter, one thing for Parliament to enact that parishes should keep their highways in repair, and quite another thing to get it actually done. We have now to describe how the various legal obligations cast upon the Parish were fulfilled, and how far the system of compulsory and gratuitous amateur service succeeded in producing the roads that were required. And in this description we shall roam over the whole country, piecing together the contemporary testimony as to what was actually done in this parish or that, and seeking to convey an impression of parochial road administration as it was during the whole period between 1660 and 1835.

To begin with the Parish as a whole, and its duty of nominating persons as Surveyors of Highways—called also

Overseers or Supervisors of the Highways, or, more familiarly, Waymen, Waywardens, Boonmasters, Stonewardens or Stonemen—we gather that, except perhaps during the dislocation of the Commonwealth, such nominations were made with decent regularity, though the occurrence of complaints by some persons of having to serve continuously indicate that it was not easy to find a sufficient rota of suitable and willing inhabitants. In a grumbling, but on the whole good-tempered sort of way we see the farmers, in the rural parishes, taking it in turns to serve the office, occasionally pressing into the service the village innkeeper, or a little independent craftsman or shopkeeper. We do not gather that the duties were undertaken by the " gentry," even such as were not Justices of the Peace, or that the office was often accepted by clergymen or doctors, who were legally exempt, or that it was ever imposed on the not inconsiderable number of women occupiers or owners of farms.

The basis of the parochial system of road maintenance was, however, not the Surveyor of Highways, but the unpaid and compulsory labour force of all the parishioners, which he was empowered, by mere notice in church, to summon for six days' service. We have made no investigation as to how closely this system of enforced labour resembled the well-known Spring and Autumn *corvie* on the roads of France, or the compulsory road work of Ireland, or the analogous services in other countries. It is noteworthy that although the compulsory road work in Ireland was abolished by statute in 1762, and although Turgot had sought to relieve France from the *corvee* in 1764, "Statute Labour " lasted in England and Wales right down to 1835. The English system was carried to America by the seventeenth century emigrants, and it still exists, for the maintenance of the roads outside the cities, in all but five of the United States.

In England, at least, this Statute Labour seems in the sixteenth and seventeenth centuries to have been performed with the utmost remissness. Whether there was ever a time in which this work was commonly done with any degree of conscientiousness or exactitude we may well doubt. In William Harrison's wellknown *Description of England,* in the reign of Elizabeth, we read that " the rich do so cancel their portions and the poor so loiter in their labours, that of all the six, scarcely two good days' work are performed.... Sometimes, also, these days' works are not employed upon those ways that lead from market to market, but each Surveyor amendeth such byeplots and lanes as seem best for his own commodity and more easy passage unto his fields and pastures." By the seventeenth century it is clear, the highways had got into a dreadful state, as we are told in 1610, "to the daily continual great grief and heartburning of man and beast, with charges, hindrances, wearing and tiring of them, and sometimes to the great and imminent danger of their lives, and often spoil and loss of goods." By the end of the seventeenth century, notwithstanding the successive amending statutes that we have described, the futility of the Statute Labour had become a byword. One hired labourer, it was said in 1696, "will do as much work at the highways in one day than is done by six or seven others" coming in compliance with the law. The substitutes sent in by inhabitants who refused to labour in person were as unsatisfactory as the conscripted workers themselves. "These are they," we read in the same work, "that call themselves the King's Highwaymen, when they beg of all travellers that come near them; but they are commonly called the 'King's Loiterers,' who work when they list, come and go at their pleasure, and spend most of their time in standing still and prating, and looking after their fellows whom they send out from their work, most shamefully, to stop passengers for a largess."

Part of the difficulty of enforcing the six days' attendance arose from the fact that, when the relative equality of conditions of the mediaeval Manor had been left behind, the burden imposed by the law was seen to be very inequitably distributed. "To speak plain," says one of the earliest writers on the subject, "the way and manner of charging persons by the old statutes still in force seems to me as unequal and oppressive as it is uncertain and obscure.... It seems very unequal that every poor cottager and labourer who hath not bread for himself and family to eat but what he earns by his labour from day to day should be charged to labour himself, or to find a labourer, to work the six days in repairing the common highways. And therefore I cannot blame the practice of some Surveyors in this case, especially of those that live in corporate and market towns where the poor abound, in admitting the children of poor cottagers and labourers, in lieu of their parents, to labour the six days in gathering stones for repair of the highways; and in conniving at the absence of other poor cottagers that have no children to send, or in taking but a little money of them for their defect." We gather, indeed, that, in many parts of the country, the exaction of unpaid labour from the poor cottagers was altogether given up; and even the farmers were left to do as much or as little as they chose, to the highways round about their own farms. Any pretence of enforcing the statute was, in fact, abandoned. "The six days' work," writes John Shapleigh, an able Justice of the Peace in 1749, " have hitherto in most parishes been so much neglected, and so slightly performed, that I believe very few parishes can truly say, from their own experience, that the six days' work... are not sufficient." Nor was the result very different where an attempt was still made to enforce the law. The sort of promiscuous popular gathering on the roads once a year—to use the words of Littleton in 1692, "the scambling way of sending in carts and labourers "—could not be made into an effective labour force, even if the service of team and toiler had been fully and cheerfully rendered, and the Surveyor of the Highways had possessed a genius for organisation. "What is the benefit," pertinently asks Sir John Hawkins in 1763, "arising from the labour of twenty men and as many horses, occupied in four or five different stations within an extensive parish, compared with that of half the number of each, working under the immediate direction of an officer, and executing a plan which he himself has concerted." "Let us suppose," says a writer in the *Gentleman's Magazine* in 1763, " that as the statutes direct, a general notice is published, requiring the inhabitants to perform their statute work on six days properly specified, and suppose they all attend, how are the Surveyors to employ them? In most places materials must be got ready before the work can be done, gravel must be dug before it can be spread... a few hands only can be employed. When the whole parish is called out together, the Surveyor cannot avail himself of the labour which such a body might perform." As a matter of fact the duty was always shirked, and there was, to use a modern term, a persistent policy of "ca' canny." "In those few parishes," writes Sir John Hawkins, in 1763, "where the inhabitants are disposed to yield obedience to the letter of it, the days for performing the statute duty are so far from being considered as days of labour that, as well the farmers as the common day-labourers, have long been used to look on them as holidays, as a kind of recess from their accustomed labour, and devoted to idleness and its concomitant indulgences of riot and drunkenness." "Statute work," says a writer in the *Gentleman's Magazine* for December 1767, "is a burden from which everybody has endeavoured, and always will endeavour, to screen themselves and one another. Teams and labourers coming out for statute work are generally idle, careless and under no commands.... They make holiday of it, lounge about, and trifle away their time. As they are in no danger of being turned out of their work, they stand in no awe of the Surveyor... in short, statute work will never mend the roads effectually. " "One hired team," wrote John Scott in 1778, " is almost if not quite equal to two duty teams, with regard to the quantity of work done in a day." "The days set aside for the performance of the statute labour," says the reporter on the agriculture of Herefordshire in 1794, "are, by long established custom considered as allotted to play and merriment, and the man who can continue to do the least work with his master's cattle thinks he does him a kindness." "When a farmer sends his cart to perform statute duty "—to quote the reporters on the agriculture of Northumberland in the same year—" it seldom carries more than half a load, and the servants practise every manoeuvre to put off time and do as little as possible." In the nineteenth century, with the gradual adoption of other methods, contemporary criticism of "Team Duty" becomes less frequent, but it loses nothing of its indignant contempt. "In many cases," we read in 1825, " the statute duty is evaded. Sometimes it is omitted altogether; sometimes the teams do not work the statutable number of hours; sometimes they are sent by the farmer, when, from the wet state of the roads, they do more harm than good; and sometimes a considerable part of the stones and other materials provided by the parish are carted into the gateways, perhaps even the farmyard, of a man who ostensibly is engaged in the performance of a public duty." "I can mention a case," said a witness before a House of Commons Committee in 1834, "of a person going out to do his statute duty, and taking his corn to the miller as a farmer, and on his way bringing home a load of stones, which he called doing his day's statute duty; his neighbour, the Waywarden, disliking, of course, to interfere with his neighbour's proceedings, takes no notice of it—the road suffers." By 1834 it could be reported by a Poor Law Commissioner that "the Statute Labour assigned to farmers is a mere farce, and a farce attended with false pretences."

It was in vain that Parliament conferred upon the Justices large powers to compel the performance of Statute Labour on the roads. In such records of Quarter Sessions as exist we hear of comparatively few indictments, even of the most obstinate of the passive resisters that abounded on every hand. In 1576, indeed, we read of one John Johnson of London, gentleman, occupying one hundred and twenty acres at Fulham, being indicted at the Middlesex Quarter Sessions for " having neither found nor sent any wain or cart " on any of the six days notified in church as having been fixed " for mending and repairing the highways of Fulham." In 1633-34, probably as part of that general tightening up of governmental control over local administration which had its effect in producing the great Rebellion, we see a sudden rush of indictments in Worcestershire and some other counties, to be followed by a complete cessation of indictments for many years. The records of the "Hundred Court" of Pevensey, in Sussex, from 1710 to 1718 contain a few cases in which both farmers and labourers were presented and warned for not working on the highways, but no actual amercements. In 1715, one Richard Cope of Buxton was indicted at the Derbyshire Quarter Sessions " for not sending his cart to the mending of the highways according to notice given in church." The Hertfordshire archives include, under date 17th October 1780, "certificates of the conviction of R. S. and others of Tring (fined 30/), for not working with their teams on the highways in the Hamlet of Long Marsham, in the said parish, by virtue of their holdings in the said Hamlet, on the 5th, 6th, and 7th days of October." But such indictments were certainly not common, and it is repeatedly stated, as we learn from an able Justice of the Peace in 1749, "that the Justices of the Peace are very unwilling to proceed " judicially against the defaulters.

With how little knowledge of the principles of roadmaking the annually chosen, unpaid, amateur Surveyors of Highways went to work, we can dimly imagine. They had, for the most part, no idea of constructing, or even of scientifically repairing a road in any durable way. If they opened the tracks over the common lands once a year, and heaped up earth on the more frequented roads, when the ruts became exceptionally deep, they considered their duty well discharged. Instead of a steamroller, we hear occasionally of the road plough.

"People now living," wrote Albert Pell in 1887, "may have seen, decaying under the walls of a parish church, the enormous plough, girt and stayed with iron, which, as Spring approached, was annually furbished up and brought into the village street. For this the owners or their tenants, acting in concert, made up joint teams of six or eight powerful horses, and proceeded to the restoration of their highways, by ploughing them up, casting the furrows towards the centre, and then harrowing them down to a fairly level surface for the summer traffic." Right down to the opening of the nineteenth century, England had practically nothing but soft "dirt" roads, at best, as Albert Pell says, "mended with weak and rotten sand and gravel "; or, in some districts, as his biographer reminds us, with "flint or rotting pebbles, contributed by the farmers, and picked off the arable fields by the frozen fingers of rural infants For all this miserable outfit statutable books had to be kept, made up, and verified; a separate rate got out, solemnly allowed by Justices of the Peace and then collected. The whole business ended with a wrangle at the Vestry, for which the Surveyor fortified himself with a brimming jorum of brandy and water."

To the administrator of the twentieth century, it must be a subject for astonishment that so extravagant and wasteful a system as Statute Labour, involving so much injustice and personal annoyance to individuals, and resulting in such futility, can ever have been tolerated. Yet, in spite of unanimous condemnation by every competent observer, so attractive to Parliament and the agricultural classes was this device of service in kind, that it remained, down to 1835, the basis of the system of maintaining the highways. Though more and more eaten into, as we shall describe, by money payments, the farmers up and down the country continued to the last to send teams and men instead of paying rates, to the extent officially computed in 1814 of £551,241; and even as late as 1835, to an amount estimated by Sir James M'Adam at " about £200,000 per annum." And though statute after statute dealt with highway maintenance, and pamphlet after pamphlet expatiated on the need for reform, " none of the many various propositions for amending the highways," down to 1763 at any rate, as Sir John Hawkins tells us, ever " ventured to assert the expediency of annihilating" the immemorial service in kind to which the Act of 1555 had given definite Parliamentary consecration.

What ensued was not any abrogation of the law as to Statute Labour, but a steady increase in the adoption of the device of commutation. This began very early. In the "St. Columb Green Book," being the parish accounts of a Cornish village, we find, under date of 1586, an entry to the effect that" those whose names follow have made default about the mending of the said ways, viz. William Mark, Edward Beale, Martin Bysshop,

D

Edward Noye, which four have given to the parish for their default two shillings and sixpence apiece. Also John Skoin hath paid for like default twelvepence." But there came to be more systematic commutation. At Reading, as we learn from the manuscript minutes of the Vestry of St. Mary's Parish, the parishioners, on 12th April 1680—as we imagine, quite without legal authority—made the following roughly graduated scale of services and payments according to means: "The agreement of the Vestry concerning the repairs of the highways within the Parish of St. Mary's. That all persons that pay twopence a week or upwards to the poor shall pay or work six days; all such as pay one penny or three halfpence a week shall pay or work four days; all that (pay) one halfpenny a week and all such (as) above the degree of receiving collection *i.e.* Poor Law relief) shall pay or work two days. All such in case aforementioned qualifications that do accordingly shall pass upon account to the Vestry: that those that shall refuse shall be indicted at the sessions."

More usually, however, the commutation money was based on the pecuniary penalties incurred. It was, as we have pointed out, incumbent on the Surveyor to report defaulters, and their punishment took the form of a fine, "to be bestowed on the highways." And, though, as we have said, Justices were loth to enforce these penalties, we gather that it became the custom for any one who preferred to pay in money to tender the amount, and for the Surveyor of Highways to accept it, rather than be at any trouble. This custom was greatly fostered by the change in the value of money, which, by 1763 at any rate, as the *Gentleman's Magazine* observed, had made it "the interest of the party to incur the penalty rather than perform the duty. The farmer can earn with a cart and one man ten shillings, which will pay the whole penalty he incurs by not employing a team and two men on the highway; and the labourer, if he works, incurs a certain loss of a week's subsistence to his family, but if he omits to work the loss is contingent." When matters had got thus far, it occasionally occurred to the Parish Authorities, especially in towns where the enforcement of Statute Labour had fallen into disuse, to take advantage of the objection to personal service in order to raise parish revenue. Thus, at Manchester, about the middle of the century, when it was desired to improve the Rochdale road, " the expedient was hit upon of summoning all households to Statute duty... and accept of money in commutation, which not only cleared off that arrear, but enabled the managers to make other improvements on the avenues of the town. " "Custom," says the *Gentleman's Magazine* in 1763, "has... in many places converted the labour into a rate as the law now stands; for the Surveyors, as soon as they enter into their office, assess every inhabitant in a sum proportioned to the labour required of him, and proceed to collect it as regularly as the proper officers do the poor's rate; but this practice is illegal; and if it was not, a rate thus accruing is by no means equal... and the Surveyors having, under pretence of favouring those who suffer by the inequality, assumed a power of commuting with the inhabitants, are very frequently guilty of partiality, exacting the full sum when there are equitable pretences for commutation, and commuting where the payment of the whole sum would be less felt." Loud became the complaints of the " corruption " of the Surveyors in thus, as it was termed by Sir John Hawkins, "garbling " the " inhabitants of a parish, commuting with them for their duty, receiving of some five, of others four shillings, half-a-crown, or what many of them like better, a bowl of punch. " It was doubtless to remedy this evil that Parliament, by the General Highway Acts of 1766 and 1773, regularised the practice of commutation, by fixing elaborate scales of money payments as alternatives to service in person. This legislative sanction naturally promoted commutations, and many Surveyors of Highways habitually collected money from those who preferred to pay rather than serve; whilst still making more or less effort to enforce the service in kind, at any rate as regards "team duty," on those who would not, or could not, pay what was demanded. In some few districts, we are told, in 1798, "the old inefficient custom of team-work, labourers, composition, etc. which is seldom half done, and then not in an equitable proportion," was "with consent of the Justices and the parishes" frankly left in complete desuetude, there being paid to the Surveyor instead " an equal assessment of threepence or sixpence in the pound, or more if necessary, on the fair annual value of all lands, houses, hereditaments, etc." Sometimes an old scale of commutation would be combined with an equal pound rate. Thus, the account book of the Surveyors of the Highways for the Parish of Chalfont St. Peter (Bucks) for 18251835, which we have seen, contains a bewildering array of names and figures, with each farmer in the parish debited with so much Statute Duty, apparently in proportion to his rent and tithe, to be performed by so many teams, attended by so many men, for so many days; subject to commutation, if desired, at such and such a sum; together with so much money to be paid in addition, at the rate of 2Jd. in the pound. There could be no check or audit of such accounts. Indeed, what with the lack of any definite valuation roll or fixed assessment, the complication and uncertainty of the law, and the unwillingness of both Surveyors and Justices to be at the trouble of legal proceedings against their neighbours, it is plain that under the commutation system the greatest inequality and laxness prevailed.

The persistence of such uncertain and arbitrary methods of raising funds appears to us to-day still more strange, in that, under the law as we have described it in the preceding chapter from 1691 onward, the Surveyor had, in the occasional Highway Rate, a source of revenue more easily collected than compositions and fines. Such Highway Rates, in fact, began slowly to be levied in particular parishes and townships, though always under the special authority of Quarter Sessions, given in each case as an exceptional measure. That they were greatly resented, and that the whole financial proceedings of the Surveyors of Highways were objected to, we infer from the lively comments of Daniel Defoe in 1697. "The rate for the highways," he asserts in his *Essay on Projects,* " is the most arbitrary and unequal tax in the kingdom; in some places two or three rates of sixpence per pound in the year, in others the whole parish cannot raise wherewith to defray the charge, either by the very bad condition of the road or distance of materials; in others the Surveyors raise what they never expend; and the abuses, exactions, connivances, frauds, and embezzlements are innumerable." But Defoe's complaint led to no reform in assessment or audit, and from the very beginning of the eighteenth century the number of Highway Rates steadily increases. The student of the proceedings of Quarter Sessions is always coming across these separate orders authorising special Highway Rates, usually on the application of the parish Surveyor of Highways, who found himself otherwise unable to perform the necessary repairs. Thus, at the Essex Quarter Sessions in 1700, we read that " Upon application made to this Court by the Surveyors of Highways of the Parish of Purleigh in this County, showing that the statute work for teams and labourers within the said Parish hath been done and performed by the inhabitants of the said Parish, and not sufficient to repair and amend the same for this present year, and humbly praying a rate of sixpence per pound upon all the inhabitants and landowners within the said parish, for the better repairing and amending the said highways. It is ordered by this Court that the said rate of sixpence in the pound be proportionately rated and collected upon the inhabitants of Purleigh accordingly." Such a rate could, at any rate after the Act George I. c. 52 (1716), be equally made in any Municipal Borough having a Court of Quarter Sessions, and thus we find the Ipswich Quarter Sessions ordering in 1727, apparently for the first time, or the first time for many years, a rate of fourpence in the pound in each of the four wards of the borough, to be assessed by the Surveyor of Highways and expended on the thoroughfares of the town. It is impossible, in the absence of any statistics, to ascertain how many parishes had recourse to these rates. Our impression is that, during the first half of the eighteenth century, at any rate, the number in rural districts was exceedingly small—perhaps averaging in any one year fewer than half a dozen in each county— and that more than nine-tenths of the parishes and townships contrived to avoid the noxious impost unwillingly imposed by the Justices, " whose authority in this branch of their jurisdiction," it was said by Sir John Hawkins in 1763, "carries the appearance of great oppression, and can seldom be exerted to any beneficent purpose." Thus, even as late as 1794, the roads in the Cleveland district of the North Riding of Yorkshire were reported as being good and " still maintained in the same state by voluntary subscriptions and the Statute Duty of the "inhabitants." So, at Spilsby (Lincolnshire) in 1796, we learn incidentally that "the highways are maintained by Statute Labour without a rate." In Pembrokeshire, "the gentlemen above the mountains declined including their roads in any of the various Turnpike Acts, alleging that they could keep them in repair by the Statute Duty "—a sanguine idea which experience proves to be futile. The Highway Rate seems, however, under the Acts of 1716 and 1735 to have rapidly become a matter of course in some of the boroughs, where the performance of Statute Duty was obviously unsuitable. After the peace of 1763—the era of many improvements in Local Government—these rates become more frequent, though they were still demanded only by a small minority of parishes. Not until England had settled down after the Napoleonic Wars do we gather that the annual levying of a Highway Rate of some sort had become the normal, and even then not the invariable, method of providing the greater part of the Surveyor's resources.

But, even if the obsolete device of Statute Duty had been universally exchanged for a regular money income, there could have been in the absence of skill, continuity, and integrity of management, little real improvement in the roads. Such superior persons as Justices of the Peace and clerks in Holy Orders, barristers and physicians, were exempt from the obligation to serve in this, as in other parish offices, whilst most other wellto-do inhabitants managed to escape their turn of service, either by paying a fine, purchasing a "Tyburn ticket," or some less legitimate device. The office of Surveyor of the Highways had, in fact, as we are told by the pamphleteer of 1825, "generally to be taken in turn by the farmers of the parish, and held for one or two years, as the custom of the parish or of the county may be. " Leaving on one side the modern requirement of technical science in road construction, as irrelevant to eighteenth century standards of administrative efficiency, the plan of relying for any kind of effective superintendence on a casually chosen inhabitant, absorbed in his own affairs and dependent on the goodwill of his neighbours, was, it is needless to say, foredoomed to failure. Many and bitter are the complaints from the middle of the eighteenth century onwards, of the inevitable inefficiency of the Surveyor. "Those spiritless, ignorant, lazy, sauntering people, called Surveyors of Highways," ejaculates the learned Dr. Burn, whom the farmers in Vestry persisted in nominating, "just such as themselves, that will let them go on in their ancient course, and frustrate the very purpose they are intended to serve." The great survey of English agriculture conducted in 1794 under Sir John Sinclair and Arthur Young, produced almost unanimous testimony from the skilled investigators of the various counties as to the "farce of appointing Surveyors in the respective parishes. " "I cannot see any probability," sums up John Clark, one of the best of the County investigators, "of making the parochial roads in this country even tolerably safe until... the ridiculous farce of appointing one of the parishioners annually (at no salary) to enforce from his relations, friends, and neighbours a strict performance of a duty which probably he never performed himself; and from which, by showing lenity to his neighbours, he will expect to be excused in his turn when they shall respectively succeed him in the office of Surveyor." Assuming that the Surveyor was honest and capable he quickly discovered, as the pamphleteer of 1825 aptly observes, that " the active exercise of his powers,' would expose him ' to the imputation of officiousness, and of an unneighbourly interference with private property." Hence, in the vast majority of cases, the Surveyor did not even attempt to enforce the obligation of the owners of the land adjoining the highways to remedy the active and passive nuisances, which prevented, as it was thought by so representative a writer as John Godschall, "the roads from growing better of themselves." As was observed by the critic of 1825 whom we have often quoted, "the Parish Surveyor... was, before his appointment, in the habit of being guilty of many of the delinquencies pointed out by the Highway Act, and will be guilty of them again when his term of office has expired. The consciousness of this induces him to view the delinquencies of his other brother farmers with a very lenient eye." Under these circumstances the majority of Surveyors, " wishing to avoid quarrels with their neighbours," as we are expressly told with regard to the County of Durham in 1794, did not trouble to exact the Statute Duty, or the fines on defaulters—still less to apply to Quarter Sessions to afflict the parish with a new rate. The ordinary Surveyor adopted the easy policy "of not doing anything till it is necessary, viz., till the way is nearly impassable," with the result, as was said by the reporter on Cheshire, that " there is little chance of roads left to the care of officers so chosen ever being properly taken care of. " Even if, by good luck, the parish got, in one year, an enthusiast for road repair, it quickly lost him again. "The present mode of committing the care of the roads to an officer chosen annually and by rotation," writes the same investigator, " without any regard to abilities, etc. , in each parish or township, seems to be one chief cause of the neglect and insufficiency of their repairs. Sometimes, though seldom, an active intelligent man is in that office; but no proper system of repairs being laid down and pursued, an ignorant or indolent officer succeeding the former suffers what has been properly done to go to decay." "The annual choice of Surveyors," observed, in 1778, the ablest of eighteenth century writers on Local Government, " is in itself an impropriety. There are perhaps few offices wherein more skill and attention are required... yet before this officer is half master of his business, he is discharged and a fresh ignoramus chosen; consequently the work is never done as it ought to be." This testimony was repeated by subsequent observers with almost wearisome iteration. "The reluctant and evasive manner in which Statute Duty Labour is performed, and the want of power in Surveyors, in most cases, to call for even an adequate composition in lieu thereof," is emphatically denounced by an experienced administrator to the House of Commons Committee in 1806. "I can only hint," he adds, " at the want of abilities, or the requisite general knowledge, too general among Surveyors, particularly of parish roads, who... serve gratis, and perform their duties exactly as such a mode might lead us to expect. " "Parochial Surveyors," reports a witness before another Committee in 1808, "are generally the principal farmers, or persons substituted by them, and who are interested that the least possible expense shall be incurred."

This continuous and almost universal neglect by the bulk of the inhabitants, and by the Surveyors of Highways themselves, to fulfil their statutory obligations with any completeness, or to render with any zeal their unpaid service, is, in itself, evidence that the Justices of the Peace were at least equally remiss. For, as we have described, on this governing class had been cast the residual obligation of seeing that the labourer, the farmer, and the appointed Surveyor each and all performed their several parts of the common task. For this purpose the Justices had, as we have seen, been furnished with a fine array of legal instruments— powers of appointment and direction, instructional charges, disciplinary fines, compulsory rates, and, in the last resort, the presentment and indictment of the parish as a whole.

The extreme rarity of any records of the proceedings of Petty or Special Sessions deprives posterity of the means of discovering how regularly the Justices met, and whether they did more than walk perfunctorily through their parts. All the indirect evidence indicates that, as in the case of the prisons and the Poor Law, the vast majority of the eighteenth century Justices never realised that they had any administrative responsibility at all for the management of the roads. They persisted in regarding themselves as a judicial tribunal, called upon only to listen to such complaints as might be brought before them of any positive breach of the law, and then impartially to adjudicate upon them. So little did the Justices exercise their power of selecting the Surveyors that it came habitually to be supposed that their duty was limited to the formal ratification of the choice indicated by the lists sent in by the Vestries. The significant fact that, in the consolidating Highway Acts of 1766-73 the useful power to insist on written reports being handed in by every Surveyor at every meeting was omitted—apparently by mere inadvertence— goes a long way to prove that listening to and criticising a series of these forms had not actually formed part of the business of the typical bench of magistrates. In one instance only have we ever found these written reports by the Surveyor so much as mentioned. We see no sign that the Justices took the trouble to give the newly appointed Surveyors any useful "charge," or to direct them which roads to repair first, or to advise them how to proceed. Apart from this negative evidence there is a continuous stream of testimony, in the pamphlets and newspapers of the eighteenth century, as to the remissness of the Justices in enforcing the highway law. To their disinclination to enforce Statute Duty on the ordinary citizen we have already referred; and for this lenity there was, in the opinion of Sir John Hawkins, himself an active magistrate, ample excuse. Consider, says this learned writer, the excuses urged by the poor man,—" poverty, a numerous family, a wife, and four, five, or more small children, sickness, lameness, and an income of nine shillings a week... and think whether that authority is to be envied which the magistrates are sworn to exert in enforcing obedience to perhaps one of the most oppressive statutes that ever yet received the sanction of public assent." And if the labourer could appeal to the compassion of the Justice, the unpaid Surveyor of Highways — possibly a tenant of his own—could play upon the English dislike to be hard on neighbours. Other writers, such as John Shapleigh, in 1749, attribute the negligence of the Justices to "the making so many vague and seemingly inconsistent laws on this head " of highway administration, which " hath tended much to the weakening instead of the strengthening the power of the Justices of the Peace, and hath so perplexed their thoughts that they care not to act under them." In short, whatever may have been the cause of this inaction, all the available evidence confirms the statement, made by the same authority, "both from observation and experience," that the Justices of the Peace are "very unwilling to proceed according to the methods prescribed" by the Highway Acts.

There are, however, two directions in which the Justices of the Peace seem to have exercised their functions in road administration with complacency, and occasionally with zeal—the sanctioning of the supplementary Highway Rate and the presentment or indictment of the parish as a whole, for the non-repair of its highways. We have not discovered a single recorded instance of Quarter Sessions refusing the application of a Surveyor of Highways for the statutory rate to cover the excess of his expenses over receipts, or of the rate so demanded being cut down in amount. But we are inclined to think that this easy acquiescence in the Surveyors' applications indicates only that Quarter Sessions chose to regard its function in the matter of Highway Rates as merely ministerial. There is no sign of the Justices initiating these rates, and ordering the Surveyors to expend them. This is perhaps due to the fact that the few Justices who were keen on bettering the roads seem to have found a more convenient channel for their reforming energy in the roundabout and antiquated procedure of presentment or indictment of the parish as a whole. To this peculiar device we devote the next chapter.

APPENDIX TO CHAPTER III

Notes And References

Page 27. There is less literature by or about Surveyors of Highways than by or about such other parish officers as Churchwardens or Overseers of the Poor, or even Parish Clerks. Many particulars as to the office and its duties will be found in our book *The Parish and the County* (see Index of Subjects). It was often included with other parish offices in popular legal manuals, of which we may mention the following: *The Duties of Constables, Borsholders, Tithinymen, and such other low Ministers of the Peace; whereunio be also adjoined the several Offices of Church-*

warden, etc., by William Lambard, 1582. Other editions, 1583, 1599, 1610, etc. Also *The Office and Duty of Constables... with the Office of Surveyors of the Highways,* by John Layer, 1641; and *The Offices, and Duties of Constables, Borsholders and other lay Ministers; whereunto are adjoined the several Offices of Church Ministers and Churchwardens,* by William Sheppard, 1641. Other editions, 1652, 1657, etc. Also *The Exact Constable ... as also the Office of... Surveyors of the Highways,* by E. W., 1682.

The statutory title is Surveyor of the Highways. But "overseer of (or for) the highways" was frequently used at an early date; see, for instance, the *Churchwarden's Accounts* (Surtees Society) for entries under 1662, etc., "chosen overseers for the Highways for this present year." "Boonmasters" is, of course, derived from "boon," or work given gratuitously, whether to a landlord, an employer, or a friend; whence we get in Lincolnshire dialect, "to boon the roads," meaning " to repair the roads."

We note frequent complaints in the middle of the seventeenth century, amid the dislocations of the Civil War and the Commonwealth, that Bedfordshire and Yorkshire parishes were not appointing Surveyors of Highways (see *Growth of English Industry and Commerce in Modern Times,* by Dr. W. Cunningham, vol. i., 1903, p. 535).

Page 28. For the old French, *corvee,* see the interesting works by A. Babeau, describing village life under the *Ancien rigime,* and the various lives of Turgot. What Turgot did was to substitute a tax on land for the personal services on the roads. His reform was undone on his dismissal from oflSce, and the *corvee* reimposed. The present system is describod in the bluebook, *Report on the Construction and Maintenance of Public Roads in European States,* 1882; and specifically in "Local Government and County Councils in France," by S. Waddington in *Nineteenth Century* for June 1888. Each head of a household may be required to render three days' personal service, and to supply three days' work of all the horses, asses, and carts that he possessed, and of all the male persons between 18 and 60 resident with him as servants or otherwise; but he may avoid these "prestations" by payment in money at a defined rate. Apparently, most of the peasants, and altogether more than half the persons liable, still prefer to give the service in kind (see also the accounts given in the special Consular Reports on Streets and Highways in Foreign Countries (United States Bureau of Foreign Commerce, 1887); *A Treatise on Roads and Pavements,* by Ira Osborn Baker, 1903, p. 43; and the section on " Highways" in *Local and Central Government,* by Percy Ashley, 1906, pp. 120-4). A proposal for the abolition of the "prestations" in 1898 found support only in nine out of eighty-six departments *(ibid.* p. 124).

The Irish "roadwork" was practically brought to an end by 3 George III. c. 8 of 1762, which placed all roads under the Grand Jury of the County. That statute was re-enacted in 1765 by a great consolidating measure (5 George III. e. 14), which repealed all previous Acts on the highways, from 11 James I. (1614) to 3 George III. c. 8 (1762), and definitely swept away all obligation of service in kind.

For the "Labour Tax" existing in all but five of the United States—a poll tax, outside the cities, payable in labour at the option of the citizen, and by the farmers usually so paid; see *Road Legislation for the American State,* by Jeremiah W. Jenks (American Economic Association, May 1889, voL iv. No. 3); *A Manual of Roadmaking,* by W. M. Gillespie, 1853, pp. 341-7; and *A Treatise on Roads and Pavements,* by Ira Osborn Baker 1903, pp. 41-2. In six of the Southern States there was, in 1889, still no money tax or rate for road maintenance. Yet the "Labour Tax" is apparently as remissly rendered as it was in the England of the eighteenth century. "Under cover of this tax," we read, " many men simply waste, a day in telling stories and pretending to work" *(Road Legislation for the* iX, *American State,* by J. W. Jenks, 1889, p. 34).

On American road construction and maintenance a fund of information is now available in the valuable reports of the United States Department of Agriculture (Office of Public Roads), and in those of the Massachusetts State Highway Commission (from 1893); of the New York, Virginia, and Maryland State Highway Commissions, and the Rhode Island and Washington Highway Boards; and of the individual Highway Commissioners for Connecticut, Maine, Michigan, New Jersey, Ohio, and Pennsylvania. These are to be found in the British Library of Political Science at the London School of Economics.

Page 28. The quotation is from a short book entitled *A Profitable V Work to this whole Kingdom concerning the Mending of all Highways, as also for Waters and Ironworks,* by Thomas Procter, 1607 and 1610. This is the earliest work on highway maintenance with which we are acquainted, and ita publication at the beginning of the seventeenth century is probably significant.

Page 28. "An Historical Description of the Islande of Britayne," by W. Harrison, written between 1557 and 1587; first printed in Holinshed's *Chronicle,* now republished as *Elizabethan England,* edited by L. Withington, 1889; and more elaborately edited by F. J. Furnivall, in three volumes, by the New Shakespeare Society (1877-1908).

Page 29. For this description of "the King's Highwaymen" and of the hardship of Statute Labour to the cottagers, we are indebted to an / interesting little treatise, entitled *Of Mending and Repairing the Highways,* by E. Mather, 1696.

S page 29. *Highways,* by John Shapleigh, 1749, pp. 56-7; *A Proposal for the Highways,* by E. Littleton, 1692; *Observations on the State of the* v *Highways,* by Sir John Hawkins, 1763, p. 28.

Page 30. *Gentleman's Magazine,* May 1763, p. 236; *Observations on the State of the Highways,* by Sir John Hawkins, 1763, pp. 27-8; *Gentleman's Magazine,* December 1767, p. 573.

Page 30. *Digests of the General Highway and Turnpike Laws,* by John Scott, 1778, p. 307. This old law book, compiled by "the Quaker Poet" of Amwell (died 1784), who was an able and zealous Justice of the Peace for Hertfordshire, contains many shrewd and humorous observations, and throws considerable light on contemporary local administration. With its appendix on the construction and preservation of public roads, it forms a work of no little merit which was at that time, as his biographer observes, "probably the only scientific treatise on the subject." See Hoole's "Account of the Life and Writings of John Scott," prefixed to his *Critical Essays,* 1785, p. 60; the life of Scott in Dr. R. Anderson's *Poets of Great Britain,* vol. xi., and that in *The British Poets,* vol. lxx.

Page 31. *General View of the Agriculture of Hereford,* by John Clark, 1794, p. 55; *General View of the Agriculture of Northumberland,* by J. Bailey and G. Culley, 1794, p. 56.

Page 31. The quotation of 1825 is from an anonymous work entitled *Highways Improved,* 1825, p. 8. The others are from the evidence of the Hon. E. B. Portman, in *Report of House of Commons Committee on County Rates,* 1834; and from the *first Report of the Poor Law Inquiry Commissioners,* Appendix A (Wilson's Report), p. 130, 1834.

Page 31. For the Fulham case, see *Middlesex County Records,* by J. C. Jeaffreson, 1886, voL i. pp. 100-1.

For the great stir up as to the roads in Worcestershire in 1633-4, and the many presentments and indictments of parishes and individuals just in those years, see *Worcester County Records,* by J. C. Willis Bund, voL i., 1900, pp. mix, xl, Ixxvi, lxxviii, etc. The same records give us a case of a man prosecuted and fined for not working, who defended himself by the plea that he did some work, and that the real reason of his being proceeded against was " that he would not let his team draw a load of wood for the Surveyor gratis" *(ibid.* p. 176).

We owe the references to the MS. records of the Pevensey Hundred Court to the Rev. W. Hudson, from whose valuable works on Norwich we have learnt much.

For the Buxton *Three Centuries of Derbyshire Annals,* by J. C. Cox, 1890, vol. ii. p. 61.

For the Tring case, see *Hertfordshire County Records,* 1905.

Page 31. The full title of the work of this able Justice of the Peace is *Highways: a Treatise showing the Hardships and Inconveniences of Presenting or Indicting Parishes, Townships, etc., for not repairing the Highways,* by John Shapleigh, 1749. The unwillingness to enforce the fines he attributes in some measure to the uncertainty of the law, as the procedure specified in the various statutes of 1563, 1670, 1691, and 1715 varied slightly, so as to make it dubious whether the power to fine was in Quarter Sessions, Special Sessions, or Petty Sessions *(ibid.* p. 30). We see this doubt as to the law in Marylebone in 1730, where the Justices were willing to go as far as a summons, but uncertain as to any further proceedings. It was resolved in Petty Sessions: "That all such persons in arrear to the highways that have not been already summoned to attend a Special Sessions next Tuesday to show cause why they should not pay their several proportions "; but also "that Mr. Deschamp, Surveyor of Highways, do disburse a proper fee to counsel for his opinion concerning the validity and form of a warrant of distress and manner to levy the penalties of persons refusing to pay the charge set upon them for the repairing of the Highways, etc., and that he be allowed the same in his accounts" (MS. Minutes, Petty Sessions, Marylebone, Middlesex, 15th December 1730).

Parliament was, during the eighteenth century, always passing amending Acts, so that the exact state of the law was perpetually changing. The alterations made by the Highway Acta of 1714, 1718, 1733, 1736, 1741, 1742, 1743, 1745, 1751, 1753, 1755, 1757, 1765, 1766, 1767, 1773 and 1794 are bewildering in their detail, their repetitions and their confusion, but, so far as the system of Statute Labour is concerned, they did not effect any alteration in principle. The Act of 1766 (7 George III. c. 42) attempted a codification of the law, but this left so many questions unsettled that a renewed attempt at codification was made in 1773 (13 George III. c. 78), only to be overlain by the successive statutes to which " the vicissitudinous disposition of the Legislature," as John Scott remarks, soon gave rise. We owe these attempts at simplification of the law to such men as Thomas Gilbert and Sir John Hawkins *(Memoirs of Sir John Hawkins,* by Letitia Hawkins, vol. ii. p. 3), aided by such zealous local Justices as John Scott « (see his *Digests of the General Highway and Turnpike Laws,* 1778). We may note some of the detailed changes. The special " Highway Sessions" of the Justices, at which the Surveyors were appointed, was transferred from January to October (7 George III. c. 42). At this or any other Special Sessions the Justices were expressly empowered to direct which roads should first be dealt with, and when and how (1 George I. st. 2, c. 52); except that it was not to be in the seed month, the hay harvest month, or the corn harvest month (13 George III. c. 78). Four days' notice at every house was substituted for the public notification in church (7 George III. c. 42). The vague classification of the sixteenth century statutes into persons occupying ploughlands, persons keeping teams, forty shilling occupiers, and mere cottagers, was expanded so as to include, as contributories, all "occupiers of lands, tenements, woods, tithes, and hereditaments " (7 George III. c. 42 and 13 George III. c. 78); all persons keeping teams, draughts or ploughs in the parish, though occupying lands elsewhere; and all persons, however small their occupation, keeping a horse and cart, a coach, a post-chaise, or other wheel carriage, or even a sedan chair (34 George III. c. 74); from ail of whom either Team Duty or definite money contributions were required On the other hand, the class of persons who could fulfil their obligation fcy mere personal service for the six days (or by sending a substitute)—to Vhom, in practice, this actual manual labour came to be confined—was precisely defined as inhabitants (from 1766 to 1773 it was male inhabitants), between 18 and 65 years of age, not being apprentices or menial servants, and occupying premises worth less than £4 a year (13 George III. c. 78). Moreover, persons actually serving as privates in the militia (30 George II. c. 25), or later on, noncommissioned officers or privates from the time of their enrolment in the militia down to their discharge (42 George III. c. 90), were entirely exempted; and in 1794 any two Justices were empowered to exempt any poor person whom they thought "deserving such relief" (34 George III. c. 74). For all occupiers, team owners, and carriage-keepers there came to be elaborately graduated scales of contribution, varying, in Scott's table, from 6d. a year for a nonresident occupier of £1 annual value, who kept no team, carriage, etc., up to £10:16s. a year for an occupier of £400 annual value *(Digests of the General Highway and Turnpike Laws,* by John Scott, 1778, pp. 63-71).

Page 32. Naturally the critics of the roads put all the blame on the Surveyors of Highways. "It is a shameful thing," said a peer at the end of the seventeenth century, "to see how very much the highways are generally neglected and out of repair; the fault of which does mostly lie at the door of the Overseers i.e. Surveyors, whose chiefest care in them nowadays is how to shuffle off the matter for their time, being very little concerned for what comes after them; and by this means they bring at last a great burden upon their townships, which would have been prevented by a small charge, if but taken in time; and so the township suffers through their neglect" *(A Collection of Speeches of the late Earl of Warrington,* 1694, p. 25).

For their proceedings in the early part of the nineteenth century, see the interesting artiole on " The Making of the Land in England," by Albert Pell, M.P. , in *Journal of the Royal Agricultural Society* (2nd series, vol. xxiii. part 2, 1887); and *Reminiscences of Albert Pell,* by T. Mackay, 1908, p. 330.

Page 33. The official estimate of the value of the service in kind in 1814 is quoted in *History of the English Constitution,* by Rudolph von Gueist, translated by P. Ashworth, 1891, p. 637.

Page 33. For Sir James M'Adam's estimate of the value of Statute / Labour, see *Report of House of Commons Committee on Turnpike Trusts,* _ 1839, p. 3; *Road Reform,* by William Pagan, 1845, p. 215. The quotation from Sir John Hawkins is from his *Observations on the State of the Hightcays* j/ *and on the Laws for amending and keeping them in Repair,* 1763, p. 35.

Page 33. "The St. Columb Green Book," containing the accounts of the Parish of St. Columb, Cornwall, from 1585 to 1900, is described (and the entries from 1585 to 1604 are transcribed) by Mr. Thurston Peter, in the *Journal of the Royal Institution of Cornwall* (vol. xix. of its Reprints, 1912), to whom we are indebted for this and other information.

Page 34. For the Reading case, see MS. Accounts of the Churchwardens of St. Mary's, Reading, 12th April 1680.

Page 34. *Gentleman's Magazine,* May 1763, pp. 236-7.

For the case of Rochdale Road, Manchester, see *A Description of Manchester,* by James Ogden, 1783; see the new edition, by W. E. A. Axon, under the title of *Manchester a Hundred Years Ago,* 1883, pp. 16-17.

Page 35. *Observations on the State of the Highways,* by (Sir) John Hawkins, 1763, p. 38.

Annals of Agriculture, voL xxxi. p. 423, 1798.

Page 36. The account book of the Surveyors of Highways of Chalfont, St. Peter's, lies among the parish archives there.

Page 36. *An Essay upon Projects,* by Daniel Defoe, 1697, p. 69. Page 37. For the Purleigh Highway Rate, see MS. Minutes, Quarter Sessions, Essex, 16th July 1700; for that of Ipswich, see MS. Minutes, Borough Quarter Sessions, Ipswich, Suffolk, 27th March 1727. *Observations on the State of the Highways,* by (Sir) John Hawkins, 1763, p.2.

General View of the Agriculture of the North Riding, by Tuke, 1794, p. 85. "Cleveland," said its historian in 1808, "had long to boast of what no other district, perhaps, in England of equal extent could do, viz.; excellent roads extending in different directions for nearly sixty miles in length, without any tolls, being maintained by voluntary subscriptions and the

Statute Duty of the inhabitants. This circumstance so creditable to the district can no longer be boasted of, as two tollgates have been lately erected upon a piece of the road, made by Act of Parliament in 1803 between Yarm and Thirsk" *(History and Antiquities of Cleveland,* by Rev. John Graves, 1808, p. 39).

Page 37. For the Spilsby roads, see *The State of the Poor,* by Sir F. M. Eden, 1796, voL ii. p. 398; for those of Pembrokeshire, see *General View of the Agriculture of Pembroke,* by Charles Hassal, 1794, p. 30. The borough rate for highways will be found in the MS. Minutes Borough Quarter Sessions, Ipswich, Suffolk, 1727-1760.

Page 38. We have tried in vain to ascertain, from the MS. archives of Counties and Boroughs, in what proportion of cases Highway Bates were made at different dates. Of the making of rates in reimbursement of outlay on road material, we have, in the absence of records of the proceedings of Special Sessions, absolutely no statistics. Our impression is that, in the first half of the eighteenth century very few rural parishes, if any, dreamt of such an extravagance as purchasing road material The second rate, for general repair, had, down to 1773, to be made at Quarter Sessions, and was recorded in the Minutes. We have gone through these Minutes for more than a dozen counties, without finding more than a small proportion of the parishes applying for, or ordered to make, this Highway Bate. Thus in the Minutes of the Essex Quarter Sessions between 1700 and 1711, we noticed only two or three cases a year; and in 1711, 2 parishes (6d. each); in 1712, 3 parishes (1 @ 3d., 2 @ 6d.); in 1713, 8 parishes (1 @ 2Jd., 7 @ 6d.); in 1714, 5 parishes (1 @ 3d, 4 @ 6d.); in 1715, 2 parishes (6d. each). In 1736, a sixpenny rate was ordered in 4 parishes; in 1756 in 6 parishes; in 1766 in 14 parishes; and in 1771 in 21 parishes. The total number of parishes in the county was over 400. In Suffolk, which had about 575 parishes, in 1760-1761 the Quarter Sessions authorised Highway Bates in 10 parishes only. In the careful analysis of the Quarter Sessions records of Derbyshire only one such case is mentioned *(Three Centuries of Derbyshire Annals,* by J. C. Cox, 1890, voL ii. p. 230, where it is assumed, we think wrongfully, that the normal course was for the parish to make its own rate under the Act of 1662; which, as described in the preceding chapter, was only a temporary statute, not much employed even during its brief validity). Hackney had a sixpenny rate as early as 16991700, but we do not feel sure whether any other parish in Middlesex had one so early (House of Commons Journals, 4th May 1713). In Berkshire, at the beginning of the eighteenth century, a Highway Bate was plainly regarded as an exceptional event. In 1707 there is entered on the Quarter Sessions Minutes an elaborate petition from the Surveyors of Highways of Pusey, showing that they had spent £3:1:8, which had been allowed by two Justices, and asking that a rate might be sanctioned (MS. Minutes, Quarter Sessions, Berkshire, Midsummer 1707). Maidenhead gete a rate allowed in 1708 on the plea that it has had to pave its street *(ibid.* Epiphany, 1708). Speen gets one in 1709, subject to verification by the local Justices *(ibid.* Midsummer 1709). During the following thirty years there are only about a dozen cases *(ibid.* 1710-1740). In Hampshire we noted one case in 1699, two in 1704, and not half a dozen down to 1720. In 1723 we learn from the wording of the order that, in two cases at any rate, application had been made by counsel, and witnesses were heard for and against a rate being made, the Court deciding in favour of it (MS. Minutes, Quarter Sessions, Hampshire, 23rd April 1723). As late as 1768-70, only five such rates were made in three years, and these were confined to three market-towns *ibid.,* 1768-70). In Kent, which had over 1100 parishes, the power to rate seems to have been rather more early used than elsewhere, there being, between 1692 and 1695, as many as 8 cases recorded; then there are none till 1697-98, in each of which years one was made. Early in the eighteenth century they continued to be made at the rate of about one a year. In 1727 no fewer than 13 parishes were rated, and in 1729 as many as 24. Between 1730 and 1736 only 12 rates were made for 9 different parishes, and down to 1746 they average less than one a year. In 1747, however, 6 parishes were rated. Between 1747 and 1751 there were only 7 cases. In 1766-69 the number goes up to between 10 and 20 annually (MS. Minutes, Quarter Sessions, Kent, 1692-1769).

The Highway Bate, unlike the Poor Bate, and unlike nearly all other rates in England, was, from first to last, limited in amount to sixpence or a shilling in the pound. Under 3 & 4 William and Mary, c. 12, there was no limit to the frequency with which a Highway Bate could be levied; and we read, in 1738, that "there are numberless instances where the roads are so bad that Justices are obliged to allow that in two rates which they are prohibited doing in one" *(An Enquiry into the Causes of the Increase and Miseries of the Poor of England,* 1738, p. 8).

Page 38. For the "Tyburn Ticket"—the certificate of exemption from parish offices given as a reward for the successful prosecution of a felon—see our book, *The Parish and the County,* 1906, p. 19; *Highways Improved,* 1825, p. 9; *History of the Poor Laws,* by Bev. Dr. B. Burn, 1763, p. 239.

Page 39. The quotations from the Agricultural Survey are from *Central View of the Agriculture of Brecknock,* by John Clark, 1794, p. 44; and *General View of the Agriculture of Hereford,* by John Clark, 1794, p. 55; *Highways Improved,* 1825, p. 4; *A General Plan of Parochial Police,* by Godschall, 1787, p. 60.

Page 39. *Highways Improved,* 1825, p. 9. *General View of the Agriculture of the County Palatine of Chester,* by Thomas Wedge, 1794, p. 63.

Page 40. The "ablest of eighteenth-century writers on Local Government " was, in our opinion, John Scott, whose *Digests of the General Highway and Turnpike Laws,* 1778, we have already referred to (p. 44).

Page 41. The supineness of the ratepayers, no less than of the Justices, with regard to the inefficiency of the Pariah Surveyors, is all the more remarkable in that, in 1766, it was provided by the General Highway Act (7 George HL c. 42. sec. 2, re-enacted by 13 George III. c. 78, sec. 5) that, if two-thirds of the ratepayers in Vestry agreed, they might nominate a person to be appointed as a paid Surveyor, and suggest the salary to be paid to him out of the penalties, forfeitures, and composition money of the parish; whereupon the Justioes might, if they thought fit, appoint such salaried Surveyor. In 1773 it was added that, if the Vestry negleoted to furnish a list of persons to serve as unpaid Surveyors, or if the persons so

E nominated refused to serve, the Justices might appoint some other person, and assign to him a salary, payable by the parish, not exceeding one-eighth of a sixpenny rate (13 George III, c. 78, sec. 1), at the same time appointing also Borne inhabitant to act, gratuitously and compulsorily, as Assistant to such paid Surveyor! *(ibid.,* see. 2 and 4)—an extraordinary provision, "likely," says Scott, "to produce private animosity instead of publio benefit" *(Digests of the General Highway and Turnpike Laws,* by John Scott, 1778, p. 107). We know of no case in which, during the eighteenth century, a salaried Surveyor was appointed; and we believe that, at any rate in rural parishes, this provision remained a dead letter, its very existence being forgotten by parishioners and critics alike.

Page 41. The following entry in the Essex Quarter Sessions Minutes is, so far as we know, unique. "Whereas John Chewby Esq., has presented to this Court that great part of the highways within the half-hundreds of Waltham and Harlow and the Hundred of Ongar are very much out of repair and that the Surveyors of the Highways have been very negligent in performing their duty enjoined them by the several Acts of Parliament... this Court doth recommend to His Majesty's Justices of the Peace of that Division the putting the said laws in execution, and to cause the several Surveyors... to make due returns of the state and condition of their highways, and of all such persons as shall make default of doing their work on the said highways" (MS. Minutes, Quarter Sessions, Essex, 18th April 1721). The instructional charge contemplated by the Act of 1691 dwindled, we are told, into the perfunctory delivery, by some minor official, of a printed extract containing " the most material portions" of the General Highways Act, contained "in a broad sheet, ill-printed on bad paper, with a very small type, the matter very much crowded, the several articles difficult to be distinguished, and the whole but badly calculated to engage the attention or satisfy the enquiries of the Surveyor respecting his duty" *(Gentleman's Magazine,* November 1798, p. 971).

Page 41. *Observations on the State oj the Highways,* by (Sir) John Hawkins, 1763, p. 36; *Highways,* by John Shapleigh, 1749, p. 30, and p. 28.

Occasionally we notice a spurt of zeal on the part of the Justices. We may, perhaps, ascribe to the stimulating effect of the Royal Proclamation of 1787, which Wilberforce and Zouch got sent to all Quarter Sessions (see our *History of Liquor Licensing in England,* 1903, pp. 50, 143,144), the exceptional activity of the Essex Justices in that year. They strictly enjoin the several Surveyors within the said Division to take special care that the ruts are stubbed, the water let off, the ditches properly scoured, the fences kept low, and the pollard trees taken down or primed up, so that the roads may have the full benefit of the sun and air; for the due performance of which " essential parts of their duty they will be called upon to make a return upon oath, and in default of such duty being done, preferments will be made against the parishes so neglected at the next or any subsequent general quarter sessions" (Petty Sessions, Deny Division, Essex, October 1787; see *Chelmsford Chronicle,* 9th November 1787).

CHAPTEB IV ROAD ADMINISTRATION BY PRESENTMENT AND INDICTMENT

In the device of the legal presentment or indictment of a parish as a whole, for neglect to maintain its highways, we find ourselves back again in the domain of the Suppression of Nuisances. Under the Common Law it was open to any one to indict, at Quarter Sessions or the Assizes, the parishioners or others responsible, whenever " a common and ancient King's highway" became, to use the form given in Burn's *Justice, "* ruinous, miry, deep, broken and in great decay," so as to be "to the great damage and common nuisance of all the liege subjects of our said Lord the King." This criminal procedure had been, as we have already described, sharpened and strengthened by the successive highway statutes, one of the earliest of which (5 Eliz. c. 13 of 1563) had given to every Justice of the Peace the power "to make presentment... on his own proper knowledge... of any highway not well and sufficiently repaired." Originally, we gather, this presentment by a single Justice may have been made in person at the Quarter Sessions with little formality, the assembled magistrates then and there proceeding to fine the parish in default. Presently, however, this presentment was dealt with more formally, and was treated merely as equivalent to the finding by the Grand Jury of a true bill on an indictment of the parish. The Grand Jury could itself originate proceedings, and its formal presentment was dealt with similarly to that of a single Justice. And the Grand Jury might be moved to make such a presentment by a report laid before it by the County Surveyor, or even by one of its own members. Finally, any person, proceeding by way of indictment, would have his complaint submitted to the Grand Jury in ordinary course, whose finding of a "true bill" was equivalent to their presentment. The Grand Jury presentment, or the indictment on which a "true bill" had been found, being then formally "traversed" on behalf of the defendant parish, was put down for trial at the following Quarter Sessions. At the trial, if the parish could not show that the obligation to repair rested by tenure or immemorial custom on some particular landowner, Quarter Sessions imposed a substantial fine upon the inhabitants generally, but usually deferred the levying of the fine for three months, in order to give the parish time to put the road into proper repair. If in the meantime they did the work, and one or two Justices gave a certificate that it had been done to their satisfaction, the fine would be excused. If not, the Sheriff would be directed to levy it by distress upon any of the occupiers of the parish, and to pay it, either to the Parish Surveyor of Highways or to some other person named by Quarter Sessions, to be by him applied to the mending of the highway.

The archives of Quarter Sessions contain abundant references to this criminal procedure by presentment and indictment, and seldom distinguish between proceedings initiated in one or other of the ways described. Thus, in the published extracts from the Derbyshire archives, we find printed side by side contemporaneous presentments by a single Justice, and presentments by the County Surveyor. We may instance "the presentment of John Spateman, Esq., one of ye Justices of peace of this County of Derby... upon his own view" in 1656. "I present," wrote he, " the inhabitants of ye parish of Chesterfield for not repairing of ye highways leading betwixt Wingerworth and ye town of Chesterfield, and being within ye said parish." At Midsummer 1658, the County Surveyor made various presentments, which the Grand Jury adopted by endorsing, "We find this a true presentment." We give one of these as a sample of many. "We present the inhabitants of the parish of Duffield... for not repairing Cowhouse Lane being in the said parish, and in great decay, and ought by them to be repaired being used for all carts and carriages."

Already in 1749, as we learn from John Shapleigh, it could be said that there were "some parishes which have presentments or indictments almost perpetually hanging over their heads." We can best give an accurate idea of the working of this procedure by transcribing a few specimen entries from Quarter Sessions minutes and other documents. We give first a sample of the grant of time. At the Essex Quarter Sessions in 1745, it is "ordered... that Mr. Zechariah Button, Chief Constable of Barnstaple Hundred, do not levy the fine of £20 set on the inhabitants of... South Benfleet... for not repairing their highways, till after the next General Quarter Sessions." But the fine was actually levied if the work was not done. Thus, at the Suffolk Quarter Sessions in 1765, we read, " This Court doth order and direct the Sheriff of this County to levy the fine of fifty pounds, set upon the inhabitants of the parish of Brent Ely, in this County, for not repairing a certain road... which is and stands presented by the Rev. T. T. &c. for being out of repair, no Certificate being produced to this Court of the said road being amended and repaired pursuant to an Order of. .. Quarter Sessions... on the 8th of October last." In other cases the repairs are found to have been executed within the period of grace. Thus, in the Derbyshire archives are numerous certificates by Justices, testifying to their personal inspection of roads for which parishes were under indictment. One William Richardson about 1727 seems to have been particularly active in this business of road supervision. We may reproduce one of the many certificates by him which have been preserved: "This is to certify that the highway within Horseley Woodhouse in the said County of Derby leading from that vill to Smally Common in the said County is amended and put into very good repair. Viewed by me this 14th day of September 1727.—William Richardson." So in 1766, we see the Suffolk Quarter Sessions resolving that, " It appearing to this Court that the road in the parish of Westerfield, presented by Mileson Edgar, Esq., for being out of repair, is duly and sufficiently repaired and amended, this Court doth therefore remit the fine of £40 set upon them for that offence." At varying dates in the different counties, but eventually, we gather, nearly all over England, it became the regular thing for a parish periodically to find itself indicted at the Sessions for neglecting to keep its highways in repair; for the Vestry to instruct the Surveyor of Highways to make any defence that might seem plausible to the Court, and at any rate to plead for time; for Quarter Sessions to find the parish guilty and inflict a substantial fine, which might be anything from £10 up to £2000, but to respite its levy to give the parish an opportunity to mend its ways; and for the fine eventually to be levied by the Sheriff—usually acting through the High Constable of the Hundred—in the form of an additional rate on all the occupiers in the parish, the proceeds being paid over to some person designated by Quarter Sessions—it might be the Parish Surveyor of Highways, it might be the County Surveyor, it might even be two or more Justices selected for the purpose—to be expended on the particular highway in question. So habitual became the appointment of " expenditors," or persons to see to the laving out of the fine upon the road, that the Somerset Quarter Sessions formally ordered in, 1802,"that henceforward in all prosecutions for public nuisances respecting highways and bridges, that, after judgment upon verdict found, or upon plea of guilty, no proof shall be received in this Court by Certificate or otherwise that such highway or bridge is in repair, unless the defendants prove to the Court that notice in writing has been given to each of the expenditors appointed to lay out the fine imposed for the repair of such highway or bridge, of their appointment for that purpose."

This cumbrous and antiquated procedure had become, at the opening of the nineteenth century, almost the normal course of road repair. The Quarter Sessions Minutes of Lancashire and Northumberland, Gloucestershire and Wiltshire, in particular, abound in orders of this sort—sometimes a score of parishes at every sessions. A parish would occasionally be under indictment for years together. Thus, Tynemouth in Northumberland was indicted in 1796, and it was ordered that £50 be levied, which was laid out leisurely by the Surveyor of Highways. By 1802 he had more than exhausted that sum, and Quarter Sessions ordered a second £50 to be levied; in 1804, a further £50, together with £100 more to be dispensed by the Clerk of the Peace; in 1805 yet another £30 to settle up their respective accounts, the case not being finally disposed of until 1807. The process of indictment was, in fact, frankly made use of by all the parties concerned, as a means of levying rates. In 1784, for instance, the great Parish of Manchester found itself indicted and fined by Quarter Sessions for not repairing the thoroughfare called State Lane. In the following year the same thing happened, and two unfortunate inhabitants were actually apprehended under Bench warrant to answer to the indictment—thus proving very practically that the obligation could be brought home to each and every parishioner. A "Parish Meeting" was accordingly " held at the Parish Table in the Collegiate Church," when a rate was made, on the assessment to the Land Tax, to yield an amount sufficient to cover the fine, the expenses of the two unfortunate defendants, and the cost of repair. In a few years we see the procedure reduced to common form. Thus, in 1817, the important thoroughfare of Oxford Road, Manchester, was made the subject of an indictment, evidently with the assent and collusion of the parish officers and principal inhabitants. The whole of the great parish of Manchester (not merely the township) was fined £1600, of which the Surveyors of Highways for the township of Chorlton Row (in which much of the road lies), were ordered to pay £200, whilst the prosecutors themselves by agreement contributed £100. The balance was levied on the various townships of Manchester, whose officers and representatives held repeated meetings to arrange for its collection and payment. The whole sum was directed to be paid to a person appointed to be by him spent on the road. It came to be taken for granted that no other course was open to those who sought an improvement in the roads than to indict the parish. When, at the opening of the nineteenth century, it became absolutely necessary to get some better meansof communication with Ireland, "the first idea of the Government towards improving the road was to indict 21 townships between Shrewsbury & Holyhead. " In other counties the office of public prosecutor, with respect to faulty highways, was assumed by zealous magistrates who rode all over the country, noting the condition of the roads, threatening the parish officers, and, in some cases, giving (as we learn from Cumberland in 1829) "peremptory orders" to the local Surveyors, the Cumberland gentleman even adding a warning of his intention " to follow up his injunctions upon the Surveyors by a personal survey or inspection of the line of road in question previously to the commencement of the ensuing sessions to enable him to present such parts of it at Sessions as he may find out of repair, or slightly and insufficiently repaired."

From the standpoint of the local magistrate, anxious to level up the standard of road maintenance within his own district or throughout his county, the device of presentment had many advantages. Even as regards the highways of his own immediate neighbourhood, it enabled him to avoid the troublesome alternative of enforcing Statute Labour, imposing fines and superintending the behaviour of the Parish Surveyor. "I have often been surprised," writes a correspondent to the *Gentleman's Magazine* in 1794, at" observing Justices presenting roads lying in their own districts. What could be their motive? Have they not all the power necessary for doing everything that can be done by a presentment? Some, I have heard, say they do it because they do not like to impose fines on their neighbours, and to be teased with applications for remitting them; others, that they get rid of the trouble of making orders and attending to their execution." Moreover, it enabled the Justice, as we have seen, to extend his reforming activity beyond the limits of his own Petty Sessional Division, and to raise the standard of road maintenance throughout the whole county. No less important was the fact that the power to levy an unlimited fine enabled Quarter Sessions and Parishes to escape from the new statutory shackles of a strictly limited rate. "It is the avarice and obstinacy of a few individuals," observed Thomas Butterworth Bayley, of Manchester, one of the most efficient of eighteenth-century Justices, "who,... sheltering themselves behind the words of an Act of Parliament... refuse to contribute a farthing beyond the sixpenny assessment"; and this it was that necessitated "the very tedious and expensive mode of levying a fine under indictment or presentment by which a considerable part of the money raised is lost in law charges, Court fees, and poundage." The fact, moreover, that the Justices could direct the fine to be paid to whomsoever they chose enabled them, in some cases, to get spasmodically applied to the worst stretches of road more skilled management than could be afforded by the Parish Surveyors. But against these advantages there were grave drawbacks. The continuous use, for the function of road maintenance, of a procedure devised for the Suppression of Nuisances went a long way to undermine the normal course prescribed by Statute. In a parish under indictment, no one willingly did his Statute Labour or Team Duty, lest he should be afterwards called upon to pay the share of the fine, and thus be mulcted both in cash and in kind. "The law does not distinguish," remarks Sir John Hawkins, "those who have done from those who have refused to do their Statute work, but pronounces its judgment indiscriminately against the whole parish," the necessary rate being levied on all alike. The Surveyor of Highways, too, lost whatever motive for performing his duty properly that would have been supplied by fear of being fined for his neglect. "This," urged the *Gentleman's Magazine* in 1794, " is a matter of some importance, because many Surveyors, who contribute a very small proportion to the parish rates, are so little affected by the cost of a presentment that the dread of it is not efficacy enough to stimulate them to proper exertions: some of them would even like the frolic of attending at the Assizes at the expense of the parish." And the action of the reforming Justice might easily be indefinitely obstructed, or even defeated, by other Justices who preferred a policy of economy and *laissez-faire*. "Justices may sometimes have their own reasons," it was said in 1794, "for not wishing roads in their neighbourhood repaired.... Two Justices have been found to endeavour to stop the repair of a road, by certifying it to be in good repair, when on the trial of the indictment it has been proved, to the satisfaction of a Jury and a Judge, that the road was not in good repair. It is by defending such indictments on frivolous pretences, instead of at once amending the road, that enormous expenses are incurred. I could give... an instance of more than £100 being spent in this way, and the parish at last being obliged to repair, when £30 would at first have done all that was necessary; but a neighbouring Justice did not choose it should be done." The failure of the other magistrates to support their reforming colleague was often due to mere ignorance of what constituted proper repair. "We will suppose," says a witness before a House of Commons Committee in 1809, " this road to be indicted, after every method has been used to cause it to be repaired, without success; that, after harvest, the Parish Surveyor contracts for it to be done by a stout labourer who takes job work, with a special injunction 'to be sure that he throws the road up high enough, and makes the stones of the old causeway or foot pavement to go as far as they can.' This diligent operator falls to work, nor is he stopped by the equinoctial rains in September, for it must be done, as contracted for, before the Michaelmas Sessions.... The clods and rushes are thrown into the bottom and the soft soil which nourished them, and all other materials, hard or soft, form a convexity of considerable elevation, according to order. The stones from the old broken footpath duly surmount the whole, except a little gravel, which is raked over them, just to keep them together. This finished by the Saturday night, we will say, of October 3rd, for on Monday the 5th two magistrates on their way to Quarter Sessions are to inspect it, to take off the indictment. How can they possibly refuse to speak the truth, which is ' that it was perfectly smooth when they saw it, and that a vast deal indeed had been done since the last time they were there.' Besides wear and tear, however, decomposition immediately takes place in this chaotic mass." Hence, with all the appearance of vigour that was given by the frequent indictment of parishes for neglecting their duty, it remained true in the nineteenth century as in the eighteenth, to use the words of John Shapleigh in 1749, that " prosecutions, very seldom, if ever, procure the roads to be effectually mended, or thereby put into good and sufficient repair." Finally, we come to the fundamental vice of this procedure—the inadequacy of the old conception of a highway as being a mere right of passage, and of the corresponding assumption that roads needed only abstention from active nuisances and fulfilment of customary services. It was habitually taken for granted, as is noted by a critic of 1833, "that a parish cannot be indicted for a road unless it can be shown that such road has been in a better state than at the time of complaint: many of the roads in Hampshire are mere tracks over the Downs; and making them into good roads would thus entail an expense on the parishes they pass through to keep them up." A parish was not legally required to raise the public right of way from one grade to another, a footway to a bridleway or a bridleway to a cartway. But it was just this transformation of narrow ways into broad, and especially of mere beaten tracks into artificially prepared road surfaces, that the circumstances required. What the law tacitly assumed was the maintenance of some imaginary *status quo.* What was being demanded was virtually a new service—a service as different from that of keeping open a free passage as a modern railway is from a country lane.

APPENDIX TO CHAPTER IV

Notes And Refebences

Page 51. We know of no systematic or intelligible account of the procedure by presentment or indictment, as applied to administrative purposes such as road maintenance. We have had to grope our way through MS. Minutes of Quarter Sessions, with no further light than is afforded by such legal manuals as Burn's *Justice of the Peace,* the works of John Scott and Sir John Hawkins on the Highway Acts, such pamphlets as those by E. Littleton (1692), George Meriton (1694), William Mather (1696), John Shapleigh (1749), Henry Homer (1767), T. B. Bayley (1773), and the contemporary references in newspapers and the *Gentleman's Magazine.*

Page 51. The quotation is from *The Justice of the Peace,* by Rev. Dr. Richard Burn, vol. ii. p. 196 of the 1758 edition. In a good little office manual for Somersetshire Justices we read that " Magistrates intending to present highways for being out of repair may give instruction to the clerk of the indictments in the office of the clerk of the peace" *(A Guide to the Practice of the Court of Quarter Sessions for the County of Somerset,* by John Jesse, Junior, Ilminster, 1815, p. 64). We may continue the description of the formal procedure from the Wiltshire minutes. "It is ordered that whenever the inhabitants of any parish or tything shall be presented by a magistrate, or indicted for not repairing their highways, bridges or stocks, the clerk of the peace, within one month after the Sessions at which such presentment shall be made or indictment, found, to give notice to and summon the inhabitants of each parish or tything that they may appear and plead to the same at the then next Sessions." The inhabitants are then to appear or give recognisances for their appearance. No presentment or indictment is to be discharged (on the ground that the necessary repairs have been made) without formal certificate, and due notice to the magistrate who made the presentment. "And it is further ordered that before such indictment or presentment be discharged by certificate the Surveyor or Surveyors of highways of the parish or tything so indicted or presented shall appear in court and on oath set forth what sum of money has been expended in repairing such highways" (MS. Minutes, Quarter Sessions, Wiltshire, Hilary Sessions, 1808).

Page 52. *Three Centuries of Derbyshire Annals,* by J. C. Cox, 1890, voL ii p. 228. Already in 1565 we read of a " true bill" being found by the Grand Jury of Middlesex against the Parish of Islington, for non-repair of its highway up Highgate Hill *(Middlesex County Records,* by J. C. Jeaffreson, 1886, voL i. p. 53).

V Page 55. *The Holyhead Road,* by C. G. Harper (1902), vol. i. p. 19; *Cumberland Pacquei* (newspaper), 15th December 1829. *y* Page 56. *Gentleman's Magazine,* July 1794, p. 677; *Observations on*

Vwe *General Highway and Turnpike Acts,* by T. B. Bayley, 1773, p. 26. For a brief account of this indefatigable administrator, see our volume *The Parish and the County,* p. 366.

Page 52. *Highways,* etc., by John Sbapleigh, 1740, p. 15; MS. Minutes, Quarter Sessions, Essex, 23rd April 1745; MS. Minutes, Quarter Sessions, Suffolk, 21st January 1765.

Page 53. *Three Centuries of Derbyshire Annals,* by J. C. Cox (1890), voL ii. p. 231; MS. Minutes, Quarter Sessions, Suffolk, 10th October 1766; MS. Minutes, Quarter Sessions, Somerset, 6th October 1802.

Page 54. At one session in Wiltshire in 1810, no fewer than 20 parishes were indicted in respect of their highways (MS. Minutes, Quarter Sessions, Wiltshire, October 1810); MS. Minutes, Quarter Sessions, Northumberland, 10th October 1805, etc.; MS. Vestry Minutes, in Churchwardens' Account Books, Manchester, 23rd March 1784, 3rd July 1785, June 1817.

The MS. Minutes of Quarter Sessions of such Boroughs as Derby, Lincoln, Southampton, Bristol, Winchester, and Coventry, which we have specially consulted, show that it was a regular practice throughout the whole of the eighteenth century, for the Borough Justices (that is to say, the Mayor and Aldermen) to present the several parishes within the Borough whenever any highways needed repair; to adjourn the hearing if the parish officials appeared and undertook to execute the repairs at once; to inflict a fine if this was not done; to allow time for the execution of the work; and only to enforce the fine in case of default. (As to the relative position of the Borough Authorities and the urban parishes, see our volumes, *The Manor and the Borough,* and *The Parish and the County.)* y' Page 57. *Observations on the State of the Highways,* by (Sir) John Hawkins, 1763, p. 32; *Gentleman's Magazine,* July 1794, p. 121, and October 1794, p. 884.

Page 57. Appendix by Rowland Hunt, in Third Report of House of Commons Committee on Broad Wheels and Turnpike Roads, 1809, p. 107. The fact that parishes were obliged to defray the whole cost out of revenue, instead of spreading considerable works over a term of years, by means of a loan, made a policy of patching almost inevitable. This was pointed out in 1794. "There is one great obstacle to the making of strenuous exertions to put the roads in repair, which is that the landholder on whom it falls has often but a temporary interest in the parish. *Ti* his lease be within two or three years of expiring, and he expects another person to bid for his lands 'over his head,' and the roads in the parish are under indictment, he will calculate whether it would not be easier for him to pay his share of the expense of the indictment annually, and leave it as a legacy for his successor in the farm, than to go to the expense of putting the road in such a state of repair as would enable him to have it removed. ... Almost every road in this county is liable to be indicted. The money actually paid by the landholders in consequence of indictments, I am informed, would go a great way towards paying the interest of a sum sufficient to put all the roads in the county in good repair" *(General View of the Agriculture of the County oj Hereford,* by John Clark, 1794, p. 55); see also *Highways,* by John Shapleigh, 1749, pp. 30-31.

Page 58. The quotation is from the First Report of the Poor Law Inquiry Commissioners, 1834, Appendix A (Pringle's Report), p. 295.

Page 58. It would have been a good answer to an indictment to prove that the road in question was not a highway for carriage traffic, but only a "pack and prime way." Indictments for non-repair of these old packways are also found *(e.g.* many in MS. Minutes of Quarter Sessions for Northumberland, October 1799,1805, etc., and Cox cites one case in 1790, see his *Three Centuries of Derbyshire Annals,* vol. ii. p. 234). But a "pack and prime way" had only to be kept in repair as such, and the parish could not be required to convert it into a carriage road. The need for the conversion into a hard cart and carriage road of a highway which was only a " common footway, horseway and way for driving cattle"—an improvement for which the parish was not legally chargeable—is expressly given as the ground for one of the early Turnpike Acts, enabling the Bedfordshire Justices to make the road and levy tolls, viz. that of 5 Anne c. 10 (Hockley and Woburn Turnpike Act, 1706).

CHAPTER V THE NEW USERS OF THE ROADS IN THE SEVENTEENTH AND EIGHTEENTH CENTURIES

The new service, which those legally responsible for the maintenance of the roads were called upon to perform, involved the development of what were, in effect, bridlepaths into cartways: the conversion of the soft and miry tracks, which had for many centuries done duty as highways, into firm bottoms, and eventually into smooth, hard and level surfaces. These firm bottoms and new surfaces were required, first in order to withstand, in winter and summer alike, the perpetual trampling of an unprecedented succession of beasts of one sort and another, and then in order to accommodate the new traffic on wheels. If this new service had been wholly and expressly demanded at any one date, we imagine that the owners and occupiers of rural land, on whom, as we have seen, the bulk of the burden fell, would have strenuously resisted the charge. But the new traffic on the roads came about so silently, increased in volume so imperceptibly year by year, and altered in kind so gradually, that the change in the demand made upon the country was practically not noticed until long afterwards, and only its burden was complained of. /The first cause of the new demand for improved ways was, we think, the great increase in road traffic that seems to have marked the latter part of the sixteenth and, still more, the seventeenth and eighteenth centuries. The rapid growth of London and of foreign trade; the gradual uprising both of manufacturing and of local distributive centres; the steady substitution of pasture for arable cultivation; the habit of production for exchange, and the decay of the family handicrafts; together with such political incidents as the union of the Crowns of England and Scotland in 1603, and of the English and Scottish Parliaments in 1707, led to an ever-progressing increase, alike in the going to and fro of horsemen, in the driving to and fro of beasts, and in the carrying to and fro of commodities of all sorts On all the main lines of communication, what may be called the local use of the roads, by the farmers and cottagers who had to maintain them, became a steadily diminishing fraction of the total traffic.

But though the traffic was of a different nature, so far as its origin and destination was concerned, the new users of the roads were, for a long time, still, for the most part, horsemen and cattle. We can hardly imagine to-day how rare, outside the Metropolis, was any sort of wheeled vehicle, even during the seventeenth century. Right down to the middle of the eighteenth century— in remote parts of these islands we may even say down to the middle of the nineteenth century—the passage of a wheeled vehicle of any kind remained, on all but the main roads, an exceptional event of the day. To an extent that we find it now difficult to realise, the seventeenth and eighteenth century roads were trodden by animal feet.

We must note, to begin with, that throughout the whole of the fifteenth, sixteenth and seventeenth centuries, and, to a great though diminishing extent, throughout the eighteenth century, travellers went on horseback. It was in this way that Chaucer and his companions made their immortal pilgrimage to Canterbury; it was in this way that Shakespeare's characters went on their adventurous journeys; it was in this way that Henry the Eighth and Queen Elizabeth made their progresses; it was in this way that Hooker travelled to London to preach his first sermon at St. Paul's; it was in this way that John Hampden journeyed up and down England to stir up the freeholders to revolt; it was in this way that Daniel Defoe, as a confidential agent of the Government, enquired into the state of public opinion all over Great Britain; it was in this way that Samuel Wesley took all England for his parish; it was in this way that James Watt moved from Glasgow to London to learn mathematical instrument making; it was in this way that William Smith constructed for us the first geological way of England; it was in this way, as lately as our own grandfather's day, that William Cobbett made his shrewd and caustic criticisms of farming and local administration. Right down to the nineteenth century, indeed, every increase of travel meant, for the most part, an increase in the number of well-mounted horsemen, with their saddle-bags behind them, that were a constant feature of the roads. Throughout the whole of the eighteenth century, and in particular cases even into the nineteenth, judges and barristers "rode" their circuits; commercial travellers were simply " riders," or became known as " bagmen " from the two bags of samples they bore on their saddlebows; merchants and manufacturers and their customers alike visited each other on horseback; legislators and officials went to and fro in the same way. "These travellers commonly rode post-horses, changing their mounts at well-known stages by the way.... Thickly wrapped in riding cloaks, and with jackboots up to their hips, they splashed through mud and mire, making light of occasional falls, and so journeyed between London and Holyhead in perhaps sixdays, if they were both active and fortunate." /More numerous, however, than the mounted travellers were the pack-horses, with their tinkling bells, heavily laden with a pair of bales, or with "dungpota," "crooksV' or panniers, used for nearly every kind of commcKiityLjtn the Northern and Midland counties, the single pony which nod borne, to the Leeds cloth-market, the weekly product of the little farmer-clothier, gradually developed into long strings of pack-horses to and from every industrial centre, passing, in some frequented thoroughfares, in an almost continuous stream. "Fine, strapping, broad-chested Lincolnshire animals," we are told, "were these pack-horses, bearing on either side their bursting packs of merchandise to the weight of half a ton. Twelve or fourteen in a line, they would thus travel the North Road... from the North to the Metropolis, to return with other wares of a smarter kind from the London market for the country people." In the middle of the eighteenth century, the miry ways of Staffordshire and Warwickshire were constantly traversed, as we read in the *Life of Josiah Wedgwood,* by "pack-horses and asses heavily laden with coal,... tubs full of ground flint from the mills, crates of ware or panniers of clay,... floundering knee-deep through the muddy holes and ruts that were all but impassable.... The general rate of conveyance," we learn, "was nine shillings per ton for ten miles," which represents about as great an amount of human labour as the rate for haulage found by Thorold Rogers to prevail in the fourteenth century. The roads of Somerset in 1695 were, we read, " full " of " carriers " of coal; strings of " horses passing and returning, loaden with coals dug just thereabout." The traveller in the middle of the eighteenth century, reports a pamphleteer named Mathews, met great numbers of " men and women of Somersetshire and Gloucestershire, travelling to divers neighbouring towns with drifts of horses, as four, ten perhaps, more or less in number... laden with coals,... vast numbers of which were driven to Bristol, Bath, Bradford and to many other places." Every provincial town was a centre on which such lines of pack-horses and coalcarriers converged. At Exeter, for instance, which had at the end of the seventeenth century so large a trade in cloth that £10,000 changed hands weekly, a lady traveller notes in 1695 that the road was " thick " with " carriers, all entering into town with their loaded horses." In Westmorland and Cumberland, at the same date, the same traveller met innumerable "horses on which they have a sort of panniers, some close, some open, that they strew full of hay, turf, lime and dung and everything they would use... . Abundance of horses I see all about Kendal Street with their burdens." Three-quarters of a century later, the historians of these two counties preserve for us a printed time-table of the twelve regular pack-horse gangs, usually numbering twenty horses each, that went in and out of the same town weekly, serving no fewer than twelve different lines of route.

The adoption of the pack-horse as the universal means of conveyance of goods led to the construction, in the middle or by the side of the broad soft tracks which served as roads, of narrow causeways, wide enough for one horse to walk on," covered with flags or boulder stones." A causeway of this sort, " about two feet broad," says Whitaker—or, as Defoe testifies of another part, "generally about a yard and a half broad "—" paved with round pebbles, was in 1750 all that man or horse could travel upon, particularly in the winter months, through Cheshire and Lancashire." It was sometimes " guarded by posts at a proper distance to keep carts off it," or else raised " several feet" above the level of the slough of mud which did duty for a road. "Travellers who encountered each other on these elevated causeways sometimes tried to wear out each other's patience

F rather than either would risk a diversion." Two persons who rode from Glasgow to London in 1739 record that they found no hard road "till they came to Grantham, within 110 miles of London." Up to that point they travelled upon a narrow causeway with an unmade soft road upon each side of it on which "they met from time to time strings of pack-horses from thirty to forty in a gang, the mode by which goods seemed to be transported from one part of the country to another. The leading horse of the gang carried a bell, to give warning to travellers coming in the opposite direction, and... when they met these trains of horses, with their packs across their backs, the causeway not affording room to pass, they were obliged to make way for them, and plunge into the side road, out of which they sometimes found it difficult to get back again upon the causeway."

But it was perhaps the continual increase of the Metropolis, and the drawing of its supplies of food by road from the very extremities of the kingdom, that did most to transform the character of the traffic. We first hear this commented on with regard to the supply of fish. At the very beginning of the seventeenth century we read of the fish-jobbers of Lyme Regis, in Dorsetshire, who rode off regularly to London, leading long strings of pack-horses laden with the catch of the twenty-five fishing-boats of that little port. "Horses with panniers called dorsers were brought to the beach tied one to the other ready to receive the fish. When the dorsers were filled, the driver mounted the foremost horse of the train, and galloped off to London." A century later we hear of the " Rippers" of Folkestone, who rode off daily to the Metropolis with fresh fish. In 1710 there were no fewer than 320 such fish-laden horses galloping through Tunbridge every day. Presently, from every fishing village within two hundred miles, "the best and largest" of the catch of each tide were, we are told, sent " upon horses which travel night and day to London market." The centripetal attraction reached even more distant places. The plentiful salmon caught at Berwick-on-Tweed, Daniel Defoe tells us, were in his time taken on horseback to Shields, and there salted and dried, or boiled and pickled, to be shipped to London as " Newcastle salmon." But about 1740, one Marshall of Berwick was enterprising enough to organise a regular service of fast horsemen all the way to London, where the salmon were henceforth sold fresh, to the great advantage of the dealer. He soon found imitators at other ports, for the salmon from Workington and Carlisle, we are told in 1748, "they carry, fresh as they take them, up to London upon horses, which, changing often, go night and day without intermission, and as they say, outgo the post; so that the fish come very sweet and good to London."

But the cattle, sheep and pigs on the roads were as numerous as the horses. "In the Spring," we read in *The Book oj the Axe,* "the Western roads were studded with large droves of calves driven out of Dorsetshire, some for the Exeter and Plymouth markets, but the majority for rearing in the rich Devonshire pastures. On the other hand, Cornwall and its borders produced large quantities of pigs, in which a lucrative traffic was carried on by persons well known as pig-jobbers, who constantly drove herds of them into Dorsetshire and elsewhere, having regular halting-places, where the animals were either fed with horse-beans in the street, or made to halt for the night, as the case might be. At Axminster, if nowhere else, the spot where the droves were habitually fed is marked by the not very classical name of Pig Street." It was, however, the provisioning of the great Metropolis that directly set most of the droves in motion. De Quincey has described for us how the traveller, in every county of England, met great herds of cattle wending their way to the shambles of Smithfield. "Often," he says, "at great distances of two and three hundred miles or more from this colossal emporium of men, wealth and intellectual power, have I felt the sublime expression of her enormous magnitude in one simple form of ordinary occurrence, viz. in the vast droves of cattle, suppose upon the Great North road, all with their heads directed to London; and expounding the size of the attracting body, together with the force of its attracting power, by the never-ending succession of these droves, and the remoteness from the capital of the lines on which they were moving."

We may append some statistical details of this vast convergence. Already in the middle of the eighteenth century it was estimated that 40,000 Highland cattle annually tramped their way to the meadows of Norfolk, there to be fattened and sent off in weekly droves throughout the winter, to walk to the London market. "Twenty thousand head of Scotch beasts, at least," it was said in 1750 of the Wisbech highway alone, " go this road yearly." Thirty thousand black cattle from the summer and autumn fairs of Wales went, every year, in huge herds through Herefordshire, towards south-east England, choosing, like the Scotch cattle, the bye-lanes in order to avoid the turnpike tolls. Altogether, during the third quarter of the eighteenth century, something like a hundred thousand head of cattle and threequarters of a million sheep found their way to Smithfield annually, representing a daily arrival, rain or shine, of more than two thousand animals, by whose feet the highways leading to the Metropolis must have been kept constantly in a state of mud that we find it difficult nowadays to imagine.

There was yet another kind of traffic, besides horses, cattle, sheep and pigs, that helped to keep the roads soft and miry. "For the further supplies of the markets of London," we read in 1748, "they have within these years found it practicable to make the geese travel on foot too, and prodigious numbers are brought to London in like droves from the farthest parts of Norfolk.... 'Tis very frequent now to meet a thousand or two thousand in a drove. They begin to drive them generally in August, when the harvest is almost over, that the geese may feed on the stubble as they go. Thus they hold on to the end of October, when the roads begin to be too stiff and deep for their broad feet and short legs to march in." To quote another writer: "Suffolk and Norfolk seem to have supplied all the rest of England with turkeys. On the road from Ipswich to London was situated Stratford Bridge, and along this passage over the Stour some 150,000 turkeys were driven yearly," besides others which came over Newmarket Heath, and by Sudbury and Clare. From all parts, indeed, as John Scott remarks in 1778, these "devoted feathered legions, at certain seasons of the year, bespread the surface of the roads on their way to the all-devouring Metropolis."

The great development of this foot traffic, whether of man or beast, positively militated against anything that we should nowadays regard as a good condition of the roads. The constant tramping of droves of cattle, herds of sheep and pigs, and flocks of geese and turkeys; the incessant streams of walking pack-horses; the galloping relays of post-horses and fish-carriers, all tended to keep the track in a perpetual slough of mud. Moreover, the farmers, and the cattle-dealers driving their flocks and herds daily to and fro, objected to anything approaching to a metalled surface. The Sussex agriculturists actually petitioned Parliament in 1710, on this ground, against a proposed road improvement. "The roads," one of them is reported to the House of Commons as saying, " are already good enough for horses to go;... that he drives two or three hundred bullocks forward and backward;... that six or seven hundred sheep and lambs come to every market; that, in short, the roads are better for cattle to go on as they now are, than amended, because the stones will cripple and lame them before they come to market." For horse and cattle traffic, too, minor irregularities of surface; ruts and holes; unbridged rivulets crossing the track; streams to be forded; deep hollow ways; the narrowness of old causeways; ups and downs, and even steep hills, were no great disadvantages; and it was certainly not worth while avoiding such obstacles even by a short detour, let alone by anything like road engineering.

But an altogether new kind of traffic began to claim the attention of those responsible for the maintenance of the roads. We may perhaps date from the opening of the seventeenth century the beginning of any considerable use of the roads by wheeled vehicles, at any rate since Roman times. We notice these new users of the roads first in and near the Metropolis. The Thames, as a modern author reminds us, had been "for sixteen centuries the great highway of communication within London walls. London streets were mere footways or bridlepaths between house walls; when Queen Elizabeth went abroad she was carried in a litter by her gentlemen; there were on Thames side 40,000 watermen till the middle of the seventeenth century." "Suddenly," as he observes, we have, in 1622, the complaint of John Taylor, the waterman poet, that people are taking to new-fangled ways of locomotion, that" this is a rattling, rowling, rumbling age," in which "the world runs on wheels." "Road waggons," as public vehicles, seem to have been started, if we may believe the veracious Stow, as early as 1564, though they were certainly not common before the very end of the sixteenth century; and for half a century more they remained infrequent on all but the main thoroughfares. Year by year, these "great hooded waggons... with a team of eight horses... travelling at the rate of three miles an hour," often not making more than fifteen miles in a long summer's day, and grinding the soft track into deep ruts by their ponderous ironshod wheels, became more numerous. Hackney carriages were first used in and about London from 1634 onwards; post-chaises from 1664; whilst private carriages seem to have come into common use in the same generation. Cromwell, it is noted, set out for Ireland in 1649, not on horseback but in a heavy coach drawn by six Flemish mares, several other coaches accompanying him. The development of foreign trade, the growth of the great ports, and the improvement of the minor harbours, which specially characterised the early part of the eighteenth century, created new centres for the distribution of goods by carts and waggons. Thus, to give only one out of many instances, the works executed by Sir James Lowther, at the little harbour of Whitehaven (Cumberland) between 1709 and 1739, presently compelled practically a reconstruction of the roads radiating from that town, "which," we learn from Defoe's *Tour,* "were become ruinous and bad by the great use made of them since the improvement in the harbour, for before that time they were very narrow, and seldom made use of by carts and wheel carriages." Elsewhere the steadily developing nanufacturing industries kept long strings of carts laboriously dragging coal from the mines to the ironworks, glassworks and potteries. In South Essex the traveller met equally long strings of carts conveying chalk or lime from the pits. "At the end of October," we are told, " when the highways got too heavy " for the poultry to walk to London on their own feet, they were, at the beginning of the eighteenth century, sent in wheeled vehicles. At first these were huge and deeply laden waggons. The loads of ducks sent up twice a week from Peterborough and St. Ives, Defoe tells us, used to be " drawn by ten or twelve horses each, they were so heavy." Then they invented " fast carts, composed of four stories or stages," which ploughed their way through the mud with the best speed that two powerful horses could impart to them, " travelling as much as a hundred miles in the twenty-four hours." By means of other specially built carts, drawn by relays of fast-trotting horses, and going continuously night and day, the fish-dealers of Lowestoft and Yarmouth began, in the middle of the century, to supply the Metropolis with fresh herrings in quantity, instead of being limited to the amount that the galloping horsemen could carry. Latterly these fish-carts were made to do the journey at a speed of as much as eight miles an hour. The whole of this motley crowd of owners and users of newly introduced wheeled conveyances were, from the end of the seventeenth century onward, persistently denouncing the abominable state of the roads. It is significant that the earliest practical manual of road repair—a little treatise by Thomas Mace—dates from 1675. Pamphlets on the state of the roads then begin to appear. It is " most certain," we read in one of them, dated 1692, " that the highways of England are extremely bad at present. And it is as certain that this badness of the Highways is a great and public inconvenience, so that it much concerns us to have them mended." In 1694, we read that "the highways... were grown so foundrous (as the law terms it) and so extremely bad, that the owners and occupiers of lands in most places have been necessitated their fences to lie down, and to permit people to travel over their inclosed ground... by reason of the impassableness of the highways." For the first few decades of the eighteenth century the House of Commons *Journals* abound with complaints as to the " ruinous state " into which the great roads between London and such towns as Portsmouth, Devizes, Bristol, Chester and Norwich had fallen; the dangers to which carriage passengers were exposed, and the absolute impassableness, for wheeled vehicles, during nine months in the year, of some parts even of these main routes. "This road," writes Defoe of one great highway, "is not passable but just in the middle of summer, after the coal carriages have beaten the way, for as the ground is a stiff clay, so after rain the water stands as in a dish, and horses sink into it up to their bellies." The "nobility and gentry," it was complained in 1753, found it impracticable " to visit even their own estates." Squire Western, it will be remembered, had a coach and four, but, unhappily the "badness of the... roads made this of little use, for none who set much value on their necks" would have driven in it. In 1750, as the modern historian of Surrey tells us, " the people of Horsham petitioned Parliament for a passable carriage road to London, the road by Coldharbour and Dorking, which had superseded the excellent Roman road, being accessible only on horseback. If they wanted to drive to London, they gravely declared that they had to go down to the coast and round by Canterbury." Even as near the centre as Kensington, it was reported by Lord Hervey in 1736, that " the road between this place and London is grown so infamously bad that we live here in the same solitude as we should do if cast on a rock in the middle of the ocean, and all the Londoners tell us that there is between them and us a great impassable gulf of mud." The Mile End Road in 1756 " resembled a stagnant lake of deep mud from Whitechapel to Stratford, with some deep and dangerous sloughs; in many places it was hard work for the horses to go faster than a foot pace, on level ground, with a light four-wheel post-chaise."

We need not weary the reader with any further particulars about the state of the roads, familiar to us all in the oft-quoted extracts from the travels of Daniel Defoe and Arthur Young, and so graphically summed up in Macaulay's *History of England* and Smiles's *Lives of the Engineers.* It was upon highways of this kind that the first stage-coaches, driven by a coachman on the box, as distinguished from the carriers' hooded waggons, led by the riding or walking conductors, began to run. It is, indeed, usually forgotten how modern are these new users of the roads. We are told by the learned historian of the Inland Revenue that "there is no trustworthy record before 1754 of any coach with springs. " In that year several were advertised to run between London and Edinburgh, Manchester and Chelmsford. The traveller to and from Liverpool could get a coach at Warrington (Cheshire) by 1757; but none ran to or from Liverpool itself until 1766. Palmer's mail-coaches date only from 1784. With the advent of these "flying coaches," which accomplished their early journeys at the then wonderful rate of five miles an hour, and which, by 1830, expected to run (from London to Devonport) 227 miles in 24 hours, or (from London to Edinburgh) 400 miles in 40 hours, began the really imperative demand for the hard, smooth and level surface for which we now look in a road. What seems remarkable, however, is that contemporary pamphleteers and later historians alike complacently take it for granted that the new users of wheeled traffic had a grievance against the parishes which they passed through. The passengers demanded the new kind of road without paying for it. It was in vain that William Marshall protested in 1804 that, " when roads are worn by the public at large tenfold more, in some instances, than by the inhabitants of the parishes they happen to pass through, it is become unreasonable, if not unjust, to impose the task of repairing them on the individuals who happen to be possessed of a plough team, a cart, a wheel-barrow, a shovel, or a basket (what a principle of taxation in these days!), though they may never use the road they are doomed to repair." To the legislators and statesmen of the latter part of the eighteenth and the early part of the nineteenth century, it seems never to have occurred that, to use the words of Lord Macaulay, to demand "that a route connecting two great towns which have a large and thriving trade with each other should be maintained at the cost of the rural population scattered between them is obviously unjust." So ingrained was the feeling that it was the duty of the farmers and cottagers to maintain the highways that neither the aristocracy nor the legislature, neither the merchants nor the traders, neither the authors nor the journalists, ever reveal any glimmering of the idea that in expecting roads fit for fast carriage traffic, they were making an entirely novel demand on the villagers whose ancient tracks they traversed. The assumption made by "enlightened public opinion," in the latter part of the eighteenth and the early part of the nineteenth century, that a highway was not kept in proper repair unless it had at all times, rain or shine, summer or winter, a smooth, hard, dry surface, free from undue windings or inconveniently steep gradients, was an entirely new ideal of road administration, involving an unprecedented obligation of the country population, unwarranted by law or custom, and impossible of attainment by any ancient devices. The House of Commons, confronted by the abominable state of the highways, and woefully perplexed by angry petitions from the maintainers of the roads against the users, and from the users against the maintainers, passed, in the course of the eighteenth century, a bewildering series of highway statutes, which the Justices of the Peace were supposed to administer. These enactments, consolidated to date in the two successive General Highway Acts of 1766 and 1773, which we owe to the industry and zeal of Thomas Gilbert, made only minor alterations in the administration of the service of road maintenance, or in the obligations of those who rendered it. In the main, the country gentlemen who drafted these Acts sympathised with their tenants and labourers, on whom fell the obligation to mend the roads. Accordingly, they were always seeking to restrict and regulate the use of the King's Highway. There was, to begin with, the protection of the highway against the aggressions, by neglect or default, of the adjacent landowners — the insistence on the due scouring of the neighbouring ditches and watercourses; the leaving unploughed and free from hedges the fifteen or thirty feet margins of the middle of the road; and the due pruning, "plashing," or lopping of the hedges and trees on both sides. There were, of course, all kinds of obstructions to be prohibited—the laying of soil or earth on the road; the use of it for manure heaps; the leaving about of timber and stones; careless and disorderly driving; blocking the highway by standing vehicles or by ploughs or other instruments of husbandry, and ever so many analogous hindrances to free passage. This kind of regulation for the prevention of nuisances was developed, in the course of a couple of centuries, into an elaborate code which has now become so interwoven with our habits that we are barely aware of its continuous enforcement. But there was another kind of regulation, which nowadays seems without justification—injunctions and prohibitions as to the construction of wheeled vehicles, the way they were to be drawn, the weight they were to carry, and the number of horses or oxen to be used. Already, in 1621, we see James the First forbidding any four-wheeled waggon whatsoever, or the carriage of more than a ton of goods at a time, as the vehicles bearing " excessive burdens so galled the highways, and the very foundations of bridges, that they were public nuisances." And though this particular proclamation was withdrawn, a similar one was issued in the following reign, and the same kind of regulation appears in the statute book immediately after the Restoration. We do not intend to take up the time of the student, or weary the reader, by analysing or even enumerating the score or more of separate Acts, during the eighteenth century, which regulated wheels and weights, the number of horses and the manner in which they were to be harnessed. By 1755, on the single issue of the number of horses to be used, the learned Dr. Burn gave up in despair the task of stating the law with certainty and precision. "If a person," he wrote, "would know what number of horses or beasts in a cart or waggon are allowed by the statutes for the preservation of the roads, let him take what treatise at present he pleases concerning the highways, he must read over the whole, before he shall be sure that he hath found all which the law hath enacted concerning the same; and such is often the inaccuracy and confusion, that when he hath perused the whole, perhaps he may be still to seek. For as to this instance before us, there have been regulations made concerning the same by ten different Acts of Parliament at very different times. Before he can have any competent knowledge thereof he must lay all these ten Acts together, and when he shall have done this, he will find amongst them so many repeals, and revivals, and explanations, that it will even then be no easy matter to conclude with certainty how the law doth stand as to that article." But it was not merely the maximum number of draught cattle that was fixed. They were not to be allowed to straggle over the whole road, in straining to pull the vehicle out of the deep ruts, but were to be confined by shafts and poles, so as to compel them to follow in each other's steps. In defiance of warning and experience, Parliament again and again recurred to the device of limiting the load. The climax of regulative activity was perhaps reached in the detailed and ever-changing code as to the construction of the vehicle itself, and more especially of its wheels. In the interminable series of enactments, amendments, repeals, and re-enactments of the eighteenth century, we watch successive knots of amateur legislators laying down stringent rules as to the breadth of the wheel; the form of its rim; the use of iron tires and headed nails; the height of the wheel; the position of the felly, the spokes, and the axle; the space between each pair of wheels, and the respective lines of draught between back wheels and front. Throughout this tangled skein of legislation— the mass of which must be seen to be believed—we discover practically one and the same implicit assumption, that the wheeled carriage was an intruder on the highway, a disturber of the existing order, a cause of damage—in short, an active nuisance to the roadway—to be suppressed in its most noxious forms, and, where inevitable, to be regulated and restricted as much as possible. Instead of the modern purpose of providing such roads as secure the maximum mobility of men and commodities, our great-grandfathers aimed at preserving their highways from anything beyond the minimum wear and tear. Indeed, from the middle of the eighteenth century onward, they thought that they could make the traffic positively subservient to the maintenance of the road by converting every wheeled vehicle into an involuntary roller, which would consolidate and repair the surface over which it passed, instead of wearing it down or cutting it up; with the result that the tires of 2£ or 4 inch breadth of surface, on which Parliament at first insisted, passed gradually into tires of 6, 9, and even 19 inches in breadth. It is only by realising the implicit assumption, that the existing soft highways were to be protected against the intrusion of wheeled traffic, that the complicated and long-continued legislation as to wheels—never more than moderately successful in attaining its object—can be seen to lack neither ingenuity nor a certain equitable justification.

APPENDIX TO CHAPTER V

Notes And References

Page 62. We know of no adequate description of the change in the use of the roads that began about 1600; and we can refer the student only to the authorities mentioned below. Smiles's *Lives of the Engineers* (many editions) is the best single volume.

Page 64. The quotation is from *The Holyhead Road,* by C. G. Harper, 1002, voL i. pp. 2-3.

Page 64. As to the pack-horses, the quotations are from *Fragments of Two Centuries,* by Alfred Kingston, 1893, p. 6; *Life of Josiah Vfedqwood,* by Eliza Meteyard, 1865, pp. 267, 275; *Through England on a Side Saddle,... Diary oj Celia Fiennes* (1605), edited by the Hon. Mrs. Griffiths, 1888, pp. 160, 199, 205, 207; *Remarks on the Cause and Progress of the Scarcity and Dearness,* by J. Mathews, 1797, pp. 33-34; *History of Westmorland and Cumberland,* by J. Nicholson and R. Burn, 1777, voL i. p. 66. See also *Remarks made in a Tour from London to the Lakes,* by A. Walker, 1792, p. 25; *Loidis and Elmete,* by T. D. Whitaker, 1816, p. 81; *Perambulation of Dartmoor,* by Samuel Rowe, 1848, p. 87.

Pago 65. For the causeways see *Loidis and Elmete,* 1816, by T. D. Whitaker, pp. 77,81; *A Tour through the wlxole Island of Great Britain,* by Daniel Defoe, voL iii. p. 248 of 1748 edition; *Remarks made in a Tour from London to the Lakes,* by A. Walker, 1792, p. 25; *The Former and Present State of Glasgow,* by James Cleland, 1840, p. 65.

In Lancashire, records the historian of Preston, "strings of pack-horses, thirty and forty in a gang, were used for carrying coals and lime. The leading horse of the gang carried a bell to give warning to travellers coming in the opposite direction by any sharp turn or narrow pass. It very frequently happened that the Roman causeway between Wigan and Preston scarcely afforded room to pass: they were obliged to make way for each other by plunging into the side road (which was soft and sometimes almost impassable), out of which they found it difficult to get back upon the causeway" *(History of the Borough oj Preston,* by P. A. Whittle, 1837, voL ii. p. 61).

It may be observed hereon that the Act of 1691 had expressly directed that " no horse cawsey shall be less in breadth than three feet " (3 William and Mary, c. 12, sec. 19). But it is improbable that any old causeway, Roman or otherwise, was widened by the parish in which it lay, though it might be done by private munificence. "The Surveyors of the Highways," we read in 1717, "began to raise the Causey at Horeshead Still. They finished the work all at my expense " *(Memoirs of the Life of Elias Ashmole, Esquire,* edited by Charles Burden, 1717, p. 69). New causeways were, however, constructed from time to time—not always, it seems, very solidly. "Without due care," wrote a pamphleteer of 1746, "new causeways will sooner become ruinous than old roads" *(The Contrast,... with proposals how to amend and render more effectual the laws in being for the preservation of the public roads,* by Philanglus *(i.e.* Joseph Newball), 1746, p. 26). At the very end of the eighteenth century it could bo said of the Weald of Sussex and Kent that, "in winter, even carts are excluded; and it is extremely dangerous, and frequently impracticable, in that season to ride on horseback along the main roads; in consequence of which narrow paths, called horse tracks, are paved with stones, or formed with seabeach on one side of the roads, just wide enough to ride upon; but even this convenience is not general" *(General View of the Agriculture of Kent,* by John Boys, 1794, p. 98). In the Isle of Axholme, where the highways had been quite impassable in winter, even on horseback, "the causeways were completed all the distance from one village to another," during the era of distress from high prices, 1810-12, "a horse breadth," and paved with Yorkshire flags *(History and Topography of the Isle of Axholme,* by Rev. W. B. Stonehouse, 1839, p. 45).

Page 66. The badness of the roads seems to have made London dependent for its heavier supplies, down to the end of the seventeenth century, on sea and river traffic, and on what could be grown within a short radius of the city. In *The Grand Concern of England explained in Several Proposals in Parliament* (by John Gressot?), published in 1673, we are told that all sorts of supplies came from Henley on Thames and from Hull, and oats from Lynn and Boston; but that, otherwise, the hay, straw, beans, peas, and oats were raised within a circuit of no more than twenty miles.

Page 66. As to the fish trade from Lyme Regis, see *The Diary of Walter Yonge,* by George Roberts, Camden Society, 1848, Introduction, p. xxvii; and *Social History of the Southern Counties,* by George Roberts, 1856, p. 489; that from Folkestone, see *Three Years' Travels in England, Scotland, and Wales,* by Rev. James Brome, 1700, p. 274, and House of Commons Journals, 10th February 1710 (vol. xvL); that from Berwick on Tweed, *History of Berwick on Tweed,* by John Fuller, 1799, p. 390, and *History of Berwick on Tweed,* by Frederick Sheldon, 1849, pp. 277-278; that from Workington and Carlisle, *A Tour through the whole Island of Great Britain,* by Daniel Defoe, voL i. p. 8, voL iii. p. 268 of 1748 edition. "Sixteen fishermen... go with eight horses each... 320 fishermen's horses go through this road every day" (Evidence on the Sevenoaks and Tunbridge Turnpike Trust Bill, House of Commons Journals, voL xvi. p. 306, 10th February 1710). The word " dorser " is the same as " dosser," used by Chaucer, for pannier carried on the back.

Page 67. *The Book of the Axe,* by G. P. R. Pulman, 4th edition, 1875, p. 78. This excellent book contains much local information.

Autobiographic Sketches, by Thomas De Quincey, chap, vii., "The Nation of London " (voL xiv. of *Works,* edition of 1863, p. 179).

As to the number of Highland cattle, see *A Tour through the whole Island oj Great Britain,* by Daniel Defoe, vol. i. p. 63 of 1748 edition, and *Remarks on Road Bills in general, and on the Wisbech Road Bill in particular,* by James Collier, 1750, p. 4. It was computed by Sir John Sinclair, towards the end of the eighteenth century, that as many as 100,000 cattle left Scotland annually for the south. See *Notes and Sketches illustrative of Northern Rural Life in the Eighteenth Century,* by B. M. Alexander, 1877, p. 73.

For the Welsh cattle, see *Historical Memoranda of Breconshire,* by John Lloyd, 1903, vol. i. pp. 53-56. The statistics of beasts entering Smithfield are from the *Annals of Agriculture,* vol. vii. p. 64, 1786, where the total number of cattle for the ten years 1776-85 is given as 992,040, and of sheep, 6,859,990. "The greatest supply of cattle and sheep ever known was in the four years from 1780 to 1783, in which the average per annum was, of beasts, 101,985, and of sheep, 720,160" *(ibid.* p. 55).

So much animal traffic had other results, which we are apt to forget. "Everybody knows," we read in 1706, "that for a mile or two round this city, the roads, and the ditches hard by, are commonly so full of nastiness and stinking dirt that oftentimes many persons who ha ve occasion to come in or go out of town are forced to stop their noses to avoid the ill smell occasioned by it; and besides that, as the dirt is deep in some places which are full of holes, it often occasions horses to stumble and fall, and carts to overturn, whereby sometimes goods are spoiled and several persons hurt, if not killed" *(Proposals for establishing a Charitable Fund in the City of London,* 1706, p. 19).

Page 68. The marching poultry are described in "The Manner of driving Turkeys and Geese out of Norfolk and Suffolk up to London," which finds a place in *A Choice Collection of Curious Relations,* 1739: see also *A Tour through the whole Island of Great Britain,* by Daniel Defoe, vol. L p. 54 of 1748 edition, and p. 53 of 1779 edition; *Digests of the General Highway and Turnpike Laws,* by John Scott, 1778, p. 281; and *History of the English Landed Interest, Modern Period,* by R. M. Gamier, p. 279.

Page 69. House of Commons Journals, vol. ii. p. 306, 10th February 1710 (Evidence on Sevenoaks and Tunbridge Turnpike Trust Bill).

Page 69. The quotation is from *The Soul of London,* by Ford Madox Hueffer, 1905, p. 48. See the *Works* of John Taylor, "the Water Poet," V part ii. p. 242; notably *An Arrant Thief,* published in 1622, and *The World runs on Wheels, or Odds between Carts and Coaches,* 1623.

Page 70. The beginning of any appreciable use of the roads by wheeled traffic (since Roman times) may be put somewhere between 1600 and 1700, but it is difficult to give it a precise date. A paper by J. H. Markland, entitled "Remarks on the Early Use of Carriages" *(Archoeologica,* vol. xx. p. 443, 1824), may be consulted; together with the following varied compilations: *English Pleasure Carriages,* by William Bridges Adams, 1837; *The World on Wheels,* by Ezra M. Stratton, an' excellent production by a New York coachbuilder in 1878; *Early Carriages and Roads,* by Sir W. Gilbey, 1903; and *Carriages and Coaches,* by R. Strauss, 1912. "In the reign of Queen Elizabeth," it is repeatedly asserted, "very few coaches, chaises, or chairs were made use of," even in London *(The Contrast,. .. with proposals how to amend and render more effectual the laws in being for the preservation of the public roads,* by Philanglus *(i.e.* Joseph Newball), 1746, p. 10). It is said, however, that the carriers' waggons began to be freely used as public vehicles for passengers at the end of the sixteenth century *(History of .. Newbury,* by Walter Money, 1889, p. 337), though Fynes Morison says that "none but women and people of inferior condition travel in this sort" *(Itinerary, or Ten Years' Travel throughout Great Britain and other Parts of Europe,* by Fynes Morison, 1617). In 1621 we find that (under the Royal Proclamation mentioned in the text) various carriers were proceeded against at the Middlesex Sessions for injuring the highways by driving more than the lawful number of horses and oxen *(Middlesex County Records,* by J. C. Jeaffreson, 1887-92, vol. ii. pp. 159, 173, etc.). On the other hand, Swynfen's outburst in Parliament, in the discussion on the Highways Act of 1670, to the effect that "waggons have been in use these thirty years," dates them only from 1640 *(Debates of the House of Commons from 1667 to 1694,* by Hon. Anchitell Grey, 1769, vol. i. p. 233). He was perhaps referring to their use as regular passenger vehicles. Regular passenger vehicles ran in the Commonwealth. They were certainly running regularly between London and Devon, London and Preston, and London and Coventry, by the accession of Charles II. In *The Grand Concern of England explained in Several Proposals to Parliament (Harhian Miscellany),* issued in 1673, the new habit of riding in coaches and caravans is referred to, and it is proposed that they be suppressed. Coaches were then running thrice a week between London and Exeter, Chester and York respectively, making the journey in five days. An able pamphlet without a date, which seems to belong to the period 1680-1700, is entitled *Reasons humbly offered to the consideration of Parliament for the Suppressing such of the Stage Coaches and Caravans now travelling upon the roads of England as are unnecessary, and regulating such as shall be thought fit to be continued.* But no such suppression took place; and gradually the " caravan " became the regular method of cheap and slow travelling on the main roads. "A picturesque object was the old stage waggon on the road, with the bells on the harness of the leading horses, and frequently the driver in his smock frock riding by the side on a small pony, with his long waggoner's whip, a horn lantern hanging up in front to be lighted when night came on" *(Old Coaching Days,* by Stanley Harris, 1882, p. 113).

In remote parts of the country wheeled traffic remained almost unknown for at least another century. Thus in Cornwall, right down to the opening of the nineteenth century, "there wore no carriages in general use. I remember only one kept in Falmouth and one in Flushing; and their passage through the streets was followed always by a crowd of children, as if it were something wonderful " *(Autobiography of John Silk Buckingham;* see also *A Guide to*

Penzance and its Neighbourhood by J. S. Courtney, 1845). In 1813 the " slide-car," a kind of sledge, was still used in Wales instead of a wheeled vehicle *(An Essay on the Construction of Roads and Carriages,* by R. L. Edgeworth, 1813, p. 70). As late as 1843 a Banffshire parish (Scotland) had no vehicular traffic, and hence no "made roads." "The harvest was got in on sleds, *i.e.* two long poles trailing behind a horse, and connected by a cross-piece. Corn was carried to market, and lime fetched for farm purposes, on horseback" *(Annals of the Disruption,* by Rev. Thomas Brown, 1890, p. 37); see, in corroboration, *Notes and Sketches illustrative of Northern Rural Life in the Eighteenth Century,* by B. M. Alexander, 1877, pp. 38-39.

It may be added that the Sedan Chair, introduced from France in 1581, and required (in London) to be licensed from 1634, was habitually used in London at the opening of the nineteenth century, and in some northern towns till 1840; whilst it lasted with old-fashioned people *(e.g.* old Mrs. Pusey, who lived in Grosvenor Square) down to 1858 (see *Bygone England,* by W. Andrews, 1892, pp. 102-112; *Reminiscences of Oxford,* by Rev. W. Tuckwell).

Page 70. See the Whitehaven Harbour Acts of 1709,1713, and 1739; *A New Tour through England,* by G. Beaumont and H. Disney, 1768, p. 19; *History and Topography of Cumberland and Westmorland,* by William Whellan, 1860, pp. 440-460; and *A Tour through the whole Island of Great Britain,* by Daniel Defoe, vol. iii. p. 266 of edition of 1748.

As to the then newly invented poultry carts, see *A Tour through the whole Island of Great Britain,* by Daniel Defoe, vol. L p. 54 of 1748 edition; and as to the special fish waggons, *The Norwich Road,* by C. G. Harper, 1901, p. 39.

Page 71. We may cite, among the treatises on road repair of this /period, the curious little volume entitled *Profit, Conveniency, and Pleasure V /to the whole Nation, being a short rational discourse... concerning the V Highways of England,* by Thomas Mace, 1675; *A Proposal for the Highways,* by E. Littleton, 1692; and *A Guide to Surveyors of the Highways,* by rifl. Meriton, 1694. The quotations are from the latter two.

Page 71. The quotations as to the badness of the roads are from *A Tour through the whole Island of Great Britain,* by Daniel Defoe, vol. ii. p. 425 of 1748 edition; *Proposals at Large for the Easy and Effectual Amendment of the Roads,* by a Gentleman, 1753, p. 2; *The History of Tom Jones,* by Henry Fielding, book vii. chap. iv.; *History of Surrey,* by H. E. Maiden, 1900, p. 280; Lord Hervey to his mother, 27th November 1736, in *Memoirs of the Reign of George the Second,* by John, Lord Hervey, 1884, voL ii. p. 362; *Gentleman's Magazine,* March 1756, p. 102 (also in *Gentleman's Magazine Library,* by Sir G. L. Gomme, part xv., 1904, pp. 25-26). See *History of England,* by Lord Macaulay, vol. i. chap. iii.; and *Lives of the Engineers,* by Samuel Smiles, voL L part iii. chaps. L-v.

Page 72. For the beginning of stage coaches, see the *History of Taxation and Taxes,* by Stephen Dowell, 1888, vol. iii. pp. 40-41; *Life of Josiah Wedgwood,* by Eliza Meteyard, 1865, voL i. p. 295; the chapter on "Travelling" in *Autobiographic Sketches,* by Thomas De Quincey, in voL xiv. of his *Works,* 1863 edition; *Reise tines Deutschen in England im Jahre 1782,* by C. H. Moritz, Berlin, 1783.

Defoe notes the new habit, in the fast fish and poultry carts, by which "the driver sits on the top of the coach, as in the public carriages for the army" *(A Tour through the whole Island of Great Britain,* voL i. p. 54 of 1748 edition). With the old waggons, "a man on a pony rode beside the team and with a long whip touched them up.... The travellers walked, putting their belongings inside" *(The Exeter Road,* by C. G. Harper, 1899, p. 9). A pamphleteer of 1820 notices that the heavy waggons "are gradually giving way to light carriages, drawn by four horses, and driven, *like the coaches are,* by a man on the box " *(An Essay on the Construction of Wheel Carriages,* by Joseph Storrs Fry, 1820, p. 23).

Page 72. *On the Landed Property in England,* by William Marshall, 1804, p. 293.

Page 73. *History of England,* by Lord Macaulay, vol. i. chap. iii. For these Acts soe Appendix to chap. iii. p. 46. The Aot of 1766 (7 George III. c. 42) repealed no fewer than twenty-five previous statutes relating to highways, reenacting their contents so far as applicable. It was itself repealed by a new consolidating Act of 1773 (13 George III. c. 78), which remained the basis of the law until 1835. Both these efforts at codification were imperfeotly executed, as is pointed out in John Scott's excellent *Digests of the General Highway and Turnpike Laws,* 1778, with its interesting notes and observations.

Page 74. For the principal "nuisance" provisions, see 1 George I. st. 2. c. 52 (1714); 5 George HI. c. 38 (1765); 6 George III. c. 43 (1765); 7 George II. c. 9 and c. 42 (1733); and 13 George HI. c. 78 (1773).

Page 74. For James the First's proclamation, see *Social History of the People of the Southern Counties,* by George Roberts, 1856, p. 488. It was repeated in 1629 by Charles I., who ordered " that no carrier or other person whatsoever shall travel with any wain, cart or carriage with more than two wheels, not with above the weight of twenty hundred, nor shall draw any wain, cart or carriage with more than five horses at once" *f History of Commerce,* by A. Anderson, 1801, vol. xix. p. 130; *Treatise on Roads,* by Sir H. Parnell, afterwards Lord Congleton, 1834, p. 16). The Restoration enactments are 13 and 14 Car. II. c. 6 (1662), and 22 Car. II. c. 12 (1670). The student wishing to pursue the subject may refer to 6 Anne, c. 29; 9 Anne, c. 18; 1 George I. c. 2; 1 George I. c. 52; 5 George I. c. 12; 6 George I. c. 6; 7 George I. c. 9; 9 George II. c. 18; 14 George II. c. 42; 15 George II. c. 2; 16 George II. c. 29; 18 George II. c. 33; 24 George II. c. 43; 26 George II. c. 28 and c. 30; 30 George II. c. 22; 7 George III. c. 42; 8 George III. c. 5; and 13 George m. c. 78.

Page 74. As to the number of horses to be allowed, see *The Justice of the*

Peace, by Dr. Richard Burn, preface, p. viii, of 1st edition (1755). "However eligible," says a commentator, " this plan of limiting the number of horses may be in point of policy, there are certainly very forcible objec

G tions against it in point of humanity. The avaricious farmer, who finds himself restricted to a team of three or four horses, will too often load those horses beyond their ability.... Three horses straining to the utmost of their strength, and forcing their feet into the ground, will... damage a road more than five drawing a greater weight with a steady regular draught" *(Digests of the General Highway and Turnpike Laws,* by John Scott, 1778, p. 256). The limitation of the team of horses or oxen to a definite number was accompanied by permission to the County Justices to sanction additional animals for drawing up particular steep hills. Hence the student of Quarter Sessions records, from 1700 onwards, occasionally comes across orders in which the Justices, often on the application of a particular "common carrier," who alleges that the roads up the hills in question "are so very bad and ruinous and in so great decay that he cannot go and pass with his waggon and number of horses limited only to the Act of Parliament" (MS. Minutes, Quarter Sessions, Kent, 5th October 1708), "and having made due enquiry into the state and condition of such parts of the steep hills and roads... not being turnpikes, but within the jurisdiction of the court,... have found it necessary and thought fit to license,... an increase or additional number of horses for the purpose of drawing the carriages... over and above the number limited by the said statute." They accordingly allow eight horses " for a waggon having the sole or bottom of its wheels less than six inches," and so on (see MS. Minutes, Quarter Sessions, Hampshire, 13th July 1708, when seven horses are allowed for a long list of hills, apparently all that the county contains; *ibid.* 15th January 1771, when as many as ten horses are allowed for broad wheeled waggons up Kingsclere Hill; *ibid.* 8th October 1776; MS. Minutes, Quarter Sessions, Kent, 16th July 1752, when six horses are allowed on each of seven hills; *ibid.* 11th January 1763, when a like privilege is granted separately to seven different persons for a particular road; MS. Minutes, Quarter Sessions, Wilts, 3rd October 1796, in the terms given in the text). After 1773 the Trustees of turnpike roads could grant similar permission on their own roads, subject to confirmation by the Justices in Quarter Sessions, whose confirmatory orders are given in their Minutes (see MS. Minutes, Quarter Sessions, Kent, 7th October 1794; ditto, Hampshire, 16th July 1776).

Page 75. As to the position of the horses, see 7 and 8 William III. c. 29 (1695) and 6 Anne c. 29 (1707). As late as 1802 we find the Trustees of the Epping and Ongar Turnpike Trust struggling to prevent a Chelmsford man from drawing his waggon with two horses abreast (contrary to 13 George III. c. 84, sec. 20), thus doing "great damage to the turnpike road by drawing with horses abreast and thereby destroying the horsepath." At last, after four years of warnings, they indicted him at Quarter Sessions, and got him fined £5 *(Minutes of the Epping and Ongar Highway Trust, 1769-1810,* by Benjamin Winstone, 1891, p. 151).

Page 76. "Meddle not with the weight they are to carry, for it will be impracticable," said Colonel Birch, M.P., in the debate on the Highway Act of 1670 *(Debates in the House of Commons from 1667 to 1694,* by the Honourable A. Grey, 1769, vol. i. p. 233). In 1672 the Common Council of the City of London ordained that "no street cart or brewer's dray shall... be drawn with more than one horse... except where the load cannot be divided and requires more than one horse, and also except when drawing up any of the hills from Thames Street, and up Holborn Hill." No waggon or cart was to be shod with iron or spignails *(An Act of Common Council together with certain Orders, Rules and Direction touching Paving and Cleansing the Streets,* etc., 1672, Rules 3 and 23). In 1720 Parliament enacted that not more than 12 sacks of meal, 12 quarters of malt, 7J cwt. of bricks or 1 "chalder" of coals should be carried at one load, in a vehicle having iron tires, within ten miles of London or Westminster, under penalty of forfeiting one of the horses, with gear, bridle, etc., to any person who shall distrain the same (6 George I. c. 6). For Bristol, it was not only prohibited in 1749 to have wheels shod with iron streaks of less breadth than six inches, and to use more than three horses (22 George II. c. 20); but also, in 1765, to draw loads of more than 14 sacks of corn or meal in four-wheeled vehicles, or 8 sacks in two-wheeled vehicles; or to use more horses within the city than were allowed in a team on the turnpike roads of Gloucester and Somerset (6 George III. c. 34).

Page 75. The discussion as to the proper shape, size and arrangement of wheels, so as to injure a soft road as little as possible, lasted for more than half a century. See *A Treatise upon Wheel Carriages,* by Daniel Bourn, 1763; *Inquiry into the Means of Preserving and Improving the Public Roads,* by J. Jacob, 1773; *Some Brief Remarks upon Mr. Jacob's Treatise on Wheel Carriages,* by Daniel Bourn, 1773; *Remarks on the Comparative Advantages of Wheel Carriages of Different Structure and Draught,* by Robert Anstice, 1790; *Observations on the Effects which Carriage Wheels with rims of different shapes have on the Roads,* by Alexander Gumming, 1797; *A Supplement to the Observations on the contrary effects of Cylindrical and Conical Carriage Wheels,* by the same, 1809; *A Treatise on Wheels and Springs for Carriages,* by Davies Gilbert, M.P., P. R.S.; *An Essay on the Construction of Roads and Carriages,* by R L. Edgeworth, 1817; *Cursory Remarks on Wheeled Carriages,* by John Cook; and *An Essay on the Construction of Wheel Carriages as they affect both the roads and the horses,* by Joseph Storrs Fry. The subject engaged most of the attention of the House of Commons Committee on the Preservation of Roads, etc. , which published nine reports between 1806 and 1811.

One inventor went so far as to supersede wheels altogether, replacing them by two or four broad iron rollers, which it was supposed would level the ruts, clear away the mud and cement the gravel. See *A Treatise upon Wheel Carriages,* 1763, and *Some Brief Remarks upon Mr. Jacob's Treatise on Wheel Carriages,* 1773, both by Daniel Bourn; and *Digests of the General Highway and Turnpike Laws,* by John Scott, 1778, pp. 269-270.

Apart from the difficulty of getting the law enforced, the provisions as to width of wheels were largely nullified by the exception always made in favour of carts used in and about husbandry and manuring of land (see, for instance, 5 George I. c. 6, 1718), and by the use of "dishing" or "conical" wheels, with "tapering rims," by which the "tread" was reduced. "We have lately seen," writes a practical critic in 1773, "the broad wheels of waggons which, by Act of Parliament, should press a surface of nine inches, in reality bear only on one of about three; some of them by means of bevelling the edges and raising the middle of the periphery; and others by bevelling the whole periphery and having the inner edge considerably higher than the other" *(Observations on the Structure and Draught of Wheel Carriages,* by J. Jacob, 1773, p. 89). It may be said, in excuse of these regulations, that the heavy waggons were demonstrably so destroying the soft roads of the time as to cause the cost of their repair to become an intolerable burden. Certain Warwickshire roads in 1765 were actually costing £84, and even £121, per mile per annum *(Inquiry into the y/faeans of Preserving and Improving the Public Roads,* by Henry Homer, 1765, p. 78); or more than double the average cost of the far superior turnpike roads of 1815.

Page 76. A draft bill prepared in 1753 would have quite calmly required, from one end of the Kingdom to the other, "that in some short but reasonable time. .. the furrows or ridges of the deep ruts and holes in the roads and highways shall everywhere be filled in and laid level or even *for the accommodation of the wheel carriages" (Proposals at Large for the Easy and Effectual Amendment of the Roads,* by a Gentleman, 1753, Clause 9); without any sort of consideration of the burden thereby to be thrown on the farmers and cottagers.

CHAPTER VI THE MAINTENANCE OP BRIDGES

In a country enjoying a heavy rainfall, and intersected by innumerable rivers and streamlets, the bridge might easily be assumed to be an indispensable part of the common highway. We take it nowadays for granted that, wherever the road is interrupted by running water, a bridge should be provided and maintained at the expense of public funds, so as to furnish a continuous dry passage. But so far is this from being an assumption of immemorial antiquity that it can be shown to have grown up within the last few generations. The Common Law of England knows nothing of the making of bridges. Not until 1888 (Local Government Act, 51 and 52 Vic. c. 21) did any statute make their construction part of the common duty of any public authority; and then it was entrusted, not to any ancient body, but to the new County Councils. To our ancestors of the fifteenth and even of the eighteenth century, accustomed to ride or scramble through the frequent " water splashes" on the roads, and to cross most rivers by fords, a bridge appeared as an exception to the common course of things, coming into existence as the result of some extraordinary private benevolence or religious zeal. To the traveller, the new bridge might be a boon calling for a special act of devotion at the chapel or crucifixes by its side, "which were the invariable pious accompaniment of the mediaeval bridge." To the ordinary home-keeping citizen, it seemed mainly a burden, which might involve new and unaccustomed contributions, against which he sought to protect himself in Magna Charta itself.

Notwithstanding this discouragement of public enterprise, bridges existed here and there from the earliest times, and their number was gradually increased by the pious labours of the "Brothers of the Bridge" (if, indeed, this quasi-religious order did any work in England), the enterprise of particular monasteries, the benevolence of testators, and even by the interference of the monarch himself. Of such primitive British stone bridges as those still existing on Dartmoor and Exmoor; of the Roman bridges that must, here and there, have spanned unfordable streams, and of which, indeed, the foundations have been traced on the Tyne in the North and on the Teign in the South; as also of the rude wooden bridges by which the English supplemented them, little or nothing is known. The maintenance and repair of such bridges was, like that of the highways, if not undertaken by particular estates *raiione tenurae,* part of the *trinoda necessitas* enforced by the English Kings on all holders of land. Several of these ancient bridges were referred to in the *Domesday Survey,* usually with regard to their state of dilapidation. Mention must also be made of the wooden structure that had spanned the Thames at London since the tenth century. Except that (as with the highways) the common obligation to maintain them in repair was enforceable by the Court Leet, we know nothing as to the actual administration with regard to these bridges. Gradually their number increased. The first stone bridge built in England is often said to have been that erected across the Thames at Wallingford, in Berkshire; but the interesting triangular bridge of worked stone near Croyland Abbey is unquestionably older, possibly of the ninth century. We owe to the enterprise of the Empress Matilda the two stone bridges at Stratford-at-Bow, on the borders of Middlesex and Essex, which were vested in the Abbess of Barking, with lands for their support. The old London Bridge itself was burnt down in 1136, and promptly renewed; to be replaced between 1176 and 1209, out of funds raised from diverse sources, by the stone structure covered with houses that excited, for over five centuries, the admiration of the world. We hear, incidentally, in the thirteenth century, of the rebuilding of the old wooden bridge over the Cam at Cambridge, probably of Roman origin, which had been carried away by a flood. This was done by the Sheriff of the County, Roger of Estra, who levied half a crown on every hide of land within the County for this purpose; whereupon the inhabitants loudly complained, urging that he had promised to give them a stone bridge, whereas he had built only a wooden one, and had taken full seven weeks over the job! The fourteenth century saw many bridges built, or wooden bridges replaced by stone; sometimes by wealthy landowners or pious testators, sometimes at the expense of a toll or " pontages," levied by Royal licence for three, five or eight years. Thus, the very ancient bridge at Wisbech was granted in 1326 by the King to the Bishop of Ely, with liberty to levy a toll for three years, and put it in repair. But by far the most important of these works was the old wooden bridge over the Medway at Rochester, on the important London to Dover road, which was replaced, in the reign of Richard II. (1391-97), by those doughty warriors, Sir Robert Knollys and Sir John de Cobham, acting probably with royal authority. The maintenance in repair of the nine stone arches of this bridge, in succession to the wooden one which had been there time out of mind, devolved, we are told, severally upon certain dignitaries, the owners of certain estates, and certain towns within the County. Thus, the Archbishop of Canterbury was responsible, in respect of the lands of his see, for the fifth and the ninth arches and piers; the Bishop of Rochester had to maintain the first, the King himself the fourth; whilst certain manors at Gillingham and elsewhere were severally burdened with the second, third, sixth, seventh and eighth. In 1421 the Wardens of Rochester Bridge were specially incorporated by Act of Parliament. The Gild of the Holy Cross at Birmingham, which was founded in 1392 for the performance of works of charity, subsequently undertook the maintenance and repair of "two great stone bridges and divers foul and dangerous highways," in what was, already in 1547, "one of the fairest and most profitable towns... in all the shire." We read of the erection, in 1425, of a stone bridge, with the customary chapel, at Catterick in Yorkshire, where the old Ermin Street crossed the Swale; but it is difficult to believe that this was not merely in replacement of an older structure. After the middle of the fifteenth century the practice of building new bridges seems to have ceased—possibly with the impoverishment of the religious orders and the decay of faith among testators— and the very art died out in England; to be revived, mostly at the public expense, in the seventeenth and eighteenth centuries.

But though the erection of a bridge might be a matter of private or corporate bounty, the law, from the first, took cognizance of its maintenance in repair. When a bridge had once been erected, it became a matter of obvious public convenience that it should be maintained. Though the traveller had originally managed to do without a bridge at all, its coming into existence generally so altered the circumstance of the highway as to make it henceforth indispensable. The road no longer led directly to the ford; the ford itself had perhaps disappeared with the embanking of the river; the ancient ferry had been discontinued; and thus the disappearance of the bridge might involve, not a mere reversion to the ancient state of things, but the complete stoppage of the highway. Hence, though English law regarded it as no part of public duty to construct a bridge where none had previously stood, however sore might be the traveller's need, it strenuously enforced the obligation to maintain all bridges forming part of the public highway, by whomsoever they had been erected, and however moderate might be the degree of their utility to the public.

Thus it is that the failure to maintain a public bridge in good repair has been, from time immemorial, a public nuisance presentable at the Court Leet. But it was more than a manorial offence. It was a misdemeanour for which an indictment would lie, and if it was found by the Grand Jury that any such bridge was broken or ruinous, the King's Judges at the Assizes, or his Justices in Quarter Sessions, would insist on the guilt being brought home to some one, on whom they could impose a substantial fine, to be devoted to making good the defect. As with the common highway, the obligation to keep in good repair might be, *ratione tenurae,* a burden upon some particular property, which had, by grant or by immemorial prescription, been charged with this service. Or it might be that the obligation to maintain a particular bridge attached to some Municipal Corporation or other "body politic," either *ratione tenurae,* as an incident of its tenure of certain specific lands, or merely by prescription, as when a Municipality, a Parish, a Hundred or a Franchise had, time out of mind, performed this duty. But these were exceptions. The general rule of the Common Law was that, in default of any special liability, the County was responsible for the maintenance of public bridges situated within its area. And, seeing that in many cases it could not be " proved what Hundred, Riding, Wapentake, City, Borough, Town or Parish, nor what person certain or body politic ought of right to" keep bridges in repair, it was expressly provided by the well-known " Statute of Bridges " in 1531 (22 Henry VIII. c. 5), to the end that " such decayed bridges " might not " he long without any amendment, to the great annoyance of the King's subjects," that, where no other liability could be definitely proved, the burden of maintenance should, for bridges outside corporate towns, always be held to fall upon the County, and for those within corporate towns, on such towns. So far, it might be said, as in the case of highways, that the procedure contemplated for securing the maintenance of bridges was merely that of enforcing, by the machinery of the criminal law, definite obligations to repair. Those who were liable for the maintenance of any public bridge, including the inhabitants of the County or "Borough Corporate" themselves, were to be presented or indicted for their neglect, and punished for it by fine, a process to be repeated again and again until the defects were made good. But upon the Justices in Quarter Sessions, whether of Counties or Boroughs, the Statute of Bridges cast a special administrative duty—perhaps the earliest branch of municipal enterprise entrusted to their care. They, " or four of them at the least," were given power in 1531 "to enquire, hear and determine, in the General Sessions, of all manner of annoyances of bridges broken in the highways, to the damage of the King's liege people, and to make such process and pains upon every presentment, against such as ought to be charged to make or amend them, as the King's Bench usually does, or as it shall seem by their discretions to be necessary and convenient for the speedy amendment of such bridges." Their power and authority extended, not only to the bridges themselves, but also to the highway for 300 feet from each end thereof. They were authorised to appoint in each County two Surveyors, who were to "see every such decayed bridge repaired and amended from time to time, as often as need shall require." And to meet the expense of such works, the Justices were empowered, a century and a half before they were empowered to impose a parochial rate for highway repair, to levy their own rate directly upon all the inhabitants of the County, "to such reasonable aid and sum of money as they shall think by their discretion convenient and sufficient for the repairing, re-edifying and amendment of such bridges."

The chief interest afforded by the records of County bridge administration lies, not so much in the vast increase of the service, or in the methods by which it has been successively performed, as in the peculiar and unpremeditated way in which the expenses previously borne by private individuals or by parishes were, especially from the end of the eighteenth century, increasingly saddled upon the County Fund. In the earliest Quarter Sessions records that are extant, we see the Justices looking after the few County Bridges then in existence. By the beginning of the eighteenth century this had, indeed, become the principal administrative service that they actually performed. To the gaols and houses of correction, which had also fallen to their charge, they gave the very minimum of attention; their supervision of the parochial authorities in such matters as poor relief and highways was, in the reign of William the Third, at its lowest ebb; and the half a dozen squires and clergymen who, in 1700, met quarterly at the County Town, would have had but little taxation to levy on their neighbours had it not been for the constantly recurring need for " Bridge Money." In contrast, too, with later practice, we find them not waiting for the presentment of the Grand Jury, or other process of the law, but acting on what we may call an administrative interpretation of the Statute of Bridges; treating the maintenance of the County Bridges simply as a branch of the civil government of the County, for which they could give orders and spend money at their discretion, without the County being, on an indictment, found guilty of neglect, or even presented as in default. They were, in fact, sufficiently concerned about keeping open the main thoroughfare roads through their County, not only to be perpetually ordering little repairs to the County Bridges, but also to be willing to execute works of improvement out of the County Fund—to widen and extend the old bridges; gradually to replace wooden structures by brick or stone, and even to make contributions towards the erection of the new bridges that were felt to be required by the rapidly increasing traffic on the roads.

The bridge business of the County was, however, at the beginning of the eighteenth century, according to modern ideas, only a small affair. Although the law unequivocally made the County liable for the maintenance of all bridges, large or small, new or old, except those which could be definitely shown to be a legal charge on other persons, or on Municipalities, the County Justices were very far from assuming or admitting so large a responsibility. The bridges maintained at the cost of the County, and administered by the Justices in Quarter Sessions, were insignificant, alike in size and in number. The largest and most important of the bridges then in existence—like London Bridge and Rochester Bridge—were maintained out of lands given or left for the purpose; or else fell naturally, by immemorial custom, to the charge of the Municipal Boroughs which had grown up at such centres of traffic. Other bridges were, by immemorial custom, "Hundred Bridges," repaired out of a rate levied, not on the County as a whole, but on the particular Hundred, or other analogous district, and administered, in practice, by the Justices acting for that Hundred. The thousands of little streamlets that crossed the parish highways were, for the most part, unbridged; "nor was it imagined," we read, "that the County could reasonably be called upon to maintain bridges in the cross roads which were seldom used except by the inhabitants to pass from one village to another. Such bridges were generally deemed to be Parish Bridges, and were accordingly supported by the respective parishes in which they were situated, unless any other parties were known to be specially liable.... Only bridges in the great public roads leading through the County were maintained at the County expense." Thus, right down to 1786, the Middlesex Justices maintained only three County Bridges, at Brentford, Hanwell and Chertsey respectively. Larger Counties, and especially those traversed by the main thoroughfare roads, had more bridges to look after, but not many more; and these being (south of the Trent), as Defoe informs us, for the most part built of wood, over shallow streams, the repairs required, though frequent, were, on each occasion, neither costly nor difficult of execution.

The procedure adopted by Quarter Sessions for dealing with County Bridges was of the simplest. It was at the beginning of the century exceptional for them to appoint a " Bridge-master," or other officer to look after these works. In spite of the express authority to appoint Surveyors, given by the Act of 1531, " this business of surveying the bridges," writes Dr. Burn in 1754, "is usually annexed by the Justices to the office of the High Constables." What happened was that it would be reported to Quarter Sessions, sometimes by a High Constable, sometimes by a Vestry or Court Leet, sometimes merely by letter from some of the local residents—more generally, we imagine, by one or more of the Justices themselves, or by presentment of the Grand Jury—that a particular bridge was "in great decay," or "so much out of repair as to be in danger of immediate falling." If the bridge was one which had previously been repaired at the County expense, or was on a highway of any importance, and was not notoriously chargeable to some particular person or Corporation, the Justices would usually not demur to the execution of the necessary repairs, even if there had been no indictment of the County. Quarter Sessions would direct one or two of the magistrates living near to inspect the bridge in question, to give the necessary orders to some local workmen, and to supervise their work. Thus we read in the minutes of the Suffolk Quarter Sessions for 1695 that " this Court doth desire Sir Adam Felton, Bart., and Sir John Barker, Bart. , to view Shelley Bridge and Bourne Bridge, both within this Division, and to give such necessary directions for the present repair of the said bridges as to them shall seem meet, and also to give such further directions for rebuilding Shelley Bridge with brick or stone as they shall think most fitting." In 1718 the Essex Quarter Sessions orders the County Treasurer to pay £60 to four of the Justices, "to be by them immediately applied for the repairing of Ilford Bridge and Causeway as they shall think most meet and convenient." A century later exactly the same procedure was being resorted to in Wiltshire, where, in 1809, Quarter Sessions resolved "that the County Bridge at Compton Chamberlain called Horse Shoe Bridge, presented by J. H. Penruddocke, Esq., as being out of repair, be forthwith repaired under the direction and supervision of the said J. H. Penruddocke, Esq., and such Surveyor as he shall think fit to employ; and that the expenses of such repairs be defrayed out of the County Stock." In other cases the Chief Constable of the Hundred would be directed himself to get the repairs done, with some such order as the following, taken from the Suffolk Quarter Sessions records: "This Court doth order Mr. Robert Clarke of Ipswich, Treasurer of the Bridge Money of this County, to pay the sum of eight pounds into the hands of Mr. William Wincup, one of the Chief Constables of the Hundred of Blything, in this County, to be by him laid out in and about the repair of Blithborough Bridge and Causey; and the said Mr. Wincup to give an account of his disbursements at next sessions."

It was, however, not merely the lack of professional skill, and the absence of any adequate supervision of the work, that caused the steady increase in the levies of "Bridge Money." The number of bridges maintained by the County was continually growing. At first, as we have said, the existence of a bridge, and especially of a bridge repairable by the County at large, was looked upon as an exception. We see the Essex Justices in 1720 making a stand against a tendency, already recognisable, to make the County widen its responsibilities. Local and particular obligations to maintain bridges were easily forgotten, and for want of knowledge thereof " many private bridges and causeways," they declare, "have come upon the County to be repaired, and many others are out of repair, and some altogether down and demolished, the reparation of which in time may become a charge to this County." To remedy this state of things the Essex Justices made an attempt to resuscitate the old machinery of the Inquest Jury. "It is therefore ordered," they resolve, "that a precept be sent to the Sheriff... for returning the twelve men out of every Hundred to serve on such Petty Juries or Juries of Inquiry as have been out of mind used." These Juries were to inquire, among other matters, into the state of the bridges and causeways and to state who is legally liable for their maintenance. How far this revival of the Inquest Jury was effectual in enforcing the obligations of the owners of ancient private bridges in Essex cannot now be ascertained. But as the century wore on, the growth of wheeled traffic and the rising standard of road administration led everywhere to a demand for new bridges. Many roads could be made suitable for wheeled traffic only on condition that the narrow packhorse bridges were replaced by others wide enough to admit at any rate a single vehicle. Others were impassable in winter, when the water was deep at the fords, until bridges were provided. In others, again, the slight and flimsy wooden structures, which private donors or parishes had provided at their own expense, required to be replaced by larger and more solid buildings. Strictly speaking, neither Common Law nor general statute warranted either Parish or County to erect new bridges, or to contribute towards their cost. But the need for new bridges was so obvious that, in one County after another, applications poured in upon Quarter Sessions. Thus in 1708, it was reported to be absolutely necessary to bridge the Derwent at Hazelford, the ancient ford by which the packhorses bearing the woollen goods of Bradford entered Derbyshire. In 1713, " the gentlemen of Chipping Ongar and neighbourhood" represent to the Essex Quarter Sessions that their way to Ingatestone is impassable for lack of a bridge over what is now a rushing river. In 1718 the Derbyshire Justices had seriously before them the state of the ford by which the road between Manchester and London passed over the Lathkil river. "Great gangs of London carriers' horses, as well as great drifts of malt horses, and other daily carriers and passengers," came and went by this ancient way, which lay in a hollow, frequently overflowed by the swollen stream. Heavy rains had now so scoured out the channel as to render the ford impassable for eight or ten days together, whilst at all times "carriers with loaden horses and passengers cannot pass the said road without great danger of being cast away." The Suffolk Quarter Sessions, in 1726, had to face the fact that the bridges and causeways in various parishes which had hitherto been charged with their maintenance were so ruinous as to be quite beyond the means of these parishes to repair. So, in 1731, the bridge at Halesworth, over the main road, but not a County Bridge, was in such a state that much more had to be spent upon it than the parish would consent to afford.

The Justices in most Counties seem to have yielded to such requests, and to have made grants somewhat freely in aid of the erection or improvement of bridges that were not strictly County Bridges, but were nevertheless of distinct public utility. The applications recounted above were all met by the grant, out of the Bridge Funds of the County, of sums varying from £10 to £60, in aid of the subscriptions raised by the local inhabitants, or of the rates levied by the parish officers; in each case (as in Essex in 1742-43) on condition of the subscribers or the parishioners "undertaking to repair it for the future, it being no County Bridge "; or else (as in Derbyshire in 1714) with the express stipulation that for the future " there never be any more money given by the County "; or to quote the more elaborate words of the Suffolk Justices in 1737, making the grant "in such manner as may not incline posterity to accept or refute the same in the nature of a County Bridge, but to esteem this as a voluntary gift only." But, useful as were these bridges, and carefully as the Justices guarded themselves against incurring any future liabilities in connection with them, the inevitable rise in the periodical levies of "Bridge Money" led to objections to their action. The objectors, whose case is fervently put in a contribution to the *Gentleman's Magazine* in 1759, admitted that the "bridges called County, Riding or Wapentake Bridges are commanded to be, and ought to be, repaired, by several statutes." But the action of Quarter Sessions had, they complained, created a new category of bridges other than County Bridges. "Besides these," continues the writer, "we have had bridges of another denomination for many years, and of such kind as are not to be found in our common or statute law. These bridges are erected by the legislature of the Court of Quarter Sessions; they are the bounty of that court, not only without power delegated by the statute, but in express violation of the Great Charter of our liberties which says, 'No town or freeman shall be distrained to make bridges but such as in old time were made.'... The inhabitants of many parishes withheld for several years the money demanded of them for the erection of Gratuity Bridges, which were granted with warrants of distress, which neither the Chief nor the Petty Constables, nor even the legislature of the Quarter Sessions thought proper to put into execution. Bridges of this order are numerous, and have been in fashion above eighty years, occasioned by thunder showers and sudden rains, the brooks overflowing for a few hours, through the idleness of the people to restrain them in their proper channels. These bridges are not in the least necessary for public commerce; they are chiefly for private convenience and communication of neighbouring houses; and if any gentleman is disposed to oblige himself or his friends with a bridge, he must be of little interest or address if his petition is refused. In the eighth year of the reign of Queen Anne (1710), I remember a gentleman went to the Quarter Sessions, holden at Easter in a Northern County, to oppose the erection of one of those bridges, in no shape useful to the public, for which £130, as an introductory sum, had been paid by the Petty Constable to the Chief. The lawyer he retained, addressing himself to the Court, said: 'Gentlemen, you must maintain the ancient bridges, but have no authority to build new ones where there never were any, without an Act of Parliament.' Then moved for a discharge of the order granted before, and for repayment of the money, which were agreed to without objection, every Petty Constable soon after receiving his respective share. At the next Quarter Sessions, a petition being preferred for another of these bridges, the same gentleman opposed it, and obtained an order as follows:—' Whereas Gratuity Bridges have been complained of to this Court as a burden and oppression to the people, it is ordered by this Court that for the future no sum of money shall be granted as a gratuity to any place or person whatsoever for the building of such bridges.'... Notwithstanding all this, how many of these bridges have been erected since? What great sums of money granted, levied and misapplied?. .. When by distress, or menaces of distress, money is wrested out of the hands of the people, not only against common law, but a strong denunciation of the statute, the case of many individuals may be made truly deplorable.... The repair of these bridges may in time be entailed on one estate, but though we have been so ductile and slavish as to build them, we are not yet obliged to maintain and uphold them,... but may be, in a generation or two, if these impositions are not opposed before they become immemorial." It was, we assume, with the object of checking this liberality and enterprise of Quarter Sessions in the matter of bridges that Parliament inserted in the County Rate Act of 1739, a clause expressly prohibiting any money being " applied to the repair of bridges until presentment be made by the Grand Jury, at the Assizes or Sessions, of their insufficiency, inconveniency, or want of reparation."

From this time forth, though mere administrative orders do not cease, nor even the grants of money towards "Gratuity Bridges," we infer that the Justices in Quarter Sessions made more use of the cumbrous machinery of indictment or presentment, by which alone, so Parliament had declared, they could lawfully spend the county funds on the maintenance of bridges. The High Constable, or sometimes one or more of the jurymen themselves, would bring before the Grand Jury, at the Sessions or the Assizes, the ruinous or decayed state of such and such a bridge, whereupon the Grand Jury would make a formal presentment of the fact, stating also who in their opinion was liable to maintain such bridge. Some Counties found a simpler form of obeying the letter of the law. Any one Justice of the Peace might, as we have mentioned, make presentment of a highway not properly kept in repair, which presentment had been, long before, by statute of 1563, expressly made equivalent to one by the Grand Jury. By the General Highway Act of 1773 this power of a single Justice to make a presentment was extended to bridges. Though we cannot help doubting whether Parliament then intended this to apply to anything more than presentment of the Parish for little bridges forming part of the parish highway, it was in some Counties extended to County Bridges and utilised as a device for complying easily and promptly with the terms of the Act of 1739. In other Counties, however, the proceedings took a more elaborate form. The High Constable or the Bridgemaster, if such an officer existed, or perhaps one or two Justices themselves, would make a report (often called a presentment) to Quarter Sessions that a particular bridge was out of repair. Upon this, the Clerk of the Peace would prepare a formal indictment of the person or "body politic" liable to maintain the bridge, this being in most of the cases, "the inhabitants of the County" in question. This indictment of the County itself would be solemnly laid before the Grand Jury at the Assizes, a true bill would be found, no defence would be made, and the Justices on the Bench would proceed formally to give judgment against their own County, for neglecting to maintain its bridge, postponing the case until the following Sessions in order to allow the necessary repairs to be executed. On a certificate being then produced that the bridge was in good order, the indictment would be formally discharged. In Lancashire and Northumberland, and doubtless in other Counties, it seems to have been the practice, at the end of the eighteenth and beginning of the nineteenth century, to make every case of bridge-repair the subject of such an indictment. The voluminous and well-kept minutes of the Lancashire Quarter Sessions record, at every sessions, scores of cases in which "the inhabitants" of the

H

County or the Hundred were presented for not repairing particular bridges, it being ordered by the Court that a fine be imposed and estreated unless cause be shown at the next Sessions. At the single Midsummer Sessions, 1799, "the inhabitants of the County of Northumberland" pleaded guilty to no fewer than twelve indictments for not repairing various County Bridges, or ends of roads adjoining such bridges—the cases thereupon standing automatically referred to the "Bridge Surveyor for the North" or the "Bridge Surveyor for the South" as the case might be, who got the necessary work done, and received payment at the subsequent Sessions "for the repair of bridges as per his Report Book... they being under presentment for want of repairs."

The clause in the Act of 1739, confining the Justices' expenditure on bridges to those which had been made the subject of legal proceedings, was doubtless intended to restrain an increasing item of County expenditure. How far it had the desired effect of limiting the number of so-called " Gratuity Bridges " we have no means of determining. Nor can we ascertain in how many cases the County in defending itself managed to fasten the legal liability to repair a bridge on some other shoulders. What was, however, not anticipated was that the formal transfer of the business of bridge repair, from the domain of the Justices' civil administration to that of a judicial determination of the legal liability to repair, was eventually to lead to an enormous extension of the County obligations. What had perhaps not been foreseen was that the judicial decision, unlike the exercise of an administrative discretion, might become the subject of appeal to a higher tribunal. The indictment was not always a matter of form, instigated by the County itself, but sometimes a genuinely hostile action, set on foot by some one who wanted to get a local bridge repaired at the County expense. In 1780 the West Riding of Yorkshire was indicted for not repairing a little carriage bridge in the township of Glasburne. The Riding denied liability, as the carriage bridge had been notoriously erected within comparatively recent date, by the Township in which it stood, in substitution for an ancient footbridge sixty yards lower down the stream, which the Township had always maintained. To the consternation of the County authorities, the Judges unanimously held the Riding liable, in spite of its having neither built nor sanctioned the bridge. "If a man build a bridge, and it becomes useful to the County in general," said the Court, " the County shall repair it." In the case of a bridge recently erected, it could not be said that the Township or any one else was liable by prescription; it was not liable merely by reason of having constructed the bridge; and there was equally no question of liability by tenure. Hence, under the plain words of the Statute of Bridges, it was the County that was liable for maintenance.

This interpretation of the law, which was adopted in various succeeding cases, clearly involved Counties in the liability for all bridges, large or small, erected since the beginning of legal memory, which could not be said to be maintainable by prescription, if they were not maintained as an incident of the tenure of specific lands, provided that they had come to form part of the common highway, and were of distinct public utility. The full effect of the doctrine was not, at first, realised. Gradually, however, it came to be understood; and those who had erected and hitherto maintained small local bridges, hastened to shuffle off their liability to the more capacious shoulders of the public. The next half century produced, accordingly, a crop of indictments against Counties, in which the latter were nearly always found liable. Parishes and Townships made the County repair their little highway bridges; Turnpike Trusts (which we shall describe in the next chapter) shifted shamelessly the charge of those which they had themselves constructed to reap their tolls; millers who had deepened fords and substituted bridges for their own profit, all repudiated their obligations to maintain them— even King George himself, in the case of a bridge at Datchet built by Queen Anne for her own convenience, of which he had appropriated the materials to his own use, refused to be at the charge of keeping it up. "Lords of Manors," subsequently declared the Committee of Middlesex Justices, "and other persons deemed liable to the maintenance of bridges, and who had actually maintained them, have, by their influence and connection, induced Parishes and Turnpike Trusts to indict the County; and by withholding the necessary information (seldom known except to the parties locally interested) have frequently succeeded in obtaining a verdict." Literally hundreds of small bridges were, in this way, gradually transferred to the charge of the Counties in which they were situated. It was, indeed, as the Middlesex Justices declared, "a very easy and convenient method" of shifting a liability; "because if it be not proved on behalf of the County what other party is liable, the County is fixed with the burden." Moreover, "this facility of indicting the County " was found to operate " on the most trifling occasions; for in 1815 the Trustees of the Kensington Turnpike Road indicted the County for the non-repair of a culvert only two feet six inches wide, under the road between Kensington and Hammersmith. This culvert, although dignified with the title of Counter's Bridge, was scarcely known even to the inhabitants. But the indictment having, through inattention, been undefended, a verdict was obtained in the Court of King's Bench, and the County was consequently declared liable to the repair of the said culvert, misnamed a bridge."

It was naturally pointed out to the Judges, in connection with these cases, that their decisions were upsetting the long customary practice, and imposing heavy charges on the County rate. But the law was clear, and the Judges could only declare, as one of them said, that " if any inconvenience arises from this decision, the Legislature must provide for it in future Acts." Some of the Counties did, at last, bestir themselves to get the law altered. In 1799, as we learn from the *Manchester Mercury,* the Clerk of the Peace for Staffordshire incited the great County of Lancaster to take the matter up. The Lancashire Justices had just found themselves legally saddled with charges amounting to £1000 for the repair of small bridges not heretofore chargeable either to the Hundred or to the County; and they discussed the whole position at a special meeting, adopting a resolution in the following terms: "The determination of the Court of King's Bench on the Glasburne Bridge case in the year 1780, and some subsequent determinations founded on that case, have had the effect of making Counties subject to the charge of rebuilding and supporting all new bridges of which the public have had the use, built by subscription or otherwise, without the knowledge or approbation of the respective Counties. The extent that has been given to these determinations has already subjected the County of Lancaster to great expense, and if not restrained may lay an incalculable burden on the County Rate, by proceedings which previous to these determinations were unknown. The Court is willing that the inhabitants of the County should be accommodated with new bridges on proper conditions where they are really wanted, but the Court conceives that it is equitable... that bridges which are afterwards to be upheld and supported at the expense of the County should be built by the authority of the County. The Court therefore recommends that in the bill intended to be presented to Parliament for the amendment of the law respecting County Bridges it should be provided that when any new bridge should be intended to be built for public use, application should be made in the first instance to the General Annual Session for the County, first giving public notice of such application, and if the magistrates then assembled should be of opinion that it was expedient that the bridge should be built, they should settle with the petitioners the money that they were to pay towards defraying the expense of erecting the said bridge, which money should be paid into the hands of the Treasurer of the County, the deficiency being supplied from the County Rates, and the County building the bridge, which should afterwards be deemed and taken to be a County Bridge; and no bridge built otherwise than under the above regulations should be deemed or taken to be a County Bridge." A Bill was accordingly prepared, and Thomas Butterworth Bayley—the able and zealous magistrate whom we have already mentioned as a road reformer—was sent with it to enlist the support of the West Riding of Yorkshire. But Parliament was, at that date, not disposed to interfere with the freedom of landowners and townships to improve the means of communication by local bridges. All that it would do (by Lord Ellenborough's Act, 43 Geo. III. c. 59, sec. 59, 1803) was, whilst making some minor amendments in the Justices' powers of repair, to enable Quarter Sessions to require that new bridges, thereafter erected otherwise than by the County itself, should, as a condition of their becoming repairable by the County, be constructed in such manner as the Justices might approve, and under the inspection of the County Surveyor. With this meagre protection the Counties had to content themselves; and the number of small bridges thrown upon the County Rate continued, by frequent indictments, annually to increase. The Justices seem in each County to have made the best terms they could. In Lancashire, the Deputy Clerk of the Peace was instructed, in June 1806, "in future in all cases where indictments shall be preferred for not repairing" bridges built by private subscriptions, to "consult with the magistrates assembled at the General Quarter Sessions within the district wherein such indicted bridges shall lie, and shall take their direction as to the propriety of defending or submitting to such indictments." Quarter Sessions accepted, with little demur, the charge of all substantial bridges, which were distinctly of public utility, but they continued to resist attempts to make them take over mere culverts or tiny arches in local highways. They had, moreover, as in Northumberland in 1827, frankly to accept the unsatisfactory position that new bridges would be built, whether the County paid for them or not, and to make the best of the statutory requirement that they should be constructed to the satisfaction of the County Surveyor. But, as the Middlesex Justices found in 1820-26, even this protection availed the County little. If the builder of a new bridge did not trouble to inform the County Surveyor, or persisted in disregarding his instructions, the bridge, once built, would have to be maintained somehow; and in the absence of any special liability, could, if of any public utility at all, hardly fail to fall to the charge of the County, in spite of the fact that it had been built without its approval. The Judges seem to have suggested in 1821 that the remedy of the County was to indict the too zealous bridge-builder for committing a common nuisance in erecting a bridge which, though serving possibly an urgent public need, was likely at some future time to throw upon the County the burden of repairing it. It is needless to say that no such indictment took place. It would, say the Middlesex Magistrates, "be considered very invidious to prosecute a man for building a bridge on his own land for the use of the public, and therefore they conclude, "it is not likely that any bridge which ought to be the subject of an indictment would be brought to the notice of the magistrates. "

In this unsatisfactory and illogical condition the law as to the erection of new public bridges by other than the public authority has ever since remained. But even before the exact effect of the law had, in the various cases between 1780 and 1821, been thoroughly explored, the need for more bridges and better ones had led many Counties voluntarily to assume the duties of general bridge authorities. For more than a century hardly any bridge had been built in England, when, in 1611-37, the remarkable long stone bridge at Berwick-on-Tweed was erected in substitution for the ancient wooden bridge which had fallen down; and in 1634 Inigo Jones was commissioned to design the charming little bridge over the Conway River at Llanrwst, in North Wales. A persistent agitation for additional bridges over the Thames, carried on from 1660 to 1769, led, at last, to the erection of Westminster Bridge (1738-50) out of moneys granted by Parliament, and of Blackfriars Bridge (1760-69), built by the Corporation of the City of London out of its trust funds. From the middle of the eighteenth century, with the steady increase of carriage traffic, which could not conveniently ford streams, nor yet use the old packhorse bridges, we see a general movement for bridge construction setting in. Between 1746-55, when the marvellous stone bow bridge over the Tafi at Pontyprydd was finished, and 1789, when he died, the "bridge-building mason," William Edwards, constructed more than a dozen stone bridges in South Wales. In 1779 the first iron bridge was constructed, over the Severn at Coalbrookdale. But the most remarkable development was in Shropshire, where the County Justices seem to have been inspired with the most praiseworthy zeal for bridging all the streams in the County. Appointing in 1786, as Samuel Smiles graphically relates, another promoted stone-mason, Thomas Telford, to the post of County Surveyor, they allowed him, within the next fifty years, to put up no fewer than forty-two new County Bridges, five of which were of iron and the others of stone. Even in so apathetic a county as Buckinghamshire we find Quarter Sessions, in the early part of the nineteenth century, busying itself constantly about getting new and additional bridges. Up and down the country we see such bodies as Municipal Corporations, Turnpike Trustees, or Improvement Commissioners obtaining Special Acts of Parliament authorising them to construct new bridges, or to rebuild old ones. This desire for better means of communication within the County may well have prevented the Justices from offering any very strenuous opposition to the ever-increasing transference of bridge maintenance from parishes and private landowners to the County Funds. Even where some sort of bridge was in existence, it was frequently necessary to build a new one, in order to replace a foot-bridge, or a packhorse bridge, or a narrow carriage-bridge with inconvenient gradients, by the broad and level roadway called for by the new coach traffic. In the absence of any general statutory authority to build a new bridge, the most convenient course may well have been for the County to allow itself to be made legally chargeable with the maintenance of the old one, and then to execute the improvement in the guise of the ordinary work of repair or " re-edifying," contemplated by the Act of 1531. Be this as it may, we infer that, by 1835, outside the Municipal Corporations, the great majority of bridges other than those owned and maintained by statutory bridge companies, to which we shall allude in the next chapter, those belonging to the Turnpike Trusts, which we are about to describe, and those specifically charged on particular bodies by their respective private Acts, had come to be maintained out of County Funds.

APPENDIX TO CHAPTER VI

Notes And References

Page 85. By far the most useful single volume on the maintenance of Bridges is the extensive quarto *Report of the Committee of Magistrates appointed to make enquiry respecting the Public Bridges in the County of Middlesex,* 1826. The first volume of *Lives of the Engineers,* by Samuel Smiles (1801) contains (pp. 237-275) three admirable chapters on the early bridges, of which also J. J. Jusserand's *English Wayfaring Life in the Middle Ages,* 1892, gives interesting glimpses; whilst Smiles's second volume gives, in the Memoirs of Telford and Rennie, much information as to the later bridge-building. The modern technicalities of bridge-building may be seen in such works as *The Theory and Practice of Bridge Construction,* by M. W. Davies, 1908, or *A Practical Treatise on Bridge Construction,* by T. C. Fidler, 4th edition, 1909. The law as to bridges is to be found, characteristically enough, partly with that of nuisances, partly with that of highways; see, for instance, *The Law of Highways, Main Roads and Bridges,* by J. Tidd Pratt, edited by W. W. Mackenzie and J. Weir, 1897; *The Law of Nui-*

sances, by Edmund W. Garrett, 1897; Pratt and Mackenzie's *Law of Highways,* 16th edition, 1911; *The Law relating to Highways,* by W. C. and A. Glen, 1897; or *The Law relating to Waters,* by H. J. W. Coulson and TJrquhart Forbes, 3rd edition, 1910. But we have had, for the most part, to seek our material on the administration of bridges in the MS. Minutes of Quarter Sessions.

Page 85. As to the " pious accompaniments of the mediaeval bridge," see *Three Centuries of Derbyshire Annals,* by J. C. Cox, 1800, vol. ii. p. 225. Picturesque chapels "on the bridge" still exist at Wakefield *(Old Yorkshire,* by William Smith, 1884) and Derby *(Notts on the Churches of Derbyshire,* by J. C. Cox, 1875-79).

Page 85. As to the burden, compare " No town nor freeman shall be distrained to make bridges... but such as of old time, and of right, have been accustomed to make them " (9 Henry III. c. 15, 1224; 15 Edward I. c. 12,1287). "None can be compelled to make new bridges where never any were before, but by Act of Parliament" (Lord Coke's *Institutes,* vol. ii. p. 701). See Caiman's *History of Local Rates,* 1912, pp. 30-33.

Page 86. For the " Brothers of the Bridge," *fratres pontiflces,* to whom the French traveller was indebted for the bridges at Avignon and Lyons and many others, see the extracts quoted in Herbert Spencer's *Descriptive Sociology* (No. viiL, France, by James Collier), and *Recherches historiques sur les Congregations hospitalieres des Frires Pontifes,* by M. Gregoire, Bishop of Blois (Paris, 1818). Although their work extended to Italy, Spain and Germany, and continued throughout the twelfth and thirteenth centuries, it seems doubtful whether they built any bridges in England *(English Wayfaring Life in the Middle Ages,* by J. J. Jusserand, translated by Lucy Toulmin Smith, 2nd edition, 1892, p. 41); though individual bridge constructors in the England of that time may have belonged to the Order.

Page 86. For early instances of bridges see *Lives of the Engineers,* by S. Smiles, 1892, vol. i.; *History of Private Bill Legislation,* by F. Clifford, 1887, vol. ii. pp. 23-35. For the Roman bridges over the Tyne, the Teign, and the Cam, see *The Celt, the Roman, and the Teuton,* by Thomas Wright, 2nd edition, 1861, p. 225. For Queen Matilda's bridge at Wallingford, see *History oj Wallingford,* by J. K. Hedges, 1881. For the two bridges at Stratford at Bow, see *Archaologia,* vols. xxviL p. 77 and xxix. p. 380. For London Bridge, see especially (among the endless literature) *Chronicles of London Bridge,* by Richard Thomson, 1827; *History oj London,* by W. J. Loftie, 2 vols., 1884; *A Survey of the Cities of London and Westminster and the Borough of Soulhwark,* by John Stow, 1598 (latest edition). For the extortions of the Sheriff over the bridge at Cambridge, see *Rotuli Hundredarum,* edited by W. Dlingworth, 1812-18, voL i. p. 54; *The Growth of English Industry and Commerce during the Early and Middle Ages,* by Dr. W. Cunningham, 1890, p. 202. For the bridge at Wisbech, see *History of Wisbech,* by N. Walker and T. Cradook, 1849, p. 417. For Rochester Bridge, "finer than that of London," see *Monsieur MissoiCs Memoirs and Observations on his Travels over England,* translated by Ozell, 1719, p. 278; *Rotuli Parliamentum,* vol. iii. pp. 289, 354, vol. iv. p. 149; *History of Private Bill Legislation,* by F. Clifford, 1887, vol. ii. pp. 22-23; *The Growth of English Industry and Commerce during the Early and Middle Ages,* by Dr. W. Cunningham, 5th edition, 1910, voL i. p. 450. For the Gild of the Holy Cross at Birmingham (and Lenche's Trust), see *English Gilds,* by Joshua Toulmin Smith, 1870, pp. 238-261; and "The Gild of Holy Cross, Birmingham," by Lucy Toulmin Smith, in *Byegone Warwickshire,* by W. Andrews, 1893. For Catterick Bridge, see *History of the County of York,* by Allen, vol. iii. p. 496; *A Picturesque History of Yorkshire,* by J. S. Fletcher, voL iv. p. 175; *Growth of Industry and Commerce in the Early and Middle Ages,* by Dr. W. Cunningham, 5th edition, 1910, vol. i. p. 450.

Page 87. The cessation of bequests for bridges and highways is made much of in *A Compendious or Briefe Examination of Certayne Ordinary Complaints,* by W. S. William Stafford, 1581, pp. 15, 17, etc.

The mere fact that the bridge was erected at a comparatively recent date by some private person would not suffice to impose upon him or his heirs the obligation to maintain it. "If a man make a bridge," says Lord Coke, " for the common good of all the subjects, he is not bound to repair it" *(Institutes,* voL ii. p. 701). Nor would it suffice to show that he had voluntarily once or twice repaired it. The same was true even if it were proved that he erected it wholly or mainly for his own convenience, if it had since actually been used by the public, and had been of distinct public utility (R. *v.* the Inhabitants of Glamorganshire, 1788, East's *King's Bench Reports,* vol. ii. p. 356). To make an individual liable to repair a bridge actually used by the public as part of the common highway, the obligation had to be shown to be an incident of his tenure of specific lands *(Pleas of the Crown,* by Sir Matthew Hale, voL ii. p. 181; R. *v.* Sir John Bucknall, 1702, Lord Raymond's *Reports,* voL ii. p. 804). It is, then, enforceable primarily against the occupier of the land in question, who can obtain reimbursement from the owner (Baker *v.* Greenhill, 1842, 3 Q.B. 148). As to obligation to repair *ratione lenurae,* see Lord Coke's *Institutes,* vol. ii. p. 700; Wood's *Institutes* (1763), Book I. chap. viL The obligation of a Municipal Corporation, or other body politic, *ratione tenurae,* is merely that to which a private owner would be subject in like case. It therefore differs from an obligation to repair by prescription, in that the remedy is by indictment against the Corporation, as owner, not against the inhabitants of the locality, and in that it is not necessarily confined to a bridge situated within the limits of the borough, etc. The ancient bridge over the Thames at Kingston, mentioned as existing in the time of King John, was, in 1813, held by the Court of King's Bench to be maintainable by the Municipal Corporation of Kingston, which had vainly tried to throw the burden on the counties of Middlesex and Surrey. The Corporation had had an estate settled upon it in 1565 by one of its Bailiffs, upon trust to support the bridge, and had frequently repaired it *(History of Surrey,* by Owen Manning and William Bray, 1804-1814, vol. iii. , Appendix, p. 146; *Report of Committee of Middlesex Magistrates on Public Bridges,* 1826, p. 284). Cities or Boroughs which are "counties in themselves" or "counties corporate" (as to which see our book, *The Manor and the Borough,* 1908, vol. i. p. 328, etc.), have always been held liable to maintain any public bridges within their limits (not repairable by private persons) as if they had been ordinary counties. See the cases fought out by Norwich and Southampton, R. *v.* Norwich, I. Str. 177; R. *v.* Southampton, 17 Q.B.D. 424; 55 LJ.M.C. 158; 55 L.T. 322; 35 W.R. 10; 50 J.P. 773; 16 Cox C.C. 117. And "towns corporate" generally were made so liable by 22 Hen. VIII. e. 5 (1531).

Page 89. "Towns corporate," or municipalities, even when not "Counties in themselves," were exempted from contributing to the County "Bridge Money," where, as was usually the case, they maintained the town bridges. Under the Statute of Bridges, the duty of administration of such town bridges fell, in the absence of any special liability, upon the Borough Justices in Quarter Sessions, and the burden on the inhabitants at large. But the Municipal Corporation itself was usually liable by prescription. Thus, at Ipswich (Suffolk) we see the Corporation, in 1708, acting on this assumption as a matter of course: "Whereas we are credibly informed by the complaint of divers persons and otherwise that the several town bridges are greatly decayed and out of repair, to the endangering those persons that pass and repass over them with horses, carts and carriages, for the timely remedying whereof it is ordered and agreed by this Court that (10 names) shall be a Committee to inspect and view the breaches and decays in and about the said several bridges, and report thereof to the next General Court to be held for this town with their opinion what necessary repairs must forthwith be done for preserving the same" (MS. Minutes, Town Council, Ipswich, 12th November 1708; see other entries, 12th August 1761). Norwich had six large bridges within its walls, which the Corporation maintained, obtaining an Act in 1726 to authorise the levy of tolls for the purpose *(Tour through the whole Island of Great Britain,* by D. Defoe, vol. L p. 61 of 1748 edition). The ancient Corporation of Sudbury shared, by prescription, with the County of Essex, the cost of maintaining its bridge over the Stour; and was, in 1803, so bankrupt as to be utterly unable to pay. How it was settled we do not know; but Counsel advised the Suffolk Quarter Sessions that distraint could be levied on everything the Corporation owned, even to the mace! (MS. Case Book, in Suffolk County archives).

Page 91. The practice with regard to " Hundred Bridges" differed from County to County, and is wrapped in obscurity. Traces of separate chargeability by Hundreds, Wapentakes, Rapes, Lathes, Liberties or Franchises occur in many Counties, in respect of various other services besides bridges. A separate rate would often be levied on the Hundred or other district, without any distinct separation in administrative jurisdiction between the Justices of the County, meeting in General or Quarter Sessions, and the Justices acting for the particular Hundred, meeting to administer the funds of the Hundred. Probably we may say that the financial separateness survived long after such administrative separateness as may once have existed (see R. *v.* Inhabitants of Charl. 39 L.J. M.C. 107; R, *v.* Inhabitants of Oswestry, 1817, 6 M. & S. 361). "Hundred Bridges" existed in the eighteenth century, principally in Lancashire, Shropshire, Suffolk, Kent, Sussex and Hampshire (as regards Isle of Wight), where they were administered by the County Justices in General or Quarter Sessions, though the business was usually transacted at a meeting held by adjournment in the Hundred in question, and attended only by the Justices acting for the Division. But with the growing systematisation of County rating, the separate Hundred Rate was found inconvenient; and the growth of County establishment charges made the calculation difficult. Hence most Counties seem silently to have merged their Hundred Rates in the general County Rate. Kent did so as late as 1875, by a clause inserted in a Turnpike Continuance Act (38 & 39 Vict. c. cxciv. sec. 10), formally converting its Hundred Bridges into County Bridges. The Isle of Wight long paid for its own bridges (as well as for its House of Correction); see the order of the Hampshire Quarter Sessions of 1774, fixing the quotas payablo by each parish to the County Bate, and leaving the cost of the island bridges and bridewell to be levied as an extra local rate. The island bridges were formally made County Bridges in 1812 (53 Geo. III. c. xcii. sec. 67), but the Hampshire Justices continued the separate island rating until 1886, when it was upset by an important legal decision, in which the whole position of these bridges was reviewed (B. *v.* Inhabitants of the County of Southampton). Sussex, by ancient custom, levied separate rates for bridges, as for some other services in its various Hundreds or "Bapes" until 1865, when the County was divided into East and West Divisions as regards bridges, by 28 Vict. c. 37; twenty-three years before this was done for all purposes, except the Lord Lieutenancy, by 51 & 52 Vict. c. 41 (1888). In Suffolk, the Liberty of Bury St. Edmunds insisted on maintaining its own bridges in 1697, and the other three Divisions did the same about 1739. The Bridge Bate seems to have been made separately for the four Divisions until 1888, when the County was divided into two for all purposes but the Lord Lieutenancy (51 & 52 Vict. c. 41). The Cinque Ports had been treated, as regards bridges, as a distinct County in 1531 (22 Hen. VIII. c. 5, sec. 5); and so continued until 1888, when thenbridges were made County Bridges of Kent, East Sussex, and the County Borough of Hastings respectively (51 & 52 Vict. c. 41). Hundred Bridges now survive chiefly, if not exclusively, in Lancashire, where their continuance was expressly secured by 41 & 42 Vict. c. 77, sec. 20, of 1878 (see Local Government Board Circular of 18th September 1878; *The Law relating to Highways,* by W. C. and A. Glen, 1897, pp. 873-874, 1152).

Page 91. *Report of the Committee of Magistrates appointed to make enquiry respecting the Public Bridges in the County of Middlesex* (1826), p. 3.

Page 91. Defoe notes as a remarkable fact that the bridges of Yorkshire and Durham were of stone, so that he does not " remember to have seen one of timber from the Trent to the Tweed" *(A Tour through the whole Island of Great Britain,* vol. iii. p. 124 of 1748 edition).

Page 91. *The Justice of the Peace,* by Dr. B. Burn, voL i. p. 190 of edition of 1758.

Page 92. MS. Minutes, Quarter Sessions, Suffolk, held at Ipswich, 19th July 1695; MS. Minutes, Quarter Sessions, Essex, 14th January 1718; MS. Minutes, Quarter Sessions, Wilts, Easter, 1809; MS. Minutes, Quarter Sessions, Suffolk, at Beccles, 15th July 1695.

Page 93. MS. Minutes, Quarter Sessions, Essex, 12th January 1720.

Page 93. In 1670, as an exceptional measure, in order to get replaced the bridges "demolished in the late wars," and provide others over the "many and sundry great and deep rivers which run cross and through the common and public highways and roads" of Cheshire and Lancashire, "which many times cannot be passed over without hazard of the lives and goods of the inhabitants, for want of convenient good and sufficient bridges in the said highways and roads, to build and erect which there is no law in force," Parliament authorised Quarter Sessions, on presentment of the Grand Jury, to build such bridges at the expense either of the County or Hundred. So the Monmouthshire Quarter Sessions was specially authorised to spend up to £40 a year on the Usk and Basalegg Bridges " which are situated upon great rivers, and lie on very great public roads of that county." But in both cases this power was limited in duration to ten years (22 Car. II. c. 12, sec. 13 and 14).

Page 94. Quarter Sessions, Derbyshire, 1708-10; *Three Centuries of Derbyshire Annals,* by J. C. Cox, 1890, voL ii. pp. 221-222.

Page 94. MS. Minutes, Quarter Sessions, Essex, 14th July 1713; Quarter Sessions, Derbyshire, July 1718; *Three Centuries of Derbyshire Annals,* by J. C. Cox, 1890, voL ii. p. 223; MS. Minutes, Quarter Sessions, Suffolk, 13th July and 5th October 1726; *ibid.* (Halesworth Bridge), 12th July 1731; MS. Minutes, Quarter Sessions, Essex, 13th July 1742, 12th July 1743; Quarter Sessions, Derbyshire, Michaelmas, 1714; *Three Centuries of Derbyshire Annals,* by J. C. Cox, 1890, vol. ii. p. 222; MS. Minutes, Quarter Sessions, Suffolk, 18th April 1737 (condition of grant towards amending Potters Bridge in Raydon parish).

Page 95. *Qentletnan's Magazine,* November 1759, p. 518.

Pago 96. 12 Geo. II. c. 29, sec. 13, 1739 (The County Rate Act). As a result of this Act, it followed that, if no one troubled to make a presentment or an indictment, no money was spent on the County Bridges. In fact, the Staffordshire Justices seem, in 1792, to have spent only £298 on all the bridges of the County.

Page 97. 5 Elizabeth, c. 13 (1563); 13 Geo. III. c. 78, sec. 24 (1773). In 1803 it was expressly declared to apply to County Bridges by 43 Geo. III. c. 59, sec. 1, and this has not been abrogated by the Highways Act of 1835 (R. *v.* Brecon, 15 Q.B. 813). We find in the Minutes of the Gloucestershire Quarter Sessions many orders like the following: "The Court taking into consideration the Presentment made and filed at this Sessions by the Rev. Wm. Hicks, one of the Justices of the Peace for this County, against the inhabitants of the County, for not repairing a certain common public stone bridge situate over the river Colne, in the several parishes of Shipton, Sollers and Withrington, near to a certain turnpike gate there, called Frog mill Gate, in the King's highway, leading from the market town of Northleach toward and into the town of Cheltenham; and having received a report from Mr. Collingwood, the County Surveyor, that the probable expense of rebuilding and repairing the said bridge will not exceed the sum of £30—Ordered that the said work be executed immediately at the said expense" (MS. Minutes, Quarter Sessions, Gloucestershire, 16th October 1821). So, in Shropshire in 1809, one Justice made presentment upon his own view against the county for not repairing Pilson Bridge (R. *v.* Salop, East's *King's Bench Reports,* vol. xiii. p. 95).

Page 97. See, for instance, MS. Minutes, Quarter Sessions, Lancashire, at Preston, 17th July 1810; MS. Minutes, Quarter Sessions, Northumberland, 18th July 1797. The " Bridge Cess " levied to cover these expenses was twenty shillings in the pound.

Page 98. An old order of the East Riding Quarter Sessions shows how the "Gratuity Bridge" could be combined with adequate legal protection to the County against future liability. "No allowance from the Riding towards building or repairing any bridge, which the East Riding is not liable to support, shall be granted until the person or township who ought to repair the same hath been indicted and submitted to such indictment" *(The. names of the Acting Magistrates and Public Officers of the East Riding of the County of York, with several matters relating to the Practice and Proceedings of Quarter Sessions,* Beverley, 1824).

Page 98. This momentous case, which imposed an incalculable burden upon the County ratepayers, was R. *v.* West Riding of Yorkshire (the case of Glasburno Bridge), 1780; Burrow's *Reports,* voL v. p. 2594; Sir Willima Blackstone's *Reports,* vol. ii. p. 685. What was novel in the case was the ignoring of the fact that the bridge in question had been only recently erected by a Township, in substitution for an old bridge which the Township had heretofore maintained as by prescription. Already, in 1705, it had been held in the case of Laycock Bridge in Wiltshire, that the County could not cast the burden on the Parish *(A Digest of Adjudged Cases,* 1775, p. 515).

Page 99. We give one case from

Wiltshire, in 1797 — " It having been represented to the Court that the County of Wilts stands indicted in the Court of Assizes for not repairing a certain bridge in the Parish of Oldstock," the Clerk of the Peace is directed to enquire, and either to defend the indictment, or to get it discharged by repairing the bridge (MS. Minutes, Quarter Sessions, Wilts, 11th July 1797).

Page 99. R. *v.* West Riding of Yorkshire (the case of Pace Gate Bridge, 1802), East's *King's Bench Reports,* vol. ii. p. 342; Petersdorff's *Abridgment of Cases,* voL iv. p. 693. See also the action of the Kensington Turnpike Trust, *Report of the Committee of Magistrates appointed to make enquiry respecting the Public Bridges in the County of Middlesex,* 1826, p. 5.

Page 99. R. *v.* Kent (the case of Foots Cray Bridge, 1814), Maule and Selwyn's *Reports,* voL ii. p. 513.

Page 99. R. *v.* Bucks (the case of Datohet Bridge, 1799), East's *King's Bench Reports,* vol. xii. p. 192.

Pago 99. *Report of the Committee appointed to make enquiry respecting the public bridges of the County of Middlesex,* 1826, p. 5.

Page 100. Le Blanc, in R. *v.* West Riding of Yorkshire (the Pace Gate Bridge case, 1802), East's *King's Bench Reports,vol.* ii. p. 342; Petersdorff's *Abridgment of Cases,* voL iv. p. 693.

Page 100. *Manchester Mercury,* 4th February and 11th March 1800; MS. Minutes, Quarter Sessions, Lancashire, 20th February 1800; and ditto, West Riding, December 1801; *Leeds Intelligencer,* 30th November and 21st December 1801.

Page 101. MS. Minutes, Quarter Sessions, Lancashire, 26th June 1806. We find the Suffolk Justices, in 1813, standing out against the demand of parishes that these "small arches" should be deemed County Bridges. The Justices protested that " the erpenses to Counties for repairing and rebuilding County Bridges are become a very serious and heavy charge upon the Counties where they are situate, and in consequence of the decision whereby the liability of the inhabitants of Counties to repair the same is so fully recognized, parishes now appear in many cases to endeavour to extend the principle of those decisions beyond what should seem could ever have been in the contemplation of the legislature. In most public roads there are small arches thrown over certain parts for the current of water for the adjoining lands." Now parishes were claiming that even these were bridges, and so repairable by the County. Counsel, on being consulted, advised that they were not bridges, but only part of the King's Highway, and repairable by the parish (MS. Case Book, Quarter Sessions, Suffolk, 31st July 1813).

Page 102. In Northumberland, in 1827, "It is ordered by this Court that in future when any person shall be desirous to erect or build any bridge within this County at their own expense, and shall in pursuance of the statute of 43 Geo. III. c. 59, apply for one of the Bridge Surveyors of this county to inspect the same, such Bridge Surveyor shall report to the next Quarter Sessions in writing, whether he approves of the site, foundation and detail of the same, and that when such bridge shall be completed to his satisfaction he shall deliver in a report in writing to the then next Quarter Sessions which shall be entered in the records of this County" (MS. Minutes, Quarter Sessions, Northumberland, 11th January 1827).

Page 102. R. *v.* St. Benedict, Cambridge, 1821, 4 Barn and Aid. 447. Page 102. *Report of the Committee of Magistrates appointed to make Enquiry respecting the Public Bridges of the County of Middlesex,* 1826, p. 46.

Page 103. *Lives of the Engineers,* by Samuel Smiles, 1861, vol. ii. p. 361. We shall refer to toll bridges in the ensuing chapter.

Page 104. The narrow pack-horse bridges still survived, in many places, well into the nineteenth century, as the only means of crossing streams. De Quincey remarks that "even in the nineteenth century, I have known a case in the sequestered district of Egremont in Cumberland, where a post-chaise of the common narrow dimensions was obliged to retrace its route of fourteen miles on coming to a bridge built in some remote age when as yet post-chaises were neither known nor anticipated, and unfortunately too narrow by three or four inches" (" Travelling," being chap. ix. of "Autobiographic Sketches" by Thomas De Quincey, 1790-1803, in vol. xiv. of 1863 edition of *Works).*

The absence of bridges, and the frequency with which deep pools or streams of water had to be regularly forded by travellers, even on turnpike roads as late as 1773, is shown by the fact that in that year Turnpike Trustees were required by statute, "at all approaches to, or entrances on such parte of any highways as are subject to deep or dangerous floods, to fix graduated posts denoting the depth of water at the deepest part of the same, and likewise such direction posts or stones as they shall judge to be necessary for guiding travellers in the safest track or passage through such floods or waters" (13 Geo. III. c. 84, sec. 41 (General Turnpike Act, 1773)). "These graduated posts," observed Scott, to whom they were evidently quite familiar objects on the roads, " are a miserable substitute for bridges. In the dark they can be of no service; and in the light they may sometimes induce strangers, depending on the depth specified by the graduations, to ford waters with the strength of whose current they are unacquainted, at the hazard of their lives." So near London as Stamford Hill, he mentions, there had long been " a very dangerous water" on the turnpike road. "I passed it myself," he sayB, "about ten years ago with no small risk" *(Digests of the General Highway and Turnpike Laws,* by John Scott, 1778, pp. 298-300).

Page 104. In Middlesex, the Justices in Quarter Sessions were maintaining, down to 1786, only three bridges. Indeed, at an earlier date they do not seem to have maintained any; for, in 1624, when there was a batch of indictments for non-repair, three were against individual landowners, three against particular parishes, and none against the County *(Middlesex County Records,* by J. C. Jeaffreson, vol. ii. pp. 237-238). Yet the Justices in 1821-25, found existing no fewer than 175 public bridges, "exclusive of Buch culverts, tunnels, etc., as from their small dimensions are ' considered to be drains only.'" Of these, about 30 had admittedly become chargeable to the County, whilst about half as many more had no known persons or authority to whom their repairs could be charged, and hence would in all probability become a County burden. About 40 were chargeable to parishes, usually under Inclosure Awards, whilst the majority were maintained by canal, dock and water companies under their respective private Acts. A small and diminishing number were still maintained by lords of manors and other landowners, *rations tenurae (Report of the Committee of Magistrates appointed* to *make enquiry respecting the Public Bridges in the County of Middlesex,* 1826). The tendency to cast the burden on the County continued. For instance, the " list of County Bridges" in Wiltshire in 1859 comprised no fewer than 88, nearly all tiny structures *(Rules and Standing Orders of the Wilts Sessions,* 1859, Appendix IX. pp. 118-120). Subsequent legislation, whilst not professedly relieving private persons or parishes of their burdens for bridges, has tended in the same direction. By an Act of 1870 (33 & 34 Vict. sec. 12) all the bridges heretofore maintained by Turnpike Trustees gradually, on the joads being "disturnpiked," became County Bridges; and by Aots of 1878 (41 & 42 Vict. c. 77, sec. 21), 1888 (51 & 52 Vict. c. 41. sec. 6), and 1891 (54 & 55 Vict. c. 63) Counties were enabled by agreement, to take over Non-County Bridges, by whomsoever erected, even if in disregard of the Act of 1803. The result has been that the County Bridges of Nottinghamshire rose, within the decade ended 1881, from about 50 to about 150; those of Norfolk from about 130 to about 170 *(Report of House oj Commons Committee on Highway Acts,* 1881, pp. 125, 201). It should be added that, in 1887, after practically all bridges had become chargeable to the County, as the result of over a century of law as laid down in the Glasburne Bridge case, the Judges seem slightly to have varied their statement of the law. In R. *v.* Southampton (1887) it was held that utility to the public at large and public user as part of the highway do not *ipso facto* make the County liable, assuming that there is no one else on whom the liability can be cast, and that all the conditions of the Act of 43 Geo. III. c. 59, sec. 5 have been complied with. These facts are only evidence on which the Jury *may* find that the bridge has been expressly or implicitly *adopted* by the County (19 Q.B.D. 590). This seems to be the first time, at any rate for a century, in which an express or implied adoption by the County is stated to be required to make the County liable (Pratt and Mackenzie's *Law of Highways,* 16th edition, 1911, p. 103; *The Law relating* to *Waters,* by H. J. W. Coulson and W. A. Forbes, 3rd edition, 1910, pp. 590-591). Meanwhile, Bo diligently has the former construction of the law been acted upon, that but few cases are left on which any question can be raised!

Page 104. For the bridge-building exploits of William Edwards and Thomas Telford, see the woll-known chapter in *Lives of the Engineers,* by Samuel Smiles, 1861, voL L For the bridge at Berwick, see *History of Berwick on Tweed,* by John Scott, 1888, p. 417. Charles EL granted the Municipal Corporation in 1667 an annuity of £100 a year towards its maintenance, which is still paid by the Treasury.

We deal with toll bridges in Chap. VII., The Turnpike Road.

CHAPTER VII THE TURNPIKE ROAD

Meanwhile a new principle of road maintenance was being adopted. The device of levying from the passengers a toll for "pavagft." or /pontage," where some special works of repair or improvement had been made to the highway, was, of course, an old onepr Littleton, in 1692, proposed that in order to meet the heavy/charges involved in the new traffic on the roads, such a toll should be authorised wherever a piece of road was made good, and wherever a ferry was replaced by a bridge. The landowners and farmers were not backward in pressing for power to exact from the new users of the King's Highway a novel contribution towards the heavy expense of the repairs that they rendered necessary, and of the new standard of road maintenance that they we're setting up. 'LE,Yery_4)_erson_it _ was urged, "ought to jContribute to the repair of roads in proportion to the use they make of, or the convenience which they derive from them.' This assumption naturally commended itself to the country genraemen who sat in Parliament, and led, as we shall describe,- TM the creation of Turnpike Trusts, and to a prodigious multiplication of these new authorities in the second half of the eighteenth century. But before these new *ad hoc* bodies were created, Parliament had already endowed the Justices of the Peace of certain Counties or Divisions with power to levy tolls, to be spent on the repair of some unusually frequented highways. In 1656, the Vestry of the little parish of Radwell, in Hertfordshire, petitioned Quarter Sessions for help with its roads. In vain had the inhabitants tried to keep them in order; these highways still " stand in much need of repair, which they are no ways able to perform (though the whole revenue of the parish should be employed), the Great North Road lying for two miles together in the said parish, and the nature of the soil being such as the winter devours whatsoever they are able to lay on in the summer, and the parish is so small that it hath in it all but two teams." In 1663, perhaps as a tardy outcome of this petition, it was represented to Parliament by the Justices of the Counties of Hertford, Cambridge and Huntingdon that "the ancient highway and post road leading from London to York, and so into Scotland... byjeasoofejgreatnd _manyJoads which are weekly drawn in waggons to Ware (whence there was water carriage to London), and " the great trade of barley and malt... is become so ruinous and almost impassable that the ordinary course appointed by all former laws and statutes of this realm is not sufficient for the effectual repairing of the same." On this petition Parliament fell back on certain mediaeval precedents, and authorised, by a special statute, each of these three Quarter Sessions to erect gates and levy tolls at Wadesmill (Herts), Caxton (Cambridgeshire), and Stilton (Huntingdonshire) respectively, for the next eleven years, and to devote this revenue to specially repairing the parts of the Great North Road within their respective jurisdictions. Only one of these three gates was successful. That at Stilton excited so much local opposition that it was never erected. That at Caxton was put up, but was so easily evaded that practically nothing was collected. The tbird,_iikJVadesmill, was thus the first effective toll-gateTh England. A generation later, when, as we have seen in a preceding chapter, the state of the roads was exciting much attention, Parliament gave similar powers by special statutes, in respect of other pieces of road, to the Justices of Essex, Norfolk, Surrey, Gloucestershire, Somerset, Cheshire, Bedfordshire, Wilts, Hampshire and Kent; sometimes to the Justices of a particular Division of the County in special Highway Sessions, sometimes to a certain number of Justices representing different Counties, but more usually to the Justices of the whole County in Quarter Sessions assembled. For fifteen years it looked as if the maintenance of the high roads was to become a function of the County Justices, either in Quarter Sessions or in special Highway Sessions. Suddenly the course of legislation changes. After 1711, so far as we have been able to ascertain, Parliament no longer resorted to the County Justices for its new road authorities. In 1706, in the case of the highway between Fornhill in Bedfordshire and Stony Stratford in Buckinghamshire, in 1709, in the case of the Sevenoaks and Woodsgate Road, and again in 1710 for certain highways leading from Hertfordshire into Huntingdonshire, forming part of the Great North Road, we have the creation of new statutory bodies, consisting of so many named persons, not necessarily or exclusively Justices of the Peace, who were empowered to levy tolls and to fill vacancies by co-option. These Acts appear to have been the first of what proved to be a long series of statutes creating special bodies of Turnpike Trustees, which came, eventually, to number over eleven hundred, administering twenty-three thousand miles of road, constructed at the cost of an accumulated debt of seven millions sterling, and raising and spending an annual revenue of more than one and a half million pounds.

These Turnpike Trusts, established by, literally, thousands of separate Acts of Parliament from 1706 onwards, were given almost identical constitutions and functions. In each case a certain number of persons of local position were named in the Act as the first Trustees, with a few specified *ex-officio* members. These persons were authorised to fill vacancies arising in their membership by the co-pption of others possessing a specified property qualification/ The Trustees were always empowered to construct and maintain a specified piece of road, to which their powers were especially confined, and to levy tolls on that piece I of road upon certain kinds of traffic. The powers were invariably I given only for a limited term of years, usually twenty-one; but every Trust, in due course, applied for a new Act containing its existence for another term, so that they became virtually permanent Local Authorities, entirely unconnected with either jlounty or Parish, Manor or Borough. The powers of these separate bodies of Turnpike Trustees, conferred upon them as they were in the first instance by these separate local Acts, varied indefinitely in detail, but showed in the course of the eighteenth century certain general lines of development. The main purpose of these Acts was, as regards the particular piece of road dealt with, to bring additional revenues and additional powers to the re-inforcement of the general highway law. It was not the intention of Parliament to exempt the parishes from their duty of maintaining the roads, nor to excuse any person from the performance of Statute Labour or Team Duty. It seems to have been assumed at the beginning that the modicum of repair to be rendered by the Parish Surveyors of Highways and the unpaid Statute Labour and Team Duty of the inhabitants would have been completed before the special Surveyors appointed to lay out the proceeds of the new revenue came on the scene. These Surveyors were authorised to require the performance of such additional labour as they thought necessary, "for which the said Surveyors," declared Parliament, " shall pay unto such labourers and to the owners of such teams, carts and wains according to the usual rate of the country." Presently the situation is simplified. The power to exact extra labour compulsorily is dropped, and whatever additional service is required has to be hired in the open market. On the other hand, in all that concerned the maintenance of the special length of road— the "turnpike road "—the Surveyor appointed by the new road authority is gradually invested with nearly all the powers of the Parish Surveyor of Highways appointed from among the inhabitants. He is authorised summarily to suppress nuisances, and enabled to take compulsorily without compensation from the common or wastes, within the parish or without, or out of any river or brook, whatever "gravel, chalk, sand or stones" are needed for the mending of his road; and to resort for this purpose also to private grounds, on payment merely of the actual damage done. More important still, from 1714 onwards, he is given express power to require the performance under his own direction of a specific proportion of the ordinary Statute Labour and Team Duty of the parishioners. The proportion of the six days Statute Labour to which the turnpike road was entitled was sometimes specified in the Act at two, three or four days; or was left to be fixed by the Turnpike Trustees or their Surveyor, with an appeal, in case of difference, to the Justices in Petty or Special Sessions. Gradually the apportionment comes normally to be settled by two Justices, on the application of the Parish Surveyor of Highways. Sometimes the Justices were empowered to allot particular parishioners, as many as they thought fit, to labour on the turnpike road; or otherwise to settle what proportion of the whole six days due from all the inhabitants should be so directed. From 1716 onward the Turnpike Surveyor was, in many cases, even given power to agree with the parish for an annual amount to be raised by the Parish Surveyor by a rate, and to be paid in a lump sum to the Turnpike Surveyor, in lieu of this specific share of the Statute Labour. Hence the new turnpike authority found itself in possession of a money income derived, not only from its own tolls, but also from the parish rates on occupiers. This income from rates was, however, at no time anything but a lump sum composition of the Statute Labour and Team Duty. In no case that we have found were the Turnpike Trustees entitled themselves to levy a rate, or even to share in the various Highway Bates made by the Justices in particular parishes. It is this incapacity to levy a rate that distinguishes the Turnpike Trustees (together with the Court Leet) from all other local governing bodies.

For the fulfilment of their special task of "effectually repairing and amending. .. very ruinous" and " impassable " stretches of the King's Highway, the new road authorities were given exceptional powers both of raising and of expending their new form of revenue. They were empowered to erect " toll-houses," "tollbars," "turnpikes," "crates" or " gates" on any part of the road under their jurisdiction, and to exact, as a condition of passage, a toll on all vehicles, horsemen and cattle passing through. This novel impost differed radically from the ancient due, custom or toll which some manorial or corporate authorities levied under royal grant, in that it was strictly limited in duration, minutely specified in amount, and legally applicable to a given public service. Thus, as we have already stated, all Turnpike Acts were temporary only, the usual period of their validity being 21 years, after which, it was fondly assumed, the special need for extraordinary repairs would have passed away, and the road might be maintained free of toll by the ordinary highway revenue. For over half a century it was even enacted, in most of the Turnpike Acts, that if the roads were sufficiently repaired, and all debts paid, before the end of the term, the Justices should order the toll-gates to be removed, and bring the tolls to an end. The number and position of the toll-gates was usually left to the discretion of the Trustees. But every Turnpike Act-specified the maximum toll that might be levied _on _vehicles, horsemen or cattle (usually doubled on Sundays), and many of the Acts included provisions against the exaction of repeated tolls on the same day, or in respect of passage along the same stretch of road, whilst others contained elaborate exemptions in favour of persons who used only minute portions of the road (as, for instance, in crossing from one field to another), or who were engaged in particular occupations, or, in some cases, who owned, occupied or inhabited particular premises. It was always the intention of Parliament that the payers of the toll should get *quid pro quo* in useful improvements. The tolls were, in some cases, not to be levied until Quarter Sessions had bound some "able and sufficient persons" in sureties to put the road in sufficient repair within five years. In most of the early Acts it is expressly provided that the Justices in Quarter Sessions may appoint fit persons to " survey the highways and enquire of the toll, and in case of misapplication... they are to certify the same to the Judges of Assize."

From the standpoint of modern administration, there were, however, glaring shortcomings in the provisions of these Acts, which, as we shall see, went far to frustrate the good intentions of Parliament. The equitable incidence of the toll was undermined by clauses enabling the Trustees to grant preferential rates to particular individuals or classes. There was no limit to the amount of borrowed capital for which the Trustees could mortgage the tolls, so that the mere interest on the mortgage debt might easily absorb the whole revenue destined for current repairs. Each generation of Trustees succeeded in obtaining a greater measure of freedom from legal limitation or executive supervision in the expenditure of their income: they could spend what they pleased, borrow what they pleased and manage the business as they pleased. They might, at their option, have their own official establishment of collectors and surveyors, or farm out both toll collection and road repair for lump sums. And whilst the control given in the early Acts to the County Justices over turnpike roads, and over the Trustees who managed them, was, in the middle of the eighteenth century, gradually removed, no new provisions were inserted requiring the Trustees to account for their receipts and expenditure to any public authority. Not less important were the powers gradually conceded to these new authorities to alter, at their own discretion, the means of communication between one place and another. In the course of half a century they not only accumulated, in their successive statutes, all the powers of the Justices under the General Highway Acts but even added new ones. They could buy land compulsorily in order to widen narrow ways and improve gradients. They could erect bars against byelanes, close up ancient highways, divert others at their pleasure and *y* compel every one to travel by the new road they had constructed. *h* In this way an ancient hamlet might find itself suddenly deprived *If* of a public road, in order that the journey from one town to another might be shortened or straightened, or even so that a particular mansion or farmhouse might be favoured with easy access to the market town.

Across this mass of Local Acts, each applicable only to a few miles of road, there came, between 1727 and 1766, nearly a score of general statutes for the "more effectual preservation" of the turnpike roads. Two of the earliest of these were directed against the " ill-designing and disorderly persons who associated themselves together both by day and night, and cut down, pulled down, burnt and otherwise destroyed several turnpike gates and houses "—the alarming frequency of this offence between 1727 and 1735 inducing an eighteenth-century legislature to raise the sentence, from three months hard labour and a public whipping, to death without benefit of clergy. But the County Justices and Turnpike Trustees who swarmed on the benches of the House of Commons discovered more insidious enemies of their turnpikes than mere rioters; and from 1741 onward we see them passing Act after Act to protect their roads against the wear and tear of heavy weights and narrow wheels. These Acts gave all bodies of Turnpike Trustees power to erect weighing machines, to exact prohibitive tolls for extraordinary weights, to seize horses in excess of the lawful number, to charge double rates for narrow wheels, and altogether to exempt the broadest wheels from their tolls. To quote the words of an able commentator, the users of wheeled vehicles were to be "in some instances compelled to obedience, like slaves, by severe penalties; and in others enticed to it like children with a sugar plum." Unfortunately for all concerned these amateur " Act-constructors," as John Scott terms them, were as unskilful as they were irresolute. "Sometimes one is at a loss to conceive the end at which they were aiming," continues Scott; "and sometimes when their end is obvious one can find no reason for their choice of the means that are designed to accomplish it." "If the Parliament would but fix on any one reasonable plan," the farmers remarked to Scott, " and keep to it, let it be what it might, they should be satisfied; but that such perpetual alterations as they had for some time experienced, were inconvenient beyond expression, for they never knew what they had to do for two years together." At the conclusion of peace in 1763, after the Seven Years' War, the chaos of statutes had become so intolerable that a publicspirited knot of local government reformers, headed by the wellknown Thomas Gilbert, set themselves to consolidate the whole of the general law relating to turnpikes, concurrently with their similar effort with regard to the highway law that we have already described — an arduous and complicated enterprise which, after an unsatisfactory essay in 1766 (7 George III. c. 40), eventuated in the comprehensive General Turnpike Act of 1773 (13 George III. c. 84).

This Act, which was made to apply to all turnpike roads, existing or thereafter constructed, was, like the legislation which it superseded, framed rather in the interest of the Turnpike Trustees and the mortgagees of their tolls than in that of the users of the roads or the public at large. It was, indeed, in the main, merely a consolidating Act. In so far as it altered the powers of Turnpike Trustees, it strengthened their control over . their own officials, and enlarged the authority of these officials over the community. To strengthen the position of the Trusts— possibly with a view to improving their credit as borrowers— it included the old clauses requiring a high property qualification for Trustees, and disqualifying publicans from serving as officials, whilst incorporating new provisions formalizing their procedure, and making it incumbent on them, whenever they leased the tolls, to lease them to the highest bidder. But the obvious defects in the Local Acts that we have already pointed out were not remedied.

No provision was made to prevent malversation or extravagance by the Turnpike Trustees; there was required no audit of their accounts; no check was imposed on the amount of their borrowings, or the rate of interest to be paid; and no curb was placed on their uncontrolled power to divert, alter or close the ancient highways at their will. The bulk of this wordy, complicated and badly arranged statute consisted, in fact, in a mere stringing together of the existing clauses relating to wheeled vehicles— prohibitions, exemptions, special tolls, fines and forfeitures, one piled on top of another until, as John Scott heard "a very respectable and intelligent gentleman now in the House of Commons observe,... the Trustees would have enough to do if they were bound to reconcile all the contradictions of the Act and make sense of its nonsense." It was this statute that, with only trifling modifications, remained the basis of turnpike administration right down to 1822, when it was superseded by another hardly less complicated.

The optimistic assumption of Parliament that the turnpike and its toll would be but a temporary device to meet an exceptionally ruinous state of a particular bit of road was, we need hardly say, everywhere falsified. Whenever the term for which Parliament had granted a toll drew near to expiry, the particular turnpike authority invariably petitioned for a renewal of its Act. The power to take toll, it was alleged, had " been of great benefit to all carriages and persons travelling those roads; the said roads are not fully repaired, nor all the moneys borrowed by virtue of the said Act paid "; "sometimes the deep and long commons over which the roads went were so impassable " as to require the construction of a causeway or other new work. After a while the application for renewal becomes so much a matter of course that no special reason is alleged for it, and the new bill "for enlarging and continuing" the powers of each Turnpike Trust appears automatically as the term comes to an end. And these renewal bills generally included new powers, either in the form of a schedule of augmented tolls, or by extension to additional lengths of roads, or through the concession of more drastic means of enforcing payment. In the first half of the century, these steadily extending powers of taxation did not fail to arouse complaints from those who had hitherto used the roads free from toll. As the number of turnpike bills increases, the applications to the House of Commons are met by counterpetitions from groups of users alleging, as in the case of the fishermen of Hastings, that the proposed tolls will " discourage them from following their employment," and will "impoverish the greatest part of the inhabitants," or, as in the case of inhabitants of Gloucestershire, declaring that the highways remain, in spite of the toll, "in a ruinous and almost impassable condition," so that they see no benefit in a renewal of the impost. The third decade of the century, which is noted as a period of expansion and active experiment in the administration of the Poor Law, was marked also by a rapid multiplication of Turnpike Trusts. Between 1720 and 1730 no fewer than 71 new

Trusts were established, the total mileage under toll being thereby more than trebled. This great extension of taxation on the users of the roads did not fail to arouse resistance, especially in districts where small holdings or cottage manufacturers prevailed. Serious riots broke out in Somerset, Gloucestershire and Herefordshire in 1726, and continued spasmodically for a whole decade, in the course of which turnpikes were destroyed, and the pikekeepers ill treated. "Great numbers of riotous and rebellious persons," we read, in 1732, "armed with firearms and other dangerous weapons have... frequently assembled themselves together in the nighttime, and marched in formidable bodies into that City Hereford and pulled down and destroyed the turnpikes erected on the roads leading thereto, and the houses of the said turnpike keepers... after they had plundered the same, and fired their guns into the windows of several other dwelling houses and in the public streets... threatened and declared that they would not only destroy the turnpikes but would murder the keepers thereof, and all such Trustees who should presume to act under the Act of Parliament; and at the public market place... have given notice in a most audacious manner that if the magistrates or any other persons should interrupt or oppose them, they would set the said City on fire." Similar riots broke out at Bristol in 1749, in which turnpikes were tumultuously demolished. The rioters were "armed with rusty swords, pitchforks, axes, guns, pistols, clubs, etc., and called themselves Sack a Lents.... They ranged themselves in the main street before the George Inn, by beat of drum, huzzas and a hunting horn, three drums attending them. Here they drank freely, with much noise, and then broke the windows of one Mr. Durbin, Tithingman of the Hundred who had, by order of the Turnpike Commissioners, carried persons concerned in destroying the turnpikes before two Justices, by whom they were committed to Newgate." After the disorder had lasted a fortnight, the rioters were dispersed by the arrival of the soldiers. A few years later there were turnpike riots at Leeds, in which the military had to fire on the rioters, with some loss of life. About the middle of the century, in spite of the annually increasing mileage of road subjected to toll, and the automatic renewal and extension of the powers of the various bodies of Turnpike Trustees, opposition, either by petition or riot, dies away, and Turnpike Acts multiply fast. After the Peace of,1748 a perfect mania seems to set in, and the number of new I Trusts rises suddenly from about three a year to nearly twenty a year. Between 1748 and 1770 the number of separate Trusts I in existence rose from about 160 to about 530, whilst the mileage subject to toll was quadrupled. When we remember the Eighteenth Century impatience of new taxation and hatred of restraints on personal freedom, this acquiescence in the extension, all over England, of an entirely new impost, is, we think, a matter for surprise. We attribute it less to a conviction in the payers of the toll that they were actually getting *quid pro quo,* than to certain common features in the constitution and working of the various Turnpike Trusts themselves. It must, in the first place, be remembered that the tolls were never levied on foot passengers, and were thus unfelt by the labouring poor. The projectors of each new Turnpike Trust were so anxious to secure local support that they included among their proposed Trustees every one of local influence or authority—noblemen, clergy, squires, farmers and even traders—a constitution of the governing body which, at whatever cost of efficiency, at any rate went far to secure assent. But it was not merely the principal inhabitants who were placated. The new source of road revenue promised to relieve the parishioners of their ancient Statute Labour. The little farmers and cottagers looked forward to the cost of repairs being henceforth met out of the tolls to be paid by the carriage folk and the London carriers. "As soon as a turnpike Act is obtained," it was said in the *Gentleman's Magazine* for September 1754, "all the parishes through which the road passes consider the Act as a benefit ticket, and an exemption from their usual expenses, and elude the payment of their just quota towards the reparation of the road, by compounding with the Trustees for a less sum, or by doing their Statute Labour in a fraudulent manner; and in both these cases they are generally favoured by the neighbouring Justices and gentlemen, for the ease of their own estates." Hence the very defects in structure and function of the Turnpike Trusts served to prevent resistance to the new impost which they levied.

From the standpoint of a national system of road communication, the Turnpike Trusts had, from first to last, many grave defects. Foreign critics complained that, instead of the main routes of through traffic, from one end of the kingdom to another, being systematically dealt with, the abandonment of the subject by the English Parliament to local initiative and local public spirit resulted, at best, in a strange patchwork. Whether or not a particular bit of road remained in the ruinous and impassable condition implied by parish management depended, not on the needs of the users, or the national importance of this particular link, but on the degree of enlightened self-interest or public spirit of the squires, farmers, and traders in its immediate neighbourhood. If, during the eighteenth century, any one had taken the trouble to make a turnpike map of England, this would have shown, not a system of radiating arteries of communication, but scattered cases of turnpike administration, unconnected with each other; appearing at first as mere dots on the map, then gradually increasing in number and size so as to form continuous lines; and only by the end of the century becoming, as John Holt somewhat optimistically declared in 1794, " so multiplied and extended as to form almost an universal plan of communication through the kingdom." It took, in fact, practically a whole century of disconnected effort before even such national arteries of communication as the Great North Road from London to Edinburgh, the Irish road from London to Holyhead, or the Great Western Road from London to Exeter came, for the whole of their lengths, under the administration of Turnpike Trusts. The travellers from Glasgow to London in 1739 found "no turnpike road till they came to Grantham, within 110 miles of London." A foreign visitor in 1752, travelling on the Great Western Road, declares that "after the first 47 miles from London, you never set eye on a turnpike for 220 miles.... What fine roads," he exclaims satirically, "from London to Land's End, or even to Exeter, Plymouth or Falmouth; you have such roads as the lazy Italians have fruits, namely, what God left them after the Flood." And yet, as another traveller observes, "there may be a profusion of too many turnpikes round a single city, half of which carried on in a straight line would have proved a national rather than a private good." For even in those districts in which Turnpike Trusts had been established, there was no security, or even likelihood, that the most frequented, the moat direct and the easiest right of way would be selected for improvement. The Commissioners employed by the Board of Agriculture in 1794 are continually remarking on the "malignant degree of ingenuity... displayed in sending them *i.e.* the turnpike roads up hills," or "over such a dreary, dangerous and hilly common." The motives for this inconsiderate choice of routes were varied and diverse The old pack-horse track which went up hill and down dale wherever the surface was good enough, was often converted into a carriage road without regard for the fact that its gradients made it a quite unsuitable route for wheeled traffic. The first waggon highways were, moreover, as a House of Commons Committee was informed in 1806, sometimes deliberately "carried up steep ascents to gain the open country and avoid the valleys, because the roads through the latter could not easily be made passable in the wet seasons of the year." More sinister motives were found in the "partiality" and "selfishness" of individual landowners, who sought, it was complained in the *Gentleman's Magazine* in August 1754, " to make turnpikes avenues, more or less, to this or that country seat." "If the great man," it was said in 1794, " who generally takes the lead in laying out the turnpike road has no immediate interest himself, he has often a friend to oblige, or an enemy to mortify, by sending the road up hill to save the land of one, or through the middle of a meadow to hurt the other. A tippling house on the top of a hill, or a favourite piece of land at the bottom, compels the husbandman at this day, in many parts of this kingdom, to keep one-third more cattle in his team than there would otherwise have been occasion for." Even as late as 1828, when the efficacy of public opinion had enormously increased, we see no less a personage than Sir Robert Peel, the elder, not scrupling to attempt to divert the new turnpike road between London and Liverpool out of its way, in order that it might pass close to his own residence and cotton-mills, to the ruin of the town of Tamworth—an attempt frustrated by counter-petitions from Tamworth and, most potent of all, an able letter to the *Times*. Nor was it always powerful individuals who perverted the action of Turnpike Trustees. The whole of the inhabitants of particular towns frequently asserted their separate interests to the detriment of a national service. "Local interest," said John Scott in 1778, "often produces strange distortions. A few years ago a new turnpike road was made from St. Alban's to Reading... designed to open an easy communication between the East and West of England, and had the straight line been preserved, would have been many miles nearer than the way through London. It was, however, found necessary to make a zigzag line by Watford, Amersham, High Wycombe and Marlow, solely to oblige the inhabitants of those towns, by which means the difference between the two roads is rendered inconsiderable." In other cases the reverse would happen, and a powerful corporation would try to prevent the new impost being levied on its own inhabitants. "The town of Liverpool," it was reported, "is a great enemy to turnpikes: there are only three toll-gates within eight miles of it, none within four." The result was that the road revenue was so much lessened that the Turnpike Trustees found themselves unable to keep any part of the roads in good repair. "Most of the great towns" of Lancashire, it was said in 1794, "have had sufficient interest to place the toll-bars at some miles distance from them"; and this, it was alleged, was "almost the sole cause of the wretched condition of the turnpike roads " in that county as late as 1808.

The narrow limits of each Trust, and the pecuniary interests involved, not only militated against the wisest choice of a route, but also obstructed the further increase of lines of communication. "Instead of Turnpike Acts being obtained for particular roads," wrote an able critic of road administration, in 1765, "they ought to have been made general throughout counties. As things are at present conducted, the Commissioners of particular roads, in order to enhance their revenues, generally take the liberty of blocking up the principal avenues of every other road which falls into or leads across theirs... so that, in fact, every Act which passes for the repair of a road, with the usual extensive powers to Commissioners to erect gates, is an Act also to prevent any of the roads leading into or across it, be they ever so bad, from receiving the same remedy." The Turnpike Trustees went, however, further in their obstructiveness. Towards the latter part of the eighteenth century, when the several oases of turnpike administration were impinging on each other, the Trustees of every existing Trust, in conjunction often with their mortgagees or other creditors, were quick to petition Parliament against any proposals for new turnpike roads which threatened to compete with their line of route. Thus, in 1780, when a new road was projected from Horsley to Dudbridge in Gloucestershire,. the Trustees of the Gloucester and Stroud Turnpike complained loudly to the House of Commons that this new road would " open up a communication of road from Gloucester to Dudbridge, and through the parishes of Standish and Stonehouse, by which means," it was said, the traveller from Gloucester to Bath would be able to go more quickly and easily, " as by the intended road several steep hills would be avoided." If the bill passes, they ask that their own tolls may be increased. The Trustees of the Cirencester and Stroud Turnpike go further, and demand the entire rejection of the project. So, in the same year, the Trustees of Newcastle-under-Lyme and Macclesfield Turnpike petition vehemently against a projected extension of the territory of the Macclesfield and Buxton Trust, as the proposed improvement of certain branch roads "will materially interfere with the petitioners' trust, as they will be a means of lessening the tolls." In the very middle of the eighteenth century there seems to have been a pitched battle in Parliament—reminding us of similar railway struggles a century later—as to the direction to be taken by the main line of road from London to the North-Western Counties. We see Sheffield and Derby petitioning in favour of rival projects, via Leicester and via Bedford respectively, and enlisting, each of them, the support of wayside parishes. Out of many similar petitions we quote the following in 1800. The Trustees of the Maidenhead and Reading Turnpike, having under its charge part of the Great Western Road, strongly oppose a projected new turnpike road from New Windsor to Longford in Middlesex, because it would make the road from London by that way considerably shorter, which might tempt the traveller to avoid Maidenhead altogether. If we remember that the Trustees, mortgagees and creditors of an existing turnpike road would certainly include the county members, the resident Justices of the Peace, the local landowners, and the more substantial farmers of the neighbourhood, we shall be able to estimate how effective was the obstruction to the Parliamentary sanction, or even to the initiation, of a shorter or easier line of communication than that to which the inhabitants were accustomed.

We may here notice the somewhat analogous development of toll bridges. The privilege of levying bridge toll, or " pontage," had been conceded by the King in special cases, notably during the thirteenth and fourteenth centuries, by way of indemnity for erecting particular bridges; but such a grant was, we understand, always limited in duration to three, five or eight years. Except for such cases, the bridges that existed seem to have been free from toll. In Lancashire in 1621, and again in Essex in 1746, we hear of attempts by neighbouring landowners to exact tolls, which are repressed by Quarter Sessions. In the eighteenth century, however, under the influence of the imperative demand for better means of communication, and of the new idea that the actual users of the highways should be made to bear the expense of their maintenance, we see erected, from 1725 onward, a whole series of new toll bridges, corresponding with the new turnpike tolls. Such a levy of tolls required statutory authority, which was granted by Local Act, sometimes (as in the cases of the City of London, Bristol, Norwich, Windsor and other corporate towns) to the Municipal Corporation; sometimes (as in the cases of Westminster and Putney Bridges, Preston Bridge, Deritend Bridge at Birmingham and Bishopwearmouth Bridge at Sunderland) to public bodies of Commissioners incorporated for the purpose; and sometimes (as in the cases of the bridges at Walton on Thames, Hampton Court and several of those within the Metropolis) to individual landowners or groups of speculators. These Corporations, Commissioners or Companies differed from the Turnpike Trusts in securing powers unlimited in duration, and in levying tolls on pedestrians. They seem to have resembled the Turnpike Trusts in the general inefficiency of their administration, in the frequent farming of their tolls, in the complications and extortions of the imposts that they levied on vehicular and animal traffic, and in the delays to which, in London at any rate, the congestion at their toll gates eventually gave rise.

When we consider the administration of the various Turnpike Trusts of the eighteenth century, from the narrower standpoint of the repair and construction of particular bits of road, we find ourselves in the midst of the haphazard and anarchic diversities characteristic of an age lacking alike in technological and administrative science. The County Justices in Quarter Sessions who,

K as we have seen, controlled the earliest of the turnpike roads, sometimes appointed an officer at a small fee to lay out the proceeds of the toll as he thought fit; or, in other cases, contented themselves with ordering the Treasurer of the moneys arising from particular turnpikes to pay lump sums to the Parish Surveyors of Highways "after the said Surveyors have made it appear... that the inhabitants of the said parish have done their full six days work, pursuant to the statute, of teams and labourers, and have expended a sixpenny rate in repairing their highways." Occasionally Quarter Sessions would request the Justices to "view the roads in their several Divisions and to cause the Surveyor to measure such parts of the roads as are out of repair, and to report at the next Quarter Sessions." But we do not gather that, for the first half of the century at any rate, Quarter Sessions, where it was responsible for a turnpike road, gave any directions, either to its own officer or to the parish Surveyors of Highways, as to the way in which the work was to be done. Some of the early bodies of Turnpike Trustees seem to have shown rather more activity, if less discretion, than the County Justices. The active Trustees, often, as we gather, the farmers and tradesmen of the neighbourhood, added petty jobbery and a foolish officiousness to their ignorance. Nor were the proceedings made any better by the intervention of the ordinary eighteenth-century squire. "We may blame," says a graphic but inelegant critic in the *Gentleman's Magazine* for August 1754, "the ignorance and obstinacy of John Trot, and reflect on Tom Buttertub, the grocer, the booby Trustee of the next parish; of course the profile of the road is injudiciously constructed. ... John Trot is not so much the object of contempt for being an incorrigible blockhead, as Squire Satskull and Sir

John Shallow are, for their pride, avarice, insolence, ignorance, petulancy and meanness.... This meanness in our gentry brings it about that a tenant shall be employed in repairing the road upon his own terms, and the more he cheats the turnpike, the better he will be able to pay his rent. The squire likes his proposals, and the rest of the Commissioners acquiesce, being either farmers or tradesmen.... We cannot justly wonder that turnpike roads should be in such bad condition as they are, when we find such meannesses amongst those who ought to be examples of public spirit and virtue." "At the first erection of turnpikes," reports another critic in the same journal for September 1754, "the road-makers *ex professo,* who perhaps were yeomen-like farmers and gentlemen's bailiffs, made a very poor figure in their undertaking; witness, amongst others, that great road from London to Bath; it errs and blunders in all the forms; its strata of materials were never worth a straw; its surface was never made cycloidal; it hath neither good side ditches, nor footpaths for walkers; no outlets were made for water that stagnates in the body of the road; it was never sufficiently widened, nor were the hedges ever cleared—of course it is the worst public road in Europe, considering what vast sums have been collected from it." Other Turnpike Trusts shifted the whole work and responsibility to their Treasurer, a gentleman whose custody of the turnpike moneys brought him a small profit, and who was therefore considered as remunerated for his trouble. "For several years past," we read about Surrey in 1794, "the turnpike roads of this county have been under the direction of Treasurers, who are Trustees of the roads, and are appointed by the Trust at large, at a meeting held for that purpose. A knowledge of the fundamental principles of making roads is not deemed at all necessary to the election of such Treasurers, but they are generally some respectable gentlemen in business (if near town) and whither perhaps they go every day. Each appoints some inferior tradesman of the district in which he lives to be the Surveyor, and who may be a carpenter, a bricklayer or any other profession, as it may happen, so that without a particle of knowledge in the maintenance and principles of roads on either side, is the expenditure of hundreds of pounds committed to the day labourers, who are for the most part old and decrepid, and who, being generally left to themselves, take every advantage; and as the Surveyor does not know how much should be done, he is easily imposed upon by the men; and as the money does not come out of his pocket, it is not very material for him to give himself much trouble about it. Thus, from the want of experience in the Surveyor, and the want of leisure in the Treasurer, these roads which, from their proximity to the gravel on all sides, might, under a proper system, be kept sound and in a good condition all the year round, are found to be daily diminishing, and the public will, ere a few years longer, findit expedient to take some steps to remedy so great a defect." Under such circumstances it was almost inevitable that many bodies of Turnpike Trustees, especially in the latter half of the century, should fall back on the common administrative expedient of the period, that of " farming" which was at the time so much resorted to in the administration of prisons and the Poor Law. As applied to turnpike roads, this meant that some local farmer or jobbing craftsman would undertake, for a lump sum, to keep a given stretch of highway in repair. According to the ablest contemporary road administrator, this practice proved as ruinous to the roads as it had to the workhouse and the prison. It was to "a desire in Trustees to be exonerated from trouble" that John Scott ascribes "that most pernicious practice of farming roads, which, like farming the poor, is the disgrace of our country. The Trustees, when once a road is farmed, have nothing to do but meet once a year to eat venison and pay the farmer his annuity; the farmer has nothing to do but to do as little work and pocket as much money as he possibly can; he has other fish to fry, other matters to mind, than road-mending. Incroachment after incroachment takes place, the hedges and the trees grow till they meet overhead, the landholders are excused from their Statute Duty, and the water and the narrow wheeled waggons complete the business. At length, perhaps, the universal complaint of travellers or menaces of indictment rouse the Trustees for a moment, a meeting is called, the farmer sent for and reprimanded, and a few loads of gravel buried among the mud, serve to keep the way barely passable.... These practices of farming roads and farming the poor ought to be prohibited by law."

With such primitive views of administration, we can understand how many of the earlier Turnpike Trusts hardly conduced to the actual improvement of the roads. Thus, Robert Phillips, in his dissertation of 1737 to the Royal Society, " concerning the present state of the high roads of England," complains that the "turnpike roads, instead of being mended, have been made bad by art. .. so that all the money that has been laid out in such roads... has been rather of prejudice than service." The people who have had the care of the roads, he explains, have heaped loamy gravel on them, deep hard-baked ruts have been formed, which are constantly filled with water. "If the turnpikes were taken down," he Bums up, " and the roads not touched for seven years, they would be a great deal better than they are now." These haphazard methods of road maintenance continued to prevail in the smaller and more remote Turnpike Trusts right into the nineteenth century. From about 1750, however, we watch the larger and more important Trusts—those administered by active and intelligent Justices or by the principal inhabitants of populous districts—enlisting in their service permanent salaried officials who proceeded to experiment in road construction and repair, without engineering knowledge, it is true, but at any rate according to some deliberate policy, which was consistently followed. The result was an amazing variety of shapes and surfaces, each for a time believed in by its inventor. The "road laid wavy," or " trenched road," with a "continuation of little hills and valleys "; the "angular road sloping like a pantile roof from one hand to the other "; the "concave road," or "hollow way," into which a stream was periodically turned to clean its surface; the built-up " horizontal road," flanked by deep ditches, sometimes a "causeway from 20 to 30 feet wide, nearly horizontal on the top, with precipices on each side of four or five feet perpendicular depth,"—could all be seen within a day's journey of the Metropolis. Regarded in the light of the modern art of road construction, all these fantastic forms and surfaces were grotesquely inconvenient and wasteful. But we may well believe that they were all of them improvements on the deep holes and inevitable ruts which resulted from the careless dumping of clay, dirt and rubbish by the little road-farmer or the ignorant workman who carried out the orders of the local Trustee. And the constant observation and comparison of these deliberately shaped roads seems to have produced, by the end of the century, something like a consensus of opinion, among the more intelligent Trustees and Surveyors, in favour of a moderately convex surface, artificially constructed of small pebbles and gravel—an immeasurable improvement on both the "natural" surface and the heaped-up dirt, which it superseded.

But the richer and larger turnpike authorities did more than merely improve the surface of the roads. Here and there we find them widening and straightening the narrow and crooked bits of their thoroughfares; bridging the numerous "watersplashes" through which generations of travellers had passed; improving gradients by cutting through the hilltops and raising the valley bottoms; and, in the latter half of the century, constructing entirely new roads from place to place. Thus, as early as 1708, we find an order made at the Hertfordshire Quarter Sessions " for the widening by eight yards, of the highway from Ware to Wadesmill... for the length of 25 poles, and for a jury to be empanelled to assess reasonable compensation not exceeding 25 years purchase." In Essex, in 1725, the parish of Chelmsford petitioned Quarter Sessions " to grant them some supply towards the charges of purchasing and pulling down the old houses in a row called Middle Row, and lay the ground into the highway for enlarging thereof, it being but nine feet wide. " It was thereupon ordered by Quarter Sessions "that the sum of £50, more and besides the sum of £100 given them last Sessions, be given to the Churchwardens, Overseers and Surveyors of the said Parish for the time being, after they have purchased and pulled down all the said houses and made a highway there. " But, as might have been expected, it was the Turnpike Trusts in the distinctly urban districts that were most energetic in this work of road improvement. The Trustees of the main road from London into Kent had, about the middle of the century," widened several places in the road to Dartford, being,"says the *Gentleman's Magazine* for May 1753, "perhaps the first who began to widen and make the roads straight." They "likewise widened and mended some narrow and bad ways from Lewisham to Bromley and Beckenham... and added a new bridge." Presently, as we learn, the local Turnpike Trustees widened the road " going off of Clapham Common to Mitcham." "The gentlemen of Camberwell" did the same for " a very bad hollow way leading by the Fox & Goose near that town." In country districts this most necessary work of widening and straightening the roads was often obstructed by the selfishness of landowners. "If," it was said in the same journal in September 1754, "there be necessity of a small strip of land to make a road more commodious sometimes it is peremptorily refused; and if you would obtain it legally it would cost twenty times as much as it is worth. If to obtain a short cut, or avoid a morass, you want to pass through a field, you are generally refused, and put to three times as much expense as the thing is worth. " But the greatest obstacle to improvement was found in the lack of administrative ability among the Turnpike Trustees themselves. It practically never occurred to such Trustees to get a professional survey made of the road to be improved; they never saw the importance of getting competent advice as to the engineering problems to be solved; and when they did have some person in their employment who was called a Surveyor, they failed to realise that it would not do to let him at the same time act as contractor for the execution of the work which he was required to supervise. In the interesting published account of the Epping and Ongar Turnpike Trust, we are able to watch the spurt of activity made by a public-spirited body between 1769 and 1786 in widening roads, levelling steep ascents, and making better connections from point to point, and to realise the difficulties which brought them presently to a standstill. Sometimes they would put the work out to contract; sometimes they would do it by direct employment, both systems proving equally unsatisfactory. What was constant was their reliance on the survey and report of individual members of their own body, supplemented by the advice of their " Surveyor "—a gentleman to whom they gave the handsome stipend of £25 a year, and at the same time allowed to undertake the execution of the work for a lump sum. At other times they gave him thirty shillings a week for superintending the labourers whom they themselves engaged. When the Trustees put out the work to their Surveyor for a lump sum, it happens more than once that it is subsequently found to have been badly done or left altogether unfinished. When they engage their own labourers under such superintendence the work invariably proves to cost enormously more than the original estimate. These administrative failures led first to repeated changes of Surveyor, and presently to an abandonment of the task in despair, practically no improvements being undertaken for a whole generation. At length in 1830, when the then Trustees nerved themselves to renewed activity, they began by engaging the services of Macadam as Consulting Surveyor, and at last made something like a good job of the business.

The most defective side of turnpike administration was that of finance.

There was, to begin with, in nearly all Turnpike Trusts, the usual eighteenth-century jobbery in the purchase of materials, in the connivance at bad work by contractors, and in the appointment of the officials of the Trust itself. In these respects, however, so far as our information goes, there is no reason to suppose that the Turnpike Trustees were either better or worse than contemporary local authorities generally. It was in the method of raising their resources that the Trusts were most open to criticism. Their relation with the compulsory Statute Labour, to be rendered by the parishes through which the road passed, was, with the uncertainty as to the amount that they could exact and the method of obtaining it, in the highest degree unsatisfactory. But the special source of revenue of Turnpike Trustees was, of course, the toll, the collection of which led to endless evasions, inequalities and favouritisms of all kinds, arbitrary exactions, and systematic petty embezzlements. We need not here dwell on the various devices by which the legislature and the Trustees tried to protect themselves against the ingenuities of those seeking to avoid the tolls—the vigilant closing up of bye-lanes or side roads, and the perpetual shifting or multiplication of the gates in order to counteract the inveterate desire to go round; together with the long array of penalties on such dodges as taking off the supernumerary horses, or lightening the load where going through the turnpike gate, dashing through without payment, or fraudulently pretending to come under one or other of the categories of exemption. What made the incidence of the tolls specially inequitable, and created a permanent sense of injustice, was the multiplicity of exemptions and abatements that were allowed to favoured trades or individuals. There were, to begin with, any number of exemptions in favour of agriculture; ploughs and implements of husbandry of every kind, carts carrying manure, cattle going to pasture, waggons bringing home the harvest were all privileged to pass and repass free of toll, however much they wore out the road. Sometimes other local industries would be specially favoured; round Evesham, in Warwickshire, the flour-millers were secured freedom of access for their customers and for the materials needed for the repairs of their mills; in Berkshire, in a vain attempt to resuscitate a decaying local manufacture, it was stipulated that "any cart or horse carrying or bringing back any cloth, drugget, serge or other woollen manufacture, to or from any fulling mill," should be free from toll. The conveyance of coal was specially favoured in some districts, and that of " peat, peat ashes, or turf " in others. A particular town would insist on the exemption of " carriages carrying hay or straw to be used within the said borough." More general was the exemption—specially useful because most tolls were doubled on Sundays—of local residents riding or driving to and from church, or attending a funeral. Most Acts forbade the taking of toll on the days of Parliamentary elections in the district, the borough and county elections being sometimes both particularly specified. Post-horses carrying mails, waggons transporting the baggage of soldiers on the march, and carts used for the passing of vagrants were almost universally exempted. What was, however, more invidious was the special privilege of exemption which influential inhabitants were sometimes able to secure, for themselves, their families, their workmen, their servants, and their agents, and for those of all successive owners and occupiers of their premises, as the price of abstaining from Parliamentary opposition. These specific Parliamentary exemptions by no means exhausted the list of favours. The Trustees were authorised, both by general statutes and by their own Local Act, to compound for the tolls; and this power was very generally exercised, not only in the case of regular and frequent users of the road, but also in favour of the inhabitants of particular parishes, and even of individual Trustees themselves. In the records of the Epping and Ongar Trust, for instance, we find, between 1769 and 1789, from a score to fifty compounders, paying from 5s. 3d. to 21s. each a year, for exemption from all tolls on themselves, their horses, their carriages, their families and their servants. In 1789 the Trustees seem to have realised how seriously their revenue was being curtailed by these nominal compositions, for they resolve " that it will be very beneficial to the Trust not to permit any person to compound for their tolls in future." The list of compounders thereupon disappears from the Minutes. But this self-denying ordinance was vehemently objected to by some of the Trustees, and one leading landowner and, it so happens, the Treasurer of the Trust, insisted on the resolution being rescinded. Within a year he carries his point, subject only to the composition rates being doubled, and the list of compounders reappears. But the exemptions and compositions accounted only for a small part of the Trustees' loss of revenue. The men whom they appointed as toll collectors—turnpike gate-keepers, or "pikemen," as they were called—were mere labourers, paid a wage of ten or twelve shillings a week, often unable to read or write, and usually incapable of keeping accounts. It was found necessary in 1763 elaborately to forbid them to absent themselves from their posts during their periods of duty, and to require them to remain until they were actually relieved. The varying rates of charge, the exemptions and compositions, the validity of tickets for return journeys or other gates, and many other complications of the toll made it impossible to devise any effective check on their receipts. It was notorious that they habitually kept back part of each day's collection for themselves. Hence, from the very first, many Trusts resorted to the plan of "farming," leasing each gate with its power of exacting toll for a definite sum per annum. At first the gates were let by private contract by the personal negotiations of the Justices of the Peace or Turnpike Trustees themselves, to any one who would make himself responsible for a lump sum,—sometimes to a publican, a little tradesman, or even a labourer. Presently it became customary, and Parliament made it compulsory, to resort, for the letting of the tolls, to public auction and to accept the highest bidder as lessee. As the mileage of turnpike roads increased, there grew up a whole class of professional toll-farmers, often men of large capital, farming tolls amounting to many tens of thousands a year, and employing under them small armies of professional "pikemen. " Old prints and descriptions enable us to visualise these men, whom Dickens loved to describe, and who have long since disappeared from among us. "A pikeman... wore a tall black glazed hat and corderoy breeches, with white stockings. But the most distinctive part ©i his costume was his white linen apron." Both masters and men quickly becoming notorious for every kind of sharp practice, illicit collusion and embezzlement. At the periodical auctions at which the tolls were let, Parliament had been careful, in 1773, to specify with minuteness that elaborate public notice was to be given, that the highest bidder was to be accepted, and that "to prevent fraud or undue preference in letting the said tolls, the Trustees must provide a glass, with so much sand in it as will run from one end to the other in one minute; which glass, at the time of letting the tolls, must be set upon a table and immediately after every bidding the glass must be turned, and as soon as the sand is run out, it must be turned again, and so for three times unless some other bidding intervene." What it probably did not contemplate, and certainly did not succeed in preventing, was the series of elaborate combinations and private "knock-outs" among the toll-farmers, which often prevented the full value of the tolls being obtained. "The tolls," it was said in 1809, "are annually farmed or let to individuals by auction, according to the last year's produce. This the farmers keep as secret as possible, and the amount can only be inferred from the increase of the terms he proffers for the ensuing year. It is then his interest to make the tolls as productive as possible; but the gate-keepers he must employ are more exposed to temptation, and over them exists less control, than perhaps occurs in any other condition of men in society. The only check their masters have upon them is by reserving, upon detached days in the year, the tolls themselves, and averaging by the produce the annual receipts, by changing their stations almost daily, and by arbitrarily discharging them if their returns do not reach the estimated amount. This becomes equally well known to the gatekeeper, and he withholds all beyond that amount. Instead of preventing, by information, the violations of the laws limiting the number of passengers, they are paid by the coachman to connive at the abuse; and the nature of their office renders them ready and constant channels for the circulation of base coin."

To the student of public administration, it is interesting to see how the imperfection of the financial machinery destroyed the whole efficacy of many of the Parliamentary devices for preserving the roads. When the simple prohibition of narrow wheels, heavy loads and excessive teams had been proved to be ineffective, the country gentlemen who drafted the various highway and turnpike statutes fondly thought to achieve their end by imposing extra rates of toll for every narrow-wheeled vehicle however loaded, and for every hundredweight of loading on any vehicle, over and above a legally specified amount, varying according to a complicated scale depending on the kind of vehicle, the breadth of its wheels, the distance between them, and even the season of the year. For this purpose Turnpike Trustees were, from 1741 onwards, authorised, and might by Quarter Sessions be required, to erect "a crane, machine or weighing engine " to weigh the loads—not the convenient modern weighbridge, which had not then been invented, but a huge and complicated structure, rising high over the road, and actually lifting the vehicle and its contents from the ground. One such machine may still be seen *in situ* at Woodbridge, Suffolk, and a weird and incomprehensible structure it is. Its erection was costly, and the expense of keeping men to work it was still greater. It was never very accurate, and was always getting out of order. "It is a very common case," it was said in 1796, "that a load will pass at one engine, when the same load at another will be subject to an increased toll." It was, moreover, hugely inconvenient to the users of the road, especially as it was practically impossible to be always sure that a load was under a given weight. There was thus every inducement to evasion and neglect; and the Trusts soon found that, apart from the ordinary charges, the weighing machine did not yield enough in extra tolls to pay for the necessary attendance and upkeep. On the other hand, the toll-farmer was willing to give a considerable additional price for the tolls if he was permitted to rent also the weighing machine. The Trustees, in fact, were in a dilemma. "If," it was acutely pointed out to a House of Commons Committee in 1808, "the engine continues in the hands of the Trust, its purpose is completely defeated by the corrupt connivance of the keeper employed; not only may he allow overweight to pass for a small reward, but he may share profits with the driver carrying extra weight unknown to his employer, and thus both the Trust and the master carrier will be defrauded. If the weighing machine is let by the year for a certain sum, nearly equal to its supposed receipts, to an individual whose own interest will keep him vigilant, that very interest will lead him to compound with the carriers of overweight; indeed composition is the only way by which he can repay himself for the rent of the engine. Were he to be rigid in the exaction of every penalty he would put a stop to overweights and to his own profits together. If, in a word, the weighing engine constituted an effectual check to overweighted carriages, the penalties exacted would amount to a very trifling sum. But they are let or farmed out for considerable sums, which completely proves that, instead of operating as a prevention, they only become an additional toll for extra load." Assuming that, on the soft surface of the period, it was desirable to discourage the conveyance of heavy weights, especially on narrow wheels in winter, it is impossible to avoid the conclusion, drawn by an able critic, in 1808, that, as actually worked, the whole system of extra tolls and weighing machines was "injurious to the roads instead of tending to their preservation, because being rented, the renters compound with the owners of waggons to receive double tolls going and returning, on permission to carry any weight. The immense rents given for weighing machines could not be raised by any other means."

The most serious of all the financial defects of the Turnpike Trusts was, however, the deficit into which many of the bodies of Trustees fell. The new revenue of tolls seemed, at first, to promise inexhaustible annual resources, which Parliament allowed to be mortgaged without check or limit. Already by 1773, the effect of reckless finance had made itself apparent in many Trusts. "At the first erection of turnpikes," wrote Thomas Butterworth Bayley, "the people imagine the roads are to be made and kept in repair by the very charm of the word turnpike, and not being obliged to continue their statute work with so much attention as formerly, depend entirely on the tolls, and fall into a state of negligence and indifference till at length the first materials are worn out, and then the tolls being mortgaged to the height, the whole burden of renewing and supporting the roads again is laid upon them with the additional tax of the tolls." By the end of the century the mortgaging of tolls had been carried to a great height, and many Trusts made default in the payment of interest on their bond debt. Sir James Macadam stated in 1839 that he knew of some Trusts which had paid no interest for over sixty years. "In some instances," reported the House of Commons Committee in 1808, " they have contracted debts bearing an interest nearly equal to the amount of their tolls, and when those have been increased fresh debts are incurred; so that the contributions levied on individuals using the road become directed to purposes wholly different from their repair."

With the whole or the greater part of the tolls thus alienated for payment of interest on past indebtedness—sometimes even with the mortgagees in possession, taking the whole money revenue for their arrears of interest and heavy legal expenses— the expenditure on the repair of the road was naturally reduced to a minimum, and it may well be that the last state of such turnpike roads was worse than the first. Arthur Young, in his travels about England, clearly implies that the great majority of the turnpike roads were far better than the parish highways, but occasionally he comes across one in Wales, in Lancashire or in Suffolk which he cannot believe to be a turnpike, so vile is its conditions of disrepair. It was, indeed, as was subsequently perceived, a "great defect in the system of turnpike laws" that there was an utter lack of " provision to compel each trust to account before some competent tribunal. Road Commissioners," said the *Edinburgh Review* in October 1819, "are the only persons entrusted by Parliament to levy a large revenue from the public without being required to account in any way for what they receive. A still greater defect is the want of any proper remedy when a set of commissioners abuse their trust. They may suffer their road to become a perfect ruin; they may embezzle funds and commit every sort of malpractice, and yet go on levying tolls, keeping possession of the road and defying all complaints." There was, in fact, no practical method of bringing a defaulting, hopelessly incompetent or dishonest Turnpike Trust to book. Subject to no official superintendence or central control, under no inspection, rendering no accounts, it could use or neglect its powers as it chose. A Turnpike Trust could not even be indicted for letting its roads become impassable. The only legal remedy was the presentment or indictment of the parish or township within which the road lay. The creation of a special statutory trust had left unimpaired the liability of the parish to maintain " the good passage " on all parts of the King's Highway, whether or not some other persons had received a statutory right to exact tolls from those who travelled on it. Spasmodically the law would be put in force. Some public-spirited Justice of the Peace would formally present an exceptionally neglected bit of turnpike road, or the parish would find itself indicted at the suit of some aggrieved user of the road, with the result of a fine, a special highway rate, a momentary spurt of activity in enforcing Statute Labour, and an early reversion to the former neglect. It is true that, from 1773 onward, the Court could apportion the fine and costs between the parish and the Trust, but only "in case it shall appear to the Court from the circumstances of the Turnpike debts and revenues that the same may be paid without endangering the security of the creditors who have advanced money upon the credit of the tolls"; and the parish, in practice, never got reimbursed the expense to which it was put. So flagrantly unjust was it to punish the local parishioners, who had nothing to do with the administration of the Turnpike Trust, for the default or neglect of a separate authority, which still went on exacting its tolls, that this procedure of presentment and indictment was, in practice, even less effective for turnpike roads than for parish highways. The injustice moved even the Yorkshire antiquary, Whitaker, to an outburst of indignation amid his church annals and genealogies. "It is a great iniquity," he says in his *Loidis and Elmete,* " as well as absurdity, that parishes and townships should be indictable or presentable for the neglect or passive defaults of others over whom they have no control, while they are condemned to be passive in the introduction of expensive and burdensome roads through their respective districts, and at the same time actively responsible for all the consequences occasioned by the fraud or negligence of strangers." Public opinion was arrayed against it, and in 1809 it was definitely discouraged by a Committee of the House of Commons.

The foregoing description of the theory and practice of turnpike administration, and our analysis of its defects, might lead the student to assume that all the effort and money lavished by the eighteenth-century Turnpike Trusts resulted in no net advantage to the community. This would be a false conclusion. The parish highway often consisted, as we have already described, of a mere horse track across a miry common, or a watery hollow lane twisting between high banks and overhanging hedges. So deep and narrow were these ways that " the stag, the hounds and the huntsmen," Edgeworth tells us, "have been known to leap over a loaded waggon in a hollow way without any obstruction from the vehicle." Such a highway was practically impassable for wheeled vehicles, and sometimes even for horsemen, for half the year. With the coming of the Industrial Revolution, with a rapidly increasing population, with manufactures ready to leap from the ground, with unprecedented opportunities for home and foreign trade, improvement of communication between different parts of the kingdom became, from the standpoint of material prosperity, the most urgent of national requirements. To-day, the railway and the tramway, the telegraph and the telephone, have largely superseded roads as the arteries of national circulation. Put, barring a few lengths of canal in the making, and a few miles of navigable river estuaries, it was, throughout the eighteenth century, on the King's Highway alone that depended the manufacturer and the wholesale dealer, the hawker and the shopkeeper, the farmer, the postal contractor, the lawyer, the government official, the traveller, the miner, the craftsman and the farm servant, for the transport of themselves, and the distribution of their products and their purchases, their services and their ideas. Hence, to open up even some of the ways between the Metropolis and the rest of the country, between the ports and the landward counties, between the food-producing districts and the new manufacturing centres, was worth almost any money cost, however vexatiously it might be raised or however wastefully it might be spent. And all contemporary evidence indicates that, what with surface-making and embanking, widening and straightening, levelling and bridging, the mileage of usable roads was, by the eighteenth-century Turnpike Trusts, very greatly extended. The frequent complaints of the local absence of turnpikes indicate in themselves how completely the new system had commended itself to the ordinary traveller. Before the middle of the century particular roads are marked out for praise. Between 1750 and 1770, when the number of Turnpike Trusts was actually trebled, the contemporary self-complacency over the new roads rises to dithyrambic heights. "There never was a more astonishing revolution accomplished in the internal system of any country," declares an able and quite trustworthy writer in 1767, "than has been within the compass of a few years in that of England. The carriage of grain, coals, merchandise, etc., is in general conducted with little more than half the number of horses with which it formerly was. Journeys of business are performed with more than double expedition.... *Everything wears the face of dispalch.* .. and the hinge which has guided all these movements and upon which they turn is the reformation which has been made in our public roads." Thirty years later, when the standard of efficiency in roads had greatly risen, the reports by the critical surveyors of the Board of Agriculture are more grudging. But with the exception of Wales, they everywhere report a substantial improvement and development, by the agency of the Turnpike Trusts, of the means of communication within each county. And we have the significant fact that the most eminent observers of, and participators in, the local government of the latter half of the century—Sir Henry Hawkins, Dr. Richard Burn, John Scott, and Arthur Young—all expressly assert, or at least unequivocably imply, the expediency of the Turnpike Trust and its toll. Our own conclusions coincide with this verdict. The intense jealousy of any increase of the national executive government, and the abhorrence of new local rates would have made-impracticable any project for a centralised road administration, or for raising the necessary income by direct assessment. "If rates on land had been resorted to," said Sir Henry Parnell, "the measure would inevitably have failed, because the landowners would, beyond all doubt, have preferred bad roads and low rates to good ones and high rates; in point of fact, very indifferent roads would have answered all their local purposes. If the roads had been vested in the hands of government, it may safely be said that this plan would also have failed, for government would never have been able to obtain the consent of Parliament to vote upwards of a million and a half a year for those roads only which now are turnpike roads. It is therefore to the turnpike system of management that England is indebted to her superiority over other countries with respect to roads.... Nothing but leaving the management of the roads to those people who live in their neighbourhood would ever have induced the people of England to pay, as they now do, a road revenue, arising from turnpike tolls, to the amount of £1,500,000 a year; for, though tolls are in every respect fair and proper for maintaining a road; and although Government by employing scientific engineers, might have expended the produce of them with greater skill than country gentlemen; the hostility to pay them, if they had been wholly at the disposal of government, would no doubt have prevented the making of useful roads so universally over the whole country as they have been made under the established system." The Turnpike Trust and its toll was, in short, the only way open. Without the local initiative

L and local support fostered by the thousand separate Trusts; without the emulation and mutual instruction which their several experiments promoted; without the large revenues which the toll drew from the multitudinous but politically helpless road users, no considerable improvement in the highways of England would have taken place for, at any rate, the first three-quarters of the eighteenth century, and very little would have been achieved before the passing of the Reform Bill.

APPENDIX TO CHAPTER VII

Notes And Refebenoes

Page 114. Of the Turnpike Trusts no systematic history has been written, and the student can only be referred to such general references and descriptions as are to be found in the *History of Private Bill Legislation,* by F. Clifford, 1885-87, voL ii. chap. vii.; *A Treatise on Roads,* by Sir Henry Parnell, afterwards Lord Congleton, 1st edition, 1833, 2nd edition, 1838; *Life of Thomas Telford, Civil Engineer, Written by Himself,* edited by John Rickman, 1838; *Voyages dans la Grande Bretagne,* by Baron Charles Dupin, 1824, troisiome partie, "Force Commerciale," vol. i. p. 33; *Descriptive and Statistical Account of the British Empire,* by J. R. M'Culloch, 1846, vol. ii. chap. v. sec. 3; and to the almost innumerable Parliamentary Reports on Highways and Turnpikes throughout the eighteenth and nineteenth centuries. A good vision of the working of a Turnpike Trust is afforded by the two Reports of a Select Committee on various Metropolitan Turnpikes, one printed at length in the House of Commons Journals for 1763 (vol. xxix. pp. 645-664), the other presented in 1765; in the brief account of the " Whetstone Turnpike Trust, 1754-1863," in *Middlesex and Hertfordshire Notes and Queries,* vol. iv. pp. 91-94; in *A Turnpike Key, or /an Account of the Proceedings of the Exeter Turnpike Trustees, 1753-1884,* by W. Buckingham, 1885; and in the interesting volume entitled *Minutes of the Epping and Ongar Highway Trust, 1769-1870,* by Benjamin Winstone, 1891. Much incidental information of all sorts is afforded in the excellent manual, *Digests of the General Highway and Turnpike Laws,* by John Scott, 1778. The MS. Minutes of the eleven hundred Turnpike Trusts, where they are preserved at all, are mostly hidden away in solicitors' offices, but they are occasionally to be found among municipal or county archives. We have had access to the MS. Minutes of the Oldham Turnpike Trust, 1806-30; the Dursley and Berkeley Turnpike Trust, 1779-1874, and a few others; but we have found most information in the (literally) tens of thousands of bills, petitions, reports of committees and proceedings in Parliament relating to roads during the past two centuries,

Page 114. Littleton's suggestion of a toll is in *A Proposal for the Highways,* 1692, p. 11. The quotation as to a toll is from *An Enquiry into)f the Means of Preserving the Pvblick Roads,* by Rev. Henry Homer, 1765, V p. 18. Road tolls seem to have been unknown in England in 1650, as they had been for a century or more, except where a Municipal Corporation charged a " Through Toll" or other *octroi,* and possibly in the cases of a few private franchises as to bridges. Various isolated precedents for their levy, by royal license, on particular stretches of road, can be found in the records of the thirteenth and fourteenth centuries. Authority seems to have been given in 1267 to levy a toll in a Gloucestershire manor; "capiat in feod unum dener, le quelibet caracte transeunte per manerie qua de Thormerton et Littleton "; see Index of the Patent Rolls, Henry VII., and *Notes and Queries,* 27th December 1851. "In 1346 a toll for pavage was levied by the City authorities on vehicles passing from " St. Giles in the Fields to Temple Bar" *History of Private Bill Legislation,* by F. Clifford, 1885-87, vol. i. pp. 4-5, vol. ii. pp. 3-8).

The name "turnpike" was given from the adoption of "horizontal tapering bars of iron or wood suspended upon a rigid perpendicular pillar, around which, as an axis they revolved. They corresponded," says an author of 1845, " with those modern cross wickets or sidegates, which may be seen in the vicinity of certain towns, with this difference that, until the dues or toll was paid, these pikes or styles could not be made to turn either to right or left" *(Road Reform,* by William Pagan, 1st edition, 1845, 3rd edition, 1857, p. 1). "A turnpike road," said a learned judge in 1840, "means a road having toll-gates or bars on it, which were originally called,' turns.'... The distinctive mark of a turnpike road is the right of turning back any one who refuses to pay toll" (Lord Abinger, C.B., in Northam Bridge Co. *v.* London and Southampton Railway Co., 1840, 6 M. & W. 428). "Pike " came popularly to be used for the toll bar or tollgate; and also for the toll itself.

Page 114. *Notes from the Hertfordshire County Records,* p. 6; *Bygone Hertfordshire,* by W. Andrews, 1898, p. 264.

Page 115. 15 Car. II. c. 1 (1663) renewed by 26 Car. II. (1674) 4 & 5 William and Mary (1692), and again by 6 Anne (1707), as to which see House of Commons Journals, 8th, 21st, 27th January and 6th March 1707. The 1663 Act is described in the *History of Commerce,* by A. Anderson, vol. v. p. 44; *A Treatise on Roads,* by Sir Henry Parnell, afterwards Lord Congleton, 1833, p. 17; *History of Private Bill Legislation,* by F. Clifford, 1885-87, voL ii. pp. 12-14; and in " The Old North Road," by J. H. Hinde, in *Archceologia Aeliana,* part ix. , 1858, pp. 237-255. But most of these Acts have remained unnoticed, and the whole episode deserves further study.

Page 115. The Harwich road, Essex (7 & 8 William III. c. 9, 1695, containing the first statutory mention of the word "Turnpike "); the Wymondham and Attleborough road, Norfolk (7 & 8 William III. c. 26, 1695; renewed by 7 Anne, c. 4, 1708, 12 George I. c. 22, 1729, and 20 George II. c. 16, 1746); the Reigate and Crawley road, Surrey (8 & 9 William m. c. 15,1697); the Birdlip and Gloucester road, Gloucestershire, (9 & 10 William III. c. 18, 1698, renewed by 9 George I. c. 31, 1723 and 16 George II. c. 21, 1742); the Minehead roads, Somerset (12 & 13 William III. c. 9,1701); the Woodford road, Essex (1 Anne, s. 2. e. 10, see House of Commons Journals, 19th November 1702, renewed by 10 George I. c. 9, 1723, and 17 George II. c. 9, 1743); the Barnhill to Hatton Heath road, Cheshire (4 & 5 Anne, c. 9, 1705); the Hockley and Woburn road, Bedfordshire (5 Anne, c. 10, see House of Commons Journals, 22nd February 1707); the Sheppard's Shord and Devizes road (5 Anne, c. 26, see House of Commons Journals, 13th, 26th and 31st March 1707); the Bath roads (6 Anne, c. 1, 1707, renewed by 7 George I. c. 19, 1721); the Portsmouth road (9 Anne, c. 8, 1710); the Gravesend and Rochester road (10 Anne, c. 34, 1711). Almost the only mention of these Acts, and then only of one or two of them, is that in the *History of Private Bill Legislation,* by F. Clifford, 1885-87, voL ii. pp. 15-16.

Page 115. 5 Anne (1706), not printed, but mentioned in House of Commons Journals 3rd and 27th March 1707, 15th and 24th February 1710, and in preamble of 3 George I. c. 15 (1716); 8 Anne c. 15 (1709); renewed by 11 George I. c. 15 (1725); 9 Anne, c. 7 (1710), of which we may quote the quaint preamble: "Whereas by the happy union of this kingdom the great post road from London to North Britain is become much more frequented than the same formerly hath been, and a great part of that road... is become very ruinous, insomuch as without very great hazard and danger members coming up to Parliament and other persons cannot pass that way... for remedy whereof, &c."

Page 116. The arrangement of the statute law is so defective that it is difficult to state with absolute certainty what Acts were passed. Down to 1702 turnpike statutes were "public," and easily accessible; from 1702 to 1720 they were all classified as "private" and were not always printed, so that our information may be incomplete; from 1720 to 1753 they were printed and bound with the ordinary public general statutes; from 1753 to 1798 they were bound separately, and are described as "Publio Aots not printed in the collection," or, more succinctly, as " Road Acts "; whilst from 1798 to 1868 they wero included among " Acts Local and Personal." After 1868 there are three divisions, viz. , Publio General Acts, Local Acts and Private Acts (see House of Commons Journals, vol. lii. p. 413; *History of Private Bill Legislation,* by F. Clifford, 1887-89, voL i. p. 269; *Legislative Methods and Forms,* by Sir C. P. Dbert, 1901, pp. 26-27; *Municipal Origins,* by F. H. Spencer, 1911, pp. 46-48).

Page 117. So by the Act of 15 Car. II. c. 1 (1663); but no one was to be compellable to travel above three, four, or five miles from home, nor to work more than two days in any one week, nor on any day in seed-time, hay-time or corn harvest (7 & 8 William III. c. 9, 1695; so also 7 & 8 William III. c. 26, 1695). The power of the Surveyor to require this extra labour is given without limit in 9 & 10 William III. c. 18 (1698). In the Kent County records in 1729 we read that " it is ordered by this Court that it be referred to Thomas Marsh, Esq., one of His Majesty's Justices of the Peace for this County, and the rest of the Justices of the Division wherein Longport lies, to sett le and set the price of labourers employed in and about the repairing, surveying and looking after Boughton highways, in this County, on the London road," the amount so set to be paid by tho County Treasurer (MS. Minutes, Quarter Sessions, East Kent, 10th October 1729).

Page 117. As regards these powers, see, for instance, the nuisance and obstruction clauses in 7 George II. c. 13 (1733); 1 George II. c. 33 (1727); 17 George II. c. 29 (1743); and especially the very comprehensive powers given in 20 George III. c. 71 (1780).

Page 117. As regards powers over private property, see, for instance, 15 Car. II. c. 1 (Great North Road Turnpike Act, 1663); 7 & 8 William III. c. 9 (London and Harwich Turnpike Act, 1695); 6 Anne, c. 1 (Bath and Kingsdown Hill Turnpike Act, 1707). Subsequently, private interests are better safeguarded. The Surveyor has to pay reasonable rates for the material so taken from private land (6 George I. c. 25, Stevenage and Biggleswade Turnpike Act, 1720); later on, express notice must be given to the owner, and specific order made by Justices, after hearing objections (39 & 40 George III. c. 3, Leicester and Hinckley Turnpike Act, 1800). The 1663 Act had required pits from which materials were dug to be filled up and levelled, "or else railed about... so as that the same may not be deemed dangerous or prejudicial to man or beast" (15 Car. II. c. 1); an obligation not made usual until the Public General Act of 1753 (26 George II. c. 28), which required any holes or pits made in commons or wastes for this purpose to be fenced; and specific clauses to this effect again appear in many subsequent Turnpike Acts, "so that " these pits "may not be dangerous to passengers or cattle " (see 10 George III. e. 54, Norwich and Block Hill Turnpike Act, 1770).

Page 117. The relations between the Parish Surveyor and the Turnpike Surveyor thus became complicated. The Parish Surveyor of Highways was to deliver a list of persons liable; the Turnpike Surveyor was to give him notice of the time and place for them to come; he was then to summon all persons liable; and they were to put in three days' work on the turnpike road; see 1 George I. sess. 2, c. 25 (Tyburn and Uxbridge Turnpike Act, 1714, for what is now the Bayswater Road, Notting Hill and Uxbridge Road); see also the detailed clause in 13 George II. c. 9 (Hockliffe and Stony Stratford Turnpike Act, 1739). As late as 1800 there was an appeal by a Parish Surveyor of Highways against a conviction by Petty Sessions for not having summoned, in response to a demand from the Turnpike Surveyor, certain inhabitants "to perform their statute work upon part of the said road" (MS. Minutes, Quarter Sessions, Lancashire, 15th July 1800).

For oases in which the Justices were left to fix the number of days' labour to be given to the turnpike road or by whom it should be given, see 7 George I. c. 18 (Highgate and Barnet Turnpike Act, 1720); 16 George II. c. 21 (Birdlip and Gloucester Turnpike Act, 1742); 13 George II. c. 9 (Hockliffe and Stony Stratford Turnpike Act, 1739); 17 George II. c. 9 (Harlow and Stump Cross Turnpike Act, 1743).

Page 118. For power to require a money composition, see 3 George I. c. 4 (Highgate and Hampstead Turnpike Act, 1716); 4 George I. c. 4 (London and East Grinstead Turnpike Act, 1717); 4 George I. c. 5 (Southwark and East Greenwich Turnpike Act, 1717); and many subsequent Ajts. In 19 George II. c. 19 (Liverpool and Prescot Turnpike Aot, 1745), the power to raise the composition money by rate is expressly given to the Parish Surveyor of Highways. These compositions naturally led to embittered negotiations between the Parish and the Trust. Hackney, for instance, was made to pay £100 a year towards the Kingsland Road Turnpike Trust, and this arrangement was embodied in 12 Anne, st. 1, c. 1 (1714). In 1741-44 payment was, on some pretext, withheld by the parish, and to compel the parish officers to collect the necessary rate required a special Act (17 George H. c. 41, 1743), which changed the composition for the future to 200 days' work of eight hours, by teams of three good horses, able to carry 24 bushels each load, each to be attended by two able men. Twenty-three years later, the Vestry Minutes show the parties to be again at issue. "The parishioners present were acquainted that the Trustees of the Kingsland Turnpike Road were making an application to Parliament to enlarge the term and powers of the Acts relating to that Trust, and that by the said Acts the Parish of Hackney are to do yearly 200 days' statute work with teams on that road, or pay to the Trust the sum of £100 in lieu thereof, and that by an Act of the last session of Parliament relating to the public highways, and the determination of His Majesty's Justices of tho Peace in consequence of it, every person liable to do statute work with a team might compound for the same for 4s. 6d. a day instead of the former penalty of 10s.; and that if the said Trustees should obtain a clause in the said intended Act for this Parish to pay the Trust £100 per annum in lieu of statute work, it would be a net loss to the Parish, as the Parish must by composition lose 5s. 6d. in every ten shillings." The Vestry thereupon appointed a committee to watch the bill (MS. Vestry Minutes, Hackney (Middlesex), 12th December 1767). Twelve years later the Vestry opposes another Bill of the same Trust, because it was proposed to fix the rate of composition for the parish contribution of statute labour at too high a figure *(ibid.* 23rd March 1789). Tho sum of £100 seems to have been a favourite one for the annual composition of a large parish. The Surveyor of Highways of the Township of Manchester had, down to 1812, for many years paid to the Trustees of the Oldham Turnpike Roads a lump sum of £100 a year by agreement in "lieu of statute labour and liability, by indictment or otherwise" (MS. Minutes, Oldham Turnpike Trust, 29th August 1806, 11th September 1812).

Page 118. The usual toll was from one to «ix pence. Thus, whilst a horse was charged a penny, every stage coach, hackney coach, carriage, waggon or cart was charged sixpence, every score of sheep a penny, every score of calves or hogs twopence, and every score of cattle sixpence (8 & 9 William III. c. 15, Reigate and Crawley Turnpike Act, 1697). Double tolls were usually charged on Sundays. A later specimen makes the toll on a carriage drawn by six or more horses one shilling, by four sixpence, by two or three threepence, by one three halfpence; a one-horse cart or waggon paid a penny; a two-horse ditto, three halfpence; a horse, mule or ass, a halfpenny; a drove of meat cattle, fivepence a score; a drove of calves, hogs, sheep or lambs, twopence halfpenny a score (11 George II. c. 33, Loughborough and Derby Turnpike Act, 1737).

We do not find in England the ordinary French provision for exacting double tolls at the entrance to the Metropolis, or any place at which the King or Queen is staying (see, for instance, *Liste General des Posies de France dresses par ordre de... Comte Dargenson,* 1751).

Page 118. For power to bring the Turnpike Trust prematurely to an end, see, for instance, 15 Car. H c. 1 (1663), 8 & 9 William HI. c. 15 (1697). A similar power is given to Quarter Sessions in many Turnpike Acts down to the middle of the eighteenth century; but we have not noticed it in any later Act.

Page 118. The regulations as to tickets were varied. A ticket was given on each payment of toll, and this freed the payer from any further payment for the same animal or vehicle during the same day, according to the terms of the particular Local Act and the orders of the particular Trustees, either at that gate, or at that gate and some others, or at all gates on a particular section of road, or at all the gates of the Trust. The "day " usually ended at midnight (sometimes at midnight in summer and 10 P.m. in winter; see 3 George I. c. 4, Hampstead and Highgate Turnpike Act, 1716). A more complicated arrangement prevailed on the Kensington road, where it was expressly ordained " that for all droves of cattle passing through the turnpike gates, the tickets that shall be delivered on Saturday shall be in force till Monday noon following; and the tickets that shall be delivered for droves of cattle every other day besides Saturday shall be in force till the day following at noon" (House of Commons Committee on the Management and Application of money collected during the last eleven years for repairing any particular highway; see House of Commons Journals, 19th April 1763, voL xxix. p. 646).

Page 119. For the provision making the levying of the tolls contingent on sureties for the repair of the road, see 9 & 10 William IH. c. 18 (1698). In an early Bedfordshire Act it was provided that " No turnpike is to be erected nor toll demanded... nor shall the said causey, without the consent of the lord.. . of the... manor.. be laid open for... carriages, until sufficient security be given by able and sufficient persons to the Justices of the Peace... that the said way. .. shall within three years be sufficiently repaired and amended " (5 Anne, c. 10, Hockley and Woburn Turnpike Act, 1706). The Justices' power to investigate the state of the road and the amount of the toll was given, generally, in 9 George I. c. 11 (1722).

Page 120. The general statutes relating to turnpike roads, prior to the consolidating Acts of 1766 and 1773, were 1 George II. c. 19 (1727); 5 George H. c. 33 (1731); 8 George II. c. 20 (1734); 14 George II. c. 42 (1740); 21 George II. c. 28 (1747); 24 George *JL* c. 43 (1750); 26 George II. c. 30 (1753); 28 George II. c. 17 (1755); 30 George H. c. 27 (1757); 30 George II. c. 43 (1757). The Act imposing the penalty of death for destruction of turnpike property was that of 1734. These statutes, together with the consolidating Acts of 1766 and 1773, were made the subject of an able and instructive commentary by John Scott, in his *Digests of the General Highway and Turnpike Laws,* 1778, from which the quotations in the text are taken (pp. 277, 265, and 259). The 1773 Act, together with fifteen subsequent statutes of 1774 (4), 1776 (2), 1777, 1778 (2), 1781, 1785, 1812, 1813, 1815 and 1817, were repealed and re-enacted by 3 George IV. c. 126 (1822); see *The General Turnpike Road Act,* by Joseph Bateman, 1822, and *A Supplement to the General Turnpike Road Act of 3 George IV. c. 126,* by the same, 1823, and, as to the muddle, *An Argument for more of the Division of Labour in Civil Life in this Country,* by William Wiekens, 1829, pp. 67-73.

Page 122. The quotations from petitions for and against Turnpike Bills are from the House of Commons Journals (8th January 1707, 24th January 1709, 20th December 1709 and 3rd February 1710).

Page 123. For the successful turnpike riots at Kingswood in 1727, see Oldmixon's *History of England,* 1735, p. 804; for those at Hereford, see *Read's Weekly Journal,* 25th November 1732, and House of Commons Journals, 2nd and 28th March 1732; compare also the account of those at Ledbury in 1735 in *Daily Gazetteer* for 8th October and 9th December 1735, given in *The Law of Highways,* by W. C. Glen, 1865, pp. 53-5. For the riots at Bristol in 1734 and 1749, see *Annals of Bristol in the Eighteenth Century,* by J. Latimer, p. 157, and *Gentleman's Magazine,* August 1749, p. 276; for that at Leeds in 1753, see *Loidis and Elmete,* by T. D. Whitaker, 1816, p. 77.

Page 125. The optimistic statement of John Holt is in his *General View of the Agriculture of Lancashire,* 1794. It was quoted in Second Report of House of Commons Committee on Highways, 1808, Appendix 7a, p. 183.

Page 125. For the condition of the Glasgow to London road in 1739, see Dr. Bannatyne's scrapbook, quoted from in Cleland's *Statistical Account of Glasgow; Penny Magazine,* 16th March 1833; Place MSS. 27828-10. For the foreigner's acoount of the road from London to Land's End, see *Gentleman's Magazine,* November 1752. Two years later, another correspondent stated that, out of the 172 miles to Exeter, there are "no turnpikes more than 40 miles from London, except... people go round by Bath or Wells" *(ibid.* August 1754).

Page 125. The reference to the multiplicity of turnpikes around one particular city is in the *Gentleman's Magazine,* August 1752.

Page 126. For the opinion of the Commissioners employed by the Board of Agriculture in 1794, see, for instance, *General View of the Agriculture of Hereford,* by John Clark, 1794, p. 51; *General View of the Agriculture of Northumberland,* by John Bailey and George Culley, 1794, p. 56; *General View of the Agriculture of Durham,* by John Granger, 1794, p. 26. "Had... plans and sections," sums up Thomas Butterworth Baylcy, "been sent with the petitions for Turnpike Acts during the last 40 or 20 years, Parliament would not have sanctioned the enormous waste of public money in carrying on the schemes of ignorant projections or interested individuals."

Page 126. The quotation from the House of Commons Committee is from the Second Report from the House of Commons Committee on Broad Wheel Acts, 1806, p. 12.

Page 126. The quotation as to the wilful diversion from the straight course is from the *General View of the Agriculture of Hereford,* by John Clark, 1794, p. 53.

Page 126. As to the Tamworth case, see *Times* of 31st May and 16th June 1828, which explains that "It so happens... that the residence of Sir Robert Peel is distant from Tamworth about 2 miles and immediately adjacent to his cotton and spinning factories at Fazeley, a village almost exclusively Sir Robert's own property, with a population consisting of his artisans. Under these circumstances Sir Robert has been using his powerful interest to exclude Tamworth in order to bring the road through Fazeley, and the proposed line is now changed accordingly, by which Tamworth will be entirely ruined."

Page 127. The quotation from John Scott is from his *Digests of the General Highway and Turnpike Laws,* 1778, p. 317.

Page 127. The exempted areas of Lancashire are described in the *General View of the Agriculture of Lancashire,* by John Holt, 1794, and in the Second Report of House of Commons Committee on Highways, 1808, Appendix A, p. 182. Another case may be cited from Yorkshire. When in 1802 the trustees of a certain twenty miles of the Great North Road in the North Riding got their Act, the inhabitants of the two little villages of Thirsk and Yarm, which formed the terminal points, secured clauses inserted forbidding the erection of toll gates within four miles of each place. The result was that all local traffic was able to use eight out of the twenty miles free of toll, and cunning travellers managed even to get free of the toll on the other twelve, by using slightly longer parallel bye-lanes *(Statement concerning the Thirsk and Yarm Road,* by the Committee of Trustees, etc., Stockton, 1823).

Page 127. The quotation is from *An Inquiry into the Means of Preserving and Improving the Public Roads,* by Rev. Henry Homer, 1765, pp. 21-2.

Page 128. For the petitions against the new Horsley to Dudbridge road, see House of Commons Journals, 25th and 28th January 1780. A new road, admittedly advantageous, might even be opposed by a rival trader. In 1760 there was a petition presented against a new Turnpike Bill by an individual Derbyshire coalowner on the plea that the new road would "give such advantage to the proprietors of the collieries" near it as to be detrimental to his trade (House of Commons Journals, 22nd February 1760). For the petition against the Macclesfield and Buxton Turnpike Trust Bill, see *ibid.* 21st February 1780. For the struggles between the rival roads between London and the North, see *ibid.* January and February 1750. For that in protection of Maidenhead, see *ibid.* 9th June 1800.

Page 129. For cases of the grant of

"pontage" during the fourteenth century, see the references to the Parliament Rolls in *History of Private Bill Legislation,* by F. Clifford, 1887, voL i. pp. 25-35.

Page 129. It was in 1621 that the Lancashire Quarter Sessions was seeking to suppress the exaction of tolls on County Bridges. "The Justices here present are of opinion that if any toll or stellage be taken for the carriage over Crosford Bridge or any other bridge repaired by the common charge of the County the same is extortion, and ought not to be taken or paid, and that the takers thereof shall be dealt with withall by indictment of extortion *quo warranto* or otherwise as the law will warrant, yet nevertheless all bridges shall be repaired by the charge of Counties and Hundreds as formerly they have been accustomed" *(Manchester Sessions Notes of Proceedings, 1616-16S3,* edited by Ernest Axon, 1901, p. 142). More than a century later, the Essex Quarter Sessions had expressly to require the "owners of any bridge or bridges built over any river or stream running across any highways. .. immediately (to) take or cause to be taken the chain or chains from off the same" (MS. Minutes, Quarter Sessions, Essex, 15th July 1746).

Page 129. Among the Local Aots authorising toll bridges to be built by Municipal Corporations may be mentioned those of Norwich (1726), Windsor (1735), London (1756, 1768, 1762, 1767, etc.), Maidenhead (1772). Special bodies of commissioners were incorporated by Local Acts for the purpose of building and maintaining Westminster Bridge (1741, 1744, 1745); Putney Bridge (1725); Preston Bridge (1750); Deritend Bridge at Birmingham (1788, 1792, 1813 and 1822; see *Old and New Birmingham,* by R. K. Dent, pp. 421-2; *A Century of Birmingham Life,* by J. A Langford, pp. 68-71); Bishopwearmouth Bridge at Sunderland (1792, 1814). To these must be added the Local Acts obtained by landowners or private speculators, such as those for bridges at Walton-on-Thames (20 Geo. II. c. 22,1746) and Hampton Court (23 Geo. II. c. 37, 1749), and those relating to the various toll bridges built by joint-stock companies in the Metropolis (Report of House of Commons Committees on Metropolitan Bridges, 1854, 1876, 1877 and 1881). The most valuable toll bridge, still existing as private property, is probably that of Lord St. Levan, connecting Plymouth with Devonport, and yielding a revenue of many thousands a year. In 1800 the tolls were rented from year to year at the "immense sum of £2500 " *(The Plymouth Dock Guide,* 1800, p. 28; *A View of Plymouth Dock,* 1812, p. 53).

Page 130. It would be wrong to imply that the establishment of the Turnpike Trust did not lead to some improvements in road-making. Thus, the remarkable work of " Blind Jack of Knaresborough " (1717-1810), the self-taught genius at simple road construction, was wholly executed for the Turnpike Trusts of Yorkshire, Lancashire, Derbyshire and Cheshire *(John Metcalf, His Life,* 1795; *Lives of the Engineers,* by Samuel Smiles, 1861; *Old Yorkshire,* by William Smith, 1883, pp. 170-74; *Road Making and Maintenance,* by Thomas Aikken, 1900, p. 11). But only very slowly and gradually does the idea arise that the construction and maintenance of roads requires expert knowledge and professional training. The eighteenth-century roads had not the advantage even of such engineering skill as then existed, as road-making was regarded as beneath the dignity of a civil engineer; and right down to the nineteenth century this profession," says Sir Henry Parnell, "has been too commonly deemed by Turnpike Trustees as something rather to be avoided than as useful and necessary to be called to their assistance" *(A Treatise on Roads,* by Sir Henry Parnell, 1833, p. 291). "Every ignorant peasant," it could be said in 1818, " considers himself competent to lay out and execute roads in all /directions " *(Practical Directions for laying out and making Roads,* by James V Clarke, 1818, p. i). Even so wise a man as John Scott could imagine no better road engineer than himself, or any other country gentleman who would apply himself to the details of road administration. Even the art of taking levels," it was said in 1765, "was at first above the capacity of country surveyors, whose contracted ideas extended no further than to the surface of the land which was the scene of their operations. To them it would have appeared a chimerical undertaking to have attempted to execute any plan for reducing ground to a regular descent when it was to be effected by raising valleys and sinking hills" *(An Inquiry into the Means of Preserving and Improving the Public Roads,* by Henry Homer, 1765, p. 33).

In 1800 we find a Turnpike Trust suggesting the engaging, "at least experimentally," of "some person or persons scientifically acquainted with and practically experienced in the formation and management of turnpike roads. Without hastily abandoning the present system, a trial might be made by the mile on certain parts of the road... and thus your surveyor might be improved in theory and in practice, and a desirable emulation be excited " *(Report of Committee of Trustees of (he Hammersmith and Brentford Turnpikes,* 1800, p. 17).

Page 130. The examples of the Justices' action are taken from the Minutes of Quarter Sessions, Essex, 1704-75. In 1704 "it is ordered that Mr. L. and Mr. E. A. of Coxford in this County are hereby appointed Surveyors for the road lying between Kelvedon and Strennaway, commonly called Domsey Road, for one whole year, and... that all the moneys now in the hands of... (the) Receivers of the toll at the turnpike be by them paid unto the said Surveyors and by them... to be employed and laid out in repairing Domsey Road " (MS. Minutes, Quarter Sessions, Essex, 25th April 1704). For 15 Orders for payments to as many parishes, see MS. Minutes, Quarter Sessions, Essex, 5th October 1725. For the order to the Justices to view the roads in their Divisions, *ibid.* 15th January 1722.

Page 131. The quotation is from the *General View of the Agriculture of Surrey,* by W. James and Jacob Malcolm, p. 62.

Page 132. The quotation as to "farming" is from *Digests of the General*

Highway and Turnpike Laws, by John Scott, 1778, p. 345.

Page 132. *Dissertation concerning the Present State of the High Roads oj England, especially those near London,* by Robert Phillips, 1737, pp. 3, 4,15.

Page 133. As to the fantastic shapes of roads, see *Digest of the General Highway and Turnpike Laws,* by John Scott, 1778, p. 322. "Some roads in England... are laid wavy, or rising and falling, and men attend... after rain, to let out the water with their spades" *(Gentleman's Magazine,* May 1749, p. 218). "In level countries, where the roads are cut, these waves are absolutely necessary.... The first waving of the roads was begun in Whitechapel on the Essex Road," or else in Leicestershire. "The waves were then short and high, and soon were found so excessively inconvenient to the travellers, both on foot and horseback and in carriages, that they were discarded.... The Hackney road... followed the waving method, but made the ascents and descents longer" *(ibid.* November 1759).

"The angle in the pantile roof road," observes Scott, " is often so great as to endanger overturning on the least collision of carriages, and always enough to occasion anxiety to the timorous passenger" *(Digests of the General Highway and Turnpike Laws,* by John Scott, 1778, p. 320). For the concave road or hollow way, see *Dissertation concerning the Stale of the High Roads of England,* by R. Phillips, 1737, p. 15. This is, we imagine, the "washway" referred to in the *Inquiry into the Means of Preserving and Improving the Public Roads,* by Rev. Henry Homer, 1765, p. 30. In such a road, "instead of the water being thrown off, it is here made the repairing agent, by being conducted from the sides to the centre, and from thence to the lowest part of the road, where a side outlet is made for it; in its course the water washes the whole surface, carries off the mud, and leaves the road firm and clean " (C. M. Ward to Sir John Sinclair in Report from House of Commons Committee on Broad Wheels and Turnpike Roads, 1809). The wilful obstruction of any "water which, by order of the Trustees or their Surveyor, shall be reserved to run or be let in upon any part of the said road " was often made punishable by fine and imprisonment (see, for instance, 17 George III. c. 20).

Page 133. See, for the best opinion on road-making in 1778, the admirable Appendix "On the Construction and Preservation of Roads," in the *Digests of the General Highway and Turnpike Laws,* by John Scott, 1778, pp. 313-52.

Page 134. For the cases of road-widening cited, see *Notes from the Hertfordshire County Records,* p. 39; and MS. Minutes, Quarter Sessions, Essex, 5th October 1725; and *Gentleman's Magazine,* May 1753.

Page 135. See, for all this, the *Minutes of the Epping and Ongar Highway Trust, 1769-1870,* by Benjamin Winstone, 1891.

It may be here noted that it is to the turnpike roads that we owe the general establishment of milestones, which (if we ignore those which were placed by the Romans on their roads) date from about 1720. At first they were put up voluntarily on a few roads. "At every mile from Grantham to Stangate," says Defoe, "are stones set up by Mr. Boulton which he designed to have carried on to London for the general benefit" *(Tour through the whole Island of Great Britain,* by Daniel Defoe, vol. iii. p. 28, edition of 1748). Prom about 1744 most Turnpike Acts contain a clause (see, for instance, 17 George II. c. 4, Chatham and Canterbury Turnpike Act, 1744) requiring the Trustees to measure their road and set up stones or posts stating the distance. In 1766 this requirement (including also those of direction posts at crossways and " graduated posts or stones " where the road was subject to "deep or dangerous floods ") was made universal by 7 George III. c. 40, sec. 30 (the General Turnpike Act, 1766), re-enacted by 13 George III. c. 84, sec. 41 (the General Turnpike Act, 1773). The "milestones" were sometimes wooden posts; those of the Epping and Ongar Turnpike Trust in 1787 were to be of oak, 5 feet high and 11 inches wide; angular, with letters and figures on each side denoting the distance from Epping and Chelmsford respectively *(Minutes of the Epping and Ongar Highway Trust, 1769-1870,* by B. Winstone, 1891, p. 138).

The signpost is earlier than the milestone. Paul Hentzner, the German traveller, was directed by a signpost in Kent in 1598 *(ItinerariumGermaniae, Galliae, Angliae, Italiae,* by Paul Hentzner, 1612). In 1695 we read of Lancashire, " they have one good thing the most parts of this Comity... that at all cross ways there are posts with hands pointing to each road with the names of the great town or market towns that it leads to " *(Through England on a Side-Saddle... Diary of Celia Fiennes,* edited by the Hon. Mrs. Griffiths, 1888, p. 157). As early as 1697 the Justices in Special Highway Sessions were authorised to require Surveyors of Highways to put up a " direction stone or post" at " cross highways" (8 & 9 William in. c. i6).

Page 135. With regard to jobbery, it seems to have been quite usual for a Turnpike Trust in spite of an express prohibition by Parliament, to give orders for materials or work to individual Trustees. Thus, when a House of Commons Committee looked into the accounts of the Kensington Turnpike Trust for 1764, it was found that an incredible number of loads of gravel were entered as put on three-quarters of a mile of road (Piccadilly) between Clarges Street and Knightsbridge; and further enquiry revealed that the gravel was supplied by one of the Trustees. All the carpenter's work of the same Trust was contracted for by the partner of another Trustee (Report of House of Commons Committee appointed to enquire into the application of money collected within the last twelve years, by virtue of any Act of Parliament, for repairing any particular highway, 1765; see House of Commons Journals, vol. xxix.). Adam Smith had, it will be remembered, the meanest opinion of the financial management of Turnpike Trustees. "The money levied is more than double of what is necessary for executing, in the completest manner, the work, which is often executed in a very slovenly manner, and sometimes not at all" *(Wealth of Nations)*. John Scott, who knew them at first hand, remarks that "the Surveyors of turnpike roads... are frequently decayed farmers or tradesmen, recommended by some friend or relation to an office they are absolutely unqualified to execute."... Some "Trustees... are most earnest to provide a maintenance for their poor favourites by recommending them to offices they are unfit for" *(Digests of the General Highway and Turnpike Laws,* by John Scott, 1778, pp. 255, 350).

Page 136. Evasion by taking off supplementary horses before coming to the turnpike gate was specifically forbidden by 24 George II. (1750). There is a reference to this practice in *Gentleman's Magazine,* September 1752. Lightening the load in the same way was prohibited by 13 George III. c. 84, sec. 10 (General Turnpike Act, 1773). "Returning by way of frolio," relates Sir Nathaniel Wraxall, " very late at night, on horseback, to Wimbledon from Addiscombe, the seat of Mr. Jenkinson, near Croydon, where the party had dined, Lord Thurlow the Chancellor, Pitt and Dundas found the turnpike gate situate between Tooting and Streatham thrown open. Being elevated above their usual prudence, and having no servant near them, they passed through tho gate at a brisk pace, without stopping to pay the toll, regardless of the remonstrances and threats of the turnpike man, who running after them discharged the contents of his blunderbuss at their backs. Happily he did no injury."

Page 136. The exemption found most serious to the Turnpike Trustees seems to have been that in favour of manure carts, perhaps because of the fact that, with the increasing use of town manure (which Arthur Young found still unusual in most parts of England), this exemption became greatly stretched. "It would undoubtedly be a real hardship on a farmer," said Scott already in 1778, " to pay toll for bringing dung a few poles' length from his own yard to his own fields... but the matter is quite dissimilar when old rags, chalk, lime, bones, etc., are carried, in heavy loads, ten, twelve and perhaps twenty miles, and at once reap the benefit of the road and contribute to damage it" *(Digests of the General Highway and Turnpike Laws,* by John Scott, 1778, p. 276). It was just these "narrow wheeled waggons carrying muck from Norwich" that were complained of in 1808 as perpetually cutting up that turnpike road. "The damage which this never-ceasing wear and tear does to the road," it was said, "is much greater than arises from all the other traffic upon it put together" *(Second Report of House of Commons Committee on Highways,* 1808). Attempts were made to get also exempted carts and waggons going empty to town in order to bring back manure; see the report of the meeting of "gentlemen, farmers, gardeners, and landowners" held in London, *Morning Advertizer,* 4th April 1810. This was conceded by Parliament under complicated restrictions. The toll was to be paid, and a special " manure ticket" given in exchange, on production of which on the return journey with manure, the money was to be repaid by the tollcollector (52 George III. c. 145, 53 George III. c. 82).

Page 136. Special exemptions in the interests of particular trades inoluded the following: (a) flour-milling: Exempted from toll were "all persons who shall carry any grist to be ground for their own private use, and all horses (called the load horses) employed by any miller to carry grist belonging to any private family to or from the mill," as well as "horses and carriages " used to carry materials for " building and repairing mills," 17 George II. c. 13 (Evesham Turnpike Act, 1743); (6) cloth making: 20 George II. c. 6 (Reading and Puntfield Turnpike Act, 1746); (e) coal-carrying: 24 George II. c. 11 (Lancaster and Richmond Turnpike Act, 1750); *(d)* peat-carrying: 20 George II. c. 6, 1746; (e) hay and straw carrying: 17 George II. c. 13 (Evesham Turnpike Act, 1743).

Page 137. The invariable provision as to doubled tolls on Sundays did not satisfy the Sabbatarians, and it was frequently urged that there should be "a great additional toll at each turnpike gate," on carriages passing through on Sunday; see for such a recommendation in 1800, *Anecdotes of the Life oj Richard Watson, Bishop of Llandaff,* by his son, Richard Watson, 1817, p. 342.

Page 137. As to exemption on election days, see, for instance, 24 George II. c. 29 (Ludlow Turnpike Act, 1750), we append a specimen exemption clause: "No toll shall be taken for any person... carrying any quantity of materials for repairing the said road; or for carrying dung, mould, soil or compost of any kind for manuring lands or gardens; nor for carrying hay or corn in the straw being the product of... the said townships... to be laid up in the houses, etc., of the... inhabitants... nor shall toll be taken for any ploughs or other instruments of husbandry... nor for any person residing in the townships... passing. .. to and from church... or who shall attend the funeral of any persons who shall die or be buried in either of the said townships; or for post-horses carrying the mail or packet; or for any cattle going to or from water or pasture; nor for the horses of soldiers on the march or carriages attending them; or for horses, carta or waggons travelling with vagrants sent by legal passes" (24 George II. c. 13, Stretford and Hulme Turnpike Act, 1750). As regards soldiers, " in early Turnpike Acts, as for instance local statutes passed in Charles II.'s and later reigns, the army upon its march was exempted from the tolls thereby imposed. In 1778 the General Turnpike Act (18 Geo. III. c. 63) contained the first general exception in favour of the Army, which in the year 1799 was inserted in the Mutiny Act" *(Military Forces of the Crown,* by C. M. Clode, 1869, vol. i. p. 214). The exemption in favour of the Post Office had a similar history. Practically all Turnpike Acts contained clauses exempting the mails, but some mentioned only post-horses, others also carriages carrying mails. A General Act of 1785 made the broader exemption universal (25 George III. c. 57).

Page 137. We append some particulars as to these compositions. In a 1746 Act a clause was inserted exempting from toll " the owners, occupiers and inhabitants of Coley House and of the farm adjoining thereunto... their several workmen, servants and agents... with horses, cattle, coaches, carts and carriages" (20 George II. c. 6, Reading and Puntfield Turnpike Act, 1746).

In lieu of erecting a new turnpike gate at a certain point, the Trustees of the Lincoln and Peterborough Road were authorised to agree with the inhabitants of fifteen specified parishes for an annual payment of not more than £40 each, in lieu of toll; so long as this sum is paid, the gate is not to be erected (39 & 40 George III. c. 70, Lincoln and Peterborough Turnpike Act, 1800).

In 1764 the "compositions" received by the Kensington Turnpike Trust amounted to £326, or 8 per cent of the total receipts from toll; and those of the Marylebone Turnpike Trust to £308, or 13 per cent (Report of House of Commons Committee to enquire into the application of money, etc., 1765).

For the Epping and Ongar case, see *Minutes of the Epping and Ongar Highway Trust, 1769-1870,* by Benjamin Winstone, 1891, pp. 103-104, 137-138, 154.

Page 138. For the prohibition of "pikemen" to leave their posts, see Report of House of Commons Committee on tho management and application of money collected during the last eleven years for repairing any particular highway; House of Commons Journals, 19th April 1763, vol. xxix. p. 646.

Page 138. Letting of Tolls.

In 1709, the turnpike on the " Mountnessing road... with its profits and tolls " was let by the Essex justices to a man for £400 per annum; and in 1710 the lease was renewed to the same tenant at the same rent for three years (MS. Minutes, Quarter Sessions, Essex, 12th July 1709, 11th July 1710).

"Ordered... that it be referred to the Justices of the Peace of Chelmsford Division or to any two of them at their Petty Sessions... to treat with the present tenants of the profits of the Turnpike arising at Mountnessing or with any other person for the letting the same for a term of years, and that they endeavour to procure the best rent and tenants that can be got for the same, and do mako report thereof at tho next General Quarter Sessions" (MS. Minutes, Quarter Sessions, Essex, 7th October 1718).

The West Kent Justices in Quarter Sessions let the " profits and tolls" of the turnpike at Chalk in 1747 to the local alehousekeeper for £260 a year, and in 1750 to "James Pearson of Chalk, Labourer," for £300 for a year (MS. Minutes, Quarter Sessions, West Kent, 6th June 1747, and 11th January 1750). In 1773 alehousekeepers were prohibited from being either Turnpike Trustees, or surveyors or toll-collectors; but they might become toll-farmers, if they employed others as collectors (13 George III. c. 84, sec. 46, General Turnpike Act, 1773).

Page 138. The quotation as to the pikeman's costume is from *The Exeter Road,* by C. G. Harper, 1899, p. 4.

Page 138. The statutory requirement of a minute-glass at toll auctions is in 13 Geo. HI. c. 84, sec. 31. For specimen advertisements of such lettings, see that of the Trustees of the Whetstone Turnpike, *Morning Adverlizer,* 25th January 1806; the Trustees of the Marylebone Turnpike, for two newly erected " weighing engines or bridges," *ibid.* 19th May 1806; the Trustees of the Old Street Road Turnpike, *ibid.* 22nd March 1810; the Trustees of the Surrey New Roads, and those of the Old District of Brentford (including weighing engine), *ibid.* 13th February 1818. The toll auctions wore frequently made scenes of convivial festivity, in order to attract possible bidders. In one case, in 1814, £10 was granted for a dinner to those who attended the auction *(Minutes of the Epping and Ongar Highway Trust, 1769-1870,* by Benjamin Winstone, 1891, p. 172). A graphic description of a letting of tolls in the early part of the nineteenth oentury is given in *Records oj Old Times,* by J. K. Fowler, 1898, chap. ii. The sums involved were sometimes very large. One gate on the Brighton road was said to take £2400 a year in tolls. Levy, who was the Napoleon of toll-farmers, is said to have contracted at one time for as much as half a million a year, being a third of the aggregate toll revenue of the Kingdom; as well as for £300,000 a year post-horse duty *(Highways and Horses,* by Athol Maudslay, 1888, pp. 84-85; *Old Coaching Days,* by Stanley Harris, 1882, p. 188). The tolls of the Whetstone Turnpike Trust, for 8 miles in Middlesex of the London and Holyhead road, were let by auction in 1831 for no less than £7530 per annum *(Middlesex and Hertfordshire Notes and Queries,* vol. iv. pp. 91-94). At this time there were daily on the road to Barnet "18 mails and 176 other coaches, besides road waggons, postchaises and other vehicles" *(Tl«e Holyhead Road,* by C. G. Harper, 1902,. vol. i. p. 27).

Page 139. As to "knock-outs" and other conspiracies with regard to toll auctions, it was definitely said in 1833 that " combinations have been... successfully organized to defeat the provisions of the said Act... with regard to the letting of tolls" (Second Report of House of Lords Committee on Turnpike Trusts, 1833). One such combination or " knock-out" we see in the case of the letting of the Epping and Ongar Turnpike tolls in 1801, when the two pretended rivals in the auction-room afterwards come forward jointly to take up the contract which had been knocked down to one of them for £1055. The Trustees "suspected that there had been underhand proceedings... collusion between those bidding for the tolls." This was eventually admitted by the parties, who agreed to an increase in the price to £1201, at which a lease was granted to them *(Minutes of the Epping and Ongar Highway Trust, 1769-1870,* by Benjamin Winstone, 1891, pp. 162-164).

Page 139. The quotation as to fraud by pikemen is from a letter of C. M. Ward to Sir John Sinclair; see Report of House of Commons Committee on Broad Wheels and Turnpike Roads, 1809, Appendix A. There are frequent complaints as to the arbitrary exactions of the " pikemen" from inexperienced or timid travellers; see letter to *Times,* 18th June 1824. The lessee of the Epping and Ongar tolls in 1816 was found persistently "taking more tolls on coaches, postchaises, etc., than he was entitled to." Criminal proceedings against him were begun, but subsequently compromised *(Minutes of the Epping and Ongar Highway Trust, 1769-1870,* by Benjamin Winstone, 1891, pp. 173-174).

Page 140. The provision as to a weighing machine is in 14 Geo. II. c. 42 (1740); the power was often specifically repeated in Turnpike Acts; see, for instance, 20 George II. c. 7, Essex Turnpike Act, 1746; it was afterwards embodied in the General Turnpike Acts, 7 George III. c. 40, sec. 1, and 13 George HI. c. 84, sec. 1. For the uncertainty of such weighings, see Report of House of Commons Committee on the General Turnpike Acts, 1796, p. 749. "The persons concerned in the trade of market gardeners never are able to know the weight of their articles, for sometimes it happens from a shower of rain a loading of 2 tons 5 cwt. will be increased three or four hundredweights."

Page 140. As to the dilemmas presented by the weighing machine, see letters from C. M. Ward and F. Dickins to Sir John Sinclair, in Report of House of Commons Committee on Broad Wheels and Turnpike Roads, 1809, Appendix A. The Clerk to the Trustees of the Stamford Hill roads said that he was satisfied that the lessees of the weighing machines suffered "carriages to pass through upon a certain weekly sum without weighing them," though he could not prove it. This led to the recommendation: "that... as weighing engines are intended to prevent excessive weights, and not to increase the revenue of the turnpikes, the trustees of road should be restrained from leasing or otherwise letting the same " (Report of House of Commons Committee on the General Turnpike Acts, 1796).

It was perhaps in consequence of this dilemma that these costly weighing engines were sometimes left, like one at Hammersmith in 1800, "for many years disused and suffered to fall into decay " *(Report of a Committee of the Hammersmith and Brentford Turnpike,* 1800, p. 7). Already in 1796 the Trustees of the Surrey Turnpike had removed their engine seven or eight years before (Report of House of Commons Committee on the General Turnpike Acts, 1796). A Committee in 1833 recommended the total "abolition of the use of weighing engines" (Second Report of House of Lords Committee on Turnpike Trusts, 1833).

Among other heavy vehicles objected to came, in the latter part of the century, the heavily laden stage coaches, which were exempt from subjection to the weighing engines. An Act of 1788 restricted them to six outside passengers, in addition to two on the box by the driver (28 George III. a 57). A more stringent measure in 1790, known as " Gammon's Aot,"

M attempted to reduce this to four and one respectively, or fewer if under three horses, and did its best to prevent drivers allowing more by imposing a toll of five shillings on every passenger in excess (30 George III. c. 36). But, as with the excess tolls for overweight, it was soon found that the pikemen "notoriously compound with the drivers of coaches," and the practice continued unabated *(Report of Committee of Hammersmith and Brentford Turnpikes,* 1800, pp. 18, 33). "Mr. Gammon's Act," it was pointed out in 1794, "is now openly set at defiance, and sometimes 20 persons are to be found at the outside of a stage coach on the roof which by law is limited to six " *(Times,* 19th April 1794). "The salutary regulations provided by these Acts," reported a Committee of 1806, " have been by a variety of contrivances most grossly evaded, insomuch that instead of 6 (the number limited by the original Act) 20 passengers and more are often carried on the outside of stage coaches" with results not only " extremely destructive" to the roads, but also dangerous, as " scarce a week passes without some of these carriages breaking down" (First Report from House of Commons Committee on Broad Wheels and Turnpikes Roads, 1806). A further Act was then passed, facilitating the enforcement of the preceding ones (46 George III. c. 136). See *The Danger of Travelling on Stage Coaches and a Remedy Proposed,* by Rev. W. Milton, 1810, and *Brief Considerations on the Present State of the Police of the Metropolis,* by L. B. Allen, 1821.

Page 141. *Observations on the General Highway and Turnpike Acts,* by Thomas Butterworth Bayley, 1773, p. 52. "Cases may be found," said the House of Commons Committee, "where persons taking the management are rather disposed to maintain establishments beneficial to themselves, than to relieve... the public burdens" (Second Report of House of Commons Committee on Highways, 1808). "There is not a gentleman in the Kingdom," writes one who was himself a squire, "who cannot bear testimony to the lax manner in which the duties of turnpike road commissioners are discharged, to the total absence of all personal responsibility... and to the general improvidence of the expenditure" *(A Letter to the Right Hon. C. B. Bathursl, M.P., on the subject oj the Poor Laws,* by Richard Blakemore, 1819, p. 32).

Page 142. When the Post Office wanted to extend its mail coach service from Shrewsbury to Holyhead, and found the turnpike road actually unsafe, the Postmaster-General began by sending letters to the Treasurers of the several Turnpike Trusts on the route, asking them to effect improvements. This producing no result, he had 21 parishes indicted, and thus compelled them to do some repairs, though they proved insufficient to bring the road up to the requirements of a fast mail coach route (Second Report of House of Commons Committee on the Holyhead Road, 1810; *Her Majesty's Mails,* by W. Lewins, 1864, p. 142).

The provision as to apportioning the fine and costs is in 13 George III. c. 84, sec. 33, General Turnpike Act, 1773. "As the Law now stands," wrote Sir J. C. Hippisley to Sir John Sinclair in 1808, "if any part of a turnpike road be out of repair, remedy is given by presentment or indictment of the parish in which such road is situate, subjecting the parish to great exponse and inconvenience, although the nuisance be wholly imputable to the trustees of the turnpike. ... It is true that... Quarter Sessions may apportion fines and costs between the Parish and Turnpike Trust, yet this power can afford very inadequate relief or compensation in many cases, where the parishes have been harassed by prosecutions for nuisances for which they have in no respect been equitably responsible, for their parish officers, travelling thirty or forty miles to the Quarter Sessions, for loss of time, &c." (Sir J. C. Hippisley, Bart., M.P., to Sir John Sinclair, 4th April 1808; Second Report of House of Commons Committee on Highways, 1808, Appendix A., p. 136.)

Page 143. *Loidis and Elmete,* by T. D. Whitaker, 1816, p. 82.

"That it is the opinion of this Committee that, in the case of any presentment or indiotment of any highway being a turnpike road, the said presentment or indictment should be preferred against the treasurer of such Trust, instead of the parish through which such roads run " (Report of House of Commons Committee on Broad Wheels and Turnpike Roads, 1809).

Page 143. The quotation from R. L. Edgeworth is from *An Essay on the Construction of Roads.*

Page 144. Praise of particular roads. "The Commissioners of the road from Whitechapel into Essex very well understand and perform their office.... Justico ought to be done also to the Commissioners of the Turnpikes leading into Kent over Shooters Hill, who endeavour to make the road straight, by cutting off all angles, and widening it" *(Gentleman's Magazine,* May 1749). Speaking generally of the roads in England, a writer declares in 1754 that "amendments made of late years... have been very considerable.... The turnpike now forming from Truro to Falmouth, on the West, and to Grampound on the East, I look upon as a very masterly and complete piece of workmanship; and indeed, it must be acknowledged that the new turnpikes are better than the old. Thus, the Taunton Turnpikes are better than the Bath or Bristol; the Exeter better than either; and the Truro in a fair way to exceed them all" *(Gentleman's Magazine,* October 1754). The dithyrambic quotation is from *An Enquiry into the Means of Preserving and Improving the Public Roads,* by Henry Homer, 1765, p. 8.

We may quote a few of these statements of the surveyors employed by the Board of Agriculture in 1794. Of Kent we read that "the turnpike roads, and those most frequented, are kept in tolerably good order; but the bye-roads of West Kent are frequently impassable for postchaises" *(General View of the Agriculture of Kent,* by J. Boyes, 1796, p. 90). Of Westmoreland it is said that " the great roads leading through the county are kept in excellent repair by the sums collected at the turnpike gates" *(General View of the Agriculture of Westmoreland,* by A Pringle, 1794, p. 37). The Nottinghamshire reporter testifies that " the roads of this country are of late years much improved, many parishes having learnt from the example of the turnpikes to form them properly, and have them executed under an understanding surveyor" *(General View of the Agriculture of Nottingham,* by R. Lowe, 1794, p. 53). Of Northumberland it is said that "the turnpike roads are most in good order, but badly designed" *(General View of the Agriculture of Northumberland,* by J. Bailey and G. Culley, 1794, p. 56). As to Lancashire, where manufactures had so enormously increased, and turnpikes were almost universal, we are told that " Great exertions have been of late years at very considerable expense to improve the roads, the effects of which are very apparent" *(General View of the Agriculture of Lancashire,* by John Holt, 1794, p. 64).

Page 145. *A Treatise on Roads,* by Sir Henry Parnell, afterwards Lord Oongleton, 1833, pp. 263-264, 288-289.

CHAPTER VIII

"PONTIFEX MAXIMUS TELFORD" AND "MACADAM THE MAGICIAN"

With the opening years of the nineteenth century we become conscious of a change in opinion as to the whole system of road communication. What were then the best-kept turnpikes, once thought something like perfection, come now to be deemed only passable, whilst the condition of the worser sort of roads is again felt to be an intolerable public nuisance, much as it had been at the close of the seventeenth century. It is plain that a much higher standard is being set. We ascribe this onward stride of public opinion to many converging influences. The political necessity for improving the means of communication in Scotland and Ireland had led to successful road-making experiments in those countries, planned by expert engineers, and executed by the regular labour of hired workers. These roads were reported to be better than the best of the English turnpikes. "For a country so far behind us as Ireland," exclaims Arthur Young, in 1780, "to have got suddenly so much the start of us in the article of roads is a spectacle that cannot fail to strike the British traveller." The Irish gentlemen who now came to Westminster found, like R. L. Edgeworth in 1817, "on a journey of many hundred miles, scarcely twenty miles of well-made road," according to the standard set in Ireland. "Comparing all the roads in that country with the roads in England," he continues, "the shameful inferiority of the latter would evidently appear." Englishmen who had seen the Highlands of Scotland reported that the roads laid out by Lord Daer, the eldest son of the Earl of Selkirk; by Abercromby, a gentleman by birth who became a professional road engineer, and especially those executed for the Government Commissioners of Highland Roads by Telford, had effectually opened out those hitherto inaccessible regions. Meanwhile the urgent need for a better system of land communication in England was being consciously felt by powerful sections of the community. The rapid multiplication of public coaches, the development of the postal service, the growing multitude of men and beasts ever on the move from place to place, the huge tonnage of goods now dragged by wains and carts—all this was enormously augmenting the use of the English roads. The agriculturists sending crops to market, the merchants and manufacturers intent on disposing of their greatly augmented output of wares, the newly enriched classes hankering after the luxuries of the East and the West, were none of them in the humour to put up with the constant delays and extravagant cost of land carriage to which the previous century had been accustomed. This new note of discontent with the roads is heard in evergrowing strength in a series of House of Commons Committees extending, almost without interruption, from 1806 to 1830. "It is a matter to be wondered at," reports the Committee of 1808, "that so great a source of national concern has hitherto been so much neglected." "The many important advantages," reports the Committee of 1811, "to be derived from amending the highways and turnpike roads of the kingdom need hardly be dwelt upon. Every individual in it would thereby find his comforts materially increased and his interest greatly promoted. By the improvement of our roads, every branch of our agricultural, commercial and manufacturing industry would be materially benefited. Every article brought to market would be diminished in price; the number of horses would be so much reduced that by these and other retrenchments the expense of five millions would be annually saved to the public. The expense of repairing roads, and the wear and tear of carriages and horses, would be essentially diminished, and thousands of acres, the produce of which is now wasted in feeding unnecessary horses would be devoted to the production of food for man." For the first few years the deliberations of these successive Committees seenTto have been dominated by the old assumption that what had to be discovered was some way of regulating the use of the roads so that their maintenance should involve the minimum of cost. Hence we find elaborate resolutions, appendices and notes of evidence concerned with the shape of wheels, the weight of waggons, the defects of weighing machines and the overcrowding of passenger coaches. The impression which these voluminous discussions of archaic technique leaves on the student is that, in the matter of road administration, the landed interest in the House of Commons had made scarcely any intellectual progress during a whole century. Only very gradually does there arise a suspicion that even economy might be furthered by putting more thought and care into the actual construction of the roads. But this leads to nothing more practical than haphazard resolutions condemning the scandalous negligence of the Surveyors of Highways, the slovenly performance of Statute Labour, in-j capacity of the men jobbed in as turnpike officials, the circuitous and badly constructed roads which they provided, and the reckless finance which was steering more and more of the Turnpike Trusts into bankruptcy. It is difficult to see how the House of Commons would have got out of these meanderings, if it had not been for the energetic intervention of two Government departments, and the emerging, under the patronage of the chiefs of these departments, of two experienced enthusiasts, Thomas Telford and John Loudon Macadam.

The first effective step forward came from the General Post Office. The growing postal business of the country, at a time when all mails were road-borne, and, since the union between England and Ireland, the need for improving the means of travel between London and Holyhead, had, from the very beginning of the nineteenth century, been leading the Postmaster-General to interest himself in the state of the main lines of road. We see him writing to different Turnpike Trusts, stirring up Quarter Sessions, indicting parishes and sending his " riding surveyors" to inspect the principal routes. Whatever success these measures may have had elsewhere, they proved quite ineffectual in getting anything like a decent road between London and Holyhead, which the Postmaster-General found actually unsafe for a mail coach. The Irish Members of Parliament, and all who had occasion to use this route perpetually complained of "the extreme inconvenience, difficulty and danger of travelling it." A Special Committee of the House of Commons in 1810 reported strongly that something must be done. The Government then bethought themselves of the promoted stone-mason and County Surveyor, Thomas Telford— Southey's "Pontifex Maximus "— who had been, since 1803, successfully overcoming the hills and bridging the streams for the Commissioners of Highland Roads; and in 1810 he was set to work to make a complete survey of the line. In 1815 the Treasury summoned up enough courage to ask the House of Commons to grant £20,000 towards the construction of the necessary lengths of new road, as an enterprise transcending the capacity of any existing local road authority. As in the case of the Highland Roads, the work was entrusted to a special body of commissioners, established by Act of Parliament. These commissioners, ten in number, had at their head three Ministers of the Crown, but the really active member, to whom in practice the administrative work was left, and who for twenty years seems to have devoted nearly the whole of his energy to it, was Sir Henry Parnell, Bart, M.P. , afterwards Lord Congleton, who had been, we read, "the principal instrument in carrying the Holyhead Road Bills through Parliament."

In the annual reports of these Holyhead Road Commissioners, and in the proceedings of the various Parliamentary Committees which considered the matter between 1810 and 1830, we see all concerned falling more and more under the influence of Telford, and becoming more and more convinced that what was necessary to improve the roads was engineering skill and organised professional administration. The particular task which they had taken in hand was, indeed, one of difficulty. They found the Welsh part of the road "in the worst possible condition,... exceedingly narrow,... carried unnecessarily over hills, the ascents... often... 1 in 10,1 in 8, and even 1 in 7, many parts... very dangerous to travellers... along the side of precipices." The English part of the road, from London to Shrewsbury, was, in many parts, seriously defective, soaring over unnecessary hills, wandering about in circuitous routes, and having so bad a surface as to be perpetually out of repair. The whole line of 194 miles was divided among no fewer than 23 separate Turnpike Trusts, which the

Commissioners had no authority to supersede. Each of these Trusts had to be separately argued with, and persuaded to allow the Government Engineer to execute the works necessary to improve its bit of line. The 17 English Trusts were, with two exceptions, left undisturbed in their authority. But in each of their bits of road Telford had a free hand in carrying out the particular improvement—lowering a steep ascent, raising a hollow way, embanking a slough, cutting through a hill, building a bridge, or making an entirely new line of road—which he thought necessary. When the work was done, an addition of fifty per cent was made to the local tolls, and the proceeds of this surtax were handed over to the Parliamentary Commissioners. And although the various Trusts retained their own Surveyors for current maintenance, Telford was always up and down the road acting as inspector, advising here, criticising there, and presently coming to be virtually in the position of consulting engineer all along the line. In two cases, indeed, those of the Whetstone and St. Albans Trusts, administering highly important stretches of road between London and St. Albans, the road was so bad, and the management so hopelessly incompetent, that a House of Commons Committee proposed, in 1828, that both roads should be taken away from the Trustees for three years, and vested for that time in the Holyhead Road Commissioners. We do not gather that this drastic step was actually taken; and we imagine that the Trustees were by this threat induced to put them into somewhat better order. With the six little Welsh Trusts, controlling the most difficult 85 miles of the line, more severe measures had to be taken. It became clear to Telford and Parnell that the majority of the Trustees, and all the Surveyors, were quite incompetent, under the ordinary machinery of a Turnpike Trust, to manage even the current repairs of their roads with either honesty or efficiency. It was resolved practically to get rid of them all. By one means or another Sir Henry Parnell, who devoted the spring of 1818 to attending their meetings, induced them to allow their Trusts to be merged by Act of Parliament into a single body of fifteen Trustees only, over whom the influence of Telford and his Commissioners was supreme. It is significant of the dominant idea of the moment that it was deliberately enacted by statute that these Trustees should employ a professional civil engineer as their Surveyor for the whole of their mileage of road. Under Telford's superintendence an entirely new system of road management was introduced. The 85 miles of road were divided between three assistant surveyors, each having under him about half-a-dozen foremen, and each of these being made definitely and permanently responsible for four or five miles of road and the superintendence of an adequate gang of hired labourers employed at piece-work rates. But all this work took both time and money. So successful were the first pieces of improvement undertaken by Telford, and so unreserved was the confidence which he inspired, that Parliament voted larger and larger annual grants and loans towards the complete reconstruction of this main artery of national communication, until, by 1830, no less a sum than three-quarters of a million sterling had been expended on it, including, as it is only fair to observe, extensive improvements at Holyhead harbour and the erection of the suspension bridge over the Menai Strait. In return for this large sum the Commissioners of the Holyhead Road had reconstructed, through Telford's engineering skill and Sir Henry Parnell's energy, a continuous line of road from London to Holyhead, which—though doubtless far inferior to what would now be produced by a French, a Swiss or a Norwegian road engineer—could be fondly regarded in 1830 as affording "an example of road-making on perfect principles," a model of " the most perfect road-making that has ever been attempted in any country," and which was at any rate far and away the best piece of land travelling of its time.

Meanwhile another department of the National Government had been bestirring itself in the attempt to get a better administration of the roads. The Board of Agriculture, inspired by the practical genius of Sir John Sinclair, Bart. (1754-1835) and Arthur Young, had, from 1794 onwards, been incidentally reporting on the unsatisfactory condition of the English highways and constantly pressing for their improvement. Early in the Session of 1806 Sir John Sinclair, the Chairman of the Board, laid before the House of Commons a Bill for reforming highway administration generally, a step which produced, not an Act, but the first of the series of Parliamentary Committees on roads to which we have already referred. In the proceedings of the Committees of 1806, 1808, 1809, and 1811 we see Sir John Sinclair inviting communications from Justices of the Peace, Turnpike Trustees, County Surveyors and all sorts of cranks and enthusiasts; and getting these, with other materials, sifted by the staff of the Board of Agriculture for presentation to the committees. Among the communications addressed to the Chairman of the Board of Agriculture there came, in 1810, a long memorandum from a fellow-Scotsman, one John Loudon Macadam, giving it as his opinion that the whole system of road-making was fundamentally erroneous, and begging to be allowed to bring under public notice a new plan which he " had been long endeavouring to get... fairly tried." "Sir John," we are told in his *Memoirs,* " being pleased with the suggestions in his letter, "resolved to bring them under the notice of a Parliamentary Committee on Highways, which was then sitting, and of which Sir John Sinclair was Chairman. To give the new method a better chance of success (he) caused the information sent by Mr. Macadam to be arranged and condensed, and had it printed in the Appendix to the Report of the Committee." From this time onward, until his death in 1836, Macadam occupied, towards successive Parliamentary Committees on general road administration, much the same position of expert authority as did Thomas Telford in those concerned with the Scottish and Holyhead roads. And it is thus to Macadam, rather than to Telford, that we owe such modicum of reform as was effected in the general law and administration of roads between 1810 and 1835.

John Loudon Macadam, when he first gained the attention of the public in 1810, was, unlike Telford, not a professional road constructor. He belonged, on the contrary, to the much larger class of unpaid, amateur administrators, who, as Justices of the Peace and Turnpike Trustees, were giving orders to parish Surveyors and turnpike officials. Returning to Sauchrie in Ayrshire in 1783, with a moderate competency gained at the early age of twenty-seven as agent for the sale of prizes at New York during the American War, he was appointed a member of one of the local Turnpike Trusts; and when, in the closing years of the eighteenth century, he moved to the West of England, he became a Justice of the Peace and a member of various other Turnpike Trusts. His ostensible profession during the Napoleonic war was that of victualling agent for the Admiralty; his hobby, to which he seems to have given his whole thought, was the administration of roads. Like the great prison reformer, John Howard, Macadam had a passion for concrete investigation. "I have travelled at various times," he tells a Committee of the House of Commons in 1819, "to ascertain which are the best roads, and which the best means of road-making, over the whole kingdom, from Inverness in Scotland to the Land's End in Cornwall." The materials locally available, those actually used, the times and seasons chosen for repairing, the instruments employed, the cost per yard of road under each system or lack of system, the respective value of Statute Labour, pauper labour, and labour hired in the open market, by time or by the piece, the salaries and qualifications of turnpike Surveyors, the amount of the tolls, the frauds of the toll-farmers and pikemen, the account-keeping of Turnpike Trusts, the effect on traffic and on the roads of the regulations concerning wheels, weights, and draught horses—all this mass of technological and administrative detail was absorbed and retained by his intensely practical intelligence. Like John Howard, he was inapt at literary expression, and not till after middle life did he succeed in giving vent to his enthusiasm and experience. But eventually there emerges, after thirty years of this incessant observation, a new set of assumptions and maxims as to the object and methods of road-making, which, like those of Howard in prison administration, were destined to be revolutionary in their results. /The first and most significant of these was the conception that roads_must_be made to accommodate the traffic, not the traffic regulated to preserve the roadsy The reports of the Committees of the House of Commons,' he quietly remarks in 1810, "seem to have had principally in view the construction of wheeled carriages, the weights they were to draw, and the breadth and form of their wheels; the nature of the roads on which these carriages were to travel has not been so minutely attended to.... Is it not time to enquire whether the system of road-making now in use is good?... to consider the making, the form and surface of roads scientifically? If it is found that a smooth hard surface is the most convenient for a carriage to pass over, and that it is drawn with the smallest effort of animal strength, then it will be profitable to enquire by what means this smooth hard surface is obtained." The new ideal which Macadam set before the road administrator was not the mere keeping open of a passage over the natural surface cleared of obstructions, but the construction of "an artificial flooring, forming a strong, smooth, solid surface, at once capable of carrying great weight, and over which carriages may pass without meeting any impediment. " To attain this end he devised his celebrated technique of surface-making—a technique which, whatever may have been its shortcomings, was an enormous improvement, alike in efficiency and in cheapness, over any method commonly used by contemporary road officials. To his particular device for surface-making he attached fanatical importance; whilst he seems to have ignored, or greatly underestimated, the larger problems of road engineering. As a mere road constructor he was, it is clear, inferior to Telford, and doubtless to other civil engineers of the period. But it was rather in the art of road administration than in road technology that Macadam so greatly served his day and generation. Besides providing a novel objective or ideal, he furnished both legislators and administrators with sound maxims and new devices of general administration. Without undervaluing the initiative of the unpaid amateur, he persistently urged that the essential feature of any efficient administrative service must necessarily be the trained professional official, paid a salary which enabled him to live without corruption,—Macadam said he must be of good social status,—giving his whole time to his duties, and held responsible by the governing body for the success of the undertaking. "Gratuitous services," he urged, "are ever temporary and local; they are dependent on the residence and life of the party; and have always disappointed expectation. Skill and executive labour must be adequately paid for if expected to be constantly and usefully exerted; and, if so exerted, the price is no consideration when compared with the advantage to the public." Equally scientific were his views with regard to the employment of subordinate labour. Statute Labour, and all service in kind, he unhesitatingly condemned as a relic from a time " when a fair quantum of labour could not in many parts of the country be obtained for money." He objected equally to employing paupers "as inefficient both to the improvement of the roads and to the object of relieving the parishes.'' He always advocated the employment of fully competent labourers, using the best implements, and paid at the market rate, according to a fixed schedule of piecework prices. He recommended the appointment of them as " milemen," so that each might have the undivided responsibility for a mile of road. And, like his contemporary Edwin Chadwick, he saw that Local Government could not be carried on efficiently without central direction and control. He was always in favour of bringing the

Turnpike Trusts under the supervision and control of Parliament. He insisted on the absolute necessity of their being compelled to report annually their receipts and expenditure. What he seems to have contemplated was the establishment of a strong central department, which should keep an eye on the operations of all the Trusts, make known their several experiments, advise them in their difficulties, and report on their defects. In short, he adumbrated, in his confused and unliterary way, a system of government which should retain the utmost local autonomy and personal initiative, whilst utilising efficient bureaucratic organisation, and subject to "a general superintendence which would have an interest in the whole."

Macadam's enlightened ideas as to the proper organisation of Local Government services were barely understood, and certainly not adopted, by his contemporaries. The reforms proposed by Sir John Sinclair's Committee were insignificant, and failed to get embodied in law. But the Report of the Committee incorporated Macadam's main assumption that roads ought to be made to stand the traffic instead of vehicles being constructed to preserve the roads; and from that time forward Parliamentary Committees ceased to recommend the enforcement and extension of the eighteenth century regulations as to wheels and weights, number of horses and lines of draught, or even to trouble themselves to enquire into their working. Moreover, the publication of Macadam's memorandum, and the influential approval of the Board of Agriculture, served to bring Macadam and his particular device of surface-making under the notice of the larger and more progressive bodies of Turnpike Trustees. In January 1816 he definitely transformed himself from being an unpaid amateur administrator into a professional official and expert consultant. At the request of his co-trustees he undertook, at a salary of £400 a year, the office of "General Surveyor of the Roads" to the largest of the Turnpike Trusts to which he belonged, that of the Bristol District, which had, since 1799, with 148 miles to look after, become the most extensive single road authority in the Kingdom. In the course of two or three years he revolutionised the administration of this important body, securing a greatly improved surface of road at a considerably lower cost. The fame of this achievement spread far and wide, and he was pressed to advise Turnpike Trustees in all directions. By 1819 he was acting, with the assistance of his son, as salaried Surveyor to no fewer than "thirty-four different separate sets of commissioners," having simultaneously "328 miles under repair," according to his system, and another 300 miles under survey with a view to his advising upon them. The public, we are told, looked upon him almost as a magician, so novel and extraordinary were the results that he was believed to have achieved. He was popularly regarded as a great public benefactor. "Our shops," said Charles Dickens, "our horse's legs, our boots, our hearts have all been benefited by the introduction of Macadam. " In 1819 his friends in Parliament succeeded in getting a Committee appointed, nominally to enquire into the state of the highway law, but really to make known Macadam's successful administration. The report of this Committee is one long eulogy of Macadam and of the efficiency and economy of his improved system of road maintenance. They recommended the payment to him of a Government Grant which was eventually made up to £10,000, in recognition of his eminent public services. His administrative maxims gain their emphatic approval. "There is no point," say the Committee, "upon which a more decided coincidence of opinion amongst all those who profess what may now be called the science of road-making than that the first effectual step towards general improvement must be the employment of persons of superior ability and experience as superintending Surveyors." Hence it is suggested that, in each county, Quarter Sessions should appoint and pay one or more County Surveyors, to have the superintendence and management of all the turnpike roads within the county, but to act under the direction of the several Trusts. The Committee also advocated the consolidation in one body of the numerous Turnpike Trusts in and around the Metropolis, which Macadam had reported to be the worst in the kingdom, though they controlled several hundred miles of most profitable road, yielding the high average of £500 a year per mile in tolls. They recommended also a renewed consolidation of the various Turnpike Acts. In the succeeding committees of 1820 and 1821 all these recommendations were repeated and emphasised, and Sir Henry Parnell and Telford were both brought to testify, from their experience of the Holyhead Road, to the advantage of professional skill and of combining Turnpike Trusts into larger areas. Thus, the two distinct movements of reform, that initiated by the Post Office and carried out by Telford and Sir Henry Parnell, and that originating in Macadam and patronised by Sir John Sinclair and the Board of Agriculture, became united in a formidable innovating force, which promised extensive changes.

The legislative results with regard to Turnpike Trusts were disappointingly small. It was not found possible even to remedy the more important defects of the general turnpike law. The various Public General Acts on the subject were, it is true, strung together in 1822 into mechanical unity by a consolidating Act, carried through Parliament by Sir Frankland Lewis; but this left the real complications practically unchanged, and was itself promptly overlain by a new set of little amending Acts. In spite of repeated recommendations Parliament failed, until 1831, to devise any remedy for the trouble and expense annually wasted over the periodical renewal of the Local Acts of the eleven hundred Turnpike Trusts; or to protect their promoters from being mulcted in absurdly heavy fees by the officials of the two Houses of Parliament; and even in 1831 could find no more efficient reform than the inclusion, each year, of all the expiring Acts in one annual renewal bill. No attempt was made by Parliament to effect any general reform in

the administration of the existing Turnpike Trusts. Committee after Committee vainly urged the desirability of "consolidation of areas," but made no practical proposal for bringing it about. The great difference in financial position between the various Trusts, and the natural reluctance of every solvent body to take over the liabilities of a bankrupt concern, prevented anything of the kind taking place. The obvious and perhaps the only possible way of surmounting the financial entanglement of the thousands of separate mortgages of tolls remaining unpaid, of the great and growing arrears of interest owing by some of the Trusts, and of the pledging of particular tolls for separate debts, was compulsorily to amalgamate all the various Trusts, so as to give each of the mortgagees and other creditors a superior security, and so as to bring the total expenditure within the aggregate income. This meant, in effect, the merging of them all into a national department of toll-supported roads, a project frequently recommended by outside critics and irresponsible advisers. But under George the Fourth as under George the Third no Ministry was ever found willing to undertake such a reform, and no Parliament to sanction such an increase in the executive power and Government patronage. As an alternative to any scheme of consolidation under a national department, some substantial progress might have been made in compulsorily consolidating the Trusts of particular districts, a policy which had been strenuously recommended by the Committee of 1819, with respect to the Metropolis, and had been repeated by successive Committees in after years. In London, indeed, where "great dissatisfaction prevailed," owing to the "multiplicity of the different Turnpike Trusts,. .. great interruption of the traffic,... frequency of turnpike gates," and with all this, roads of exceptional badness, some measure of consolidation was at last achieved. In 1820 an energetic knot of members, headed by Davies Gilbert and Sir Henry Parnell, made an heroic attempt to roll up all the various Trusts surrounding the capital into a single effective body—a reform to which the Committees of 1819 and 1821 had attached particular importance in the hope of rendering "the roads round the Metropolis," on which an "immense revenue" was " collected from the public," a " pattern for the kingdom," so that " the spirit of improvement radiating from this centre may... spread with rapidity throughout the country." This bill was an extensive proposal, which would have wiped out more than fifty separate Trusts in Essex, Middlesex, Surrey and Kent, comprising several thousands of Trustees, who were to be permitted to select a small body from amongst themselves as the new Trustees. Though the second reading was carried by a large majority, the measure naturally met with "a very great opposition by the several Trusts that were proposed to be consolidated, and there was no party possessing the means to forward the measure." Left entirely to the energy of a few private members, without Government support, it was obstructed, postponed, and eventually defeated in the House of Commons by 72 votes to 71. But the question was not allowed to drop. Some of the Metropolitan
N

Turnpike Trusts were raising incomes from tolls far in excess of their requirements, and rendering no public account of their disbursements. The renewal, in 1824, of the Kensington and Hyde Park Turnpike Act led to some damaging criticism. In the following year Viscount Lowther, M.P., moved for a committee of enquiry into the turnpikes in and near the Metropolis, alleging that no less than £200,000 a year was being levied within a radius of ten miles from St. Paul's; that much of this enormous income was wasted or misappropriated, and that some Trusts were paying as much as 10 per cent interest on money borrowed from their own members. As a result of this enquiry a modest measure of consolidation, confined to the principal Trusts in the County of Middlesex, was carried into law in 1826. By this Act fourteen of the Metropolitan Turnpike Trusts north of the Thames were consolidated into a single authority, consisting of 46 named Commissioners of eminence and distinction, administering under a carefully drafted statute, 172 miles of streets and roads, which yielded an annual revenue in tolls of between sixty and seventy thousand pounds, and became by far the wealthiest and most important road authority in the Kingdom.

The movement towards consolidation went no further than this imperfect Metropolitan achievement. Another alternative might have been found in the Parliamentary grant of funds to improve a particular line of road, as had been so successfully done in the case of the Holyhead road. For a moment it looked as if the importunities of some of the great towns and the necessities of the Post Office might lead to the formation of a second Parliamentary Commission, dominating into some sort of unity the Trusts along another great line of road. Repeated memorials from the municipal Corporations of Newcastle, York and Hull, and from the chief Yorkshire landowners between 1823 and 1827, had induced the Government to allow the Postmaster-General to get Telford to survey the whole line of the Great North Road from London to Edinburgh. Telford's plan, which would have saved twenty miles of distance, and substituted for the existing windings a hundred miles of road from York to Peterborough as straight as a French *chauss6e,* commended itself to a House of Commons Committee, which recommended that the successful precedent of the Holyhead road should be followed. When, however, the Northern Road Bill was submitted to the House of Commons in 1830, it aroused a storm of opposition. Petitions poured in from the towns on the existing Great North Road, alarmed lest they should find themselves "side tracked " by one of Telford's diversions of route. Mortgagees and Trustees of the Turnpike Trusts marshalled strenuous opposition. The House of Commons was indisposed to begin a work which might possibly involve a cost as great as that incurred over the Holyhead road. Meanwhile the important trials of the new locomotive engines had taken place at Rainhill in 1829; and the amazing success of Stephenson's engine, with the progress of the new railway schemes, made people think that road travelling might in a few years become obsolete. The project was therefore presently abandoned, almost by common consent.

In the sphere of turnpike administration there was, it must be said, a certain amount of improvement taking place. The successful operations of Telford and Parnell between London and Holyhead were year by year extending to neighbouring branches of road—to Chester, to Liverpool and so on—whilst their influence on the Trusts nearer London was leading to constant improvements. The two Macadams, father and son, were annually extending their range of work and " macadamizing" an ever increasing mileage of the roads. The Middlesex roads were, from 1827 onwards, being transformed by the Commissioners of the Metropolitan Roads, whilst the 63 miles of the Surrey and Sussex Turnpike Trust—the aggregation second in importance in revenue (£19,000) — were steadily improved by the force of example. The same may be said of the Middlesex and Essex Trust (£11,000) with its 31 miles, and of the New Cross Trust (£14,000) with its 49 miles, both yielding exceptionally large toll receipts. "The whole of the south and south-western roads," as we learn incidentally from the historian of our taxes, " benefited by the impulse to locomotion in those parts, due to the patronage of Brighton" by George the Fourth. The much frequented roads about Bristol, where the consolidation of small Trusts had put 172 miles under one management (revenue £15,000), were brought to a high state of excellence by the Macadams, and vied with those of the Bath Turnpike Trust (51 miles of very remunerative roads yielding £8000). Other extensive Trusts were those of Worcester (160 miles, £5000), Hereford (156 miles, £5000), Exeter (146 miles, £6000), and Alston in Cumberland (130 miles, £3000); whilst the Manchester and Buxton Trust, with only 45 miles of road, stood sixth in aggregate receipts (£8000). These eleven great Trusts managed, in the aggregate, 1165 miles of road (or about 6 per cent of the total mileage), but collected no less than £166,000 in revenue (or about 12 per cent of the whole turnpike receipts). Elsewhere, especially in the more remote and less frequented parts of the Kingdom, the thousand and odd little Trusts remained unconsolidated, each administering its ten or twenty miles of road, and its thousand or two pounds of revenue, by its miscellaneous fifty or a hundred Trustees; gradually executing, it is true, the most elementary improvements, but for the most part squandering their tolls in extravagant administrative expenses, and piling up their debts until actual insolvency beset them, much as they had done for the previous couple of generations.

APPENDIX TO CHAPTER VIII

Notes And References

Page 164. For tho contrast between Irish and English roads, see *Tour in Ireland,* by Arthur Young, 1780, vol. ii. p. 56; and *An Essay on the Construction oj Roads and Carriages,* by R. L. Edgeworth, preface to edition of 1817, p. 7; also p. 46.

Page 165. The government road-making in the Highlands of Scotland, begun in 1732, went forward with great energy after 1745, with the stimulus of funds derived from the forfeited estates, under the conviction that the opening up of the inaccessible districts was the best security for the prevention of further Jacobite risings. The 1500 miles of military roads constructed by General Wade and his troops, going recklessly over hills and seeking fords rather than build bridges, were, however, very far from sufficing for nineteenth-century mail-coaches. In 1802 the problem was taken up afresh, and, under the authority of an Act (43 George III. c. 80) of 1803, a special body of Commissioners was created, authorised to provide, from national funds, half the oost of each new work decided on, if the balance was found by individual landowners. From 1804 onwards, the counties sought and obtained Parliamentary powers to contribute towards the latter half from the local rates. These new roads were designed and executed for the Commissioners by Thomas Telford, who in the course of the ensuing fifteen years constructed nearly a thousand miles of road, and more than as many bridges over streams and mountain torrents, at a total expense of about half a million sterling, of which the national government paid only a half. In 1816 a new Act (56 George III. c. 83) empowered the same Commissioners to reconstruct the Carlisle and Glasgow road. See the nine Reports of the Commissioners of Highland Roads between 1804 and 1821; the Thirtieth Report of the House of Commons Committee on Finance; *Voyages dans la Grande Brelagne,* by Baron Charles Dupin, 1824, voL v. pp. 47-51; *A Treatise on Roads,* by Sir Henry Parnell, 1833, pp. 2930; *Lives of the Engineers,* by Samuel Smiles, 1861, voL ii. (Telford); */Highways and Horses,* by Athol Maudslay, 1888, p. 53.

Page 166. The mere trouble and delay caused by having to stop at the tollgates begins, at the opening of the nineteenth century, to be seriously complained of, particularly in the neighbourhood of the Metropolis, where the road traffic had become large and incessant. The numerous tollbars round London, says a writer of 1816, "in a crowded situation, become no small nuisance. Eastward of the Tower of London stoppages of this kind exist even in the paved streets, and the populous villages which encircle the Metropolis are beset in such manner as if locomotion were an offence prohibited by fine or imprisonment.... Within six miles of London there cannot be less than twenty tollgates on the ten principal roads, requiring two able-bodied men for each gate, and not fewer side bars on the crossroads, requiring one man each—in all 60 men, whose wages or profits are not less than £50 per annum each of them." Passengers on horseback, or in coaches, he continues, would "rather pay double the present sum than be put to the delay and interruption now incurred" (Letter by "X. Y. " to *Times,* 8th February 1816).

Page 166. The quotations are from the First Report of the House of Commons Committee on the State of the Highways of the Kingdom, 1808; and the Report of House of Commons Committee on the Acts now in force regarding Highways, 1811.

Page 166. "Our object," it was said in 1809, "must be to encourage the carriage of the lightest weights on the broadest wheels" (Report of lHouse of Commons Committee on Broad Wheels and Turnpike Roads, 1809, Appendix). "A proper construction of carriages," reported one authority, "is certainly the most easy, and of all others the most effectual means of security to the roads, but then it should not be such a construction as will enable them to carry heavy, but such a one as will oblige them to carry light loads" (T. F. Erskine to Sir John Sinclair, in First Report of the House of Commons Committee on the State of the Highways of the Kingdom, 1808, Appendix II.). It needed to be pointed out in 1809, in an able letter to Sir John Sinclair, that " hitherto the attention of the legislature has been principally confined to a few restrictive regulations upon carriages.... The important points of the subject, the selection of the best lines for new roads, or the improvement of the present ones, the best form of construction, means of repair... have been in a great measure left to chance without any superintending power to control the want of intelligence or ignorance of individuals" (C. M. Ward to Sir John Sinclair, in Report from House of Commons Committee on Broad Wheels & Turnpike Roads, 1809, Appendix A).

Page 167. The complaints of the Irish members are referred to in the First Report of the House of Commons Committee on the Holyhead Road, 1817, p. 3. The Statute was 55 George EEL c. 52, 1815.

For the story of the Holyhead Road, see the numerous reports of special Parliamentary Committees, and of the Commissioners, from 1810 to 1830; *Voyages dans la GrandeBrctagne,* by Baron Charles Dupin (1824), voL v., Voies Publiques, pp. 41-7; *A Treatise on Roads,* by Sir Henry Parnell, 1st edition 1833, 2nd edition 1838; *Life of Thomas Telford, Civil Engineer,* by himself, edited by John Rickman, 1838; *Lives of the Engineers,* by Samuel Smiles, 1861, voL ii.; *Roadmaking and Maintenance,* by Thomas Aitken, 1900, pp. 14-26; *The Holyhead Road,* by C. G. Harper, 1902. The Commission was merged in the Office of Woods and Forests, by an Act of 3 & 4 William IV. (1833).

Sir Henry Parnell, Bart. (1776-1842), deserves a biography, which does not appear to have been written. He was elected to the Irish Parliament in 1797, and voted against the Union. From 1800 to 1832 (except 1802-6) he represented Irish constituencies in the House of Commons. He succeeded to the baronetcy on the death of his elder brother in 1812, and was created Baron Congleton in 1841. His *Treatise on Roads* (1st edition 1833, 2nd edition 1838) was long the best book on the subject; but he is now better known by his work *On Financial Reform,* which went through four editions between 1830 and 1832, and greatly influenced publio opinion in favour of the policy afterwards pursued by Peel and Gladstone (see *Finance and Politics,* by the Right Hon. Sydney Buxton, M.P., 1888, vol. i. p. 32). On the accession of the Whigs in 1831, Lord Grey offered him only a humble office in the Government, which he refused. He was, however, subsequently appointed Secretary at War *(Memoir of Earl Spencer,* by Sir D. Le Marohant, 1876, p. 271). As Secretary at War he earned the disapproval of Greville, who thought badly of him as an administrator *(Memoirs,* by Henry Greville, 1st series, 1874, vol. ii. p. 243); and Sir D. Le Marchant describes him as honest but incapable *(Memoirs of Earl Spencer,* p. 271). But nothing could well have been more successful than his management of the complicated business of the Holyhead Road Commission, whioh Greville and Le Marchant entirely ignore. His other publications (besides reports of speeches in 1810, 1814, 1824 and 1825) include *Observations upon the State oj Currency in Ireland,* 1804; *History oj the Penal Laws against the Irish Catholics* (The Pamphleteer, vols. xx. and xxi., 1813); *Observations on the Irish Butler Acts,* 1825, and *Observations on Paper Money, Banking and Overtrading,* 1827. See *Dictionary of National Biography.*

Thomas Telford takes rank as one of the very greatest of our engineers. Born in 1757 at Westerkirk in Eskdale (Dumfriesshire), the son of a farm herd, he had the minimum of schooling; was apprenticed to a stonemason; and afterwards worked at his trade in Edinburgh and London (1780-84) and Portsmouth, where he acted (1784-86) as foreman or manager, if not also as architect. Appointed, in 1786, County Surveyor for Shropshire, at a mere retaining fee, he executed all sorts of work for the Justices, and practised extensively in the County as anarchitect; erecting houses, churches, a gaol, but above all maintaining roads and constructing bridges. In 1793 he became engineer to the Ellesmere Canal Company, constructing remarkable aqueducts at Chirk and Pont Cysylltan. A project for a new London Bridge of a single span in iron attracted considerable attention in 1801. He reported on Scotch harbours for the British Fisheries Society, and on a canal through the Great Glen for the Government. In 1802 he went to Scotland for the Government, where he constructed, within the ensuing twenty-six years, nearly a thousand miles of road, erected over twelve hundred bridges, built forty-two churches, executed dozens of harbour works, great and small, and carried to completion the Caledonian Canal— thus earning from his friend Robert Southey, who visited him in 1819 amid his engineering triumphs, the jesting appellations of " Pontifex Maximus" and "Colossus of Roads." Meanwhile various canal works were constructed by him, both in England and in Sweden. From 1816 onwards he was busied also over the Holyhead Road and the suspension bridge over the Menai Strait. In 1818-20 ho was the chief founder of what became the Institute of Civil Engineers. Dying in 1837, he was buried in Westminster Abbey, where a statue was erected. See the imperfect autobiography,! *The Life of Thomas*

Telford, Civil Engineer, written by himself, edited by John Rickman, 1838; the well-known graphic account in *Lives of the Engineers,* by Samuel Smiles, 1861, vol. ii.; *History of England,* by Spencer Walpole, 1879, vol. i. pp. 85-8; *A Treatise on Roads,* by Sir Henry Parnell; Southey's account of his tour in 1819; articles by Sir David Brewster in *Edinburgh Review* for October 1839, and by Southey in *Quarterly Review* for March 1839; and the brief statements in Sir David Brewster's *Edinburgh Encyclopedia;* Cresy's *Encyclopedia of Civil Engineering,* 1847; Chambers's *Biographies of Distinguished Scotchmen,* 1870, vol. iii. p. 435; and *Dictionary of National Biography.* There exists a portrait of him painted by Sir H. Raeburn; another (in Institute of Civil Engineers) painted by Samuel Lane in 1830; and woodcuts in Caw's *Scottish Portraits,* 1903, voL ii. p. 100, and *Harper's Weekly,* voL xxxiii. p. 633 (1880).

Page 168. The need for expert engineering was now keenly felt. Thus, in 1817 we read " Your Committee have been induced to suggest the propriety of having a survoy made of each district of the road by a skilful civil engineer, under the conviction that a much higher degree of science is requisite for laying out the proper line of a road, and for forming a proper plan for its construction, than is commonly imagined to be the case; and in consequence of great sums of money being so frequently thrown away under the idea that the most ignorant and illiterate persons were perfectly oompetent to execute so easy an operation as that of road-making" (Fifth Report of H0U30 of Commons Committee on the Holyhead Road, 1817, P-VI).

Page 168. The quotation as to the Welsh precipices is from the Report of the House of Commons Committee on the Holyhead Road, 1817. "It was narrow and crooked; hills had been passed over and valleys were crossed without any regard to inclinations; no solid foundation was prepared; a very superficial coating of very bad stones or gravel was all that covered the soil; the transverse sections were often just the reverse of what they ought to be; the draining was miserably defective, and either no protecting fences or very weak ones existed along steep hill-sides and tremendous precipices" (First Annual Report of the Commissioners on the Holyhead Road, 1824, p. 17; *A Treatise on Roads,* by Sir Henry ParneD, 1833, pp. 31-2).

Page 169. Report of House of Commons Committee on the Whetstone and St. Albans Turnpike Trusts, 1828; see also the article on Roadmaking in *London Magazine,* August 1828. A description and historical account of the Whetstone Turnpike Trust is given in *Middlesex and Hertfordshire Notes and Queries,* vol. iv. pp. 91-4.

Page 169. The statutory requirement of a civil engineer is in 59 George III. c. 30 (Shrewsbury and Bangor Turnpike Act, 1819); see evidence of Sir Henry Parnell before House of Commons Committee on Turnpike Roads and Highways, 1820.

Page 170. The exact total spent on the construction and management of the works on the road from London to Holyhead, in the fifteen years 1815-29, is given as £733,502 (Report of House of Commons Committee on the amount of all sums and money received, expended and repaid by the Commissioners for the Improvement of the Holyhead and Liverpool Roads, 1830; *A Treatise on Roads,* by Sir H. Parnell, 1833, Appendix No. IV. p. 382).

The phrases describing the result are in the Report of House of Commons Committee on the Holyhead and Liverpool Roads, 1830; and in *A Treatise on Roads,* by Sir Henry Parnell, 1833, p. 31.

Page 171. No more detailed life on Macadam (1756-1836) exists than the notices in the *Imperial Dictionary of Biography* and the *Dictionary of National Biography,* together with that in Chambers's *Biographical Dictionary of Eminent Scotchmen,* 1870, voL iii. The materials for any adequate account of his activity have to be sought in his voluminous evidence before successive Parliamentary Committees from 1810 onwards; in the MS. proceedings of the Trusts for which he worked; in contemporary newspapers and pamphlets, and in the successive editions of his books, which had a great vogue between 1820 and 1830, but are now almost forgotten. He received a Parliamentary Grant of altogether £10,000 in recognition of his services, and, towards the close of his life, he was offered a knighthood (1834), which he asked might be given to his son, instead of to himself. He resigned his appointment under the Bristol Turnpike Trust in 1825, after local quarrels. Retiring to Moffat, in Scotland, he died in 1836. He published *Remarks on the Present System of Roodmaking, with Observations deduced from practice and experience* (1st edition 1816, 32 pp.; 9th edition 1827, 236 pp.); *A Practical Essay on the Scientific 'Repair and Preservation of Public Roads,* 1819; and *Observations on the Management of Trusts for the care of Turnpike Roads, as regards the Repair of the Road, the Expenditure of the Revenue and the Appointment of Officers,* 1825. See, for brief notices or criticisms, *Annals of Bristol in the Nineteenth Century,* by John Latimer, 1887, pp. 63-4; *Bristol Mercury,* 2nd August 1819, and 22nd July 1820; *Gentleman's Magazine,* 1837, part L p. 101; *Memoirs of Sir John Sinclair, Bart.,* by Rev. J. S. Sinclair, 1837, vol. ii. pp. 95-8; *"Recount of the M'Adams,* by Patcrson; *Lives of the Engineers,* by Samuel Smiles, 1861, vol. ii. p. 430 (with a portrait); *Highways and Horses,* by Athol Maudslay, 1888, p. 65; *Roadmaking and Maintenance,* by Thomas Aitken, 1800, pp. 11-14. The name was spelt indifferently in its various forms. A portrait of him is to be found in *Harper's Weekly,* vol. 33 (1880), p. 633.

Page 172. Macadam's remarks as to the character of the past legislative activity are in the Report of House of Commons Committee on Highways and Turnpike Roads, 1811, Appendix C. pp. 27-30. "The anxious provisions of the legislature for the preservation of roads," he observes elsewhere, " have unfortunately taken precedence of measures for making roads fit to be travelled upon, or worth the care of being preserved " *(Remarks on the Present System of Roadmaking,* by J. L. Macadam, 1822, p. 12).

His proposal to concentrate on making a surface are in *Remarks on the Present System of Roadmaking,* by J. L. Macadam, p. 37 of edition of 1820. "No one," he observes, "seems to have contemplated the idea of a road being made at once strong, smooth and solid."

Page 173. The distinctive feature of Macadam's system was to abstain from the use of clay, dirt, or even pebbles, but " to put broken stone on a road, which shall unite by its own angles, so as to form a solid hard surface" —to substitute " small angular stones, prepared from larger pieces, for the large rounded stones then generally made use of in road construction "— and to dispense with " binding material " or any " mixture of earth, clay, chalk or other matter that will imbibe water and be affected by frost" *(Roadmaking and Maintenance,* by Thomas Aitken, 1907, p. 12; see Cresy'8 *Encyclopcedia oj Civil Engineering,* 1847; also Report of House of Commons Committee on the Highways of the Kingdom, 1819). R. L. Edgeworth, on the contrary, " recommended that the interstices should be filled up with small gravel or sharp sand," a practice which, though it was condemned by Macadam, is now adopted by the best surveyors *(The. / Construction of Roads and Streets,* by Henry Law and D. Kinnear Clark, »" 1887, p. 9). "Telford's name is associated with the system of handset stones as a pavement foundation on which the top metal or wearing surface is placed.... Macadam was satisfied with laying the metalling directly on the surface of the ground, after the irregularities had been levelled, and side ditches formed.... A system of bottoming roads combining the methods practised by Telford and Macadam has long been adopted," though the use of the steam-roller has compelled the application of water, which was to Macadam anathema *(Roadmaking and Maintenance,* by T. Aitken, 1900, pp. 249, 251, 253; see also *The Municipal and Sanitary Engineer's Handbook,* by H. Percy Boulnois, 1883). Not only Telford, but also, it is said, "Rennie had practised the same method of making roads over his bridges long before" Macadam's publications *(Lives of the Engineers,* by Samuel Smiles, 1861, vol. ii. p. 185). So, also, it is said, did Abercromby, who constructed admirable roads in Scotland; and various French roadmakers, notably the great Pierre Tresaguet, whom Turgot employed in 1764 *(The King's Highioay, the Nature, Purpose and Develop- ment of Roads and Road Systems,* by Reginald Ryves, 1911; *The Art of Roadmaking,* by Frost, pp. 159, 160; *Highways and Horses,* by Athol Maudslay, 1888, p. 53). But in 1830 the French Government officially adopted Macadam's system, which received the highest praise in 1843 from Dumas, the engineer in chief of the department of Fonts et Chaussoes *(ibid.* p. 65).

Page 173. The remarks quoted from Macadam arc in *Remarks on the Present System of Roadmaking,* by J. L. Macadam, pp. 20-21,24,128 of 1820 edition. "Statute Labour," wrote R. L. Edgeworth a little before this time, " is a remnant of personal service. A gentleman might as well argue... that rents paid in kind are more easy and equitable than monied rents, as to defend the custom of mending highways by compulsory labour" *(An Essay on the Construction of Roads and Carriages, 18IS,* p. 34 of 1817 edition).

Macadam's fame continued to grow, and the " macadamizing " of roads spread like a mania. He is said at one time to have had as many as 300 subsurveyors acting under his directions *(Roadmaking and Maintenance,* by Thomas Aitken, 1900, pp. 11-14). So discriminating was the popular eulogy that it led to a reaction. "The public," said the *Westminster Review* in 1825, " looks on him as a sort of magician, and his invention, as it is thought, as something preternatural. Innocent of quackery himself, he has been forcibly made the great quack of the day; such is the effect of a fashion and a name. If his own name had not been Macadamizable into a verb, it is probable that his roads would, even now, have been little known. He did not invent the method in question of breaking stone, because it had long boon the practice of Sweden and Switzerland and other countries, and was long known to every observing traveller" *(Westminster Review,* voL iv. p. 354, 1825). Although Sir Henry ParneU's jealousy on behalf of Telford led him to quote the above detraction, he is fair enough to add that Maoadam "certainly had the merit, of no inconsiderable value, of being the first person who succeeded in persuading the Trustees of turnpike roads to set seriously about the improvement of them. By teaching them how to prepare gravel materials, and to keep the surface of a road free from ruts by continually raking it and scraping it, he produced a considerable change for the better in all the roads in the kingdom " *(A Treatise on Roads,* by Sir Henry Parnell, p. 25 of 1838 edition). What commended Macadam to Turnpike Trustees was that he improved the roads without increasing their cost—often, even, whilst decreasing it, and herein lay the " magic." Telford's scientific engineering of roads was costly, which led Colonel Sibthorp, M.P., to refer to him, most unfairly, as "one of those visionary gentlemen who expects to feed upon the public" (Hansard, 3rd June 1830). As a matter of fact, Telford accepted absurdly low fees, and devoted his whole energy to his various works, without accumulating, in spite of extraordinary thrift and abstemiousness, in all his long life, much more than a single year's income of a twentieth-century engineer of distinction.

The name was more quickly and more generally used as an adjective, verb and noun, and used as the stem for derivatives, than in almost any other instance. From 1821 onwards, we find, in common use by good writers, such words as macadamize and macadamite. "We shall see no more" of the Surveyor of Highways, wrote Miss Mitford in 1824, "for the macadam ways are warranted not to wear out " *(Our Village).*

Page 176. The general legislation about Turnpike Trusts between 1822 and 1834 comprised the 3 George IV.

c. 126 (General Turnpike Act of 1822); amended by 4 George IV. c. 16 (1823); 5 George IV. c. 69 (1824); 7 & 8 George IV. c. 24 (1827); 9 George IV. c. 77 (1828); 1 & 2 William IV. c. 25 (1831); 3 & 4 William IV. c. 78 (1833); 4 & 5 William IV. c. 81 (1834). In 1824 a further consolidation was attempted by J. Cripps, M.P., himself a Justice of the Peace and Turnpike Trustee, who brought in a Bill to include in a single statute the entire law relating to highways, parochial as well as turnpike. This was deprecated by Sir Frankland Lewis as unwise, and was not pressed (Hansard, 25th March 1824).

Page 176. On the vexed question of Parliamentary costs, it was pointed out in 1827 that Bills for the consolidation of Turnpike Trusts have "hitherto been visited... with the heaviest charges. Turnpike Bills generally have been always subjected to double House Fees, on some principle not sufficiently intelligible to your Committee; but when Trusts are consolidated, or when roads are divided into two or more districts... the House Fee is again doubled or trebled, and so on, as the case may be; the Committee Fees are also increased, though not in the same proportion." Yet, as was vainly urged, Turnpike Bills, being really measures for the publio advantage, not for individual profit, might proporly be relieved from all fees. The limitation of time inserted in them was "a precautionary provision of the Legislature, not at all requisite for the purposes of the Trust, but on the contrary, rather injurious to its interests, having been introduced for the sole benefit of the public, with a view to procure a periodical revision of tho powers and proceedings of the Trust." All renewal Bills should therefore be exempt from the charges on Private Bills (Report of House of Commons Committee on Turnpike Trusts Renewal Bills, 1827; see also *A Second Supplement to the General Turnpike Road / Acts for 1827,* by J. Bateman, 1827, p. Ill; *Municipal Origins,* by F. H. r Spencer, 1911, pp. 77-84).

The first of tho long series of annual Turnpike Trust Renewal Acts was 1 & 2 William IV. c. 6, 1831, entitled "An Act for continuing until the 30th day of June 1832 the several Acts for regulating tho Turnpike Roads in Great Britain which will expire at the end of the present session of Parliament."

Page 177. Irresponsible suggestions for turnpike nationalisation crop up from time to time. Thus in 1800 we have a fussy nonentity writing to Lord Auckland as follows: "Let all the turnpikes be taken into the hands of the public.... Let all sums lent on turnpikes be funded and all the tolls of the kingdom be made a security for the amount. This would be a popular measure, as many of the little turnpikes are unable to pay any interest, and many more are unable to pay off the principal; while many of the great turnpikes could pay the whole debt due on them, but are obliged not to pay it, in order to be entitled to renew their Acts when they expire.... Turnpike roads in general are now in pretty good condition and might be kept up at a moderate expense. The improvements still wanting are chiefly such as exceed tho purse of any particular district and the abilities of its Commissioners. Such are new outs, new bridges, levelling great hills, or the like, which should be done by able engineers." In 1816 the same irresponsible adviser offers the suggestion to the Chancellor of the Exchequer. "The turnpikes... might be made... a very efficient source of revenue as well as useful regulation, if Parliament would permit them to be put into the hands of Government.... Many individuals suffer by having lent money on unproductive turnpikes, to whom it would be a great relief to have their loans secured on the tolls of the whole kingdom" (John Bowdler to the Chancellor of the Exchequer, 12th January 1816; in *Memoir of the late John Bowdler, Esq.* (Anon.) 1825, pp. 166-7, 201-2). The same idea of making the roads into a revenueyielding department of government, like the modern Post Office, is expounded in *A Letter to the Rt. Hon. C. B. Bathurst, M.P., On the subject of the Poor Laws,* by Richard Blakemore, 1819, p. 33. National administration was implied, too, in the suggestions frequently made that (as in Scotland, by General Wade in 1750) the troops should be made use of. "Let the military and a proportion of militia (if wanted) be employed in repairing the roads," wrote John Bowdler to Lord Auckland in 1800, in *Memoirs of the late John Bowdler, Esq.* (Anon.) 1825, p. 166. "Whenever a peace takes place," writes a correspondent of Sir John Sinclair in 1809, "I do really think that employing the soldiers on the roads... with a daily increase to their pay while so employed, would be the best and most effectual way of keeping such roads in proper repair" (G. Orr to Sir J. Sinclair, in Third Report of House of Commons Committee on Broad Wheels and Turnpike Roads, 1809). More responsible advisers could get no further than the creation of a " Parliamentary Commission," to receive annual reports from all Turnpike Trusts (First Report of House of Commons Committee on the Highways of the Kingdom, 1808). Edgeworth proposed a National Board to supervise Turnpike Trusts *(An Essay on the Construction of Roads and Carriages,* 1813). The Committee of 1819 could not bring itself to recommend "that the turnpike roads of the kingdom should be taken into the hands of the government," fearing that" in process of time the roads might be considered rather as a source of revenue than an accommodation to the public." It therefore recommended the formation of a "Parliamentary Commission," having authority to examine complaints, audit the accounts, and conduct experiments on its own account (Report of House of Commons Committee on the Highways of the Kingdom, 1819; see *A Treatise on Roads,* by Sir Henry Parnell, 1833, p. 306).

The same indisposition to create a national department of roads continued in the Reformed Parliament. In vain did Sir Henry Parnell propose in 1833 that all Turnpike Trusts should be placed under the control of the Commissioners of Land Revenue (seeing that the latter were, under an Act of 1833, just taking over the duties of the Office of Works and the Commissioners of the Holyhead

Road), and that these Commissioners should maintain a staff of engineers to inspect all roads and advise the local officers (4 *Treatise on Roads,* by Sir Henry Parnell, 1833, pp. 301-3). When Lord Teynham asked Earl Grey whether it was the intention of the government to take over the management of the turnpike roads, the answer took the form of yet another committee, which reported once more in favour of central control without central management (Report of House of Lords Committee on Turnpike Trusts, 1833). Three years later, the Committee of 1836, whilst recommending some kind of "Boards of Control" over Turnpike Trusts, expressly " guard against being understood as conveying the recommendation of any executive power or control of management or of direction being confided to a Central Board, which might place the management of the roads of the kingdom under the same power as the roads of France or of Spain" (Report of House of Commons Committee on Turnpike Trusts and Tolls, 1836).

Page 177. The movement towards consolidation in particular districts had already led, in 1799, to the formation of the Bristol District Trust, controlling nearly 150 miles of road; and to a similar amalgamation of the Trusts round Exeter. Nine Trusts in Essex had voluntarily associated themselves to appoint a common surveyor. They held an aggregate meeting of all the Trustees, but the procedure was of doubtful legality (Macadam's evidence, in Report of House of Commons Committee on Highways, 1819).

In 1827 it was urged that, " Of all measures the most valuable would be to devise some means of encouraging a consolidation of Trusts. The advantages of a scientific superintendence, an equalisation of rates on just principles, the most appropriate disposition of gates, the purchasing of the best materials, the establishment of a uniformity of system, and a greater economy in the managemont of the fund, can only be secured by a general consolidation of Trusts" (Report of House of Commons Committee on Turnpike Trust Renewal Bills, 1827). Six years later another Committee declared that "one of the greatest evils... is the number of Trusts, as well as their limited range and extent. The Committee would recommend every consolidation of Trusts which their localities and other circumstances will permit. Such consolidation would secure more uniform and efficient administration of the Trusts by enabling the Trustees to employ more competent and skilful officers, and a reduction of useless expenditure, by diminishing the number of clerks and other officers and the outlay incurred by the renewal of so many Local Acts" (Report of House of Lords Committee on Turnpike Trusts, 1833). The multiplicity of Trusts was, indeed, carried to an absurd extreme. Within the municipal boundaries of Leeds there were 46 miles of turnpike roads and 30 tollgates, belonging to no fewer than 18 different Trusts, and collecting, in 1842, £23,251 per annum, *(Suggestions for consolidating the funds and management of turnpike roads l/ within the Borough of Leeds,* by Richard Bayldon, 1843, p. 11). Within the boundaries of the Parliamentary Borough of Stroud (Gloucestershire) there were 13 different Trusts *(Rebecca at Stroud, or a few words about the Turnpike i/ Trusts,* by David Rioardo, 1847).

Page 177. Davies Gilbert (formerly Giddy), 1767-1839, Sheriff of Cornwall 1792, President of the Royal Society in 1827 and a leading Cornish antiquary, had a seat in the House of Commons from 1804 to 1832, where he was one of the most painstaking members at the useful but unrecorded administrative and constructive committee work so typical of the time. He is chiefly known by his *Parochial History of Cornwall* (4 vols., 1838), but his interest in road reform led him to write *A Treatise on Wheels and Springs for Carriages,* and to bring his scientific knowledge to the aid of Telford in the calculations required for the Menai Suspension Bridge. See *Bibliotheca Cornvbiensis,* by Boase and W. Courtney (1874), pp. 173-5, 1194-95; *Dictionary of National Biography,* and the many references there cited.

Page 177. For the state of the roads round London see Report of House of Commons Committee on the Highways of the Kingdom, 1819; ditto, on Turnpike Roads and Highways, 1820; ditto, 1821. Before the Committee of 1819 it was given in evidence by such competent witnesses as the Postmaster-General's superintendent of mail-coaches and the leading coach proprietors, that the high roads within fifty miles of London were much worse than those in the rest of the kingdom; that ten horses were required on them to do the work of eight; that the horses lasted only three or four years on them, as compared with six years elsewhere; that the mailcoaches occasionally lost twenty minutes in labouring through a few score yards of heavily gravelled road; and that, whilst the amount paid in tolls had greatly increased, the state of the roads near London, though in a few cases improving, was either stationary or frequently retrograding.

Page 177. For particulars as to the struggle over Gilbert's abortive Consolidation Bill, see Hansard, June and July 1820; February and April 1828; and the evidence of Viscount Lowther and James Macadam before the House of Lords Committee on Turnpike Trusts, 1833. The Bill was opposed also by some of the Vestries; see MS. Vestry Minutes, Kensington, 25th March 1821; ditto, Chelsea, 29th March 1821.

Page 178. For Lord Lowther's Committee see Hansard, 5th May 1824; 17th February 1825. The consolidation of these 14 Trusts (which had 131 miles of road, extending from Isleworth and Uxbridge to Lea Bridge and Edmonton, and on which was levied, in 1826, £75,000 in tolls) that was effected by 7 George rV. c. 142 of 1826, was an immense public improvement. Viscount Lowther (1787-1872), who was M.P. for various constituencies from 1808, and who succeeded his father as Earl of Lonsdale in 1844, was a Junior Lord of the Admiralty in 1809, and of the Treasury from 1813 to 1826, but (except for very brief intervals in 1828 and 1834-35) was not again in ministerial office until 1841. He undertook the chairmanship in 1826, and, with the greatest assiduity, presided for no less than forty-six years over the new body of Commissioners, which worked energetically and efficiently. The immediate reduction in cost of official staff was some thousands a year, besides great economies in purchase of road materials. The troublesome gates, in such busy thoroughfares as the Marylebone Road and Old Street had become, were promptly removed; all weighing engines were done away with, and all additional " night tolls" abolished. By an amending Act of 1829 (10 George IV. c. 59) the tolls were greatly simplified and reduced in frequency; so that, by 1838, with a length of road increased to 172 miles, and growing traffic, the amount levied was only £66,000. The Trustees appointed, in 1827, as " Surveyor-General of Metropolitan Roads," Macadam's son and assistant, who, in 1834, became Sir James Macadam (1786-1852). On his death in 1852 he was succeeded by his son, William (1803-61), who held the office till his death in 1861, the Macadam dynasty thus continuing for nearly forty years. Notwithstanding the inroads made on their tolls by the competition of the new railways, the Commissioners managed to pay off all their debt by 1856, besides executing many road improvements. In 1864, at the instance of the Commissioners themselves, all their roads within the district of the Metropolitan Board of Works were freed from toll and transferred to the respective parishes (26 & 27 Vict. c. 78, Metropolitan Turnpikes Act, 1863). The Commission was terminated, and its remaining roads were freed, by a clause in the General Turnpike Acts Continuance Act, 1871. It thus came to an end in 1872, a few weeks after the death of its assiduous chairman, whose portrait was given in the *Illustrated London News* for 16th March 1872 (see also Bourke's *History of Whites,* 1892, vol. ii. p. 116). See, for its work, the 46 Annual Reports to Parliament of the Commissioners of the Metropolis Turnpike Roads (North of the Thames) from 1827 to 1872; *Morning Chronicle,* 6th April 1825; *Times,* 10th November 1826 and 12th June 1828; Hansard, 31st March 1829; 12th March 1830; evidence of Viscount Lowther and James Macadam before House of Lords Committee on Turnpike Trusts, 1833; *A Treatise on Road Legislation and Maintenance,* by Richard Bayldon, 1857, p. 23.

Page 179. For the abortive project of a new Northern Road, see the Report of the House of Commons Committee on the State of the Northern Roads, 1830; House of Commons Journals, May and June 1830; Hansard, 3rd June 1830; *Gentleman's Magazine,* 1861, p. 455; *Lives of the Engineers,* by Samuel Smiles, 1861, vol. ii. pp. 433-4.

Page 179. To give one instance out of many of the activities of the Macadam family, the Epping and Ongar Turnpike Trustees appointed James Macadam their surveyor in 1830, and borrowed £7000 at 5 per cent, to enable him to carry out his plan of making " an entire new line between Epping and Woodford Wells," which was completed in 1834 *(Minutes of the Epping and Ongar Highway Trust, 1769-1870,* by Benjamin Winstone, 1891, pp. 199-200).

Page 179. *History of Taxation and Taxes,* by Stephen Dowell, 1888, vol. iii. p. 45. We may conveniently notice here, as a by-product of all this coach travelling, the "road books" which, for a century and a half, served our forefathers much as " Bradshaw " does ourselves. The first of these, by Ogilvy, appeared in 1675, and ran through many editions. Paterson's work superseded it in 1771. The sixteenth edition in 1822 was edited by E. Mogg, whose name was placed on all subsequent editions. Meanwhile Owen's *New Book of Roads* was a powerful competitor between *IS* 1805 and 1827.

CHAPTER IX THE ROAD LEGISLATION OF THE NINETEENTH CENTURY

To those who watched, between 1820 and 1835, the rapid improvement of the main turnpike roads; the progressive linking up of town with town, until practically every place of importance found itself regularly connected, by the network of fast stage-coaches, with practically every other town in the Kingdom; the gradual aggregation into extensive administrative areas of such Turnpike Trusts as those of Middlesex, Surrey and Sussex, Bristol, Hereford, Worcester and Exeter; the more frequent cases in which, as on the Holyhead Road, a practical unity of technical administration was achieved by the employment of a common Surveyor; the excellence of Telford's road engineering and the success of Macadam's smooth and hard road surface; the average speed of nine or ten miles an hour, and occasionally more, which the newest stage-coaches came to maintain, even throughout the forty hours' journey to Edinburgh or the twenty hours' journey to Exeter; and who realised, on the other hand, how inefficient was the parochial administration of the byroads and side lanes outside the jurisdiction of the Turnpike Trusts, and how hopelessly incompetent the Parish Vestry and the Surveyor of Highways were still proving, it would have seemed incredible that the splendid turnpike system, which they so much admired, should be destined, within little more than a generation, entirely to pass away, whilst the despised parochial administration was to prove the germ of the new order. Yet this is what happened. In spite of the improvements here and there effected on the main lines of road, and of the really great achievements of the capitalist organisers of the stagecoach service, the historian has to record the fact that all the ferment of reform started by the Government departments between 1815 and 1828, all the genius of Telford and Macadam, and all the energies that the Sinclairs, Parnells, and Lowthers so devotedly put into the work, failed to secure to the Turnpike Trust even another fifty years' life. What this generation of road reformers accomplished was something quite different. Almost against their will, they found themselves promoting the evolution of a new system of highway administration;' based, not on tolls, but exclusively on compulsorily levied rates; governed, not by a separate *ad hoc* body, but by the general local governing authority of the geographical district in which the roads were situated; administered, not by self-selected groups of local dignitaries, but by democratically elected representatives of the whole body of citizens; acting, not through the unpaid amateur doing his term of service as Surveyor, but through permanent professional salaried officials; and getting the actual manual labour performed, not by any gratuitous common service, but by a permanently employed staff of wage earners. This evolution, which took nearly the whole nineteenth century to come about, has now to be traced.

We must begin, not with the Turnpike Trust, with its "telfordised" or " macadamised " roads, but with the humbler parish highways. If we had confined our reading between 1800 and 1830 to the voluminous Parliamentary Papers, to the reports and evidence of such experts as Macadam and Telford, and to the books, articles, and pamphlets about roads that abounded in these years, we might easily have imagined that by this time the bulk of the roads throughout the kingdom had become turnpikes, and that the condition of such byways and country lanes as still remained under the jurisdiction of the parish Surveyor of Highways was of no importance. This was not the case. Out of a total length of recognised public highway in 1820 of about 125,000 miles, only about 20,875 miles, or little over one-sixth, was under Turnpike Trusts; and even by 1838 the mileage under Trusts had only increased to about 22,000, leaving, it was computed, no less than 104,770 miles, with an annual expenditure of more than a million sterling, under parochial control. Nor did the minority of turnpike roads include all the ways much frequented by man, beast, and vehicle. The main arteries between the metropolis and the provinces. and the thoroughfares connecting one great industrial centre with another, had, it is true, at the beginning of the nineteenth century come under the management of practically continuous Turnpike Trusts. But among the parish highways were to be found miles of important streets in those suburbs of big cities, and in those industrial villages in which the inhabitants had failed to get a Local Act incorporating a body of Street Commissioners. Even across rural parishes, especially in the eastern counties and in the south-west of England, many roads of more than local importance remained outside the network of the eleven hundred Turnpike Trusts.

. These hundred thousand miles of miscellaneous streets, roads, and lanes were, in 1830, as in 1730 or in 1630, still administered by the thousands of separate parishes and townships, according to the mediaeval assumption of personal service and parochial obligation that we have in a previous chapter described. The annually chosen unpaid Surveyor of Highways, careless or timid, illiterate or corrupt; the forced Statute Labour and Team Duty unwillingly rendered on the roads on the six appointed days; the arbitrary compositions and intermittent highway rates, spent without skill or audit: this untrained, dilatory, and irresponsible service made more irritating and burdensome by threats of indictment of the parishioners and arbitrary fines levied upon any one of them—in short, the whole highway mechanism of the sixteenth and seventeenth centuries—went on for the first thirty years of the nineteenth century practically unchanged. "The legislative enactments" for the "maintenance and repair... of the parish roads," Macadam contemptuously notices in 1819, "are so inadequate to the object that they may be considered as being placed almost out of the protection of the law." For, in spite of the condemnation of this system by every road reformer, Parliament, amid all its numerous Highway Acts, had effected no substantial alteration, either in law or practice, since the opening of the eighteenth century. To this statement there should perhaps be one exception. By the General Highway Act of 1773 the Justices in Special Highway Sessions had been empowered, at the request of two-thirds of the parishioners in Vestry assembled, to appoint a salaried Surveyor of Highways for the parish, to be paid out of the local rate. For many years, as we believe, little or no use was made of this power; of a paid Surveyor of Highways we hear nothing. During the first decades of the nineteenth century, however, such an officer was occasionally appointed for specially extensive or urban parishes—sometimes acting for all the numerous townships or hamlets of a large parish— and becoming, like the permanent overseer, a servant of the Vestry, though still fully subject to the orders of the Justices of the Peace. These "standing" or "hireling" surveyors did not differ, in character and experience, from the paid officer of a small Turnpike Trust; and under the management of these promoted labourers, bankrupt tradesmen, or unsuccessful farmers, such parish roads seem often to have so far improved as to attain the low level of the minor turnpike road.

Here and there a similar degree of improvement might be brought about by the voluntary action of public-spirited individuals. Thus, we read in 1768 of a road in Hertfordshire which had "for time immemorial been suffered to remain impassable by all carriages, narrow-wheeled carts and waggons excepted." It "became the subject of universal complaint," but nothing was done. "At length... a person who had frequently suffered inconveniences from the road,. .. availing himself, as Surveyor of Great Amwell, of the powers granted by the late General Highway Act of 1766, and assisted in the execution thereof by some gentlemen in the Commission of the Peace... applied the whole statute duty of the parish, with the addition of parochial rates and liberal subscriptions of his own, to improving that part of the road... which, by these means and the generous aid of a gentleman of Ware, was completed to the satisfaction of the public.... In Little Amwell... two different subscriptions were solicited, obtained, and faithfully expended thereon. " A more highly organised voluntary effort is seen in the interesting "Vale of Evesham Road Club" established by "the gentlemen residing in the neighbourhood of Bredon Hill," Worcestershire, who found that the highways, "by long neglect become founderous and unsafe for travelling," were not only "a blemish and disgrace of this our county," and a " drawback to industry and trade," but also that they deprived " the county of its social pleasures and connections. You too well know," they urge on their associates, " that in the winter, when the cheerless season of the year invites and requires society and goodfellowship, the intercourse of neighbours... cannot be kept up without imminent danger to life and limb." They therefore declare that it is their "intention from this time to exercise our utmost influence, by advice and example, to put the laws relating thereto into strict execution; and for this purpose we will be ready and willing to serve (at least in our turns) as surveyors of the roads in our respective parishes; and we strongly recommend to the parishioners to appoint such persons as shall be most likely to execute the duties of that office with regularity, impartiality, and diligence." And they " give notice to all parishes adjacent, that if the repairs of their respective roads are not more seriously attended to than they have been (the Statute Labour for which, duly performed, will in a great measure be sufficient) they are determined to unite in indicting such defaulters." In a very few years they had "the pleasure," said the reporter for the Board of Agriculture, "of seeing their district assume a new face under their auspices, and instead of its being studiously avoided, as formerly, from the inconvenience and even danger of travelling, they have now to congratulate themselves and the public on a very safe and pleasant communication."

Such organised manifestations of voluntary activity with regard to road maintenance were, unlike the analogous associations for the prevention of crime, extremely rare, and probably very transient, for we have discovered no other traces of their activity than those above quoted. What was perhaps a little more frequent was the substitution, by voluntary agreement, of a rate for the Statute Labour, and of a road contractor for the unpaid Surveyor of Highways. Thus we read of the North Riding of Yorkshire in 1794, that " in a township on the north side of the Howardian hills" (by which, we assume, is meant the estates of the Earl of Carlisle)..." the practice is to employ a person by the year to do all the carriage work and keep the roads in repair, the expense of which is raised by an assessment laid upon the inhabitants. " Far more effective was, however, the extra-legal action taken in 1830 by the magistrates of the Southwell division of Nottinghamshire, on the inspiration of the noted poor-law, prison, and friendly society reformer, the Rev. J. T. Becher. "To facilitate information respecting the amendment of the highways, and to produce uniformity, Mr. Bonsor, the Permanent Overseer Surveyor of Highways of Southwell, who is also the Surveyor of the turnpike roads under the Commissioners, is appointed by the magistrates as their General Surveyor, to instruct all parochial Overseers Surveyors of the Highways willing to consult him, which they do very frequently. He surveys the whole of the roads in any parish requiring his inspection; reports upon the state of them to the magistrates; recommends such amendments or improvements as appear advisable, and when they have been executed, reports further; certifies the state of the highways to the magistrates so as to obtain, on behalf of such parish, a reduction of such portion of the Highway Rate as can be conveniently dispensed with. In this district the whole of the duty to be performed upon the roads is converted into money, being at the rate of 16£d. in the pound sterling, which yields for every £50 assessment £3: 8: 9, so that the value of a team for one day is estimated at lis. 5£d., being for six days £3: 8: 9, as above shown to be the representative of £50. Under this arrangement, which originated at Southwell, and has extended itself over a great part of the county, the teams and labourers are not called out, as in other counties, for a certain number of days, but the duty is converted into piecework, and the party liable is allowed to perform his team work according to his convenience, and to work out the sum due at the rate of one shilling per mile for every ton of materials conveyed.... The beneficial effects... have been considerable."

The scheme adopted by the Nottinghamshire Justices amounted, in effect, to the administration of the highways by the magistrates of each Division, under guise of their large and indefinite permissive powers of control and direction. It was, in fact, just such an appointment of a County Surveyor of Highways, constantly inspecting all the one or two thousand miles of parochial highways within the county, and supervising the action of four or five hundred parish Surveyors, that writer after writer, and Committee after Committee of the House of Commons, had recommended. The annual appointment of an unpaid officer in each parish was plainly a defect; the reliance on Statute Labour was admittedly a scandal. "But," concludes with emphasis the able report of a Committee of the Norfolk Justices in 1826, " the Committee are persuaded that no alteration in the law can be effectual unless the Magistrates are invested with a power, when assembled in their Quarter Sessions, of appointing persons of superior ability and experience as superintending Surveyors; and they are confirmed in this opinion by the authority of Mr. Macadam, who in his evidence before a Committee of the House of Commons, states that the only cure for the defects in road management would be to have people of a better station of life placed over the Surveyors, not only to direct them what to do, but to see that the work is judiciously and honestly executed; and he further states that in his opinion a very small proportion of the sum now wasted by bad management would pay for such an establishment."

In one direction only did the parishes themselves initiate a new departure at the beginning of the nineteenth century, namely, in the employment on the roads of their able-bodied poor. To the little farmer or shopkeeper who served as Overseer of the Poor or Surveyor of Highways, as to the farmers who met in Vestry at the Parish church, this policy seemed plainly advantageous. The parish found itself threatened with an indictment for the bad state of its highways. At the same time it had to maintain its able-bodied poor. By setting the unemployed labourers to work on the roads, the parochial authorities seemed completely to fulfil both obligations. They supported the poor, kept them out of mischief, and even secured something like a test of destitution. They got their roads repaired, staved off the indictment, and even carried out slight improvements in widening and levelling without cost to the ratepayers. Some enthusiastic reformers saw visions of all the highways of England being straightened and improved by this "much useful employment for our supernumerary poor." It was usually the most enterprising and progressive parishes that first started this plan. Thus, the little town of Minchinhampton, which had been for several years energetically mending and improving its roads, pitching and paving footpaths and watercourses, and even constructing " underground drains," organised in 1826 a systematic combination of road repair and poor relief. "Many of the highways in this parish requiring great improvement," runs a Vestry Minute," it is unanimously resolved that the best means of providing for the able poor will be to consolidate the highway rates of this parish, and employ such poor in repairing such highways, and in sloping the quarries of the Common, so as to render them less dangerous; that the price to be paid by the parish for labour shall be three-fifths of such sum as shall be named by Mr. Smart as a fair compensation; he so calculating as to allow an able labourer accustomed to such work to earn ten shillings per week; that Mr. Smart be appointed superintendent, and that he bring in his charge for such superintendence at every monthly meeting." By 1833 this policy of putting pauper labour on the roads had become so common that the Poor Law Commissioners made its working one of the special subjects of their enquiry. They found pauper road-mending in vogue, as the alternative to the Roundsman System and the Labour Rate, all over the south of England. Sometimes the Surveyor of Highways undertook, in the interest of the parish, to employ all men sent to him by the Overseer. Sometimes, when the Surveyor was not so compliant, or when friction arose between him and the Overseer, the Vestry would induce the Justices to appoint the same person to fill both offices. The wages paid by those Vestries that were dominated by the new school of Poor Law Reformers were reckoned by piecework at rates deliberately fixed below the market price of labour. More usually, however, a time wage was allowed, fixed according to "the Justices' Scale," and thus varying, not with the efficiency of the labourer, but with the size of his family and the price of corn. The money was taken sometimes wholly from the Highway Rate, sometimes wholly from the Poor Rate, sometimes partly from each of these rates. With regard to the results, the reports of the Assistant Poor Law Commissioners differ in their tone. When the road-work consisted of no more than strictly supervised stone-breaking, at piecework rates, fixed below subsistence level, it no doubt served as a severe test of destitution, but in that case it effected nothing for the repair of the roads. When it amounted to continuous employment at wages, of paupers who were not chosen for efficiency, and could not be dismissed for idleness, in the place of labour hired in the open market, the results were unmistakable. The dissolute idleness of the little groups of able-bodied paupers on the roads became notorious. Whenever the Surveyor is present "the men bestir themselves a little, but the moment his back is turned, a man who gives himself any trouble in working more than he can help is laughed at by his companions.... Their remark is, 'You must have your 12s. a week or your 10s. a week, whether you work or not; I wouldn't be such a fool as to work.'... Of course, under these circumstances they do anything but work." It naturally followed that, in the worst cases, the money, so far as regards any effect on the roads, was wholly thrown away; whilst even in the best cases any repair or improvement was gained at an enormously excessive cost. That the "Labour on the roads on account of the parish is generally unprofitable " is the universal testimony. "We frequently make a contract with the Parish Overseer," said the younger Macadam, speaking for his father and himself, in their operations on behalf of Turnpike Trusts, "to do a certain quantity of work for the road; in that case he employs such persons as he finds most convenient; in most cases where we have done so we find the work has cost the parish above three times what we have paid for it." There was, moreover, the further drawback that the work had often to be done at the season when it was least effective, because it was then that the labourers needed relief. Nor did the distribution of the unemployed bear any relation to that of the highways requiring repair. The parish authorities, it was said, "sent their gangs of unemployed labourers... on roads not in fact requiring repair, while the labour might be beneficially employed on the highways in adjoining parishes... there being frequently at the same time numerous unemployed labourers supported at a heavy expense... by a parish whose roads were in a good state, while those of an adjoining parish... remained neglected." Hence, however theoretically possible it might be to combine advantageously the duties of road maintenance and the relief of the destitute able-bodied unemployed, if both were perfectly administered on a national system, it is clear that, under the parochial system of 1833, with the Poor Law policy of the time, the employment of pauper labour on the roads was as ineffective a device for keeping the highways in good repair as it was for providing for the destitute. Yet we must not underestimate the magnitude, whether for good or for evil, of this employment of the unemployed on the roads. In the year 1832 work was in this way found for no fewer than 52,800 of such unemployed men, at a cost to the Poor Rate of no less than £264,800, implying something like two months' service by each man. The pauper labour on the roads amounted, in fact, at this time to about as much as the Statute

Labour and Team Duty under the 1555 statute.

We pass lightly over the dozen or so successive statutes relating to roads, by which, between 1800 and 1835, Parliament contrived to render more complicated and incomprehensible a body of law which was already beyond the comprehension of any human being. We have already said enough about the futile attempts to regulate the weight, the wheels, the team, the line of draught, and their relation to each other. We have given in as much detail as can now be endured the incessant criticisms and complaints, the perpetual stream of proposals and suggestions, as to the state of the roads, the burden of the rates and of the tolls, the manifold imperfections of all those concerned, and the various ways in which it was supposed that the evils could be cured. Starting from 1806, we have, in five and twenty years, more than twenty Parliamentary Committees hearing evidence on these things, discussing them in elaborate detail, and reporting at great length and diversely. In this and the preceding chapter we have already sufficiently disturbed the dust under which these ancient blue-books he buried.

With the reform of the House of Commons, and the greater energy in legislation of the Whig administration, we get, at last, some definite progress. It was, of course, only to be expected that the Reformed Parliament, and eventually the Whig Government, should attempt to apply to the roads the current panacea of representative institutions and a ratepaying democracy. After eight or ten abortive bills by private members in the five preceding sessions, the General Highway Act of 1835 (5 and 6 William IV. c. 50) repealed practically all the then existing statutes relating to highways (as distinguished from those relating to the roads under Turnpike Trusts), in order once more to codify the whole law in one carefully drafted Act of a hundred and twenty clauses, and a schedule of twenty-five forms. This consolidating Act set up, in each parish, the meeting of ratepayers in Vestry assembled as the supreme governing body; gave it power, in parishes exceeding 5000 inhabitants, to elect a representative board of management; authorised it to nominate a Surveyor in public meeting, who had power to levy a rate, and who might be a salaried officer; and left it free to raise all the revenue required for road maintenance with the minimum of interference from the Justices of the Peace. The Justices' power of "presentment" of the parish was taken away, and replaced by power to fine the Surveyor himself. The ancient obligation to render service in kind, by Statute Labour and Team Duty, was contemptuously dismissed. All the statutory restrictions on wheels and weights, number of horses and lines of draught, were silently repealed. The new assumption that collective provision should supersede collective regulation was, so far as regards the surface of the road, expressly embodied in law; the old expedient of amateur service by rotation was no longer relied on; and the modern administrative device of salaried officials and hired labour was definitively adopted. Where the new Act failed to carry out the reforms initiated by Sinclair and Macadam, Telford and Parnell, and advocated by the Parliamentary Committees from 1806 to 1830, was in its selection of the area of administration and of the governing body. Every committee of enquiry, like every practical expert and every pamphleteer, had asserted the supreme necessity of larger areas of administration, and had assumed that the County Justices in Quarter Sessions assembled would become inevitably the paramount governing authority, for this as for every other County service. It was plain that only by having large areas could there be any proper economy and organisation in the purchase of road materials and the employment of labour, and for large areas alone could there be secured the services of the trained professional surveyors, paid salaries sufficient to place them above petty corruption, who were admittedly required for the road-making of the kind now contemplated. Without large areas, moreover, it could never be possible for the roads to be properly graduated in " width and strength " in the order of their public importance, or for the cost of maintenance to be equitably distributed among all the inhabitants of the neighbourhood. In road administration, too, where the County Justices had actually taken it up, they had shown themselves the least corrupt and the most enlightened of contemporary authorities. Hence, had the Whig Government of 1835 been concerned exclusively with perfecting the highways, it would undoubtedly have adopted the County as the area, and Quarter Sessions as the supreme governing authority. Such a policy was, however, in 1835, politically impossible. Apart from the fact that the County Justices were predominantly Tory in opinion, it was not practically open to a Whig Parliament, so soon after the Reform Bill, to give new rating powers to a non-elective body. The steady rise in the County Rate, due to the building of gaols and lunatic asylums, was just then making Quarter Sessions unpopular as an administrative authority. There was, moreover, a special reason against giving the County Justices any further powers over roads, and (as Hansard records) one specially referred to, even by so mild a Whig as the Hon. E. B. Portman, on the introduction of his own Bill in 1831. For some time past there had been growing up in the new urban districts a volume of popular indignation against the magistrates' activity in closing public footpaths. By an Act of 1815, any two Justices had been given power summarily to close any footpath which they deemed unnecessary, subject only to confirmation by Quarter Sessions. Unfortunately, as there is reason to believe, individual magistrates up and down the country did not scruple to use this power for their own personal advantage whenever they felt inclined to exclude the public from crossing their lands. In many counties the closing orders were given with the greatest carelessness and to the utter disregard of the public convenience. It was currently reported that one magistrate would jovially ask another to dinner, giving as a reason that he wanted his concurrence in stopping up a footpath. Even the country gentlemen themselves deplored, in the House of Commons, the "facility with which public and most useful highways might be stopped up by the order of two magistrates, and the great difficulty of getting such orders quashed by appeal to the Quarter Sessions." Especially in the new manufacturing districts, where the great increase of population made the use of the footpaths a source of annoyance to the landowners, were these public rights of way arbitrarily abolished, without thought of compensation, to an extent which called forth the grave and unaccustomed censure of a legal commentator. Hence the Radical members from the newly enfranchised industrial districts had both general and particular reasons for resisting any project of increasing the power of the County Justices over the highways; there was available no other authority for the County than Quarter Sessions; the utmost that could be done to get more satisfactory areas was to give to parishes the option of combining in the appointment of a surveyor—an option practically never exercised—and accordingly, in the choice of an area for the new road authority, administrative efficiency had to be sacrificed to popular consent.

The Act of 1835 thus left intact the immemorial autonomy, as regards the roads, of each "parish, township, tithing, rape, vill, wapentake, division, city, borough, liberty, market town, franchise, hamlet, precinct, chapelry, or any other place or district maintaining its own highways"; and, indeed, by diminishing the authority of the Justices of the Peace, increased the practical independence of all these little local republics. Notwithstanding that there were at least 15,000 such separate "Highway Parishes" in England and Wales, half of them having only each a few score families, the Act of 1835 definitely secured to them the administration, free from any external supervision, control, or even audit—or, at least from any more efficient supervision than the local Justices of the Peace chose to exercise over the Parish Surveyor, or from any more practical check than the still-surviving Common Law liability to indictment at Quarter Sessions or the Assizes—of the not inconsiderable expenditure of a million a year which they were so wastefully bestowing upon the hundred thousand miles of road that lay outside the jurisdiction of the Turnpike Trusts. The story of the ensuing half-century may very largely be summed up in a series of attempts to undo this mistake in the choice of an administrative unit, and to find or construct, in lieu of the parish, some "Highway Authority" that all those concerned could be persuaded to accept as a substitute.

It was hoped, at first, that parishes would voluntarily consent to combine, as the 1835 Act enabled them to do, by application to Quarter Sessions or Special Sessions, for the formation of a Highway District, able to pay a suitable salary to a competent District Surveyor. Such a combination would have left intact the financial independence of each little parish, for the Act carefully specified that the whole of the rates levied in each parish were to be spent on its own roads, unless the Vestry meeting chose to authorise a special contribution towards some improvement of common interest. So concerned were the authors of the Act for the integrity of the parish that the only thing that the Highway District would have had in common would have been the District Surveyor and his salary. But in nearly all the rural parishes, up and down the country, the inhabitants in Vestry assembled saw no reason for incurring the expense of a salary at all, and were far too suspicious of the neighbouring parishes to combine to pay a common officer, who might be found to be spending most of his time over the highways of the other parishes. Accordingly, as we gather, there were hardly any Highway Districts—if, indeed, any at all—formed under the Act of 1835.

Another proposal had a little more success. The Act provided that, in a parish having over 5000 inhabitants, the Vestry meeting might elect a Highway Board—being, in effect, a Committee of the Vestry, which should itself exercise the powers of the Surveyor, and which might appoint and pay an Assistant Surveyor to act under the Board's orders. We see this taken advantage of at Bradford, and a few other populous places, which were not incorporated as Municipal Boroughs, nor yet managed by bodies of Street Commissioners under Local Acts. But, as the number of such Highway Boards in all England and Wales does not appear ever to have exceeded nine, this particular detail of administrative machinery need not detain us.

During the whole of the next thirty years we see one legislator after another, whether County Member or Minister of the Crown, trying his hand at the curiously narrow issue of how to enlarge the administrative unit of area for rural road management; and, as we may now discern, failing just because he could not bring himself, as regards each particular locality, to view the problem of local government as a whole. More than a dozen measures were brought in between 1835 and 1850. Prior to the year 1872 all highway and turnpike road matters were within the jurisdiction of the Home Office; and bill after bill was prepared on the lines of giving the magistrates in Quarter Sessions some general supervising and controlling authority— sometimes to combine parishes compulsorily into Highway Districts; sometimes to adopt the Petty Sessional Divisions for such districts under Highway Boards partly elected by the parishes; sometimes to give the work, incongruous though it seemed, to the Boards of Guardians of the Poor, under the supervision of Quarter Sessions. Sometimes it was proposed to deal only with the parish roads, leaving undisturbed the roads under Turnpike Trusts, a course which largely deprived the measure of the driving force of public interest. Any reform was, indeed, only too likely to be opposed by all parties—by the Tory country gentlemen, "because," notes Sir G. C. Lewis in 1848, "they are sulky about the price of corn," and by the farmers, because of their objection to " anything which appears to impose any additional 'burden' on the rates."

Sometimes, on the other hand, it was proposed to put also the Turnpike Trusts under the supervision and control of Quarter Sessions, or even to include both turnpikes and parish roads in one and the same administration, a course which inevitably marshalled against the measure the widespread influence of all the eleven hundred Trusts and their officials. "The General Roads Bill," Sir G. C. Lewis explains in 1849,—then Parliamentary UnderSecretary at the Home Office under Sir George Grey,—" was met by the opposition of the Clerks to Trusts, who are nearly all attorneys, and their influence with members—particularly as there was at Easter some expectation of a... dissolution— was irresistible. We were forced to withdraw it, and the question must now be settled in some other way."

In 1860, Sir George Cornwall Lewis, who had now become for a brief period Home Secretary, thought he had found a way in the complicated scheme of road administration adopted for South Wales. The six southern counties of Wales, as we shall presently see, had, already in 1844, as the result of a great social convulsion, transferred all their Turnpike Trusts to County Roads Boards, under which the turnpike roads were managed by District Roads Boards, and to which was at the same time entrusted a somewhat shadowy jurisdiction and control over the parishes with regard to their own highways. This organisation had, during its fifteen years of life, commended itself to South Wales. Advantage was now taken of its efficiency and popularity to bring the parish highways into virtually the same hands. The South Wales Highways Act of 1860 (23 and 24 Vic. c. 68) made more definite the control of the County Roads Boards, and provided for the establishment, in each County, of separate Highway Districts and Highway Boards exclusively for the parish highways, acting under the supervision of the County Roads Board. More important, however, than the nominal constitution was the fact that the Surveyor of each of the new Highway Districts was appointed by (and thereby virtually made responsible to), not the Highway Board whom he nominally served, but the County Roads Board, which had also its own County officers to advise it. The parochial highways of South Wales were thus, in effect, placed under a County Authority, and (as we anticipate to say) under the same County Authority that itself administered the turnpike roads. It is probable that Sir George Cornwall Lewis hoped to achieve the same sort of County control for North Wales and for England. This was, however, not to be. Any such enlargement of the powers of the Justices in Quarter Sessions always failed to secure assent; whilst the various attempts to give the County a more acceptable governing body than the Justices were no more successful.

Meanwhile the real solution had been found, though the fact was not at first recognised, in another direction. It had been persistently taken for granted—partly, no doubt, because of the historical origin of road administration in the police jurisdiction of the Manor—that the reorganisation of the administrative unit would be closely connected with the police and magisterial jurisdiction of Quarter Sessions. It proved, on the contrary, to be connected with quite a different evolution, namely, that of the slowly emerging local organisation for the purposes of Public Health. The problem of parochial highway administration was, in fact, first successfully grappled with, not in the rural parishes at all, the lanes and byroads of which had so far been most prominently in view, but in connection with the unpaved thoroughfares of the new urban areas. The first breach in the ancient parish autonomy was made by the Public Health Act of 1848, which incidentally, and without any one realising that it involved ultimately an attack on the rural parishes, made the new " Local Boards of Health " themselves the Surveyors of Highways for all the roads within the newly created urban areas. By the energy of Edwin Chadwick and Southwood Smith at the General Board of Health, a considerable number of "Local Boards of Health" were set up. In 1855, Parliament revolted against the too energetic Chadwick; and the breathless nation paused for a time in its sanitary advance. But after 1858 the Local Government Act of that year led to a renewed growth of these Local Boards, and, accordingly, to a further abstraction of highway administration from parochial and from magisterial control.

So far, however, was any one from realising that the new sanitary organisation of the Kingdom was eventually to triumph, that, in 1862, the Home Office, under Sir George Grey, at last succeeded in passing into law a General Highways Bill which adhered to the conventional lines of Highway Districts, at first sight much the same as those recently adopted for South Wales. The Highways Act of 1862 (25 & 26 Vic. c. 61), the first important amendment of the Act of 1835, empowered the Justices in Quarter Sessions compulsorily to combine parishes into Highway Districts, under Highway Boards, made up partly of Justices of the Peace *ex-officio,* but chiefly of the "way wardens" elected by the constituent parishes, which then lost the administration of their own highways. All that was left to the Vestry meeting was the actual levying of the rate to meet the precept of the Highway Board, and the power annually to elect its Waywarden, who (besides sitting as a member of the Highway Board) might, as regards the highways of his own parish, act as a volunteer unpaid assistant to the salaried Surveyor appointed by the Highway Board, for such purposes as reporting the need for repairs and supervising their execution. But, unlike the South Wales Act, the new law left the appointment of the District Surveyor to the District Highway Board, not to any County Authority. What was, however, fatal to the success of this legislation was the attitude of the Home Office—an attitude worth the notice of the student of English administration, because it was (and to this day remains) characteristic of this particular Government Department. When, after prolonged agitation and discussion, an Act of Parliament is passed giving any powers or duties to Local

Authorities, the Home Office habitually regards its own duty in the matter as completed. It may or may not notify the Local Authorities concerned of the passage of the Bill into law; for is not every one assumed to know the law? But even if it does as much as send out a circular, it seems to consider it beyond its duty to take any steps to get the Local Authorities to take action, or to call upon them to report annually what action they are taking, or to supervise, from year to year, how they are administering (or possibly not administering) the powers entrusted to them. Least of all does the Home Office seek to guide the action of the Local Authorities, or even to bring about any uniformity of policy among them; though in one field after another the lack of such direction has produced disaster.

In the case of the Highways Act of 1862, the abdication of leadership by the Home Office led ultimately to the failure of the law, and to the reversal of the action taken under it. No advice as to policy or administrative direction was given to the Justices. This naturally led to a diversity of action and a confusion of areas that made the tangle of Local Government still more involved. Some Quarter Sessions took action under the statute, and began to form Highway Districts. Others did nothing. Of those that took action, some adopted the Petty Sessional Division as the unit of area; others chose rather the area of the Poor Law Unions formed under the 1834 Act; whilst others, again, constructed brand-new areas corresponding neither with the Poor Law Union nor the Petty Sessional Division. The Northumberland Justices decided to divide their huge County into only four Highway Districts, each electing from 125 to 213 Waywardens to the Highway Board. The areas of the Districts varied, in fact, in the several Counties, from about 12,000 acres (or 20 square miles) up to 380,000 acres (or 600 square miles). At Alston in Cumberland a single large parish was made a Highway District; in many cases the number of parishes in a District was under a dozen; whilst four Districts had over a hundred parishes each. Some Districts found themselves with only forty or fifty miles of highway to look after, whilst others had six or eight hundred miles. In almost every case the constituent parishes resented being combined at all.

The first result of the Act was, however, one which had not been foreseen. The parishes did not want to lose their power over their own highways. Up and down the country, but especially in Yorkshire and Lancashire, there was a rush to "adopt" the Local Government Act of 1858 that we have already mentioned, by which the parish could become what was afterwards to be designated an "Urban Sanitary District"; substituting for its Vestry Meeting an elected Board; and gaining additional powers to execute sanitary and other improvements if and when it chose. It was, however, not for any of these objects that the parishes hurried, in 1862 and p 1863, to " adopt " the Act; but because by so doing they were enabled to retain complete and undivided power over their several highways. For it had been provided by a clause in the Highways Act of 1862 that no place under the Local Government Act of 1858 was to be included within a Highway District. Within a year no fewer than nine hundred little parishes—many having fewer than a thousand inhabitants, and being not more "urban" in character than the ordinary English village—had converted themselves into Urban Sanitary Authorities; and had so put themselves in a position to bid defiance to the desire of Quarter Sessions that their highway administration should be grouped. Then Parliament intervened. In 1863 the Home Office—still under Sir George Grey—got through an amending statute, the Local Government Act of 1863 (26 & 27 Vic. c. 17); which imposed, for the future, a minimum of 3000 inhabitants for the Urban Sanitary District; and thus stopped the loophole through which the little parishes were creeping.

The parochial opposition to the newfangled Highway Districts was, however, so strong and so universal, and it evoked so much sympathy even among Justices of the Peace, that the work of combining parishes into Highway Districts was never completed, and had eventually to be undone. During the twenty years, 1862-82, about 8500 parishes were, at one time or other, combined, for their road administration, into 424 Highway Districts; but of these a few dozen were subsequently dissolved. The progress of consolidation differed considerably from County to County. We must first note that about a thousand separate Boroughs and Urban Sanitary Districts, comprising all the populous towns in every County but Rutland (the numbers varying in the different Counties from 1 to as many as 183), managed their ocal highways for themselves. In about half the Counties of England, and throughout North Wales, the greater part of the rural parishes soon found themselves superseded, as regards road administration, by the Highway Boards. In five of these Counties this supersession of the Parish was, by March 1882, absolutely complete. There were, however, in 1879, still 5868 parishes; and in March 1882, after the much disliked financial provisions of the 1878 Act, as many as 6203 parishes, including some of quite trivial population, which maintained the autonomy of the Vestry Meeting and the Parish Surveyor of Highways. The great County of York had 759 parishes in Highway Districts and 720 separate; besides 183 Urban Sanitary Districts managing their own thoroughfares. Seven or eight Counties, including Buckinghamshire, Norfolk, Suffolk, Staffordshire and Westmorland, stood out obstinately for parish management, and would have no Highway Boards at all within their areas.

We find it difficult to account for this passionate attachment to parochial management of the highways, in spite of every argument of economy and efficiency in favour of wider administrative units. How inefficient was usually the road administration of the Parish, even in the middle of the nineteenth century, we can now only dimly picture to ourselves. Only in an infinitesimal number of extensive parishes did the Vestry dream of appointing a qualified professional expert as Surveyor of Highways: it would, indeed, seldom have been easy to secure such a person for the small fragment of his time that a single parish required. The Surveyors of Highways, it was deposed as late as 1881, were "farmers, millers, clergymen, squires "—when they were not gardeners, bricklayers, brokendown clerks or shopkeepers, or merely the incompetent relations of prominent parishioners. "I do not suppose ten per cent are competent," said the witness, "although many are paid." For, after the Highways Act of 1835, it seems gradually to have become usual for the Parish Surveyor of Highways to receive some sort of remuneration, with various minor perquisites. Until 1879, indeed, there was no efficient or external audit of his accounts. What happened, we gather, in most parishes, was that the Surveyor produced to the Vestry Meeting some sort of budget of road repair, for which a Highway Rate would be required; and the Vestry Meeting would discuss and wrangle whether this road or that needed to be dealt with, and at what cost. Eventually some general decision would be come to, a resolution would be passed approving a Highway Rate of so much in the pound, and the Surveyor would execute the work as he chose. Under such a system, each parish seems to have thought that its own highways could not possibly be so well managed as they were when the parishioners themselves saw to the repairs of their own roads—that they would certainly cost more, because it was vainly imagined that the local farmers would lend their carts free of charge to carry stones to their own roads—that to pay the District Surveyor of Highways a salary of £200 a year for a whole Highway District was more extravagant than letting a score of parish Surveyors allow themselves perquisites, or even £10 or £20 salary, for their amateur work. Above all, there seems to be everywhere a rooted distrust of the parishes at the other end of the district! This became intense after the Highways and Locomotives Act of 1878, which incidentally made a common fund for each Highway District, replenished by a common Highway Rate, instead of each parish being financially separate. Who could be sure that an unfair proportion of the common Highway Fund, and an undue share of the District Surveyor's time, was not being given to the parishes a dozen miles away, where the soil was soft, the traffic heavy, and so on? The feeling was intensified by the fact that the Highway District often extended into two or more Poor Law Unions, each with its own basis of assessment; and the common Highway Rate might accordingly fall (or be supposed to fall) with unequal burden on parishes assessed with different degrees of leniency or laxness. After nearly half a century of advocacy of Highway Districts, and nearly twenty years' experience of them, witness after witness before the House of Lords Select Committee on the Highways Acts, in 1881, argued and pleaded, almost passionately, for a reversion to parochial management.

The grouping of parishes had, however, by that time gone too far to be given up. The question at issue was only how to group, and how to complete the work. Here, again, it proved to be the Public Health organisation that cut the Gordian knot. The Royal Commission on Sanitation had reported in 1869 in favour of the complete division of England and Wales into sanitary areas on a uniform plan; and, rejecting both the County and the Parish, had finally decided on the Poor Law Union as the best available unit of area for the rural districts. This decision, which was the turning-point in the Local Government history of the nineteenth century, proved to be the turningpoint also for highway administration. In 1872, under section 36 of the Public Health Act of that year, the jurisdiction of the Home Office with regard to highways and turnpike roads was transferred to the newly created Local Government Board; which combined Public Health and Poor Law administration, and started free from the traditional bias of the Home Office in favour of the police and magisterial influence, and the County area. The Public Health Act of 1872 (35 & 36 Vic. c. 79), reenacted with amendments in 1875 (38 & 39 Vic. c. 55), ignored the County altogether, and parcelled out England and Wales, for purposes of Public Health administration, among Urban and Rural Sanitary Authorities respectively, the former comprising the Boroughs and Urban Districts already existing, or to be established, and the latter those portions of the Poor Law Unions that lay outside such urban areas. The Urban Sanitary Authorities were, as we have seen, already managing their own highways, under the Acts of 1848, 1858, 1862 and 1863. It followed, almost of necessity, that, outside such urban areas, the administration of the highways, like other local services, must fall eventually to the Rural Sanitary Authorities. This was made clear by the Highways and Locomotives Act of 1878 (41 & 42 Vic. c. 77), the first Highways Act passed under the influence of the Local Government Board. This Act directed that Quarter Sessions should, for the future, when forming or altering Highway Districts under the Highways Acts, make them as far as possible coincide with Rural Sanitary Districts. Moreover, the Justices were at the same time empowered, in all cases in which the Highway District coincided in area with the Rural Sanitary District, to dissolve the Highway Board, and transfer its powers to the Rural Sanitary Authority, which then merged the expenses of road administration in those of general sanitary services, and provided for them by a common rate. This provision came into effect with regard to forty-one Boards. Where the Highway Boards continued to exist, the separate interest of each parish in its own roads was weakened by the abolition, under the same Act, of parochial separateness as regards highway finance. Instead of charging the cost of the parish highways to the parish, the whole of the Highway Board's expenditure was thenceforth borne by a common fund, replenished by a common Highway Rate.

The parish, as the Highway Authority, and the Highway Board, as an *ad hoc* authority for the highways of a wider area, still maintained a vigorous existence, even after the heavy blows dealt to them by the Acts of 1872, 1875 and 1878. Very few additional parishes allowed themselves to be formed into Highway Boards; and in very few cases did Quarter Sessions find it practicable to coerce them. Only about ten per cent of the Highway Boards were actually merged in the Rural Sanitary Authorities. In both cases the "chaos of areas" stood in the way. Parishes and Poor Law Unions overlapped County boundaries, Highway Districts overlapped Poor Law Union boundaries, and so on. In 1894 the number of Highway Districts in existence had fallen to 357, leaving over 5000 separate " Highway Parishes," annually electing their Surveyors of Highways, and mending their own roads, as they had done since 1555, at least. The need for wider areas of administration became, however, to the country gentlemen, the Members of Parliament and the official class, more and more indisputable, with the steady increase of through traffic, as compared with local user of the highways. Presently the time arrived when drastic measures could be taken. So completely had opinion swung round to the inclusion of road management among sanitary services generally, that the very measure aiming at a rehabilitation of Parish Government could, without objection, be used to give the death-blow to parochial road administration. The Local Government Act of 1894 (56 & 57 Vic. c. 73) definitely abolished both Highway Districts and "Highway Parishes," merging them in the Rural Sanitary Authorities for their localities. This, however, it was easier to enact than actually to accomplish, because of the overlapping of areas; and each County Council was accordingly empowered to postpone the operation of the law as regards highways for three years, or for such further period as the Local Government Board might, on the Council's application, allow. Under this provision repeated postponements took place. In only ten Counties could the Act be brought into force at once for the whole area. Meanwhile many minor adjustments of parish, union and County boundaries were made. Gradually the tangle was straightened out. The number of Highway Boards sank from 357 in 1894 to 45 in 1897; and within two years more the last had been dissolved. The same years witnessed also the merging of the last surviving " Highway Parishes," which numbered 6454 in 1894, and only 1168 by September 1897. By the end of the nineteenth century, the last trace of the immemorial responsibility of the Parish for its highways may be said to have disappeared.

Meanwhile what was happening to the eleven hundred Turnpike Trusts, with their twenty-two thousand miles of relatively good roads, connecting town with town, and daily traversed in 1830, as we have described, by tens of thousands of stagecoaches, postchaises and private carriages? We must here look beyond legislation, of which, as regards the Turnpike roads, the output was small. In 1822, it is true, the whole law had been consolidated into a single statute (3 George IV. c. 126), without essential alteration. From first to last the constitution and powers of the Turnpike Trust remained singularly unchanged. Its most glaring abuses were, as we described in a previous chapter, to some extent mitigated in the principal centres of population and along the main lines of route. By 1830 the nation had come to be proud of its great lines of stage-coach communication, on which travelling seemed to contemporaries to have been brought to a high pitch of perfection. In 1837 the toll revenue rose to its highest point, exceeding one and a half million pounds.

Suddenly, with little warning, there fell, upon all concerned, what Sir James Macadam described as "the calamity of railways." The short lines between Stockton and Darlington (1825), and between Liverpool and Manchester (1830), proved to be only the beginning of a complete supersession of through passenger traffic by road, whether by stage-coach, postchaise or private carriage; and it was mainly upon the great development of this passenger traffic that the Turnpike Trusts had come to depend for their revenue. Each stage-coach journeying daily from London to Manchester was contributing over £1700 a year in turnpike tolls to the different Trusts along the route. It was computed that each coach paid something like £7 a year in tolls for each mile of road that it traversed. The transfer of this business was instantaneous and complete. Every coach had to be taken off the road the moment the railway was open to the towns along its route. No one took a postchaise when he could take the train. Whatever might be the fascination of the road, or the transient apprehension of danger by rail, no one was prepared to forgo the advantage of travelling thirty miles an hour instead of ten, at a price considerably less than that of the stage-coach. The last stage-coach between London and Birmingham ran in 1839; the last between London and Bristol in October 1843; the last to Plymouth in September 1847; the last to Bedford in 1848; the last out of Manchester to Derby in 1858. Between 1837 and 1850 the toll revenue of the Turnpike Trusts fell off by half a million sterling, or by one-third.

The weakest point of the Turnpike Trust had, as we have seen, always been its financial basis. There was no invariable relation, and no necessary connection, between the amount that it cost to keep a particular mile of road in repair, and the amount that could be collected in tolls. Moreover, the cost of collection, including the waste by peculation, fraud and the swollen profits of the toll-farmers, was relatively enormous. The tolls, too, were practically always mortgaged for the debt that had been incurred in the construction or improvement of the road; and the interest on this debt was legally the first charge on the gross receipts. Upon what remained there battened a host of treasurers, attorneys, clerks, surveyors, and road contractors, numbering between three and four thousand persons—not to mention the 20,000 "pikemen," or collectors, at the 7800 toll-gates—with very little effective supervision from the Turnpike Trustees, few of whom could even be got to attend a meeting. Under these circumstances, it is not remarkable that, whilst a few Trusts enjoyed ample incomes, most of them found it difficult to spare much money for road repair, or that many of them failed to keep up their payments of interest on their bonds. Already by 1830, notwithstanding the great increase in traffic and tolls, some Trusts had paid no interest for thirty or fifty years in succession, their bonds becoming valueless; whilst numerous others had their tolls taken possession of by their creditors, so that the whole accruing daily revenue was sequestrated towards meeting the interest on the bonds.

The "calamity of railways" that fell upon the Turnpike Trusts between 1830 and 1850 brought down a large number of them to the state of chronic insolvency into which some had already fallen. The receipts at many gates hardly paid the cost of collection. The bonds, once thought a safe security, became, in most cases, more and more depreciated. What was more important to the nation at large was the inability of the Trusts to maintain their roads in any decent rppair. This threw the burden of maintenance again on the parishes through which the roads passed. The common law liability of the parish had never been taken away; and, indeed, in many Trusts, the Surveyor had continued to insist on Statute Labour and Team Duty being done on the turnpike road, as on others, right down to the Highways Act of 1835. Since that Act, the liability of the parish for turnpike roads had, in practice, not been enforced. Now, the Legislature sought to revive it by empowering, in 1841 (4 & 5 Vic. c. 59), the Justices in Special Sessions to order a contribution from the Highway Rates to be made towards the repair of turnpike roads where the toll revenue had proved insufficient.

Any such subsidising of the Turnpike Trust by the parishes through which its roads passed—making the unfortunate parishioners pay both the cost of repair and also the toll—whilst it failed to cure the evils of Turnpike Trust finance, naturally excited local resentment. In South Wales, where the little farmers and smallholders were already suffering from adverse economic conditions, this resentment flared up, in 1842-43, into a convulsive popular rebellion known as the Rebecca Riots. Especially in Carmarthenshire had the Turnpike Trusts been oppressive, in the excessive number and close proximity of the gates and side-bars, at which every vehicle or beast was taxed; the toll-farmers had exacted heavy, and sometimes illegal, tolls; and the Trusts had required the parishes to repair the turnpike roads in ways of doubtful legality, on roads on which heavy tolls were also levied. It is impossible to read the voluminous evidence of the Royal Commission of Inquiry into South Wales in 1844 without feeling that the hard-driven smallholders of South Wales were being seriously oppressed. This was partly the fault of Parliament, which had heedlessly given vexatious and oppressive powers to irresponsible bodies. It had carefully limited the amount of each toll, but had not specified how frequently the toll might be exacted. "We know no reason," gravely reported the Royal Commissioners, "why the Trustees should not, if they thought fit, in virtue of the large and lavish powers committed to them, establish a gate and demand a toll at intervals of 100 yards each throughout the County of Carmarthen." In one unfortunate district, two rival Turnpike Trusts had both been given power to tax the traffic on roads which ran in and out of each other's territory in such a confused network that each Trust did its best to multiply toll-gates, and the public was fleeced by both. Political rivalry lent animus to this economic competition, for one of these Trusts (that of Kidwelly) was, we learn, " blue " and the other (Three Commotts) "red," the Trustees of each belonging almost exclusively to one political party. The country gentlemen were blamed for neglecting their duty as Trustees and also for expending large sums on building bridges at the public expense, mainly for greater convenience of access to each other's houses. Grievances connected with tithe, and resentment at the New Poor Law swelled the discontent. Suddenly, in the winter of 1842-43, there was an epidemic of riotous destruction of the hated turnpike gates and side-bars, especially the newest and most oppressive, throughout all the six Counties of South Wales. That winter will never be forgotten in the valleys of South Wales so long as tradition endures. Some Turnpike Trusts found every one of their gates destroyed, the gate-posts being neatly sawn across close to the ground, with more or less tumult; with their entire revenues brought at an end. Carmarthenshire alone had eighty gates destroyed. Throughout two whole Counties (Pembroke and Cardigan) not a gate was left standing. The outburst had its fantastic aspect. Wild proclamations were issued in the name of Rebecca, in allusion to the verse of Genesis (xxiv. 60) in which it is promised to the wife of Isaac that her seed should possess the "gate" of her enemies. The armed mobs, which collected suddenly on some secret signal, were often led by a man disguised in women's clothes, and they claimed to be "Rebecca and her children." The insurrection—for to that it almost amounted—was organised with a secrecy and an efficiency that have seldom been equalled. "By day," writes its best historian, "all was quiet enough. The most vigilant of the constabulary could see nothing but the ordinary sights of the roads and fields—no groups in consultation, no mysterious looks—nothing but jogging riders who duly paid their tolls, and people about their proper business in their fields or at home. If there was a suspicion of an intended attack on any particular gate, that gate was sure to be left in peace; and while it was watched half a dozen were levelled at some opposite point of the county." The unfortunate pikekeeper and his family "were roused by the blare of a multitude of cowhorns and the popping of a dozen guns; their door was burst open, and they saw a crowd, some on horses and some on foot—some in women's clothes and others with veiled faces—with the flaring torches and the glittering saws and hatchets. The toll-takers must move out their furniture or lose it; and strong hands helped to carry bed and table and utensils into the field or the dry ditch, while others were sawing off the gate-posts close to the ground and chopping up the gate. Then off came the roof of the tollhouse, and down came the walls, and up came the flags of the very floor; the road was made clear for passengers, and then the uncouth creatures leaped on their horses again, hallooed, blew their horns, fired their guns, and galloped off to some distant point which they would approach in dead stillness as in this case." The patrolling of the local constabulary was in vain. Under their protection the gates were put up again; in many instances only to be again destroyed a few nights later. One gate was thus demolished five several times. Who started the movement and who led the mobs was never discovered. Eventually a considerable force of Metropolitan Police and of regular troops had to be quartered in South Wales to maintain order. But the people had, to a large extent, won their case. The Turnpike Trusts abandoned their most oppressive gates, which were never reinstated. Only a small number of the rioters were arrested. Public opinion ran so strongly in favour of the movement that the Government preferred to act with leniency. A Special Commission, under Baron Gurney, was sent to try the prisoners, three of whom were sentenced to transportation, others to short terms of imprisonment, whilst the majority were simply bound over to keep the peace for the future. A Royal Commission of three members was immediately sent to enquire on the spot into all the grievances, and remedial legislation was promised. In the end, Sir James Graham, then Home Secretary, carried through an Act which summarily dismissed all the Turnpike Trustees throughout South Wales, merging all the Trusts in new "County Roads Boards," appointed by Quarter Sessions, and consisting of from six to twelve Justices of the Peace, with certain members *ex officio.* These County Roads Boards took over the roads, the debts, the officers and the tolls of the former Trusts; but they were assisted by a Government engineer, a "General Superintendent of County Roads in South Wales," who was appointed by the Home Secretary. The sum of £218,000 was advanced by the Government to pay off the creditors of the Trusts, the whole debt being thus consolidated, county by county, into terminable annuities at 3J per cent interest. Under what was virtually Government control, the County Roads Boards greatly reduced the tolls, the excessive number of gates, and the other oppressive exactions which had led to the popular revolt. Notwithstanding these concessions, by consolidation of areas, establishments and debts, by honesty of management, and expert direction, the County Roads Boards were able not only to pay their way, but also within thirty years to discharge their bond debt, which was practically all paid off by 1876.

If something of the same sort could have been done with the English Turnpike Trusts in 1844, they might have been spared the long-drawn-out agony of the ensuing half-century. But every attempt at legislation was defeated by the inability of reformers to agree upon the constitution of a County authority; the objection of the Justices of the Peace to any centralization or Government control; the difficulty presented by the complications of all the eleven hundred separate debts; and the interested opposition of the treasurers, attorneys and clerks of the eleven hundred Trusts. We cannot say that the episode reflects any credit on English statesmanship. So far as the Government was concerned, under the timid and unresourceful advice of the Home Office, and the refusal of successive Cabinets to trouble themselves about the subject, the Turnpike Trusts were allowed to go on just as before, annually getting their expiring terms renewed by Parliament as a matter of course, falling, most of them, progressively further and further behind their task, and many of them, deeper and deeper into insolvency.

We date from the early sixties, so far as such a change can be precisely dated, the growth of a widespread public determination, notably in Parliamentary and official circles, to get rid altogether of the Turnpike Trust and its toll. Road tolls had been wholly abolished in Ireland by 1858, and no difficulty had been experienced in maintaining the roads entirely out of rates. The sense of annoyance and impatience at the irritating impost in England was growing more and more acute. The passage of the Highways Act of 1862 made it possible to expect the formation, all over the country, of Highway Boards, to whom, more reasonably and more equitably than to the Parish Vestries, the turnpike roads might be entrusted. And though Sir George Grey remained Home Secretary continuously from 1861 to 1865, it is perhaps not altogether imaginary to date a change of policy from the retirement in 1862 of his Parliamentary UnderSecretary George Clive, M.P., to whom the Turnpike Trust business was entrusted, and who seems to have favoured the renewal of the terms of the expiring Turnpike Trusts, from inability to imagine that any other course was practicable. Immediately he retired, we seem to notice a change. In 1863 a short Act (26 & 27 Vic. c. 94) facilitated the application by the Justices in Special Sessions under the Act of 1841 of part of the local Highway Rate to the repair of a Turnpike Road which found its toll revenue insufficient. A Select Committee of the House of Commons in 1864 once more enquired into Turnpike Trusts, but this time with a significant difference. Instead of how to maintain the Trusts, the question was, practically, how to get rid of the tolls. Mr. W. B. Wrightson, M.P. for Northallerton Borough, who had had nearly forty years' experience of the House of Commons, threw himself energetically into the agitation for relieving the traveller from an unpopular impost. Practically all the witnesses before this Committee were in favour of abolishing the toll, alleging that all experience proved it to be a costly and wasteful method of raising the necessary revenue, as well as a tax extremely partial and unfair in its incidence. The Committee, unaided by guidance from the Government, reported that the turnpike tolls were "unequal in pressure, costly in collection, inconvenient to the public, and injurious as causing a serious impediment to intercourse and traffic "; that the abolition of Turnpike Trusts " would be both beneficial and expedient"; and that the most practicable course was to let the turnpike roads be vested in a public authority as had been done in South Wales.

Still the Cabinet ignored the question, and, whichever party was in power, persisted in formulating no policy. What happened, in effect, was that the House of Commons itself took the matter up. In the absence of any definite policy from the Government, either under Sir George Grey or under Spencer Walpole, and failing any direction from the Ministerial Bench, we see the House of Commons Committees hammering out for themselves a policy of gradual abolition. From 1865 onwards we get tolls abolished, here and there, in Scottish Local Acts. From 1871 onwards there was appointed annually a Committee on Turnpike Trust Bills, over which Lord George Cavendish, M.P., presided. This Committee had referred to it, each year, all the applications for the renewal of the terms of Turnpike Trusts; and every year it presented a report to the House, recommending (and thus virtually deciding) in which cases the Trusts should be allowed to come to an end, and in which cases, and subject to what conditions, a further term should be granted. The policy of this Committee, which was that of the House of Commons rather than that of the Cabinet, was decidedly in favour of winding up as many Turnpike Trusts as possible; and of conceding a renewal only where the financial position of the Trust or the circumstances of the locality made such a renewal almost irresistible. From 1864 onwards, Turnpike Trusts now dropped out at the rate of twenty or thirty a year, their roads being handed over to the Highway Districts, or to the separate Highway Parishes, in which they lay. Presently the dissolution went ahead at an accelerating rate. The Act of 1870 disposed of no fewer than 78 Trusts. The Act of 1871 ended tolls in London. From 1871, when there were still 854 Trusts existing, they had fallen by 1875 to 588, by 1881 to 184, and by 1883 to only 71. In that year the Scottish Turnpike Trusts ceased to levy tolls. In 1887 only 15 Trusts were left, and in 1890 only two. It was, however, not till 1895 that the last surviving Turnpike Trust, that for the Anglesey portion of the Shrewsbury and Holyhead road, came to an end, and on November 1, 1895, the last toll was levied— almost exactly coincident, as we have seen, with the final extinction of the Parish as a Highway Authority.

So continuous and rapid an addition to the burden of road maintenance, borne by the Highway Districts and Highway Parishes, as followed on the transfer of thousands of miles of "disturnpiked" roads, naturally excited some resentment. It formed a serious item in the increase of local burdens of which the County Members complained. From 1876 onward the burden was mitigated by a Grant in Aid of about two hundred thousand pounds, specially in respect of the "disturnpiked" roads. In 1878 an attempt was made to equalise the remaining burden, as among the different parishes in each County, by requiring (in the Highway and Locomotives Act, 1878) the Justices in Quarter Sessions to contribute from the County Fund one-half of the annual cost of maintenance of roads "disturnpiked" subsequent to 1870. Ten years later, in the Local Government Act of 1888 (51 & 52 Vic. c. 41), when additional aid was given to the County from the Exchequer, the obligation was placed upon the new County Council of entirely maintaining the " main " roads within its County; with power to add to the "disturnpiked " roads such others as it might think fit to regard as main roads; and also to contribute, at its discretion, to the District Councils for any other roads in the County (hence called "contributory" or "secondary" roads). Thus, at last, after three-quarters of a century of argument and discussion, the County became, to this partial extent, the local Road Authority.

This last reform practically brings the story down to date, so far as the constitutional machinery of local road administration is concerned. Our highways are (1913) still administered, within Boroughs or Urban Sanitary Districts, by the Town or District Council; outside these urban areas, the main roads by the County Council, the others by the Rural District Council. In each case there is a Surveyor, paid by salary, who executes the necessary work of construction or repair exclusively by hired labour at wages. The cost is provided entirely from the local rates, either of the County or County Borough, or of the Urban or Rural District, or by subsidy from the one to the other. We had by 1888 travelled so far from the demand, set up by the "new users of the roads " in the eighteenth century, for a higher standard of road administration, that we had forgotten the whole controversy. Suddenly, at the end of the nineteenth century, we found another set of " new users of the roads " invading our highways. To this phenomenon, and its immediate results on road administration, we devote our final chapter.

APPENDIX TO CHAPTER IX

Notes And References

Page 192. We have been surprised to find how obscure is the history of road administration in the nineteenth century. We know of no book in which the successive stages can be traced; and we have found it difficult, without consulting the MS. Minutes of Vestries, Highway Boards and Quarter Sessions (which we must confess not to have had time to do for the period after 1835), or the confidential archives of the Home Office and Local Government Board, which are not yet accessible, to form any oxact idea of what was happening. Our account is pieced together from statutes and Parliamentary papers, with such incidental references as we have found in the books mentioned below.

y Page 192. For a vision of the stage-coach organisation at its best, see r such books as *Coaching, with Anecdotes oj the Road,* by Lord William Lennox, ✓ 1876; *Annals of the Road, or Notes on Mail and Stage Coaching in Great y/krilain,* by Nimrod (Captain) Malet, 1876; *Old Coaching Days,* 1882; and */The Coaching Age,* 1885, by Stanley

Harris; *Brighton and its Coaches,* by /W. C. A. Blew, 1894; *Forty Years at the Post Office,* 1895, and *On the yTrack of the Mail Coach,* 1895, both by F. E. Baines; *Coaching Days and (.Coaching Ways,* by W. O. Tristram, 1901; and *Stagecoach and Mail in Days of Yore,* by C. G. Harper, 1903. "A passenger could coach from Portsmouth to Holyhead, from Barnstaple to Berwick, with changes and stoppages it is true, but by a continuous mailcoach road, without passing through London. The country resounded with the blast of the horn and the rattle of pole-chains" *(Forty Years at the Post Office,* by F. E. Baines, 1895, pp. 37-8). There was eventually coaching communication, with changes, from Falmouth to Thurso. Birmingham was, in effect, the centre of the system, at which most coach lines crossed.

Page 192. The state of the roads and lanes under the parish Surveyors of Highways, for the period between 1800 and 1835, is hardly even mentioned. Contemporary discussion and criticism of roads dealt almost exclusively with the turnpikes. Macadam scarcely ever alluded to the parish highways. The three most important contributions to current periodical literature relating to roads—the articles in the *Edinburgh Review,* October 1819, the *Quarterly Review,* May 1820, and the *London Magazine,* August 1828—are concerned only with turnpike roads. It was practically these alone that were made the subjects of Parliamentary debates and enquiries between 1806 and 1830; and there was no legislation relating to parish highways between 1814 and 1835. Practically the only author who, in these years, dealt with parish roads was the able Berkshire Justice who published anonymously a lengthy pamphlet entitled *Highways Improved,* 1825, which is wholly devoted to them.

The statistics given in the text are derived from the Report from the House of Commons Committee to consider Acts regarding Turnpike Roads and Highways, 1821; ditto, House of Lords Committee on Turnpike Trusts, 1833; ditto, Royal Commission on the State of the Roads, 1840; and *Journal of the Royal Statistical Society,* January 1839. It may be added that, whilst the 22,000 miles of the 1116 Turnpike Trusts in 1838 had 3555 treasurers, clerks, and Surveyors (besides 20,000 toll collectors, etc.), and levied £1,458,000 a year at their 7796 toll-gates and sidebars, spending in all £51 a year on each mile of road, and having over seven million pounds of debt, the 104,770 miles of parochial highways, dispersed among more than 15,000 parishes, etc., were divided among about 20,000 Surveyors of Highways, who spent upon them little over £11 per mile, and had practically no debt. With these figures may be compared the mileage for the close of the century. In 1897 there were estimated to be altogether 119,523 miles of public highways in England and Wales (apart from town streets), of which all but 1825 miles were regularly metalled. Only 21,536 miles out of the total were classed as " main roads " (i.e. were paid for by the County *(Pratt's Law of Highways,* 14th edition, by William Mackenzie, 1897, p. 7).

It may be added that, prior to 1818, there were no general statistics as to highways. The Act of 1815 (55 George III. c. 47) required returns to be made, but these were first published in 1818. The House of Lords ordered returns which were published in 1827. The next were those of 1833 and 1839, obtained by order of the House of Commons (Report of Royal Commission on the State of the Roads, 1840). The Third Annual Report of the Local Government Board (C-1071 of 1874, pp. 476-92) gives later statistics at length.

Page 193. It is difficult to realise how rare was the turnpike road in some parts of England and Wales. In the whole of the Cleveland District there was, for instance, no turnpike in 1808, apart from the Great North Road. There were no turnpikes at all in the Isle of Wight until 1813. In 1815 Cornwall had only 7-5 per cent of its total road mileage under Turnpike Trusts; and Devon only 11$ per cent; Norfolk only 7-8 per cent; Cumberland only 8 per cent; Suffolk and Essex only 10 per cent; and Lincoln only 11 per cent. On the other hand Middlesex had 31 per cent of its mileage turnpiked; Huntingdonshire (through which ran the Great North Road) 28 per cent; Herefordshire and Derbyshire 27 per cent; Monmouthshire and Staffordshire 25 per cent; and Shropshire 24 per cent (Report of Royal Commission on the State of the Roads, 1840).

Page 194. Probably, by 1830, the Surveyors of Highways had come, in most places, to enforce only the Team Duty, and had given up expecting personal labour from the cottagers. "There is a part of the Statute Duty," said a Dorset landlord in 1834, "which... no one could at this time attempt to enforce, namely, that which allows the Waywarden to call upon every labourer to contribute his portion of labour to the maintenance of the parish road" (Hon. E. B. Portman, M.P., in Report of House of Commons Committee on County Rates, 1834).

Page 194. *Remarks on the Present System of Roadmaking,* by J. L. Macadam, 1819, p. 29.

Page 195. The reform effected by the appointment of a paid Surveyor in a large Yorkshire village in 1807-16 happens to have been described. "The township of Liversedge (Yorkshire) contains 2133 acres of land, and, in 1814, a population of 3606 persons, and about 9£ miles of roads, of which part are turnpike, and the rest general highway. The usual mode of providing for the repairs of these roads was formerly the same that is understood to be commonly adopted in this country. That is to say, Surveyors, under the direction of Trustees for the different turnpike roads lying in the township, so far as their funds enabled them to do so, and the township occasionally suffered fines when the road was out of repair. The repairs of the other roads were provided for under the General Highway

Q

Act. The township was divided into different subdivisions usually called hamlets. A Surveyor was appointed for each hamlet and had his separate rate and separate share in the Statute Duty, and in the composition. At the same time the township at large was liable to any fine which might be levied in case of the indictment of any road in the township. The subdivision of the business of repairing the roads in the same township is supposed to have been greatly unfavourable to the interests of this township and to the accommodation of the public. Small tradesmen" having no time to spare from " their own business, and no practical knowledge at all of the business of repairing roads, were often appointed Surveyors.... Previous to the year 1807 the roads in this township were managed by five different Surveyors." In 1810 the Vestry was persuaded to nominate one only for the whole parish; and in 1811 to ask the Justices to appoint him at a salary. The result was a fall in the cost of the roads from an average total of expense and fines, 1797-1806, of £3560, to one of £2480 for 1807-16 *(The Select Vestry, or Parish Committee,* by Rev. Hammond Roberson, 1818).

Page 195. The quotation as to the voluntary improvement of the roads of Great and Little Amwell is from *A Letter to the Inhabitants of Hertford,* 1771, pp. 2-3. We may here find place to remind the student that the maintenance of roads and bridges, which had been a favourite object for charitable bequests by pious testators in the fifteenth and sixteenth centuries, appears to have ceased to be the subject of bequests in the seventeenth century, when the function became specifically provided for as part of Local Government. Old trusts in aid of road maintenance were usually merged in other parish or municipal property, or completely lost. In some cases, however, separate bodies of feoffees or trustees continued, during the eighteenth and nineteenth centuries, to administer considerable funds, intended, wholly or partially, for the maintenance of highways. Where the trust included other objects, such as maintaining bridges, supporting a school or providing for the poor, the tendency was naturally to drop the expenditure on the roads, and to leave these to the parish or the Turnpike Trust. The most important instance is that of the "Pious Uses Trustees" of Leeds, whose administration excited the animadversion of the Radicals of 1830. After prolonged controversy the "Board of Surveyors of Highways for the Township of Leeds" took upon itself to publish, at the public expense, *An Abstract of Accounts for Fourteen Years ending Whitsuntide 1840... of the Pious Uses Trustees,* 1841, with the following aggressive preamble: "Be it known then to all whom it may concern that there are fifteen Pious Use Trustees, self-elected, all Tories, who hold in trust a vast amount of property, bequeathed for repairing the highways, maintaining the Free Grammar School and clothing the poor." The radical grievances were the lack of publicity of the trustees' administration and, strangely enough, the fact that the funds were not spent in the relief of the highway rates, but in specific public street improvements, for which rates were not applicable.

Page 195. "Rules and Regulations of the Vale of Evesham Road Club," 1792, in *General View of the Agriculture oj the County of Worcester,* by W. T. Pomeroy, 1794, p. 23 and Appendix 5, p. 15; *Annals of Agriculture,* pp. 262-8. They added a feature vainly demanded by Dr. Burn long before, in which English villages still compare unfavourably with those of France and Germany. "An agreeable embellishment, if it may not be called an improvement, and not very expensive, is the practice they have adopted of affixing the name on some conspicuous place at the entrance of every village" *(General View of the Agriculture of the County of Worcester,* by W. T. Pomeroy, 1794). Unfortunately, this custom neither lasted nor spread to other districts. Right down to the closing years of the nineteenth century it was frequently possible to ride through an English village without seeing its name anywhere displayed. In 1897 the present writers had an opportunity of mentioning the matter to Air. (afterwards Sir) Spencer Walpole, then Secretary to the Post Office, who promptly caused steps to be taken to request every country post office to put up the name of the village in which it was situated, thus, to some extent, fulfilling the want.

Page 196. For the North Biding of Yorkshire case of a voluntary rate see *General View of the Agriculture of the North Riding of Yorkshire,* by J. Tuke, 1794, p. 86; for the Nottinghamshire (Southwell) case see First Report of Poor Law Enquiry Commissioners, 1834, Appendix A, vol. ii. p. 1069.

Page 197. For the Norfolk Justices' report as to a County Surveyor see MS. Minutes, Quarter Sessions, Norfolk, Michaelmas, 1826. An able pamphlet of 1825, by an anonymous country gentleman of Berkshire, had urged the appointment, by the Justices in Quarter Sessions, of a salaried County Surveyor, who should inspect every public road and footpath in the county at least three times a year, and give peremptory orders to the parish Surveyors, enforcible by fine at Petty Sessions. See *HighwaysX Improved,* 1825.

Such a County Surveyor had, indeed, been proposed more than a century earlier, by the House of Commons Committee "appointed to enquire into the repairing and amending of the Highways " in 1718, which recommended "that a General Surveyor should be appointed who shall be under the order and government of the Sessions" (House of Commons Journals, 31st January 1718). A recommendation for larger areas was made in 1772, when a Committee reported that the Highways Act " would be better enforced and executed if, instead of appointing Surveyors of every parish... the Justices... were to... appoint larger districts for Surveyors to act in" *(Ibid.* 3rd June 1772).

Page 198. For an enthusiastic view of what could be done, by employing the paupers on the roads, see *The Improvement of the Public Roads urged during the Existing Dearth of Employment for the Poor.* Anon. (1821). Such employment was strongly advocated by the *Quarterly Review,* December 1832.

Page 198. MS. Vestry Minutes, Minchinhampton (Gloucestershire), 14th August 1826.

Page 198. In the Isle of Wight, in

1833 (First Report of the Poor Law Enquiry Commissioners, 1834, Appendix), we read that "the able-bodied who apply for relief as out of work now receive the following ticket: 'To Mr. Surveyor of the Highways for the Parish of

Employ a pauper in your parish wanting work, and having a wife and children, for days, in the repairs of the Roads and Highways, taking care that he works the usual hours of labourers employed in husbandry, and that he be allowed half an hour for breakfast and one hour for dinner, and no more.'"

Page 200. The quotations are from the First Report of Poor Law Enquiry Commissioners, 1834, Appendix A, voL i. (Richardson's Report), and *ibid.* vol. i. (Chapman's Report) p. 431; and Macadam's statement, *ibid.* Appendix C. In the Isle of Wight it was said that the paupers " are sent to idle on the roads without having any one to control or look after them...,. The Surveyor of Roads, appointed annually, is generally a farmer, who, having other business to attend to, seldom sees these men more than once in the day. Two-thirds of the money paid to men employed on the roads is charged to Poor Rates. The sum charged under this head last year is £4732.... Therefore £7098 was the sum expended on road labour only; which, taking the highest rate, Is. 6d. per diem, represents the labour of 94,640 men for one day, or an average of 215 for each working day... notwithstanding which the roads... are far from being good" *(Ibid.* Appendix A, Pringle's Report, p. 307). The quotation as to the labour being confined to the roads of the parish is from *ibid.* voL L (Majendie's Report). On the other hand, Mr. (afterwards Sir) George Nicholls, at Southwell, had employed the able-bodied paupers on the roads, with good results, and got himself made Surveyor of Highways, as well as Overseer of the Poor, with this very object *(Eight Letters on the Poor Law,* by an Overseer). The employment of paupers on the roads continued for some time to be advocated by so-called " practical " men, see *A Practical Treatise on the Best Mode of Repairing Roads,* by Charles Penfold, 1836, p. 1; *The Practice of Making and Repairing Roads,* by Thomas Hughes, 1838, p. 1.

Page 201. The most persistent road reformer during 1831-33 was the Hon. E. B. Portman, M.P. for Dorset, who introduced a Bill in 1831 to correct the "monstrous evils which had grown up with respect to the management of the highways," on the lines of giving the Vestry in each parish complete control over the Surveyor of Highways. The Government thereupon promised to bring forward a Bill of their own (Hansard, 9th August 1831). As this did not appear, Portman reintroduced his Bill in 1833, and, with the support of Shaw-Lefevre and Sir Oswald Mosley, got it referred to a Select Committee *(ibid.* 23rd July 1833), over which Georgo Pry me presided *(Autobiographic Recollections of George Pryme,* 1870, p. 199). Portman had proposed to make it optional to each parish to abolish Statute Labour, wholly or partly; but the Select Committee thought it better to get rid of it altogether, as they found that "in every instance... where a money payment was made instead of statute duty the roads were invariably better and cheaper kept" (see Portman's evidence in Report of House of Commons Committee on County Rates, 1834). He said that, whilst unions of parishes were desirable, the country was not prepared for the compulsory formation of such road districts, but that he proposed permissive powers to unite, which he thought would lead to voluntary unions (Hansard, July 1833, p. 1144). His Bills were thus the foundation of the plan adopted by the Government in 1835.

Page 201. 5 & 6 William IV. c. 50 (General Highway Act, 1835). This Act became the subject of many legal textbooks; see *The. General Highway Act 1835,* by Joseph Bateman, 1835; *The Present General Laws f for Regulating Highways in England,* by W. F. A. Delane, 1835; *The General Highway Act of 5 A 6 William IV. c. 50,* by Leonard Shelford, 1835; a *Familiar Abridgment of the General Highways Act,* by F. A. Fry, 1836; *The Office of Surveyor oj the Highways,* by a Magistrate, 1836. The" Act (sec. 113) was not to apply to any highways managed under Local Acts, hence (besides all Turnpike Roads and all streets in places having statutory bodies of Commissioners) the Isle of Wight was entirely excluded from its operation, as its highways, whether turnpikes or not, were administered by a statutory body of commissioners for the whole island (under 53 George III. c. xcii., Isle of Wight Highway Act, 1813). The Metropolis also was virtually excluded, as it was provided that the Act should not interfere with or abridge the provisions of 57 George III. c. 29 (Michael Angelo Taylor's Act, 1817), or the privileges of the City of London (sees. 112, 115).

So fondly did the farmers cling to the performance of Team Duty as a means of avoiding payment of a rate, that, in deference to their feeling, a section was inserted in the 1835 Act enabling them to continue to avoid payment in cash. If the inhabitants agreed at a specially summoned Vestry Meeting, the ratepayers having teams might share among themselves whatever work of carrying materials the Surveyor might require, in proportion to the rate chargeable upon them; whereupon they were to be paid the value of the work so performed, at piecework rates fixed by the Justices in Special Sessions (sec. 35). This curious survival from the old Statute Labour system, rendered innocuous by the requirement that payment should be at officially fixed piecework rates, is still law, but has, we believe, usually remained a dead letter.

With regard to the repeal of the statutory regulations as to weight, etc., it should be mentioned that it was noted at the time that it had been held to be a public nuisance at Common Law to carry an unreasonable weight, with an unusual number of horses, to the injury of the publio highway *(The General Highway Act of 5 and 6 William IV. c. 50,* by Leonard Shelford, 1835, p. 90).

Page 202. In 1833 Sir Henry Parnell's authoritative manual was explicit on the question of areas. "The principle. .. of placing the highways of the kingdom under as many separate governing authorities as there are parishes is in every respect repugnant to anything like a sound principle of management; and until it is abandoned, no efforts of legislation can prove successful in introducing any real improvement.... Instead of the governing authority of a parish, that of a county should be substituted, or, when counties are very large, that of a division of a county. The private interests of a Vestry lead it to be satisfied with very imperfect highways. A road that will allow a waggon to be drawn upon it without much difficulty will answer the purpose of those who commonly compose a Vestry. But such a road need not have any other qualities than two ruts for the waggon and a trackway for the horses.... The limited extent and funds of a parish will not admit of giving such a salary to a surveyor as will secure the services of a man educated in the principles of road management" *(A Treatise on Roads,* by Sir Henry Parnell, p. 291 of edition of 1838). Macadam, in his evidence before committees as well as in his books, was always pressing the same views. "The practice of passing Road Acts as a matter of course," he wrote in 1825, "has divided the kingdom into 955 small communities for the care of roads, each having an establishment ill-paid, ungoverned, and inefficient. Such a system is as expensive as it is imbecile; half the road funds are frittered away on salaries and expenses altogether insufficient for producing any good" *(Observations on the Management of Trusts for the care of Turnpike Roads,* by J. L. Macadam, 1825, p. 33). The need for a larger area of administration than the parish had indeed been insisted upon, almost continuously, from the middle of the eighteenth century; and every writer had suggested the appointment by the Justices of a salaried surveyor for the whole county, or for each district of a large county, paid from the county rate, who should advise and superintend the parish Surveyors of Highways, direct the mode of repair, see the orders of the Magistrates properly executed, and keep them informed as to the state of the roads. Indeed, as early as 1675, Thomas Mace had expressly urged the necessity "for every hundred or two hundred miles, more or less, as may be thought fit," of having "one Surveyor-General, some active, trusty, honest man, who should constantly be on horseback himself...

, riding upon his station day after day" *(Profit, Conveniency and Pleasure vw the Whoh Nation, being a short rational discourse... concerning the Highways of England,* 1675, p. 15). The idea was persistently urged from the middle of the eighteenth century; see *Proposals at Large for the Easy vand Effectual Amendment of the Roads,* by a Gentleman, 1753, p. 27; *A Treatise upon Wheel Carriages,* by Daniel Bourn, 1763, p. 35; *History of the Poor Laws,* by Richard Burn, 1764, p. 239; *Observations on the Qeneral Highway and Turnpike Acts,* by T. B. Bayley, 1773; Second Report of House of Commons Committee on the Highways of the Kingdom, 1808; *Highways Improved,* 1825; Report of Committee of Justices as to the Highways, MS. Minutes, Quarter Sessions, Norfolk, Michaelmas, 1826.

Page 203. The Act as to closing footpaths was 55 George III. c. 68, see. 2 (1815). We see the beginning of the tendency to close footpaths described in 1809, before the facilities for legally closing them were given: "At present," writes a correspondent in 1809, "any person who may possess only a few acres of land, and finds that the footpath in his neighbourhood either spoils the appearance of his grounds, or deprives them of that privacy he wishes, immediately proceeds barricading the said footpath; puts up a board ' No thoroughfare,' 'Shut up by order of the Justices,' 'Shut up by Order of the Commissioners for enclosing Waste Lands,' threatening 'prosecution for trespass as the Law directs,' and such like intimidations, to the labouring peasant or artificer, who by such artifices are forced out of their road" (H. Clifford to Sir J. Sinclair, 21st March 1809, in Report of House of Commons Committee on Broad Wheels and Turnpike Roads, 1809). For references in debate see Hansard, 3rd and 9th August 1831. Even the legal text-book writer was moved to indignation. In the preface to a treatise on the Law of Highways, published in 1829, which long remained the standard work, we read as follows: "It may here be remarked, with regard to the diversion and extinction of highways, that it is a prevalent opinion that the powers for this purpose whioh are given to Justices of the Peace are so given to be exercised for the benefit of the proprietor, and not of the public. And this proposition has in an especial degree been reduced to practice in the instance of footpaths. The supposition... is utterly untenable.... In almost every instance the closing of a public way for the benefit of the proprietor is an absolute gift, without consideration, to an individual, out of the possessions of the public.... Justices... ought never to grant their assistance as a matter of favour. The Act expressly declares that the alteration thereby authorised is to be made only when the change will be more beneficial to the public: those who know how its provisions have been carried into execution can best tell the use which the Magistracy have made of it" / *(Treatise on the Law of Highways,* by Robert Wellbeloved, 1829, pp. viii.-ix.)

For the whole episode as to the Stopping Up of Footpaths, see *The Parish and the County,* by S. and B. Webb, 1907, pp. 599-602.

We find practically no reference to footpaths (other than footways bordering carriageways) in eighteenth-century highway literature, and the innumerable paths across private land were apparently used by the public without objection. A footpath was included in the term highway. Lord Coke in a celebrated passage said: "There be three kind of ways whereof you shall read in our ancient books: first a footway, which is called *iter, quod est jus eundi vel amb ulandi hominis..* . the second is a foot and horse way, which is called *actus, ab agendo;* and this vulgarly is called pack and prime way.... The third is *via* or *aditus,* which contains the other two, and also a cart way, etc." *(Institutes,* vol. i. p. 56). It might be inferred that the parish was liable at Common Law to maintain a footpath (lying apart from any road) like any other public highway, but we have found no case of its being required to do so; and the matter was not dealt with statutorily until 56 & 57 Vic. c. 73 (the Local Government Act, 1894), which required the now Parish Council to maintain footpaths, stiles, etc. By the General Highway Act of 1773 (13 George III. c. 78, sec. 21), express power had been given to the Justices to divert footpaths (like other highways), and to close the old ways when the new ones had been opened. In 1815 an Act (55 George III. c. 68, sec. 2) for the first time distinctly enabled a footpath to be closed merely as unnecessary, without the provision of any new way. Any two Justices, after due notice, might without any opportunity for public hearing, make a closing order, which could only be upset by immediate formal appeal to the next Quarter Sessions *(Treatise on the Law of Highways,* by R. Wellbeloved, 1829, p. 390). The 1835 Act transferred the power to make the closing order to Quarter Sessions (though two Justices could still initiate the proceedings), after trial (in case of objection) before a jury, whose verdict was decisive (5 & 6 William IV. c. 50, sec. 89).

The existence of a public right of way for foot-passengers across a field does not prevent the owner from ploughing up the field, thus obliterating the track and to some extent obstructing the passage (Arnold t. Blaker and another, L. R. 6 Q.B. 433; see *)pen Spaces, Footpaths and Rights of Way,* by (Sir) Robert Hunter, 1896, p. 294). In the Reformed Parliament so keen was the momentary feeling in favour of preserving footpaths that an amendment came near being carried, to the Highway Bill of 1833, on which the 1835 Act was founded, which would have prohibited such ploughing up a public footway. The votes were equal, and the chairman of the Committee, George Pryme, proudly relates that he gave his casting vote against the proposed clause, as one imposing a new burden on agriculture *(Autobiographic Recollections of George Pryme,* 1870, p. 199). A bridle way—the old pack and prime way, or drift way—was protected against this kind of obstruction. Thus, various persons were indicted in 1809 for " ploughing up the earth and soil in and across and along a certain part of an ancient pack and prime way" (MS. Minutes, Sessions, Northumberland, 13th April 1809).

With regard to footways by the side of roads, provision was made in both the General Highway Act and the General Turnpike Act of 1773 (13 George III. c. 78, sec. 52, and c. 84, sec. 39) for penalties against drivers damaging " causeways," and in the case of turnpikes, specifically against driving a carriage "upon such horse or foot causeways." But prior to the nineteenth century there were seldom any "footpaths along the sides of the highways, no general law having been enacted respecting either their formation or their protection afterwards, although the importance of furnishing foot passengers with that desirable accommodation can hardly be too highly appreciated" (Report of House of Commons Committee on Highways and Turnpike Roads, 1811). Such raised footpaths were thereupon often constructed, and this consideration for foot-passengers received high praise from Baron Dupin *(The Commercial Power of England,* translated from the French of Baron Dupin, 1825, p. 178). "England," he said, " is now of all countries that in which people travel least on foot, and yet of all modem nations it is that in which most has been done to secure the comfort and convenience of foot-travellers (p. 178). "Many such... footways in parish roads," says the *Quarterly Review* in 1820, "have been recently formed, either by the public spirit of individuals, or by parishes at a loss for employment for their poor, but they are out of the protection of the law, and at the mercy of every mischievous wight who thinks proper in the insolence of his heart to drive or ride upon them" *(Quarterly Review,* May 1820). Trustees of turnpike roads were expressly empowered in 1822 to construct such "causeways " (3 George IV. c. 126, sec. 111). The author of *Highways Improved* (1825) also urges that footcauseways in parish roads should have the same protection as those in turnpike roads (p. 14). This was made law in 1835 (5 & 6 William IV. c. 50, sec. 72). Some responsibility for footpaths was given to Improvement Commissioners under the Towns Improvement Clauses Act, 1847. In 1894 the Local Government Act (56 & 57 Vic. 73, sec. 25) expressly made the District Council liable for the maintenance of footpaths as of our highways; but the Parish Council was by the same Act (sec. 13) empowered to undertake the maintenance of any footpath not being by the side of a public road.

Almost the only work on the subject is *Preservation of Open Spaces, Footpaths and Rights of Way,* by (Sir) Robert Hunter, 1896; but see Benton's *Law Encyclopaedia* under "Footpath."

Page 205. For the "Board of Surveyors " formed under the Act of 1835 by the Vestry of Bradford—with a clerk at £25 a year and an Assistant Surveyor at twenty-four shillings a week—see *Historical Notes on the Bradford Corporation,* by William Cudworh, 1881, pp. 84-7.

Page 205. Among the proposals for, and attempts at legislation relating to highways between 1835 and 1872 (apart from the South Wales Highways Act of 1860 and the General Highways Act of 1862), we may mention the suggestions contained in *The Practice of Making and Repairing Roads,* by Thomas Hughes, 1838; *Road Reform: a Rate on Property more just and expedient than a Horse Tax,* by T. M. Gemmell; *Road Reform, ' A Practical Treatise on Making and Repairing Roads,* by Edmund Leahey, 1844; *Vthe Highway Surveyor's Guide,* 1852; *Rebecca at Stroud; or, a Few Words about the Turnpike Trusts,* by David Ricardo, 1847; *Turnpike Traffic and Tolls,* 1847, and *A Treatise on Road Legislation and Management,* 1857, both by Richard Bayldon.

Page 206. *Letters of Sir George Cornwall Lewis,* by Sir G. F. Lewis, 1870, pp. 187, 204, 205, 220, 223.

Page 207. The controversy as to the

reform of road administration formed only a part of that as to reform of Local Government generally. Something may bo gained from the Report of the Poor Law Commissioners on Local Taxation, 1834; *The Local Taxes,* by Danby P. Fry, 1846; *Local Self Government and Centralization,* by J. Toulmin Smith, 1851; the Tayler Prize Essay on the Local Taxation of Great Britain and Ireland, by R. H. Inglis Palgrave, in *Journal of Royal Statistical Society,* June 1871; *Local Taxation and Parochial Government,* by Thomas Sheppard, 1870; the two volumes of Cobden Club *Essays on Local Government and Taxation in the United Kingdom,* 1882; *An Outline of Local Government and Local Taxation in England and Wales,* by R. S. Wright and Henry Hobhouse, 1st edition, 1884 (with which compare the 3rd edition, 1910); the successive editions of *Local Government,* by W. Blake Odgers, 1899, etc.; and of *An Outline of English Local Government,* by Edward Jenks; *Local Government in England,* by Josef Redlich and F. W. Hirst, 1903; and *History of Local Rates,* by E. Cannan, 2nd edition, 1912. See also the full bibliography appended to *Grants in Aid,* by Sidney Webb, 1911.

Page 207. Some insight into the way the Vestry and the Surveyor of Highways proceeded may be gained from *The Parish,* by J. Toulmin Smith, 1857, pp. 331-65; *The Coaching Age,* by Stanley Harris, 1885, pp. 24-7; and, at a later date, from the evidence before the House of Lords SelectCommittee on the Highways Acts, 1881. Charles Penfold, author of w *Practical Treatise on the Best Modes of Making Roads,* and one of the ablest of the paid surveyors, described his own experience in the parish of Croydon as follows. He had held office for eight years, and had reduced the total rate from an average of £1047 during his first four years, to an average of £485 during his last four years. "I reduced the rate," he told the House of Commons Committee, "from £1000 to £500 a year. I had 100 guineas a year for my trouble. Some of the inhabitants thought that 100 guineas a year appeared a large proportion out of the £500 to give me for looking after the roads: they said ' This will not do, to give the surveyor one-fifth part of the whole; we might have done it cheaper. ' Another man jumped up who said, 'I will do it for nothing.' I said, 'Of course, if that is so I must resign; I cannot afford to work for nothing.' The Vestry gave me a vote of thanks and I retired. This man took the work for nothing: he held it one year, spent £100 more than I did, and had the assistance of many of the paupers out of employ, and also a gravel pit, which I had not. The next year he said, 'I will not carry it on by myself; I must have somebody to help me,' so they appointed a carrier travelling between London and Croydon, and gave him 50 guineas a year—with the result, as the witness declared, that the rates rose and the roads were spoilt" (Report of House of Commons Committee on County Rates, 1834, p. 8). "Many of the parish roads," we read in 1847, "are in a wretched condition. The system adopted by most parish surveyors being merely to fill the ruts and inequalities with stones picked from the surface of the land, or gravel dug in some convenient spot; this operation, repeated in the Spring and Autumn, constitutes their whole duty; no attention being paid to the nature of the soil, or the selection of the material that will bind with it to form a hard exterior crust" (Cresy's *Encyclopedia of Civil Engineering,* 1847).

Page 207. See *The Public Health Acts l848andl849,* by T. W. Saunders, 1849, and *The Laws relating to Public Health,* by Thomas Baker, 1865. For the history of Public Health legislation, see *English Sanitary Institutions,* by Sir John Simon, 1897; *The Public Health Agitation 1888-1848,* by B. L. Hutchins, 1909; *The State and the Doctor,* by S. and B. Webb, 1910.

Page 208. For the Act of 1862, together with that of 1864, and a vast amount of legal information, see *The Law of Highways,* by W. Cunningham Glen, in the edition of 1865.

Page 209. By 1865, three years after the passage of the Bill into law, only one county in Wales (Denbigh) had formed any Highway Districts; only one such district had been formed in Derbyshire, Lincolnshire, Middlesex, Norfolk, or Staffordshire; whilst none at all had been formed for Buckinghamshire, Cambridgeshire, Hertfordshire, Rutland, Westmorland, or the North or East Ridings of Yorkshire. On the other hand, nearly the whole area of the following counties had, by the same date, already been formed into Highway Districts: Bedfordshire, Cheshire, Cornwall, Dorset, Durham, Gloucestershire, Hampshire, except the Isle of Wight, Herefordshire, Huntingdonshire, Kent, Leicestershire, Monmouthshire, Northamptonshire, Northumberland, Nottinghamshire, Oxfordshire, and Wiltshire. Most of the southern counties grouped between 20 and 40 parishes together. Northumberland was exceptional in making only four Highway Districts having respectively 136, 125, 161, and 213 parishes, and governing 454, 394, 823, and 642 miles of highway.

WThe above statistics are from the official statement given in *The Law Highways,* by W. Cunningham Glen, 1865, pp. 718-28. Page 210. For statistics as to Highway Districts and Highway Parishes from 1871, down to their final supersession at the close of the century, see especially the Third and Fourth Annual Reports of the Local Government Board, C-1071 of 1874 and C-1328 of 1875; and the subsequent Reports. The only powers relating to highways now (1913) left to the parish (and exercised by the Parish Council or Parish Meeting) are (a), that of repairing and maintaining footpaths other than those alongside public roads; (6), that of veto on the stopping up or diversion of any public right of way; (c), that of refusing its consent to a declaration that any public highway is unnecessary; and *(d),* that of making a representation to the District or Parish Council as to obstructions of highways. Nevertheless, so difficult is it in England to abolish anything, that the parish is still nominally liable to be indicted at Common Law, at the suit of any person, for failure to keep its highways in repair!

Page 215. For the Act of 1822 (3 George IV. c. 126), see *The General Turnpike Road Act,* by J. Bateman, 1823.

Page 215. The heavy burden of the tolls, and the instantaneous / collapse of the stage coach as soon as a railway was opened, are described in *Old Coaching Days,* by Stanley Harris, 1882, pp. 141, 192, 193; and in *Forty Years at the Post Office,* by P. E. Baines, 1895, pp. 22-7.

Page 217. For the Act of 1841 (4 & 5 Vic. c. 59), which was amended in 1863 (26 & 27 Vic. c. 94, sec. 1), and continued by successive Acts (see, for instance, 28 & 29 Vie c. 119), the student may consult *The Law of Highways,* by W. Cunningham Glen, edition of 1865, pp. 218-24.

Page 217. For the Rebecca riots see the extensive Report and evidence of the Royal Commission of Inquiry into South Wales, 1844. (The Commissioners were Sir T. Frankland Lewis, R. H. Clive and W. Cripps; and their Secretary was G. K. (afterwards Sir G. K.) Rickaxds.) There had been a single outrage at the end of 1839, but no more until the winter of 1842-43. Though Sir James Graham as Home Secretary played a creditable part, the episode is not even alluded to in his *Life,* by W. McCullagh Torrens, 1863, nor in his *Letters,* by C. S. Parker, 1909. Nor is it easy to make good this omission. By far the best account is that given in the *Pictorial History of England,* by Craik and Macfarlane, edition of 1855, voL viL pp. 636-8. We may refer the reader also to the article " Rebecca" in *Quarterly Review* for June 1844; *The History of England,* by W. N. Molesworth, 1875, voL ii. pp. 131-3; "Rebeccaism," by R. D. G. Price, in *Nineteenth Century,* 1880; "Rebecca and her Daughters," in *LitteWs Living Age,* 1891; a mention in *On the Track of the Mail Coach,* by F. E. Baines, 1895, p. 161; and (in fiction) *The Gate Openers,* by K. L. Montgomery, 1912. The principal rioters among those whom the police succeeded in arresting were tried at Cardiff by a Special Commission under Baron Gurney in October 1843, as it was thought that no ordinary tri bunal or local j ury would convict. They were ably defended by Matthew Davenport Hill, and, as he thought, on the whole leniently dealt with (see *The Recorder of Birmingham: a Memoir of M. D. Hill,* by R. and F. Davenport Hill, 1878, p. 223). The uprising had been stained by at least one murder. A woman pikekeeper, who was rash enough to declare that she recognised the assailants of her gate, was deliberately shot dead. The state of feeling may be gauged from the fact that the Coroner's jury returned a verdict that she had died "from the effusion of blood into the chest, which occasioned suffocation. But from what cause is to this jury unknown" *(Pictorial History of England,* by Craik and Macfarlane, edition of 1855, pp. 636-8).

The County Roads Boards of South Wales lasted until 1888, when they were abolished by the Local Government Act.

Page 221. George Clive (1806-86), who was Parliamentary Under Secretary for Home Affairs from 18th June 1859 to 14th November 1862 (under Sir George Grey as Home Secretary), brought a long official and legal experience to bear on his Parliamentary duties. He was, from 1836 to 1839, Assistant Commissioner under the Poor Law Commissioners; from 1840 to 1847, a Metropolitan Police Magistrate; and from 1847 to 1857, a County Court Judge and also Recorder of Wokingham. He edited an edition of Steer's *Parish Law.* In 1857 he was elected M. P. for Hereford, which Borough he represented (except for a break between 1869 and 1874) until 1880. He was Chairman of the Herefordshire Quarter Sessions from 1871 until his death in 1880. He was described as "a Liberal, in favour of Parliamentary Reform, Vote by Ballot, and the Abolition of Church Rates."

Page 221. William Battie Wrightson, M.P. (1789-1879), sat for East Retford 1820-30; for Hull 1830-33, and then continuously for Northallerton from 1835 to 1865.

See Report of Select Committee on the expediency and practicability of abolishing Turnpike Trusts, House of Commons, No. 383 of 1864.

Page 222. George, afterwards Lord George Cavendish, M.P. (1810-80), sat continuously for Derbyshire from 1834 to 1880 as a Whig. He was raised to the rank of an earl's son in 1837, and of a duke's son in 1858.

Page 222. Ireland had abolished its last turnpike toll by 1858. The Metropolitan area was freed in 1872. Scotland had freed itself (under Act of 1878) by 1883. The Isle of Wight (see below) got rid of them in 1888.

The Isle of Wight, which had no turnpikes until 1813, then had its roads placed under a body of "Commissioners of Highways of the Isle of Wight," for the purpose of "widening, repairing, maintaining, and supporting" all the highways of the Island (the Isle of Wight Highway Act, 53 George III. c. 92). These Commissioners had power to levy tolls, and also to obtain rates by precepts to the Overseers of the parishes. The General Highways Acts of 1835,1862, and 1864 did not apply to the Island. Places within the Island (such as East Cowes, Sandown, and Shanklin), which adopted the Public Health Act of 1848 or the Local Government Acts of 1858 or 1863, or the Public Health Aota of 1872 or 1875, managed their own roads as such Urban Sanitary Authorities did in England; whilst all rural highways, however small, were under the Commissioners *(The Law of Highways,* by W. Cunningham Glen, edition of 1865, pp. 56-8). The Commissioners' powers were extended in 1883 by 46 & 47 Vic. c. 226. By the Local Government Act of 1888 (51 & 52 Vic. c. 41, sec. 12), which created a County Council for tho Isle of Wight, turnpike tolls in the Island were abolished; but the Isle of Wight Highway Commissioners were continued in existence as the Highway Authority, with the right to receive an annual grant from the Island County Council in respect of main roads. The Local Government Act of 1894 (56 & 57 Vic. e. 73) did not mention the Island; and it was held in 1895 *(In re the Isle of Wight Highway Commissioners,* 78 L.T. (N.S.) 569: 59 J.P. 438) that the Commissioners had been abolished by this Act;

which had the perhaps unforeseen effect of making all their rural highways, however small, into main roads, repairable by the County Council of the Island.

It must be noted that, even since the last turnpike toll under statutory authority on an English road was ended in 1895, we still continue to pay (a) tolls on bridges, even on pedestrians, either under Local or Private Acts (as at Newcastle-on-Tyne); or merely as private property *(e.g.* Lord St. Levan's extremely valuable toll bridge between Plymouth and Devonport); and (6) in a few cases, tolls on roads constructed and owned by individuals (as in certain highways near Harlech, near Robin Hood Bay, between Folkestone and Hythe, and near Blackpool). No statistics of these private imposts exist.

So far as we are aware, the Isle of Man, Sweden, and Norway alone stand out among all countries as never having been subjected to road tolls (noted in *Road Reform,* by William Pagan, 1st edition 1845, 3rd edition 1857, p. 134).

CHAPTER X THE NEW USERS OF THE ROADS IN THE TWENTIETH CENTURY

In the course of three centuries the horse-drawn vehicle, on two or four wheels, originally regarded as an intruder, had come to possess almost a monopoly of the King's Highway. During the nineteenth century, in particular, those who had once been denounced as new users of the roads were more and more left in sole possession of them. The tramping herds of cattle, sheep and pigs, together with the myriads of geese and turkeys, were carried by railway train; the packhorses passed silently away; gentlemen and commercial travellers alike ceased to travel on horseback; the ox-team died out and the dog-drawn vehicle was prohibited by law. Even the foot-passenger found himself increasingly relegated to side pavements or footpaths. The principal users of the roads—who habitually assumed that their own requirements were to set the standard of road maintenance—were all virtually shod with iron; they never touched the road surface otherwise than by the narrow tyres of their wheels or the sharp-edged shoes of their horseSyThis fact tacitly controlled the ideal of road maintenance,/ Macadam had prophetically declared, in words that read strangely appropriate to-day, that "a road ought to be considered as an artificial flooring forming a strong, smooth, solid surface, which should be at once capable of carrying great weights, and over-which carriages may pass without meeting any impediment. y/But Macadam for the moment forgot that such a surface—sm example of which may be found in a sheet of ice—would suit neither the iron-shod hoof nor the iron-tyred narrow wheel. And thus, instead of this "strong, smooth, solid surface," our road administrators, down to the last decade of the nineteenth century, were content (outside the asphalt, wood, or smooth stone pavement of the streets of large towns) with a more or less rough or irregular, a more or less yielding or gravelly surface, formed of imperfectly consolidated broken stone, in which the horse's hoof could find, alike in wet weather and dry, in summer heat and winter's frost, a firm foothold. And so apt are we to complacency that we might easily have remained content with such uneconomical and unpleasant traction surfaces, but for the advent of new users of the roads, having new needs, and setting up a new ideal as to what a road should be. These new users of the roads required no rugosities for foothold: they were shod, not with iron but with air-inflated india-rubber. In the story of the King's Highway their advent has opened up an entirely new era.

These new users of the roads appeared first as riders of bicycles and tricycles. We need not here trace the history of this invention, from the "velocipede" or "dandy-horse" of the eighteenth century to the first bicycle proper in 1867; nor attempt to estimate the further progress from the rubber-tyred, high " ordinary " to the low, pneumatically-cushioned " safety" in 1888. It was not until about 1895 that the world at large took to bicycling, and began seriously to demand the adaptation of road surfaces to the new traffic.

But the bicycle was a comparatively cheap vehicle; its users were mostly the young people, and, to a great extent, the poorer sections of the community. Those who sat in the places of authority despised the people who " rode ironmongery" instead of horses. Even when, by the end of the nineteenth century, the bicycle was to be found in every country house, and many a highway had more bicyclists than horse-drawn vehicles, the new users of the roads had still only the smallest possible influence on their administration.

Presently, however, the bicycle was reinforced by the automobile. Here, too, we must pass rapidly over the history of the invention, from Cugnot's first steam carriage in 1769, and Trevithick's actually running cars in 1801; over the swarm of practicable steam-cars placed upon the roads in 1826-35, by Hancock, Gurney, Dance, Summers and Ogle, Maceroni and Squire, and the rest of them—a promising enterprise so curiously strangled by high turnpike tolls, the hostility of the agricultural interest, and the popular disbelief in anything but railways; over the slow development of the road traction engine, protected against excessive tolls in 1861 (24 & 25 Vic. c. 70), but limited by the precursing " man and flag " imposed by the Act of 1865 (28 & 29 Vic. c. 83); over the epoch-making construction of the light internal combustion engine about 1885 by Daimler and Benz and Butler; and the introduction to England about 1894 of the first petrol motor cars. The "man and flag" Act of 1865 (28 & 29 Vic. c. 83) was repealed in 1896 (61 & 62 Vic. c. 29), and the motor cars and motor bicycles in use now (1913) number close upon a couple of hundred thousand. They are, however, still expensive; their owners and users include practically the whole governing class, in town and country alike; and their effect on road administration has, within little more than a decade, been almost revolutionary.

The first outcome of this new invasion of the roads was a storm of opposition, a persistent wail of complaint, from all who did not happen to use the new vehicles. It is amusing, at this point in the controversy, to look back at the abuse with which the poor bicyclist was received, for his presumption in daring to use the roads at all, seeing that he was usually " not even a ratepayer "; for his crime in being the cause of alarm to horses and to timid pedestrians; for the dust that he raised and the mud that he scattered; and for the recklessness of his excessive speed (of ten or twelve miles an hour!) It is as recent as the close of the nineteenth century, but it is difficult, in the beginning of the twentieth, to believe that it can ever have happened! Amid this storm of criticism and complaint, the bicyclist found it far from easy to get accorded equal rights with horse-drawn vehicles. It was a gain, in 1888, to get it statutorily declared that a bicycle was a carriage, even if the bicyclist was himself required to carry a bell. It must be accounted an advance that his advent brought about a universal obligation (51 & 52 Vic. c. 41, sec. 85) on all vehicles to carry lights an hour after sunset. But the bicyclist, though he suffered more than anybody from the gravelly surfaces, had no direct or very obvious effect in improving them. What the bicyclist did for the roads, between 1888 and 1900, was to rehabilitate through traffic, and accustom us all to the idea of our highways being used by other than local residents. It was the bicyclist who brought the road once more into popular use for pleasure riding; who made people aware both of the charm of the English highway and of the extraordinary local differences in the standards of road maintenance; and who caused us all to realise that the administration, even of local byways, was not a matter that concerned each locality only, but one in which the whole nation had an abiding interest.

A By the end of the century, however, the offences of the humble bicyclist, so far as the road controversy was concerned, were forgotten in the much more important issues raised by the advent of the automobile. It must be admitted that the motor car, which habitually travelled at three or four times the speed of the bicycle, with a load ten or fifteen times as great, and with fifty times the momentum, came as a serious menace both to the highways and to their frequenters. At first, at any rate, the turning loose on our roads of tens of thousands of heavy vehicles, often travelling with the speed of an express train, amounted to a real aggression on the safety and comfort of all the other users of the roads. Horses were frightened, foot-passengers were startled and sometimes terrified, the King's Highway ceased to be a place in which people could saunter, or children play, with any degree of safety. The advantages of the new traffic were paid for by a heavy toll of accidents, nearly all suffered, unfortunately, by those who had no share in the advantages. In dry weather the flying cars raised clouds of dust, and in wet weather they scattered mud, to such a degree as to cause not only discomfort but also extensive pecuniary damage. Gardens adjoining the road were sometimes greatly depreciated in value, and cottages rendered almost uninhabitable by these incidents of the new traffic. But the roads suffered as well as their frequenters. The momentum with which the wheels of a rapidly moving car struck the road surface, in its leaping and bounding motion, was many times as great as that of the leg of a horse or that of the wheels that he drew. Whether or not the pneumatic tyres really drew out the stones by a kind of suction, as was often suggested, it is clear that the armoured tyres, which were quickly adopted to prevent "side-slipping," drove their iron studs into the fragile and unconsolidated road surface with destructive effect. The amount of the dust created from the road materials was itself proof of the excessive wear and tear of the road crust. Moreover, the additional burden of road maintenance actually caused by the new traffic was quickly aggravated by the immediate rise in the standard of road administration that was set up. So great a departure from the vehicular traffic to which we had become accustomed revealed to us a whole set of unsuspected shortcomings in our highways. The narrowness of the roads, their unnecessary windings, their occasionally steep gradients, the constant irregularities in their surface, our road administrators might before have noticed, although they had seldom done so. The motor car brought home to them—in clouds of dust!—the extent to which even the best kept roads fell short of Macadam's standard of "a strong, smooth *solid* surface, which should be at once capable of carrying great weights, and over which carriages may pass without meeting any impediment." At this point the public feeling against the " new users of the roads " was strong and bitter; and there can be no doubt that many people would have rejoiced had they been excluded from the public highway. The parents whose children had been run over, the cottagers who found their roadside gardens ruined, the pedestrians deprived of all enjoyment in their Sunday promenade, the administrators responsible for the rapidly rising cost of road maintenance, all cursed the swarms of rushing motor cars that infested the great arteries of traffic. The question raised by the new traffic was, in effect, the old issue which had troubled the eighteenth century, whether the traffic was to be constrained to suit the road, or the road constructed to accommodate the traffic.

It was, we think, fortunate that calming counsels prevailed; or, as we might more accurately put it, that those who owned motor cars were influential enough to stave off repressive legislation. By the Motor Car Act of 1903 (3 Edward VII. c. 36; since 1906 continued by the Expiring Laws Continuance Acts) the new vehicles were required to be registered and licensed; to carry conspicuous identification numbers back and front; to be driven by a licensed driver; to sound an alarm when required; and to be provided with lights. They were forbidden, under penalties which might be made severe, to go at more than twenty miles an hour or, where a lower speed limit had been lawfully set, at anything above that lower limit. Subject to these limitations, the new users of the roads were, so far as the law was concerned, admitted to the fraternity of the highway.

The problem then arose of how our ancient highways could be made to accommodate the new traffic. Owing to the powerful influence of the owners of motor cars, brought to bear by an energetic "Roads Improvement Association," which had arisen originally among the bicyclists, the Government conceded, in 1902-3, an official enquiry into highway administration, through the medium of a Departmental Committee, over which Mr. Grant Lawson, M. P., the Parliamentary Secretary of the Local Government Board, presided. This enquiry brought out the fact, which remains true to this day (1913), that notwithstanding all the consolidation that had gone on since 1835, English highway administration was still split up among nearly 1900 separate Local Authorities—132 County or County Borough Councils, 279 Non-County and Metropolitan Borough Councils, 812 Urban District Councils and 661 Rural District Councils—these separate bodies actually increasing every year in number, as new urban areas are taken out of Rural Districts; exercising jurisdiction over areas having no relation to the character or extent of the highways included in them; without any organisation for common or concerted action; without anything that could be called a national policy; without outside inspection or superintendence, and without any central control. It was shown by Mr. Rees Jeffreys that even the most important main thoroughfares are still maintained and repaired along their whole length by different Local Authorities, each dealing with scraps of a few miles only. The first eighteen miles of the main road out of London westward, extending to Uxbridge, is looked after by no fewer than twelve different Authorities. The Great North Road from London to Carlisle is in the hands of seventy-two separate Authorities, including every one of the six species of Authorities, varying from the tiny Rural District Council, administering a total annual expenditure of a few hundred pounds, up to the Council of one of the largest and most important of our Boroughs, wielding the revenues of a Kingdom. Yet no one of these Authorities has power to construct a new road, however sorely the growing traffic might need it. The majority of the 661 Rural District Councils, and not a few among thesmaller of the 812 Urban District Councils, are unable to afford the salary of a qualified road surveyor or engineer. In many cases his duties are combined with others, and undertaken by officers of inferior professional status. In other Councils, we are told, they "appoint their own members; they appoint sons of members; they appoint gardeners, artisans, clerks of works, and all sorts of people who know nothing about roads "; and to them they often pay salaries of no more than £40, £80, or £100 a year. A very frequent figure is £150 a year, which does not allow the selection of a technically qualified officer. And the doings of Councils such as these, served by such officers, are not illuminated by any guidance from higher authorities. The County Council, which may employ the Rural District Council to maintain some of the main roads, has no authority over the highways chargeable to the Rural District Council itself, with the quite nominal exception that the County Council, on complaint, may hold an enquiry into the alleged neglect of the District Council to maintain a road; and, if the neglect is proved, may issue an Order for the work to be done; and, in default, may carry out the work itself, and charge the District Council with the cost. This illusory provision has, we believe, never been put effectively into operation. Moreover, the County Councils themselves are under no supervision. It is a strange anomaly that the important public service of highways, which costs us out of public funds practically as much as the whole of our payments, private and public, for medical attendance, or as much as the whole cost of our relief of the poor, and not far short of what we spend on public education, is the only public service which may never be mentioned in the House of Commons! No Minister of the Crown, and no Government Department, has any responsibility for the management of even the most important national thoroughfares. It follows, apparently, that the House of Commons has no opportunity of criticising the state of the roads, or of remedying any grievance connected with them. Except now (1913) to the limited extent of the duties of the Road Board, no item on the Estimates permits a discussion; and no question as to the state of the roads is even allowed to be put to the Government in the House of Commons. This is not due merely to the fact that road maintenance is one of the functions of Local Government. With regard to practically every other branch of local administration—police, education, poor relief, sanitation, lunacy, or liquor licensing—any malfeasance or non-feasance can at any rate be made the subject of a question in the House of Commons, so that any administrative scandal or public, grievance may be brought to light. With regard to the maintenance of roads, and it seems with regard to this subject alone, the House of Commons, the " Grand Inquest" of the nation, is, inadvertently, by the unforeseen effect of past neglect, and its own red tape, even to this day blind and deaf!

In the absence of any national policy or central control, the 1900 Local Authorities were found to be, in 1903, as they still are in 1913, pursuing the most diverse policies as to the roads committed to their charge. Some County Councils (such, for instance, as Hertfordshire, Norfolk, and Gloucestershire) have cordially accepted their function of road maintenance, and have made practically every highway of any importance into a " main" road, repairable by the County Council itself. Other County Councils (such as Surrey and Glamorganshire) have chosen to take the opposite view, and have restricted to the minimum the roads to be " mained," largely, it seems, out of a curious reluctance to bring the cost of maintaining the minor bridges and culverts upon the County, instead of on the several District Councils. The important Council of Lancashire has pursued a middle course, declaring to be " main " roads those leading to any town of 25,000 (now 20,000) inhabitants. Sometimes the County Council keeps the administration of the main roads in its own hands. In other cases (as in Devonshire) the County Council "contracts " for all its 1134 miles of main roads with the Rural District Councils, leaving them to perform the service in their several ways—sometimes even by the long-since condemned device of " farming" out the road to a little contractor for a lump sum—the Devon County Council contenting itself with paying the bill. In many cases the County Council agrees to make a contribution to the Rural District Councils towards the cost of mamtaining certain arbitrarily selected roads, which have not been "mained ": this is done to a great extent in Buckinghamshire and in Lancashire. In other Counties no such class of "secondary," or "contributory," or "Grant in Aid" roads is recognised. From the decision of the County Council upon roads, whether as to general policy, or as to the classification of a particular highway, there is—even if the highway forms part of a great national thoroughfare—absolutely no appeal.

The Departmental Committee of 1903, like every such enquiring tribunal for the preceding hundred years, shrank from the "nationalisation" of even the most important roads. Nor could its members bring themselves even to the recommendation of any effective central superintendence of local highways. They proposed merely that, following the old precedent of France, there should be a systematic official classification of roads into national and local; that the roads declared to be of national importance should be, not, as in France, administered by a national department of roads, but made the subject of specific new Grants in Aid from the National Exchequer to the County Councils, with whom their administration was to remain; and that the maintenance of these, as well as all the minor highways, should be entrusted by the various Councils to a County Roads Board, acting for the whole of a " geographical" County (thus once more including the "County Boroughs" with the rest of the County). If these recommendations had been carried out, we should have had the roads of England and Wales administered by about sixty Local Authorities, instead of by nearly 1900. But we should still have been without a central expert department to enforce, on the backward Counties, either uniformity of method or anything like a "National Minimum" of road maintenance, even for thoroughfares of national importance; and there would have been no leverage on the County Roads Boards to ensure any decent administration of the lanes and byways, which have an aggregate mileage four or five times as great as that of the main roads.

The decade which followed the recommendations of the Departmental Committee on Highways did not find, at the Local Government Board, either the statesmanship which solves national problems, or the resourceful energy which turns to account the opportunities afforded by current administration. In this branch of this work, as in others, the Local Government Board, in the twentieth century, has proved as much a failure as we have described the Home Office to have been between 1835 and 1872. Neither the recommendations of the Departmental Committee of 1903 nor any other plans of reform were embodied in legislation, or even made the subject of any Government proposal for legislation. None of the obviously required re-organisation of local road administration was even attempted. In short, it is not too much to say that, in the decade which has ensued since the Departmental Committee reported, the Local Government Board has done nothing—has never even discovered that there is any way of doing anything—to improve or to standardise local road administration. It is, in fact, apparently as unconscious as was the Home Office that it has any function or any duty in the matter. Its officers audit the accounts of four-fifths of the 1900 highway authorities; and, to those among them which are concerned with the main roads, it distributes annually large subventions which were originally granted, in part, explicitly in aid of road maintenance. But it collects no information as to the condition even of the main roads, towards which, in effect, it pays—though there is practically no other way by which the nation can learn these facts; it has never'troubled to equip itself with any staff of inspectors of roadsJby which it could inform itself of their condition; it makes no report to Parliament on roads; it publishes no such comparative annual description of the highway work of the various Local Authorities as would, in itself, be a potent instrument of standardisation; it conducts no scientific investigations into unsettled problems of road administration similar to those —all too few in number and scope—that it conducts into the analogous problems of Public Health administration; it never communicates, either to all the Local Authorities or to the most backward among them, any information as to what is being done elsewhere, or the particulars of any improvement that might be adopted; it fails, accordingly, to fulfil that function of central government on which John Stuart Mill laid so much stress, namely, the dissemination among the Local Authorities of scientific knowledge and expert criticism superior to that which they can individually command; with regard to roads, indeed, it does not even address to the Local Authorities so much as a circular of enquiry! It is fair to say that all this comes only to the one point that the Local Government Board, having no power itself to make roads, or even to order them to be made, regards it as no part of its duty to lift a finger to secure either the efficiency or the improvement of this particular branch of Local Government. But this is no more than a bad habit of the office. There is nothing in law or in the British Constitution to prevent the Local Government Board from equipping itself with a competent road staff, and efficiently exercising as much with regard to roads as with regard to sanitation, the normal functions of a central department. In consequence of its inaction, the Local Government Board has, as we presently see, been, in respect of the great and growing public service of roads, virtually superseded.

Baffled in their desire for legislation of for a wisely active use of the existing central administration, the road reformers had, perforce, to fall back on the influence they could exercise on the 1900 Local Authorities. In particular they endeavoured to encourage and influence them to deal with the problem of dust on country roads. The trials organised by the Roads Improvement Association at Farnborough in 1902 gave the start, and the tests of tar-spreading machines and preparations of tar held in Middlesex and Berkshire in 1907 by the same organisation gave the impetus, to a movement which, in spite of the imperfections of our national road organisation, has given England to-day (1913) a larger mileage of dustless roads than any other country. These and other improvements of the roads, and the corresponding increase in their cost, are not all to be ascribed to the coming of the automobile. The mere increase in the amount of traffic on the roads, especially in the neighbourhood of great centres of population, inevitably involved a steady rise in the cost of maintenance. Moreover, the new County Councils, finding themselves, from their establishment in 1888, fully responsible for the main roads, adopted, from the outset, a higher standard of efficiency in road administration than had usually prevailed. We see, in fact, the cost going rapidly up, long before the motor cars began to appear on the roads. Thus, in the twelve years between 1890 and 1902, when the traffic was still almost wholly made up of horse-drawn vehicles and pedal f bicycles, the total expenditure on main roads in rural districts was nearly doubled, the mileage being greatly increased and the annual cost per mile rising from £43 to £65. The total expenditure in these years on main roads in urban districts was more than quadrupled, the annual cost per mile rising from £49 to £207. The increase in the aggregate road expenditure in England and Wales, between 1890 and 1902, outside London and the County Boroughs, was no less than 85 per cent, or two and a half millions sterling per annum, the cost rising on an average by more than 7 per cent a year, even before the pressure of the motor cars began to be seriously felt. There was, in fact, between 1888 and 1902, a great amount of neglect to be made good, as well as an increase of wear and tear to be provided for. A large proportion of the roads were found to have " no bottom," and needed entire reconstruction. These improvements, rendered still more imperative by the rapid transformation of the traffic since 1902, have steadily continued, but, down to 1910 at any rate, with slackening speed. The County Councils—largely influenced by their powerful members who are motor car owners or users—have usually been willing to effect improvements on the main roads, in so far as their sympathy with the ratepayers »/ has permitted. Everywhere the standard of maintenance has risen, in such a way as to give us, on all the principal through routes, many miles of continuously well-made and usually fairly solid road, which is nowadays seldom allowed to become scored into ruts. The greatest advance has been that of seeking to render the surface both smooth and watertight, and practically dustless, by covering it with preparations of tar. We see now that " the English road of the immediate future must be a solid, coherent, waterproof, convex-surfaced, decently side and subsoil drained mass, secured against elemental disturbances under suitably proportioned working loads." But the adoption of this new ideal has involved a steady increase in the burden on the County Rate. The minor roads, under the administration of the Rural District Councils; and the roads and streets managed by Urban District and Non-County Borough Councils, have also felt the influence of this rising standard, to an extent varying greatly from locality to locality. Altogether, the amount spent on the English highways in 1912, outside London and the County Boroughs, which was more than double the amount spent in 1890, was probably four times the corresponding expenditure of fifty years ago. The total expenditure on the administration of highways, by the 1900 separate Local Authorities of England and Wales, during the current year (1913), probably reaches nearly fifteen million pounds, and that for the United Kingdom nearly eighteen million pounds, a sum which is apparently far in excess of the total road expenditure of any other country.

The steadily increasing cost of the roads, which the "new users of the roads " were insisting on—though the actual annual increase between 1902 and 1910 was less than between 1890 and 1902—naturally caused some discontent, especially among those who did not themselves have motor cars; and the Government was pressed to afford some relief to the ratepayer. It was felt on all hands that some contribution must be made by the users of motor cars towards the increased burden, which, even if they had not wholly necessitated, they were the most clamorous in demanding. There was, however, no convenient way by which the all-pervading motor car traffic could be taxed locally, in any definite relation to its use of the road. No one suggested a return to the toll-gate. The tax had therefore to be a national one. Accordingly, in 1909, when the Chancellor of the Exchequer brought forward the Budget by which financial equilibrium was to be secured, increased licence duties on the cars, and a new tax of threepence per gallon on petrol, were both included. But how were the proceeds of this tax to reach the roads? Mr. Lloyd George declined to set up a national road department which should itself maintain the great thoroughfares. The Local Government Board, with the characteristically British reluctance to "amplify jurisdiction," shrank even from the responsibility of superintending the road administration of the Local Authorities by means of the device of a Grant in Aid, which had, in police and education, proved so successful. What Mr. Lloyd George proposed, and what he eventually carried, was the allocation of his new road revenue, amounting normally to more than a million pounds annually, to a new "Road Board," empowered to subsidise, not the ordinary road maintenance at all, however onerous it might be, but exclusively the execution of new and specific road improvements, whether the construction of new roads, or the widening, levelling or straightening of those already existing, or the prevention of dust upon them.

The Road Board, thus appointed in May 1910, under the Chairmanship of Sir George Gibb, has gone energetically to work; devoting itself, for the present, to making grants and loans to Local Authorities in all parts of the United Kingdom—almost exclusively to County Councils—to enable them, either (a) to strengthen or create the solid " crust' of crushed granite, basalt, or other hard stone, which is the leading feature of the modern road; or (6) to make this crust smooth, watertight, and dustless, not only by careful steam-rolling, but also by the application of tar; or else (c) to widen, straighten, or level particular stretches of road where the nature of the traffic demanded it. In other cases curves or corners or gradients have been improved; bridges and their approaches have been reconstructed, and footways have been provided.

In the course of its first two years' existence as our national Road Authority, the Road Board inevitably created some disappointment among Local Authorities by its prudent financial administration. It steadfastly refused (as, indeed, the Act directs) to make any grant in aid of the ordinary maintenance of the roads, however expensive this might be proving; and it also adopted the rule of contributing, towards any proposed improvement, only to the extent of a proportion of the cost, thus in all cases leaving a portion of the expense, even of a distinctly new improvement, to be met from local funds. Hence, whilst a vast amount of improvement, distributed all over the Kingdom, has been effected in the main roads, there has been—perhaps rightly enough—no reduction of the burden on the local rates. The Board also created some disappointment among motorists by not at once taking steps, as the Act empowers it to do, for the construction of new trunk roads. This hesitation, however, is fully justified, not only by the difficulty of doing everything at once, but also by the explicit directions of the Act to the effect that, as regards any work employing a considerable amount of labour, regard is to be had to the state of the Labour Market. Since the Board has been at work, trade has been good, and the percentage of labourers out of employment has been almost unprecedentedly low. It has, accordingly, been a time when, according to the policy now officially adopted, with the approval of the economists, the Government should restrict rather than augment the volume of employment which it can influence. In 1914 or 1915, when trade may be expected to fall off, and the percentage of unemployed workmen will probably begin to rise, it will plainly be the duty of the Road Board to set going works on a large scale—not in order to employ the particular men who are unemployed, but with a view to maintain the aggregate national demand for labour approximately at a level, in bad years as in good, and thus actually to prevent unemployment from occurring. In preparation for such a time, the Board has got ready plans, and accumulated funds, for new trunk roads, such as that from London to Hounslow, which are urgently required for the relief of the present overcrowded highways. These plans, it may be expected, will be, at the first sign of depression of trade, rapidly and relentlessly carried out, irrespective of the co-operation of the Local Authorities.

Meanwhile, it is to be noted that, although the Act of 1909 (9 Edward VII. c. 47) makes no distinction between main roads and other highways, the Board, in its first two years, did next to nothing for the improvement of the 95,143 miles of roads, in England and Wales alone, maintained by and at the expense of the Rural District Councils. Its assistance was given almost exclusively to the 23,549 miles of more important thoroughfares in England and Wales, maintained by or at the cost of the County Councils; and to the corresponding roads in Scotland and Ireland. Thus, whilst the establishment of the Board has to some extent met the need, so far as the County Coimcils are concerned, of an expert central department—collecting and supplying information; furnishing skilled criticism and advice; promoting uniformity or, at least, consistency of policy; and applying incentive and stimulus—it has, up to now (1913), failed altogether in this respect so far as the more numerous and more necessitous Rural District Councils are concerned. Again, so long as its financial assistance is statutorily confined to specific new improvements, and cannot legally be extended, in the form of Grants in Aid, to ordinary maintenance, its beneficent influence on the smaller and most backward Local Authorities, who stand most in need of it, cannot be of any great effect or utility.

Moreover, the Road Board has chosen, up to the present, to adopt, as its policy, an almost complete exclusion from any participation in its grants, of the highways maintained by the Metropolis and all the County Boroughs; and even (except in so far as these form part of main roads) of all those maintained by the Urban District Councils. These Local Authorities provide for a far greater volume of road traffic than do the County and Rural District Councils; they maintain, in the aggregate, 24,747 miles of sorely tried highways throughout England and Wales; and they expended on them in 1908-9 no less than £8,164,139, being nearly twice as much as was spent on their 125,945 miles of road by all the other Local Authorities put together. These urban highways stand often as much in need of improvement as the somewhat arbitrarily selected main roads of the rural County Councils. They often need widening in places, if not also straightening. Above all, they are many of them in serious need of a strengthening of the road crust, if not also of their wood or stone pavements, to enable them to withstand the new traffic. It does not seem equitable that they should be excluded from the benefits of a fund raised by taxation that is national in its character.

The failure of the Road Board to fulfil all the functions of a central Road

Department—a failure due, as we have shown, partly to its statutory limitation to distinctly new improvements, apart from maintenance, and partly to its policy in excluding from its purview all the roads maintained at the cost of the ratepayers in London and the County Boroughs and all but those called main roads in the Urban Districts—will, we think, lead shortly to fresh developments. What is to-day (1913) bringing the question to a head is the rapid multiplication of the motor omnibuses, which have been almost suddenly introduced to our roads, chiefly in and around London. These latest of the " new users of the roads " are proving terribly destructive, not only to life and limb, but also to the road surfaces. During the year 1912 the 2500 motor omnibuses killed a foot-passenger in the London streets every other day! Such ponderous conveyances, weighing, when loaded, between six and seven tons each, and travelling at the rate of ten or twelve miles an hour, charge down the suburban roads with a momentum for which road administrators have made no adequate preparation. These motor omnibuses now contribute largely, in licences and petrol tax, towards the Road Fund; but the Local Authorities, whose highways they are destroying, receive no aid from this fund towards the heavy burden thrown on the ratepayers. The Local Authorities are slow to move, and backward in discerning exactly what to ask for. But the pressure that they can exercise, coupled with the justice of their case, will, in our judgment, soon compel the Government to redress their grievances.

Looking back on the three centuries of struggle since the wheeled vehicle began to swarm on the roads, we cannot doubt that—whatever precautions may be imposed for the protection of foot-passengers, and whatever constitutional and financial re-adjustments may be necessary as between tramways, omnibuses, and J;he public revenues—the roads have once more got to be made to accommodate the traffic, even the motor omnibus traffic, not the traffic constrained to suit the roads. This does not mean that we need submit to be put in peril of our lives. We may fairly insist on such precautions as to speed, stopping places, skilful driving, and even the segregation of particular kinds of traffic to particular thoroughfares, as will protect us from an undue frequency of accidents. We ought to insist on full pecuniary compensation being payable by the owner of the vehicle for every accident, irrespective of a proof of negligence which is nearly always impossible. If, as seems only too probable, accidents are a necessary consequence of motor omnibuses, there is no reason why the owners should be allowed to reap a pecuniary profit from their use of the roads, without fully indemnifying the sufferers and the public. Moreover, even apart from the compensation for accidents now payable by other forms of capital, we may properly, in accordance with the principle of obtaining repayment of the cost of the damage caused by extraordinary traffic, levy on the owners of vehicles of exceptionally destructive character an exceptional contribution towards the highway maintenance. Further, we ought certainly to unite under public ownership and control all the public service / vehicles primarily concerned with Metropolitan traffic, so as to get the utmost public advantage and convenience, irrespective of considerations of maximum capitalist profits, out of an in telhgent combination of omnibus, tramway, and " tube " railway. AJput, assuming these conditions to be fulfilled, history lends no 'jT support to the idea that we can, merely to save ourselves the cost 1 of reconstructing our roads, advantageously set a limit to the size, or the weight, or the character of the vehicles that lawfully use the King's Highway. Nor can we afford to let the vesid interest ofany one form of locomotion stand in the way. The motor omnibus, whether or not it is destined to be joined by the "trackless trolley car," has come itself to stay. Its murderous invasion of our streets and its specially destructive career along our suburban thoroughfares, which at present get little protection from the law and no benefit from the motor licences and the petrol tax, can hardly fail to quicken the evolution of the Road Board into an Authority of wider scope.

What is to-day required, in the organisation of our highways, we venture to suggest, is (a) such an amendment of the Act of 1909 as will permit the Road Board to make Grants in Aid, under appropriate conditions (but only to Local Authorities of sufficient magnitude—say, County or County Borough Councils, and to Borough and Urban District Councils having more than 20,000 population), for the maintenance of their highways as well as for their improvement; (6) such an amendment of the Acts of 1875, 1888, and 1894 as will enable all the Rural District Councils, and such of the Urban District Councils and Borough Councils as have fewer than 20,000 inhabitants, voluntarily to cede their road administration to the County Councils, as a means of relieving their own local rates, which would not otherwise receive any benefit from the Grants in Aid; and (c) the allocation by the Chancellor of the Exchequer to the Road Fund—a step perhaps to be facilitated by a reasonable increase in the taxation on carriages, on motor cars and on petrol—of a sum which would enable the Road Board to make its Grants in Aid of highway maintenance substantial enough to give its influence weight— perhaps equal to 20 per cent of the actual annual expenditure of the Local Authorities on this service (now nearly £18,000,000 per annum)—in addition to the present special grants for road improvements, which would, of course, have to be made available for all the highways of the Kingdom, urban as well as rural.

APPENDIX TO CHAPTER X

Notes And References

Pago 238. The period immediately preceding the present day is always that which has least history! The materials for the history of the coming on the roads of the bicycle and the motor car exist in abundance, but it is difficult to refer the reader to any convenient summary. The files of such journals as *The Cyclists' Touring Club Gazette, The Autocar* (from November 1895), and *The*

Motor Union Journal (from April 1909), representing the new vehicles; and *The Surveyor* or *The Municipal Journal,* represent ing the road administrators, are the best sources. See also the *Report of the First International Road Congress* (at Paris, 1908), by G. Montagu Harris and H. T. Wakelam, 1909; *Report of the Road Conference of the County Councils Association of England and Wales,* 1909; *Report of the Conference of Irish Road Authorities,* 1910; and the *First and Second Annual Reports of the Road Board.*

V4 *Bibliography of Roadmaking and Maintenance in Great Britain,* by S. and B. Webb,34 pp., 1905, is about to be superseded by a more exhaustive list, running to no fewer than 6000 items, to be published in the London School of Economics Series in 1913.

/ Page 238. The quotation ascribed to Macadam is given in *The Road V and Railroads, Vehicles and Modes of Travelling of Ancient and Modern Countries,* an anonymous compilation of 1839.

Page 239. For the bicycle and tricycle, see the convenient summary *y* onThe Cycle Industry" by G. R. Carter, jn *Seasonal Trades,* edited by Sidney Webb and Arnold Freeman, 1912 *y Cycles and Cycling,* by H. H. Griffin, new edition, 1903 *)/The Life and Inventions of James Starley,* 1902; *?tfistoire de la Vilocipidieybyh.* Baudry de Saunier, 1891; *cycling,* by the Earl of Albemarle, 1895 *iVfhe Complete Cyclist,* by A. C. Pemberton, 1897. Page 239. For the history of the motor car, see *Motor Vehicles and Motors,* by W. Worby Beaumont, 1st edition, 1900, 2nd edition, 1902; *XThe Motor Car,* by Rhys Jenkins, 1902; *S/Fhe Automobile,* by Paul N. Hasluck, 1902 (translation of *Manuel Thioretique et Pratique de VAutomobile en Route,* by Gerard Lavergne); *YThe Motor Car in the First Decade of the Twentieth Century,* by W. E. Hooper, 1908;fc#fotora *and Motor Driving,* by Lord Northcliffe, 1st edition, 1902, 4th edition, 1906; and the following older works of historical interest: *Narrative of Experiments with Steam Carriages,* by Walter Hancock, 1829; *Treatise on Elemental Locomotion by means of Steam Carriages on Common Roads,* by Alexander Gordon, 1832;

L *Report from the Select Committee on Steam Carriages, with Minutes oj Evidence and an Appendix,* 1834 *yfiteam Power applied on Common Roads,* by Colonel Maceroni, 1835; *Description of Cugnot's Locomotive,* by E. A. Cowper, 1853 *fOn Steam Carriages,* by A. F. Yarrow, 1863 *Report from Select Committee on Locomotive Engines on Roads,* 1873;*PThe Rise and Progress of Steam Locomotion on Roads,* by J. Head, 1873;i_ and *History of Steam Locomotion on Common Roads,* by W. Fletcher, 1891. See also *rA Comprehensive Bibliography oj Power Locomotion on Highways,* by Rhys Jenkins, 1896.

Page 239. For the controversy caused by the advent of the bicyclist on the roads, and his complaints about the low standard of road maintenance, the best single source is the file of *The Cyclists' Touring Club Gazette.*

It is often forgotten that dust on the roads is no new phenomenon. The old stage waggon of the eighteenth century, we are told, "in a light soil, and when the weather was very dry,... kicked up a wonderful dust; eight or ten heavy horses, with the large broad wheels... would raise a considerable cloud" *(Old Coaching Days,* by Stanley Harris, 1882, p. 113).

It is one more interesting parallel between the new users of the roads, at the opening of the twentieth century, and the new users of the roads two hundred years before, that we find exactly the same complaints against the horse-drawn carriage under Queen Anne as against the automobile under King Edward. In *The Taller,* an indignant correspondent complains that the vehioles " of the rich take up the whole street; while we Peripatetics are very glad to watch an opportunity in which to cross a passage, very thankful that we are not run over for interrupting the machine that carries in it a person neither more handsome, wise, or valiant than the meanest of us. It is to me most miraculous, so unreasonable an usurpation as this I am speaking of should so long have been tolerated. We hang a poor fellow for taking any trifle from us on the road, and bear with the rich for robbing us of the road itself" *(The Toiler,* No. 144; see letter to *The Times,* 7th September 1912).

Page 243. See the publications of the Roads Improvement Association, especially the papers by Mr. W. Rees Jeffreys, entitled *The Motor Problem a Road Problem,* 1903; *Programme oj Dust Prevention Experiments,* 1907; *Systems of Highway Administration Compared,* 1908; and *Dust Problem Statistics,* 1909; together with *The Development of the British Road System,* by W. Ballin Hinde, 1908.

Page 243. *Report and Evidence of the Departmental Committee on Highways,* Cd. 1973 of 1903.

Page 244. On their establishment in 1888, the County Councils were prone to " contract" with the Rural District Councils for the maintenance of the local main roads. Gradually the advantages of direct administration under the County Surveyor made themselves apparent. In 1902, however, there were still only 38 Councils directly managing their main roads. By 1908 there were no fewer than 51 out of 61 so doing; and by now (1913) the number still " contracting " is very small.

The Urban District Councils are, under the Local Government Act of 1888, entitled to manage their several lengths of main road, and to be reimbursed by the County Council the exact cost thereof. This strangely improvident arrangement, where one authority spends the money and another pays the bill, has only been made to work decently by the practical good sense of the officials and councillors concerned. Only those Councils that were in existence at the time of the passing of the Act are entitled to claim to maintain the main roads. Most of the County Councils make contracts beforehand with the Urban District Council, as to the amount to be spent on this service.

With reference to the expenditure on roads, it should be noted that (except for newstreets and expensive repaving in large cities) it is practically all charged to current revenue; and rarely raised by way of loan.

Page 249. The enthusiastic quotation as to the ideal road is from an artiole on "County Councils and Highways," by John Morrison, in *The Autocar* for 1902, p. 666.

So completely has opinion come round, from the time, a quarter of a century ago, when every consideration gave way before the suitability of the road to the horse's feet, that we now have it calmly suggested that the horse's feet must be changed to suit the new road surface 1 "The whole tendency of modern road maintenance," we find the Surrey County Surveyor declaring in 1912, "is towards surfaces less suitable for horse traffic as at present shod. Everything else has changed, but the horse shoe has not." ENGLAND AND WALES.

Page 249. We give the following instructive statistics from the Second Annual Report of the Road Board, H.C. 290, 1912.

table EXPENDITURE ON ROADS, YKAB ENDING 31st MABOH 1909. SCOTLAND.

Expenditure On Roads, Year Ending 15th May 1909.

(Compiled from Local Taxation Returns (Scotland).)

The average per mile for Burgh Councils la not filled in, because ft is obvious that a large part of the expenditure must refer to improvements and not to maintenance.

t The above figures must not be compared with the maintenance figures on the table for England and Wales. The Returns do not state the maintenance cost separately.

These figures include all expenditure (excluding loan charges).

The returns do not state the maintenance cost separately, and no miieage figures are stated. In a paper read by Mr. P. C. Cowan, Chief Engineering Inspector, Local Government Board, Ireland, at the second Irish Road Congress, it was stated that the total mileage of roads in Ireland was 55,St;2 miles.

The number of Motor Cars and Motor Cycles, excluding Hackney Carriages, in respect of which licence duty was paid during 1911-12 in England and Wales was 144,328. The number of Hackney Motors (cabs and omnibuses) was 31,260, making a total of 175,588 motor vehicles, irrespective of Scotland and Ireland.

Page 250. For the Road Board, see *The Development and Road Improvement Funds Act,* 1909 (9 Edward VII. c. 47); the series of memoranda and circulars issued by the Board; the *First Annual Report of the Road Board,* H.C. 292 of 1911; and the *Second Annual Report of the Road Board,* H.C. 290 of 1912.

Page 253. For the controversy caused by the motor omnibuses, the student should consult the London newspapers during 1912 (see the Index to *The Times);* the "Questions" to Ministers in the House of Commons during the session of 1912; and the reports of the action of Local Authorities in such papers as *The Municipal Journal,* or *The Surveyor,* for 1912.

The rapid increase in motor omnibuses in and around London in 1911 and 1912 was due to the facts—*(a)* that it was found possible to work them, even paying the new taxes, at about 7Jd. per mile run, as compared with lid. and 12d. per mile run on the tramways; and *(b)* that their development was not, as it has been in some other large cities, interfered with by a Town Council jealous for its tramway receipts. In London, almost alone among British cities, the tramway authority (the London County Council) is not the omnibus licensing authority (this being the Commissioner of Metropolitan Police). Motor omnibuses now (1913) run as far out as to Windsor, Barnet, Epping, etc. The capital invested in motor omnibuses in the Metropolis is (1913) about four million pounds; the total cost of the tramways has been about twenty million pounds. Yet the number of passengers carried by, and the gross receipts of the motor omnibuses, are in the aggregate not far short of those of all the tramcars, whilst the net profits in 1912 were apparently larger, and the percentage of profit enormously larger. See, on the whole subject, the interesting *Reports of the London Traffic Department of the Board of Trade.* t The number of persons killed in London by motor omnibuses, in 1904 and 1905 only two and three respectively, rose in 1908 to 25, in 1907 to 35, in 1908 to 62, in 1909 to 52, in 1910 to 61, in 1911 to 95, and in *the first ten months of* 1912 *to no fewer than* 143, or more than three per week! In practically none of these cases (six-sevenths of them caused by the vehicles of the principal company) was any compensation paid. It is suggested that the precedent of the Workmen's Compensation Act should be followed, and the owner of the motor omnibus made liable for all damage done to passengers and pedestrians, as he is to his workpeople, irrespective of negligence by himself or his agents. At least, this might be done for all cases except those in which definite proof of wilful negligence by the injured person could be given. The omnibus companies would easily do what to the mass of poor people is practically impossible, namely, cover the risk by an annual insurance premium, which would amount to an insignificant deduction from their profits. At the end of 1912 a departmental committee was appointed to enquire into the subject of motoromnibus traffic in the Metropolis.

Page 254. For the law and practice as to "extraordinary traffio," see *Report of the Road Conference of the County Councils* (County Councils Association, 1909), pp. 118-138; *The Practical Guide to the Administration ty'of Highway Law,* by H. Hampton Copnall, 1912; *Digest of Highway Cases,* by J. E. R. Stephens, 1903; *A Digest of Motorcar Cases* (Motor Union of Great Britain and Ireland), 1908; *The Law of Extraordinary Traffic on Highways,* by Barnard Lailey, 1912; "Theory and Practice of Special Assessments," by J. L. Van Ornum, in *Transactions of (he American Society of Civil Engineers,* vol. xxxviii.

"Extraordinary traffic" was first dealt with by way of prohibition. By the Locomotive Act of 1861 (24 & 25 Vic. c. 70) power was given to the Secretary of State to prohibit the use of any particular kind of locomotive traction engine whioh was found to cause excessive wear and tear of the roads. This was repealed by the Locomotive Act of 1865 (28 & 29 Vic. c. 83). Parliament then sought to deal with the problem by what are, technically, " special assessments." The Local Authority was empowered, by the Highways and Locomotives Act of 1878 (41 & 42 Vic. c. 77, sec. 23), to require repayment, from any one responsible for extraordinary traffic causing additional repairs, of the additional expense to which it has been put. This Act, as slightly amended by the Locomotives Act of 1898 (61 & 62 Vic. c. 29, sec. 12), has given rise to much litigation; and it has been so narrowly hedged round in the judicial decisions that it can seldom be adequately put in force by Local Authorities.

It may here be noted that opportunity ought to be taken to define, by statute, not only the rights and duties of pedestrians and drivers respectively, but also the " rule of the road." It is extraordinary that even the latter should rest on no legal authority, and be mainly a matter of custom and convention (see Finegan v. London and North-Western Railway Company, 53 J.P. 663, of the year 1889, and the authorities therein cited); except for a general injunction that the driver shall keep to the left side of the road *in* passing other vehicles, under penalty, whioh was imposed by see. 78 'of the Highways Aot of 1835 (5 & 6 William IV. c. 50). It is, of course, well known that the custom of the United Kingdom, of keeping to the left side in meeting other vehicles, and on the right side in overtaking and passing them, is the reverse of that followed in other European countries (except, we believe, Bohemia and some parts of Italy). It is, perhaps, not so well known that the English custom is only of late growth. At the beginning of the eighteenth century, Sir Roger de Coverley speaks of "the right we had of taking place, as going to London, of all vehicles coming from thence" (chap. xx. in *The Spectator).* The very phrase, "the rule of the road," seems to be quite modern. The Oxford Dictionary gives for it no earlier quotation than 1871.

Page 255. It is difficult to estimate boldly enough the increase in wealth production, the reduction in the cost of living, and the growth of freedom and amenity that would be promoted by further improvements in locomotion. A century ago the House of Commons Committee of 1811 ventured on the modest prediction that " the expense of five millions would be annually saved to the publio," by an energetic policy of road improvement *(The General Turnpike Road Act,* by Joseph Bateman, 1822, p. iii). We might to-day safely put it at many times that sum (see, for instance, the suggestive presidential address to the Society of Engineers in February 1898, by W. Worby Beaumont).

INDEX

1

THE END

Printed by R. & R. Clare, Limited, *Edinburgh.*

and the authors give us the outlines of a national campaign against sickness. The evil effects of child neglect, from infancy to adolescence, are traced in their resulting adult destitution; and the authors describe the methods of securing, from one end of the kingdom to the other, what may be called a "National Minimum" of child nurture. The dependence of destitution on feeble-mindedness and mental deficiency leads to an examination of the bearing, upon the problem, of the doctrines of Eugenics. The effects of " Sweating" and Unemployment in producing destitution are specially dealt with; and a full exposition is given of the striking plan for actually preventing the great bulk of unemployment, and for maintaining under training those whose unemployment cannot be prevented, with which the authors' names are associated The experiments and proposals in Insurance, whether voluntary or compulsory, against sickness or against unemployment, receive elaborate analysis and criticism; and the experience both of the Friendly Societies and of the German Governmeut is invoked to indicate in what way Insurance may safely be made use of as part of the provision for Old Age, Invalidity, Industrial Accidents, Sickness, and Involuntary Unemployment. The proper sphere of voluntary agencies in connection with the action of the public authorities, and as a part of the national campaign against destitution, is described at length. The grave social evil of the "overlapping" and duplication of relief at present resulting from the multiplicity of unco-ordinated authorities and agencies is described at some length; and proposals are made for preventing it by a Common Register. Finally, an elaborate chapter is devoted to "the Moral Factor," and a full examination is made of the direct and indirect effects on personal character and on family life, both of the present system of dealing with those who are in need, and of the proposed campaign of prevention. "The universal maintenance of a definite standard of civilised life is the joint obligation of an indissoluble partnership between the individual and the community."

In order to keep the page free from footnotes and references these are relegated to an appendix following each chapter.

The Prevention of Destitution—contd.

CONTENTS

 LONGMANS, GREEN & CO. LONDON, NEW YORK, CALCUTTA, AND BOMBAY

GRANTS IN AID:

A CRITICISM AND A PROPOSAL By SIDNEY WEBB

Demy 8vo, 120 pp. (1911). Price 6s. net

ADVERTISEMENT

This is the first volume dealing with Grants in Aid as an instrument of government. In the United Kingdom, at the present time, a sum of about thirty millions sterling is annually paid by the Chancellor of the Exchequer to the various Local Governing Authorities of the Kingdom This large subvention has important effects on Local Government which have never before been critically examined. The author's thesis is that in the Grant in Aid we have unconsciously devised an instrument of administration of extraordinary potency; and that its gradual adoption during the past three-quarters of a century has created a hierarchy of local government far superior to that of France and Germany on the one hand (termed by the author "The Bureaucratic System"); and to that of the United States on the other (which the author describes as "The Anarchy of Local Autonomy"). But the efficiency of our English system depends on the particular conditions upon which the Grants in Aid are made; and the book concludes with a detailed proposal for the complete revision, on novel principles, of all the existing subventions, and for their extension to other services. An elaborate bibliography is appended.

The book forms No. 24 of the Studies in Economics and Political Science, issued under the Editorship of the Director of the London School of Economics and Political Science.

CONTENTS

 LONGMANS, GREEN & CO. LONDON, NEW YORK, BOMBAY, AND CALCUTTA

In this volume, the authors of *Industrial Democracy* and *English Local Government* present what is practically a history of the English Poor Law, so far as the policy of the central authority is concerned, from the Report of the Royal Commission of 1832-4 down to that of the Royal Commission of 1905-9. For this work they have analysed, not only the statutes, but also the bewildering array of General and Special Orders, Circulars, Minutes, Inspectors' exhortations, and unpublished letters, by means of which the Poor Law Commissioners, the Poor Law Board, and the Local Government Board have sought to direct the policy of the Boards of Guardians. No such history has before been attempted. For the first time the gradual development of policy can be traced, with regard to children, to the sick, to the aged and infirm, to vagrants, to the able-bodied, etc. The reader is enabled to watch the gradual and almost unconscious evolution, from out of the "principles of 1834," of what may be called the " principles of 1907 "; being the lines of policy to which the experience of three-quarters of a century had brought the administrator, when the recent Royal Commission overhauled the subject. Two concluding chapters summarise and analyse the proposals of the Majority and Minority Reports.

LONGMANS, GREEN & CO.

LONDON, NEW YORK, BOMBAY, AND CALCUTTA

Demy 8vo, pp. xxvi and 664 (1907). Price 16s. net ENGLISH LOCAL GOVERNMENT (THE PARISH AND THE COUNTY) FROM THE REVOLUTION TO THE MUNICIPAL CORPORATIONS ACT

This work, the result of eight years' research into the manuscript records of the Parish and the County all over England and Wales— from Northumberland to Cornwall, from Cardigan to Kent—combines history and description in a continuous narrative of extraordinary interest. Avoiding the questions of the origin of English local institutions, and even of their mediaeval development, the authors plunge at once into a vivid description of the Parish Officers and the Vestry, Quarter Sessions and the Justices of the Peace, the Lord-Lieutenant and the High Sheriff, together with all the other authorities by which the internal administration was actually carried on. An entirely new view is presented of the social and political development of Parish Vestry and Quarter Sessions, of their relations to the Squire and the Incumbent, and of their attitude towards Parliament and the problems of their age. But the book is more than a contribution to history and political science. Practically all the counties of England and Wales, and literally hundreds of parishes, find place in this unique record of life and manners, in which are embedded not a few dramatic episodes of absorbing interest. It is a new picture of English life between 1689 and 1835 as it actually was in country and town, with graphic tracings of its results on national progress and on the social and economic problems by which we are now confronted.

CONTENTS

 LONGMANS, GREEN & CO.

LONDON, NEW YORK, BOMBAY, AND CALCUTTA

Demy 8vo, pp. viii and 868, In 2 volumes (1908). Price 26s. net.

ENGLISH LOCAL GOVERNMENT (THE MANOR AND THE BOROUGH) FROM THE REVOLUTION TO THE MUNICIPAL CORPORATIONS ACT

In this second instalment of their English Local Government the authors apply their method of combined history and analysis to the fascinating story of the towns and the manorial communities, of which several hundreds find mention, belonging to all the counties of England and Wales. An interesting new account is given, from unpublished materials, of the organisation and development in the seventeenth and eighteenth centuries of the Manor and its several Courts, with picturesque glimpses of the hitherto undescribed part played by the Jury in the commonfield agriculture. But the Manor is shown to be also the starting-point for a whole series of constitutional developments, passing through grade after grade of Manorial Borough, hitherto undescribed, into the complete Municipal Corporation. This, too, is analysed and described in a way never before attempted, so as to make the strangely interesting life of the towns live before us. A special chapter is devoted to the Boroughs of Wales, in which their national peculiarities are brought out. Their extensive study of the manuscript records enable the authors to set forth the inner working of the "Municipal Democracies" that existed alongside the chartered oligarchies, with their many analogies to modern American cities; and to bring vividly to notice the conditions and limitations of successive Democratic government. There is an interesting sketch of English hierarchies of town government, chief among them being the Cinque Ports, the constitutional position of which is presented in a new light. The anomalous history of the City of Westminster is explored by the light of the unpublished archives of its peculiar municipal organisation. An altogether novel view is presented of the constitutional development of the greatest municipality of all, the Corporation of the City of London, to which no fewer than 124 pages are devoted. The work concludes with a picturesque account of the "Municipal Revolution" of 1835, and the Homeric combat of Brougham and Lyndhurst which ended in the Municipal Reform Act of 1835.

CONTENTS

LONGMANS, GREEN & CO.

LONDON, NEW YORK, BOMBAY, AND CALCUTTA

ENGLISH LOCAL GOVERNMENT

"A book of the deepest, even of fascinating interest. Here for the first time we have a real study of local life in England, in village and town and country.... Everywhere we follow the gallant fights of humane and ju9t men whose stories are scattered through these pages, along with the sharp dealings of the astute. Familiar names meet us—a greatuncle of Cecil Rhodes making his 'Empire' in St. Pancras; the novelist Fielding cutting down the gains of the magistrate who preyed on the poor.... Noble figures stand out among the ignoble. As in the parish, the rulers of the county... found themselves left free... to administer as they thought fit. They used the power fully; governed, legislated, silently transformed their constitution, and showed themselves capable of the same extremes as the men of the parish, except that they never surrendered to the 'boss.'... We have only touched here on the tale the authors give, so absorbing in interest to any Englishman.... The best tribute to the writers of this most valuable work is the difficulty of turning away for comment or criticism from the subjects they present in such a vigorous and human form.... They have opened a new chapter in English history."—Mrs. J. R. Green, in *Westminster Gazette.*

"Mr. and Mrs. Sidney Webb's monumental work on our local institutions must be a source at once of pride and of something a little like shame. Here at last we have a book which is more than worthy to be placed beside those of the great continental writers on the subject.... Mr. and Mrs. Sidney Webb are as learned as the Prussian, as lucid as the Frenchman, and as scholarly and careful as the Austrian.... If it is literature to present a singularly vivid picture of a past stage of society, to render it real and lifelike by a careful selection and skilful grouping of illustrative details, and to explain its meaning with clearness, sound judgment, and not infrequent touches of quiet humour, then assuredly is this volume literary as well as learned.... Packed as it is with quotations and references, it is full of transcripts from life which one reader at least has found more fascinating than many of the efforts made to revivify the past through the medium of historical romance or romantic history. The story of the rise, the decline, and the fall of the parish autonomy and the old county oligarchy is in itself a sort of epic not wanting in the elements of adventure, and even of tragedy.... Here and there a remarkable personality emerges."—Mr. Sidney Low, in *Standard.*

"Without exaggeration it may be said that this work will necessitate the rewriting of English history.... We are ushered into a new world, full of eager and heated interest.... The authors have contrived to make these dead bones live. Everywhere are peepholes into the lives of the people, and occasionally a connected story... throws a flood of light on English society. There is not a chapter which is not full of facts of general interest, while the whole volume.. . will be altogether indispensable to the serious student.... There is a fascinating tale of the ' boss ' of Bethnal Green... . A history of the English people, richer in local colour, more comprehensive in its survey of social affairs, and more truly human in its sympathies than any treatise hitherto given to the public."—Mr. R. A. Bray, in *Daily News.*

"Mr. and Mrs. Sidney Webb continue their laborious and luminous studies of English local institutions. In the last two volumes we find the same characteristics as those already published respecting the parish and the county—a minute investigation conducted not in the spirit of the antiquary, but with an eye to realities which are of interest to the politician, the historian, and the economist; an examination of the vast mass of printed matter on the subject, much of it practically inaccessible; and exhaustive enquiry among unedited manuscript records, some of them probably never before read. A few lines in the text or in a footnote are the results of prolonged local investigation; a few unobtrusive words at the close of a sentence, or qualifying some general statement, are the fruits of a careful search among the muniments of some corporation. We cannot speak too highly of the industry and patience which these volumes attest. They possess even rarer merits. The whole subject is set in a new light. We get away from traditional formulae and conceptions. We see the local institutions at work, and they appear very different from what they are represented by lawyers to be."—*Times.*

"If it be true, as many deep thinkers maintain, that history affords the only sure key to a thorough knowledge of political institutions, then the work of which these two learned and elaborate volumes form a part is indispensable to every serious student of English Local Government, for the history of that subject has never yet been expounded with such completeness and so scientific an impartiality.... A pioneer in a new way of writing the history of institutions... . By the skill with which they present the general movement of institutional developments as the outgrowth of natural forces, and constantly illustrate it by particular points of actuality and human interest, these writers have given new life to a study too long neglected. "— *Scotsman.* "Closely packed tomes, crowded with detail, and exhibiting the result of a sum of research and investigation which leaves the indolent, irresponsible reviewer almost wordless with respectful admiration.... Such a collection of original material has been weighed and sifted as might move the envy of any German professor."—*Evening Standard.*

"For years to come they will still be sifting, amassing, arranging, but their reputation as the foremost investigators of fact now amongst Ub is likely to be confirmed rather than shaken. Their work is as minute in detail aa it is imposing in mass. In their patience they possess their intellect, and they remind us of the scholar with a magnifying glass in a picture by Jan van Eyck."—*Observer.* THE BREAK-UP OF THE POOR LAW BEING PART I. OF THE MINORITY REPORT OF THE POOR LAW COMMISSION

Edited, With Introduction, By Sidney And Beatrice Webb

Demy 8vo, xx and 604 pp. 7s. 6d net. Uniform with
"English Local Government"

Bluebooks, it has been said, are places of burial. The original edition of the Report of the Royal Commission on the Poor Law and the Agencies dealing with the Unemployed is a ponderous tome of seven pounds weight, crowded with references, footnotes, and appendices, impossible either to handle or to read. Mr. and Mrs. Webb have, therefore, rescued from this tomb the Minority Report signed by the Dean of Norwich, Messrs. Chandler and Lansbury, and Mrs. Webb herself. By omitting all the notes and references, and printing the text in clear type on a convenient octavo page, they present the reader with something which he can hold with comfort by his fireside.

This Minority Report is a new departure in such documents. More than 20,000 copies have already been disposed of, and it is still selling like the last new novel. It is readable and even exciting. It is complete in itself. It presents, in ordered sequence, page by page, a masterly survey of what is actually going on in our workhouses and in the homes of those maintained on Outdoor Relief. It describes in precise detail from carefully authenticated evidence what is happening to the infants, to the children of school age, to the sick, to the mentally defective, to the widows with children struggling on their pittances of Outdoor Relief, to the aged and infirm inside the workhouse and outside. It sets forth the overlapping of the Poor Law with the newer work of the Education and Public Health Authorities, and the consequent waste and confusion. It gives a graphic vision of the working of the whole Poor Law machinery in all parts of the United Kingdom, which is costing us nearly twenty millions sterling per annum.

The volume concludes with a Scheme of Reform, of novel and far-reaching character, which is elaborately worked out in detail, involving the abolition of the workhouse, the complete disappearance of the Poor Law, and the transfer of the care of the children, the sick, the mentally defective, and the aged to the several committees of the Town and County Councils already administering analogous services, in order that we may now, in the twentieth century, set ourselves to prevent destitution, instead of waiting until it occurs.

LONGMANS, GREEN & CO.

LONDON, NEW YORK, BOMBAY, AND CALCUTTA

THE PUBLIC ORGANIZATION OF THE LABOUR MARKET BEING PART II. OF THE MINORITY REPORT OF THE POOR LAW COMMISSION

Edited, With Introduction, By Sidney And Beatrice Webb

Demy 8vo, xvi and 332 pp. 6s. net. Uniform with "English Local Government

The Problem of the Unemployed, which the Royal Commission on the Poor Law was incidentally set to solve, is the question of the day. Part II. of the Minority Keport deals with it in a manner at once comprehensive and complete. The whole of the experience of the Poor Law Authorities, and their bankruptcy as regards the destitute able-bodied, is surveyed in vivid and picturesque detail. There is a brief account of the work of Voluntary Agencies. A lucid description is then given, with much new information, of the movement started by Mr. Chamberlain in 1886, which culminated in the Unemployed Workmen Act of 1905. The story is told of the various experiments and devices that have been tried during the past twenty years, the Belief Works and the Farm Colonies, etc. This leads up to an altogether novel descriptive analysis of the Unemployed of to-day, who they actually are, and what they really need. The final chapter on Proposals for Reform gives, in elaborate detail, the Minority's plan for solving the whole problem of Unemployment —not by any vague and chimerical panacea, but by a series of administratively practicable reforms, based on the actual experience of this and other countries, which are within the compass of the Cabinet, and could, if desired, be carried in a single session of Parliament.

LONGMANS, GREEN & (JO.

LONDON, NEW YORK, BOMBAY. AND CALCUTTA

THE STATE AND THE DOCTOR

Demy 8vo, pp. viii and 276 (1910). Price 6s. net.

In this work a great deal that will be new to the ordinary citizen is brought to light. The authors show that we do a great deal of State Doctoring in England—more than is commonly realised—and that our arrangements have got into a tangle, which urgently needs straightening out. Everywhere there is a duplication of authorities, and more or less overlapping of work. We are spending out of the rates and taxes, in one way or another, directly on sickness and Public Health, a vast sum of money annually—no man knows how much, but it certainly amounts to six or seven millions sterling. Meanwhile, as is now being revealed to us, a vast amount of sickness goes altogether untreated, with the result of grave damage to our population, and unnecessary loss of productive capacity to the community as a whole.

The authors suggest that we put up with this waste, and we allow our statesmen to postpone the task of straightening out the tangle, very largely because we are not aware of the facta There has hitherto been no popular description of our State Doctoring. Many worthy people, thinking themselves educated, do not even know of its existence. There is not even an official report setting forth exactly what is being done and left undone for sickness and the Public Health in the different parts of the kingdom.

But the authors do not content themselves with a picture of the costly and wasteful muddle that our responsible statesmen allow, session after session, to continue unreformed. The work concludes with a remarkable series of proposals for "straightening out the tangle "—proposals based on the very authoritative evidence received by the Royal Commission on the Poor Law, supported not only by the administrators, but also by a large section of the medical profession, and rapidly commending themselves to the unprejudiced enquirer.

LONGMANS, GREEN & CO.

LONDON, NEW YORK, BOMBAY, AND CALCUTTA

THE HISTORY OF TRADE UNIONISM

Demy 8vo; Tenth Thousand; New Edition, with New Introductory Chapter; Ivii and 558 pp. (1911).

Price 7s. 6d. net.

This work describes, not only the growth and development of the Trade Union Movement in the United Kingdom from 1700 down to the end of the nineteenth century, but also the structure and working of the present Trade Union organisation in the United Kingdom. Founded almost entirely on material hitherto unpublished, it is not a mere chronicle of Trade Union organisation or record of strikes, but gives, in effect, the political history of the English working class during the last one hundred and fifty years. The opening chapter describes the handicraftsman in the toils of the industrial revolution, striving vainly to retain the mediaeval regulation of his Standard of Life. In subsequent chapters the Place Manuscripts and the archives of the Priory Council and the Home Office enable the authors to picture the struggles of the early Trade Unionists against the Combination Laws, and the remarkable Parliamentary manipulation which led to their repeal. The private records of the various Societies, together with contemporary pamphlets and working-class newspapers, furnish a graphic account of the hitherto undescribed outburst of "New Unionism" of 1830-34, with its revolutionary aims and subsequent Chartist entanglements. In the course of the narrative we see the intervention in Trade Union history of Francis Place, Joseph Hume, J. R M'Culloch, Nassau Senior, William the Fourth, Lord Melbourne, Robert Owen, Fergus O'Connor, Thomas Slingsby Duncombe, John Bright, the Christian Socialists, the Positivists, and many living politicians. The hidden influence of Trade Unionism on English politics is traced from point to point, new light being incidentally thrown upon the defeat of Mr. Gladstone's Government in 1874. A detailed analysis is given of the economic and political causes which have, since 1880, tended to divorce the Trade Union Movement from its alliance with "official Liberalism." A new introductory chapter brings the story down to the last few years. The final chapter describes the Trade Union world of to-day in all its varied features, including a realistic sketch of actual Trade Union life by a Trade Union Secretary, and a classified census founded on the authors' investigations into a thousand separate Unions in all parts of the country. A coloured map represents the percentage which the Trade Unionists bear to the population of each county. A bibliography of Trade Union literature is appended (which, together with that given in *Industrial Democracy,* affords a unique index of almost every available source of information).

CONTENTS

 The History of Trade Unionism—contd. "A masterly piece of work. "—*Timet.*

"To the politician... an invaluable guide."—*Observer.*

"An admirably lucid presentation of a great mass of complicated facts. Its very footnotes display a wealth of material such as would have amply sufficed to turn each note into an article of considerable length. In the learning they exhibit, and the concise and decisive way in which they settle important subsidiary questions and side-issues, they remind us of the notes in such monuments of German industry and erudition as Zcller's *Griechhcht Philosophic....* The result is a full, clear, and condensed history such as can have few parallels.... We may fairly repeat that the book is a masterpiece of lucidity of knowledge. Every page is of value, and nearly every sentence contains a fact. "—*Speaker.* "Readable every word of it. There is plenty of excitement and plenty of romance in the book."—*Queen.*

"As fascinating reading as a well-written novel."—*Cotton Factory Timet.* "Infinitely painstaking, comprehensive, clear and acute, the first correct and scholarly history of Trade Unionism in England.... Marked by immense research.... The book must find a permanent place upon the shelf of every student of Economics.... Undeniably marked by the qualities of true history — fulness, accuracy, and clear connection in the presentation of facts."—*Newcastle Chronicle.*

"It would not be easy to overestimate the value and importance of their admirable and masterly work... not likely to be superseded for some time to come. "—*Economic Review.* LONGMANS, GREEN & CO.

LONDON, NEW YORK, BOMBAY, AND CALCUTTA

INDUSTRIAL DEMOCRACY

Demy 8vo; Tenth Thousand; New Edition in 1 vol., with New Introduc tory Chapter; Ixi and 929 pp. (1907), with Two Diagrams.

Price 12s. net.

ADVERTISEMENT

In this work the authors of *The History of Trade Unionism* deal, not with the past, but with the present. They describe, with the systematic detail of the scientific observer, and in the same objective spirit, all the forms of Trade Unionism, Factory Legislation, and other regulation of industry to be found within the British Isles. The whole structure and function of Labour Organisations and Restrictive Legislation in every industry is analysed and criticised in a manner never before attempted. The employer in difficulties with his workmen, the Trade Unionist confronted with a new assault upon his Standard Rate, the politician troubled about a new project for Factory Legislation, the public-spirited citizen concerned as to the real issues of a labour dispute, will find elucidated in this work the very problems about which they are thinking. It is a storehouse of authenticated facts about every branch of "the Labour Question," gathered from six years' personal investigation into every industry in all parts of the Kingdom; systematically classified; and made accessible by an unusually elaborate Index. But the book is more than an Encyclopedia on the Labour Question. Scientific examination of Trade Union structure reveals, in these thousand self-governing republics, a remarkable evolution in Democratic constitutions, which throws light on political problems in a larger sphere. The century-long experience of these working-class organisations affords unique evidence as to the actual working of such expedients as the Referendum, the Initiative, Government by Mass Meeting, Annual Elections, Proportional Representation, Payment of Members, and, generally, the relation between the citizen-elector, the chosen representative, and the executive officer. The intricate relations of trade with trade have an interesting bearing upon such problems as Local Government, Federation, and Home Rule. Those who regard the participation of a working-class electorate in the affairs of Government as the distinctive, if not the dangerous feature in modern politics, will here find the phenomenon isolated, and may learn how the British workman actually deals with similar issues in his own sphere. The intricate constitutions and interesting political experiments of the thousand self-governing Trade Union republics are dissected and criticised by the authors in such a way as to make the work a contribution to Political Science, as to the scope and method of which the authors, in describing their investigations, propound a new view.

The analysis of the working of Trade Unionism and Factory Legislation in the various industries of the United Kingdom has involved a reconsideration of the conclusions of Political Economy. The authors give a new and original description of the working of industrial competition in the business world of to-day; and they are led to important modifications of the views currently held upon Capital, Interest, Profits, Wages, Women's Labour, the Population Question, Foreign Competition, Free Trade, etc. The latter part of the work is, in fact, a treatise upon Economics.

A new Introductory Chapter deals at length with Compulsory Courts of Arbitration and Wages-Boards in New Zealand and Australia.

CONTENTS

"A permanent and invaluable contribution to the sum of human knowledge. ... We commend to the public a book which is a monument of research and full of candour.... Indispensable to every publicist and politician."—*Timet* (on day of publication).

LONGMANS, GREEN & CO.

LONDON, NEW YORK, BOMBAY, AND CALCUTTA

PROBLEMS OF MODERN INDUSTRY

Post 8vo; Fourth Thousand; New Edition, with New Introductory Chapter; xx and 286 pp. (1907).

Price 5s. net.

CONTENTS

LONGMANS, GREEN & CO.

LONDON, NEW YORK, BOMBAY, AND CALCUTTA

THE HISTORY OF

LIQUOR LICENSING IN ENGLAND

Small 8vo; Seventh Thousand; viii and 162 pp.

Price 2s. 6d. net.

CONTENTS CHAP.

Limited THE LONDON PROGRAMME

By SIDNEY WEBB

Crown 8vo; Second Edition (1894), with New Introductory Chapter; viii and 214 pp.

Price 2s. 6d.

"Brimful of excellent ideas."—*Anti-Jacobin.*

Published By Walter Scott, Limited

THE EIGHT HOURS' DAY

By SIDNEY WEBB, LL.B., And HAROLD COX, B.A.

Crown 8vo; 280 pp. with Bibliography

Price Is.

The unique value of this little book lies in its collection of facts. It is likely to hold the field as the handbook to one of the chief items in the social politics of the immediate future."—*Pall Mall Gazette.*

Published By Vandenhoek Und Ruprecht (gottingen) DER SOGIALISMUS IN ENGLAND. Geschildert von englischen Socialisten.

Hbrausgegeben Von SIDNEY WEBB

Lightning Source UK Ltd.
Milton Keynes UK
UKOW022116020512

191900UK00007B/41/P

9 781458 826886